the RISE and FALL of the JEWISH GANGSTER in AMERICA

REVISED EDITION

ALBERT FRIED

the RISE and FALL of the JEWISH GANGSTER in AMERICA

REVISED EDITION

ALBERT FRIED

COLUMBIA UNIVERSITY PRESS

Columbia University Press Morningside Edition

Columbia University Press
New York   Chichester, West Sussex

Morningside Edition with new preface
Copyright © 1993 Columbia University Press
Copyright © 1980 Albert Fried

Library of Congress Cataloging-in-Publication Data
Fried, Albert.
The rise and fall of the Jewish gangster in America
by Albert Fried.
Columbia University Press Morningside ed.
p. cm.
Previously published: New York :
Holt, Rinehart, and Winston, c1980.
Includes bibliographical references and index.
ISBN 0-231-09683-6 (pbk.) :
1. Jewish criminals—United States.
2. Crime—United States.
3. Jews—United States—Social conditions.
I. Title.
HV6194.J4F74   1993
364.3′4924073—dc20   93-36178
                                                                            CIP

⊚

Casebound editions of Columbia University Press books are
printed on permanent and durable acid-free paper.

Printed in the United States of America

c 10 9 8 7 6 5 4 3 2 1
p 10 9 8 7 6 5 4 3 2 1

FOR ANDREW FRIED AND BENJAMIN FRIED

Poolrooms and gangsters, brothels and cadets. Dancing academies, beckoning and calling to tired and lonesome souls sweating their flower and youth away to the time of spindles and belts and foot-powered machines.

Benjamin Antin

The criminals are themselves part of the community, in its deeper sense, and are as much its products as are its philosophers, poets, inventors, businessmen and scientists, reformers and saints.

Frank Tannenbaum

You see, studying human nature I came to the conclusion people prefer to be righteous at home and a so-called sinner someplace else. As for myself I stick to this saying: When you lose your money you lose nothing; when you lose your character you lose everything.

Meyer Lansky

CONTENTS

Twelve pages of photographs follow page 144.

INTRODUCTION

SOME QUESTIONS OF
MOTIVE AND METHOD

In the fall of 1966 I first read Michael Gold's *Jews Without Money*, a novel-memoir about a lad growing up on New York's Lower East Side before World War I. To be more accurate, it is about the suffering he sees all around him—unrelieved suffering, hopeless suffering, suffering that calls forth every horror and perversion. The streets and tenements reek with whores and pimps. Gangsters are a lurking presence: his best friend Nigger becomes a gangster, killing Louis One Eye after Louis turns Nigger's sister into a prostitute. Throughout, Gold makes no moral distinction between his underworld and upperworld characters. They are all victims of a remorseless machine; all submit to the same delusion, the false hope that a miracle will somehow release them from their thralldom.

As I read *Jews Without Money* I kept asking myself: Was the Lower East Side anything like Gold's description? Or does he present a caricature of the old neighborhood, driving certain indisputable truths to their extreme as a corrective to the romanticized image of the past? The title itself suggests bitter irony.

I was reminded of these questions a few weeks later, during a visit to New York's Jewish Museum. Featured was an exhibit of paintings, drawings, and photographs, especially photographs, of the Lower East Side when it served as the "Portal to America" (the exhibit's title) for most of the nearly two million Eastern European Jews who emigrated to the United States between 1870 and 1925. And a splendid exhibit it was. Many of the pictures were already familiar to me, but hanging there on the walls, free of surrounding text and considerably enlarged, they conveyed something new; and all of us (for the place was packed that Sunday afternoon) undoubtedly saw the squalid tenements, the noisome streets, the sweatshops, the children in school and at work and play—the overwhelming poverty and the overwhelming will to endure—with fresh understanding. I also came to appreciate more forcibly than before the artistic genius, not to say heroism (who else but a hero would have gone into such unspeakable slums in order to report the truth to America?) of those pioneer photographers, chief among them Jacob Riis and Lewis W. Hine and Alice Austen.

Still, nothing in the exhibit conveyed Michael Gold's Lower East Side, the seamy underworld part of the immigrant experience. I wondered if anyone had ever photographed pimps and prostitutes and gangsters—and, if so, where such pictures might be found. I realized, of course, that the exhibit was hardly intended to be exhaustive, and that even if the curators had wanted to include such pictures, assuming they existed, they might not have been available. All the same, my curiosity was awakened.

What I found out in the course of desultory reading over the next several years fairly astonished me. I discovered that an enormously complex, richly endowed culture of vice and criminality, made up mainly of young people, thrived on the Lower East Side, that most outsiders regarded it as a running sore of corruption and mayhem, and, not accidentally, as Tammany Hall's bastion of power, that the Jews themselves eventually came to look upon it as an insufferable burden of shame and embarrassment, and that this underworld culture, finally, did not begin to decline until World War I and then only because Lower East Siders were escaping to better neighborhoods thanks to the burgeoning prosperity, especially in the garment trades. As far as I was concerned, Michael Gold had been justified; his Lower East Side rested on solid fact.

I discovered, further, that the Lower East Side could not be isolated as a moment in time, a single habitation. Many of the children who had been nurtured by its underworld culture came into their own—inscribed their names in history—only after they had fled its precincts. So, goaded by curiosity, I enlarged my inquiry to take in some of America's greatest racketeers and bootleggers and gamblers and professional killers. Which meant finding out about Jewish neighborhoods in other cities, about the underworld cultures of Chicago, Philadelphia, Cleveland, Boston, Detroit, Newark, each a variant of the Lower East Side, but each possessing its own distinctive character, each contributing its own share of gangsters to the national pool. By the same token I had to learn about the Italian gangs, products of their ghettos, their neighborhood underworlds; more specifically, about those Italian gangsters who had teamed up with their Jewish counterparts to form the multi-ethnic syndicates of modern times.

I continued to follow the careers of these gangster-capitalists, Jewish and non-Jewish, as they passed from early manhood to middle and old age, as they went on to market other illicit goods and services (primarily gambling) after Prohibition ended, as they kept improving their system of mutual cooperation and self-governance and assumed more and more the aspect of modern business enterprises. Jewish gangsters, meanwhile, were growing less visible. There were fewer and fewer of them, and those who remained tended increasingly to occupy the strictly commercial and financial stratum of the criminal hierarchy. So that by now, entering the 1980s, all that is left is the intimation of a Jewish underworld, the residue of an obliterated past.

Four years ago I decided to resurrect that past. I decided to study the Jewish underworld from its inception to the present: from the vice-mongers of the 1880s to the last of the breed today. At first I thought I would take a single person—Meyer Lansky was my favorite candidate—who had grown up on the Lower East Side and gained prominence in the decades since as a leader of organized crime, and make him the focus of my study. But this approach, I finally concluded, was too limiting: it would mean neglecting the worst of the racketeers—Lepke and Gurrah and their murderous warriors, for example, the recitation of whose deeds still makes one shudder. I then thought of concentrating on a particular generation of criminals, those who had reached manhood in the underworld cultures of America at the time Prohibition came along and conferred high professional status upon them. That generation, born around 1900, has had no notable successors, and its passing marks the passing of the Jewish underworld in America. (Italian-American criminals, by way of contrast, have tended to keep their vocation going inside their families, often marrying into similar families, thus perpetuating the institution generation after generation, much as skilled craftsmen once did through guilds.)

Too many false starts persuaded me to abandon my single-generation approach as well. It would have forced me to slight the Lower East Side experience in all its rich squalor; I would not have been able to do justice to the earlier background of vice and crime—prostitution and gambling and street gangs—from which the argonauts of that exceptional generation emerged. So, in the end, I have chosen to trace the evolution of the Jewish underworld in its various social and economic and political settings, moving from the early Eastern European immigrant settlements to the present-day era of multinational corporations and high finance epitomized by Meyer Lansky.

One might argue that I have, at least on the face of it, only amplified or explicated a point often made by sociologists and historians of American ethnicity. It should be pointed out that the two best books on the Lower East Side mention the underworld but make little of it. Moses Rischin's *The Promised City*, a fine synoptic account, devotes only two pages to the subject of vice and crime. "Jewish criminals," Rischin writes, "regularly made newspaper headlines. The appearance of an ungovernable youth after the turn of the century was undeniable and excited apprehension." Questions immediately spring to mind. Why did so many Jewish children appear before Juvenile Court? What newspaper headlines, and referring to what stories? Who excited the apprehension, and why? How disappointing that Rischin writes not another word on the subject.

Then there is Irving Howe's vast and magisterial *World of Our Fathers*. No work has caught so abundantly the suffering and courage and genius of the Eastern European immigrants and their children and the civilization they wrought. After informing us briefly, tantalizingly, of such notorious characters as Mother Mandelbaum and Monk Eastman and Arnold Rothstein, Howe sums up the underworld culture in a sentence: "But in the life of the immigrant community as a whole, crime was a marginal phenomenon, a pathology discoloring the process of collective assertion and adjustment." Absent from *World of Our Fathers* is a discussion of the vice—prostitution and gambling mostly—or the great gangs, Kid Twist's, Big Jack Zelig's, and Dopey Benny's among others, whose misdeeds outraged the Jewish community and, indeed, the city and the entire nation. And while eloquently reminding us of the Lower East Side's remarkable legacy, its writers, artists, composers, labor leaders, and so forth, Howe neglects to mention that other legacy, the dark one left by its underworld culture. He does touch on the racketeering evil that afflicted the needle trades, manufacturers and unions both, in the 1920s, but he refers to Lepke and Gurrah and Little Augie and company only in passing, as though they were just another marginal phenomenon, a mere discoloration. And the Jewish bootleggers escape his notice altogether, a singular omission.

It is no secret that Jewish criminals did what others did before them and have continued to do, that they all have used crime as another way of moving upward and onward in the American manner. First the Irish (and to a much lesser extent the Germans); then the Jews and the Italians; and now, presumably, the Blacks and the Hispanics and the Chinese too have successively climbed the same "queer ladder." True enough. But in itself the point remains a stale generalization, a platitude. The significant question is what *kind* of underworld each ethnic group established in response to the unique experiences it encountered, who its underworld *dramatis personae* were, and what, specifically, they accomplished. This book attempts to address and answer that very question: to show in detail how some Jews followed an undying American tradition.

THE RISE AND FALL OF THE
JEWISH GANGSTER IN AMERICA

ONE

THE OLD
NEIGHBORHOOD

i

Abe Shoenfeld could not have
been completely surprised that day in August 1912 when a group of
influential New York City German-American Jews called on him to
undertake an important and highly confidential assignment. They
wanted him to head a team of private investigators who would check
out and report on the criminals and vice lords of the city's great Jewish quarter, the Lower East Side. The incidence of crime and vice
down there had gotten out of hand, had indeed reached scandalous
dimensions—so scandalous the newspapers were reporting them daily, featuring them in one headline story after another; so scandalous
they threatened to bring all New York Jews, even the most respectable (the Germans), into disrepute. The crisis demanded an extreme
response.

That Shoenfeld had been selected to carry out this grave enterprise could not have surprised him either. He had grown up on the
Lower East Side—his father had been active in the trade union movement—spoke Yiddish fluently, and knew every aspect of the community's life, its upper and nether worlds both. And he had recently
done investigative work of this sort, for a commission (financed by
John D. Rockefeller, Jr.) looking into New York's malignant "social
evil," prostitution. That work had taken Shoenfeld into the seamiest
depths of the Lower East Side. He bore the best of credentials.

One of his first reports, written only days after he was on the job, discussed a place named Segal's Cafe, located on Second Avenue, a broad boulevard filled with theaters and restaurants and dance halls and new apartment buildings and stores, the neighborhood's entertainment and social and commercial center. Segal's customers, however, were not drawn from the crowds who walked along the great thoroughfare. They usually came to Segal's when everyone else slept, when Second Avenue itself was quiet as a tomb, and there they talked and drank and gambled a little; they relaxed after their day's labor was done, for their work schedules differed from other people's: they all belonged to the Lower East Side underworld.

Months later Shoenfeld sent to his employers a list of the "habitues" of Segal's Cafe. It is presented here exactly as he wrote it:

> *Patsye Keegan*—gun–pipe fiend—mack.
> *Sadie Chink*—ex-prostitute—owner disorderly house.
> *Aaron Horlig* alias *Big Aleck*—50% owner.
> *Louis Segal* alias *Little Segal*—50% owner.
> *Charlie Auerbach*—mack—strike breaker—life taker.
> *Little Carl*—right name *Carl Hudis* alias *Harry Cohen*—gun-mack.
> *Bockso*—gun.
> *Charles Pearlstein* alias *Kopki*—mack—strike breaker—doorman.
> *Keever* alias *Little Keever*—mack-gun—gunman-strongarm.
> *McKinley*—gun and mack.
> *Mendel*—gun.
> *Lhulki*—gun.
> *Whitey Lewis* —indicted and convicted—Rosenthal Affair.
> *Lefty Louis*—indicted and convicted—Rosenthal Affair.
> *Jack Zelig*—recently murdered.
> *Dopey Benny*—guerilla—life taker.
> *Benny*—guerilla—life taker.
> *Valinsky*—gun—brother to *Harry Vallon* of Rosenthal Fame.
> *Little Mikie Newman*—gangster.

Louis Cruller—alias *Little Cruller*—gun and mack.

Candy Kid Phil—gun.

Sam Boston—gambler—owner—former fagin—fence—commission better. His wife a pickpocket.

Meyer Boston—same as his brother *Sam*—their right names are *Meyer & Sam Solomon*.

Crazy Jake—gun.

Bennie Greenie—gun.

Harry Goldberg—gun.

Markey English—gun.

Bobby Mendelsohn—mack.

Little Natie—(not the one from Broome St.)—gun. Right family name is *Lubin* being related to *Lubin* the Philadelphia Moving Film Company.

Charlie Whitey—mack and strike breaker.

Dinah Hudis—prostitute. Her mack is *Little Carl*.

Jennie Morris alias *Jennie The Factory*—former prostitute and at present disorderly house owner. Her mack is *Harry Morris*. Owner 249 Broome Street.

Bessie London—right name is *Mrs. Meyer Solomon*—her husband is *Meyer Boston*—best gun-mol in the world.

Tillie Gold—right name *Mrs. Sam Solomon*—her husband is *Sam Boston*—a gun-mol from *Bessie London's School*.

Tillie Finkelstein—gun-mol from *Bessie London's School*—married to *Candy Kid Phil*—do not know his family name.

Birdie Pomerantz—gun-mol—married to *Philly Furst*, a gun, now out of town working the rattlers and shorts and towns out west.

And other women of their calibre and men also.

At this address people of the underworld from out of town pay visits when they come here, as for instance *Celia Minsky* and *Pauline* alias *Pauline The Horse Car*—both disorderly house madams of Philadelphia. At this address *Gold* the actor plays pinochle, and *Greenberg* a city employee also. *Zelig* was "framed up" in here. *Red Phil* was in here 20 minutes before he killed

Jack Zelig. Other habitues are not yet on my lists, and whom I can think of just now are:

Big Nose Willie—gun.
Herman Scheiner—alias *Chaim The Mummey*—gun.
Yanish—gun.
Schorr—gun.
Tutsie—worker in a pool room or crap house.
Monahickey—gun.
Dan The Stud Dealer
Willie Berkowitz—gambler.*

Shoenfeld was very thorough. He wrote colorful, densely detailed and sharply opinionated sketches of many of these characters. One example, taken at random, will suffice—his account of the Solomon brothers, alias the Bostons (after the city of their birth), Samuel and Meyer, and their wives or gun-mols, Tillie and Bessie. Sam, at twenty-eight, three years older than Meyer, was short and pudgy (five feet four, one hundred sixty-five pounds) and had "rosy stout cheeks" and "a heavy underlip showing his innate lustful character." How lustful is proved by the fact that he once had been "noted for his propensities as a seducer" and deadly "maiden taker." Also, he had been a "full fledged pickpocket and fagin" who stole barrels, the zinc steps of tenement buildings, and the purses of mothers wheeling baby carriages. He had met Tillie Gold about six years earlier, when she hardly spoke English. But Tillie happened to be the friend, or rather protégée, of Bessie London who was then going with Meyer and had already established herself as "the cleverest booster gun-mol in the world" (*booster* meaning a female specialist in pilfering from department-store counters). By the time Sam mar-

---

*   Some explanation of unfamiliar terms is in order. *Gun* (derived probably from the Yiddish word *gonif*) stood for pickpocket and all-around thief; *mack* stood for pimp; *pipe fiend* for opium smoker; *doorman* for someone who warns gamblers, brothel-keepers, etc., of trouble; *guerilla* for strong-armer or enforcer; *gangster* for member of a criminal gang; *fagin* for organizer of young pickpockets; and *gun-mol* for woman pickpocket (working usually in collaboration with a man).

ried Tillie she had become an expert thief in her own right, enabling him to retire from "the gun craft" and go into a vocation worthier of his abilities, gambling. Tillie is quite a woman: "about 5 ft. 5 inches—medium color hair—good-looking—nice mannered—is considered clever—is a wise talker—walks up and down Second Avenue with thieving girls—kept women and prostitutes. . . ."

Meyer and Bessie had a roughly similar arrangement, though apparently a more successful one. Meyer, who was slim, handsome, well-dressed, and soft-spoken (Sam had "a loud mouth—nobody knows as much as he does—he contradicts everybody"), took fewer chances and played the odds more shrewdly. "Today he is a big *Second Avenue Man*," a "wise guy" (big shot) who "can play pinochle for $500 a game." What is more, Meyer had Bessie, queen of the gunmols, who lavished huge sums of money on him, beginning with an $18,000 dowry. Shoenfeld cannot help admiring her: "She is quick and clever—and had an auspicious manner—is very ladylike—has a good heart and is a good kid." Yet Shoenfeld finds on balance that "Meyer and Bessie do not live as happily as Sam and Tillie do. Sam cares somewhat for Tillie aside of [*sic*] her money stealings—and Meyer only wants money, money, money from Bessie."

Such, then, were the Bostons, typical habitués of Segal's Cafe.

During his investigation, which went on for years, Shoenfeld discovered many similar "hangouts" in the neighborhood: Gluckow's Odessa Tea House on Broome Street; the University Cafe and Simmie Tischler's hangout on Rivington; Max Himmel's and Harry Blinderman's notorious establishments on Delancey; Blattberg's Saloon, the Onyx, Sam Boske's Hop Joint, all on Stanton; Dora Gold's candy store on First Street; Gucker's Saloon on Second Street; and Sam Paul's place on Seventh Street, to name a few. All of these had their own list of habitués, each of whose life stories Shoenfeld carefully recorded. He also inquired into their occupations and modus operandi, catching them very nearly in the act itself. He compiled an endless quantity of material on whole families of prominent and long entrenched madams and pimps and procurers: Rosie and Jacob Hertz, the Rosenbachs and the Goldmans and countless others; on drug dealers, the likes of Benny Silver, Hymie Fischel, Willie Gipson, Dinny Slyfox, Little Archie, and their ilk who were "poisoning the mind and body of Jewry"; on strikebreakers and guerillas: Charlie the Expressman, Charlie Auerbach and Dopey Benny (both habitués of Segal's Cafe), Waxey Gordon, Pinchy Paul, Little Rothie, Billy Lustig, and their companions; on out and out bandits like the "Warshover Thieves"—who, as their title suggests, came originally from Warsaw, Poland, and who now comprised a vicious little group of pickpockets, their turf being the streetcars on Delancey, at the foot of the Williamsburg Bridge; and so on and on. By the time his assignment ended Shoenfeld had written biographical vignettes on some 1,900 of these people. And he had not come close to exhausting the neighborhood's subterranean life.

Conscientious as he was in gathering the facts, Shoenfeld could not help being a moralist, a scathing judge of the evildoers who brought such shame on the Jews. At one point in his essay on Segal's Cafe he recommends that a vigilante group "be formed in 4 hours and regardless of the law and order of the day . . . plant a 14 inch gun and shoot the damn basement and its hoard of carrion into perdition." His animus is understandable, implied as it is in the very terms of his mission. He must raise as high as he can the moral barrier between the men and women he is tracking down and the rest of the Lower East Side Jews, decent, hard-working, law-abiding. But this approach, valuable and even necessary as it was, scarcely did justice to the questions it called forth. If the numbers were so large, if thousands of men and women belonged to the underworld, their legions scattered throughout the neighborhood, and if they had their own solidarities, vocations, institutions, what amounted to their own society or culture flourishing at once within and beneath the community as a whole—if so, then how could one speak of a simple moral dichotomy, the "good" people versus the "bad" ones? Was it enough therefore to single out, isolate, apprehend, and punish the guilty individuals, assuming this could be done? What had brought about such a deep-rooted and pervasive underworld culture? And just how was that culture bound up with—rather than distinguished from—the community in general? These questions obviously require their own inquiry and their own answers.

We are saying that Segal's Cafe and everything it signified was the product of a history that had been germinating on the Lower

East Side decades before Abe Shoenfeld appeared on the scene in the summer of 1912.

⍥

That some men among the first wave of Jews who settled on the Lower East Side in the early 1880s turned to "disorderly women," as prostitutes were then called, is a reasonably safe assumption. Many of these men were unmarried or had left their wives (and children) behind; others went to prostitutes for occasional solace from the endless tyranny of their workaday lives. It is also safe to assume that they regarded their reliance on street women, however infrequent, as a transgression of moral and holy writ. Yet what were they to do? For married bachelors the only alternative short of self-denial was to take a mistress, an alternative which might—and often did—have unhappy consequences. As for unmarried young men, the best advice after all was to hold off marrying as long as possible, or at least until they had acquired a modest competence. Prostitution, then, had its uses, even its social virtues, on the Lower East Side as it did in all the other ghettos and immigrant habitations across the land.

Inevitably, the shame and the sense of guilt diminished, the moral proscriptions lost much of their authority, and—for the homeless and frustrated men so disposed—buying one's sexual pleasures became more and more routine. Habit has its own justification.

The women who served the Jews in the first years of their arrival were experienced, well-trained professionals. Many were brought to the Lower East Side from adjoining neighborhoods, "The Tenderloin" to the north for instance, a district full of bawdyhouses. These Irish and German and white and black American women who comprised the labor force usually charged fifty cents a trick, no small sum in those days when six or seven dollars a week was a livable wage. (The price, incidentally, remained constant for decades.) How much the prostitutes kept for themselves is another matter. It was rarely more than half the amount earned, and often less, the "surplus" going to the usual retinue, the pimps and landlords, along with the local officials from the cop on the beat to the political boss. Still, to look at the facts coldbloodedly, the average streetwalking whore ended up with more income than the average working girl, her Irish or German or rural American sister, say, who scrubbed floors from dawn to dusk in the big city for a few coppers a day.

It was not long before Jewish women began to make their appearance on the streets, too. Soon there were scores of them, then hundreds; then, by the turn of the century when the neighborhood's population was at its height, hundreds upon hundreds.* We do not have even an approximation of how many there were. No quantitative study of prostitution as such was ever done, and only a few attempts, and those on a very small scale, were made to ascertain which immigrant or ethnic groups contributed what proportion of the total. The numerous reports on the "social evil" that came out after 1901 usually skirted such questions.

The United States Immigration Commission, a body set up by Congress to investigate a broad range of immigrant and immigrant-related problems, conducted a survey of prostitutes brought before the New York City Magistrates Court between November 15, 1908, and March 15, 1909. While the survey was not a good one, the sampling being too narrow and the time period in question too brief, it does furnish some valuable data. The Commission found that of the 2,093 cases before the court 1,512 (almost three fourths) consisted of native-born women, a preponderance of whom were presumably Jewish (one can only infer this since the ethnic headings are Russian and Polish, not "Hebrew"). The data are more exact on the 581 foreign-born: 225 are Jewish as against 154 French, 64 German, 31 Italian, 29 Irish, and 10 Polish, the five next largest groups. The Commission also concluded that only a handful of Jewish women came to America as prostitutes, a total of seven in 1908–9 (most of the French prostitutes had been imported by white slave traders operating out of Marseilles).

A few years later a private New York City vice commission care-

---

* "The greatest evil the Eighth Assembly District [the Lower East Side] has to face," the *Year Book* of the University Settlement Society of New York observed in 1899, is "the evil of prostitution which seems to exist to an appalling extent, and to be on the increase."

fully examined the records of 647 New York prostitutes who were being held at the State Reformatory for Women at Bedford Hills. While that study too leaves much to be desired, so far as the ratio of Jewish inmates to the rest are concerned it more or less corroborates the Immigration Commission findings. It found that of the 290 women at Bedford Hills who had foreign-born parents, 92 were Jewish (Russian, Austrian, German and Hungarian in that order); next highest were the Irish with 65 and the German with 60. It would be unwise of course to generalize extravagantly from these reports. What they both bear out, though, is the impression—nay, the fact—that the Lower East Side had become one of the infamous red-light zones of the age.

The problem overwhelmed every effort that Jewish philanthropic and charity organizations undertook to deal with it. These organizations were created and staffed by the rich German or "uptown" Jews who had no firsthand knowledge of what life was like downtown. For their part, Lower East Siders kept their distance from the prostitutes, the scourge of the streets, a blight to every eye. Religious societies struck them from the roster of the living. Other Jews, equally appalled, had their own lives to worry about. Some blamed the women, others the circumstances. All felt helpless before the monstrous reality of prostitution.

Not until 1901 did the National Council of Jewish Women establish the Clara de Hirsch House for Immigrant Girls; and not until 1905 the Lakeview Home; each accommodated only a few hundred women at a time. Some fallen women were also admitted to the Hawthorne School, an institution built in 1906 for Jewish delinquent boys (about which more later). These efforts deserve mention here if only to emphasize the inadequacy of the response, necessarily so, given the enormity of the condition, though any response was better than none and any life saved a miracle.

A New York City police commissioner, William McAdoo, explained as well as anyone why so many Jewish women became prostitutes. "The horrors of the sweatshop," he wrote in 1906, "the awful sordidness of life in the dismal tenement, the biting, grinding poverty, the fierce competition, the pitiful wages for long hours of toil under unwholesome conditions, physical depression, and mental unhappiness are all allied with the temptation to join the better-clad, better-fed, and apparently happier [people]."* Yet the question still remains: What accounts for the high rate of Jewish prostitutes, compared with other immigrant women who suffered similar poverty and despair and were subject to similar "temptations"? Why did fewer prostitutes—fewer both proportionately and absolutely—emerge from other immigrant ranks?

The answer (one can only speculate here) may lie quite simply in the fact that prostitution was one of the ways in which Jewish women, some at any rate, expressed the contrary side of their virtues. For just as Jewish women were more independent, less passive, less bound to the constraints of traditional authority than other women (Italian, Polish, et al.), so more of them rebelled against the pinpricks, said no to the despotism that gathered about them, becoming on the one hand militant trade unionists or radical ideologues or social activists, or on the other hand (we draw the contrast as sharply as possible) streetwalkers who acted on the belief, cynical to be sure, though no more cynical than the reigning ethic of competitive individualism and Social Darwinism, that only they—those few who helped themselves by embracing the underworld culture—could be saved. Jewish women, more than any other, sought to make their own lives, for good or ill.†

We are curious nonetheless to know who they were, what prompted *them* in particular, for they were at most a tiny percentage of the Jewish female population as a whole, to choose the lives they lived, cutting themselves off from parents and community and finding comfort only among their fellow and sister pariahs, such a fate being the necessary accompaniment of their choice. And we are curious also to know what became of them. Alas, we will never learn the answers. Those who could have told us, those who represented the Jewish community as social workers and philanthropists, were

---

* Or, as Maude Miner, a probation officer in Night Court, put it: "Living in most crowded districts, with the burden of economic pressure on them, these children of Israel have almost lost that spiritual basis of life which has been their very birthright."
† Charlotte Baum, Paula Hyman, and Sonya Michel in *The Jewish Woman in America* write: "The 'new Jewish woman' originated in Eastern Europe, not America. Jewish women's political and union activities had already been established in Eastern Europe and it was carried steerage class to America."

the most eager to say nothing, to have done once and for all with these lost souls. But would it be too far-fetched to imagine that a fair number of them, even most, ceased to practice their trade after a few years (how many years it would be enormously interesting to know) and went on to marry and bear children and settle into perfectly normal and respectable lives? I do not think so.*

Like their predecessors, like their gentile sisters in other neighborhoods, Jewish prostitutes mostly worked out of crowded tenements. Typical was Rosie Solomon (no relation to the Solomon brothers), age thirty, who conducted a flourishing business in her Rivington Street flat. She was comely looking, according to the investigator's report, her shapely figure (she was five feet, eight inches tall) and dark hair set off by her five gleaming gold teeth, and she had no trouble attracting clients. Rosie Solomon had married at thirteen back in Russia and had borne a son whom she had left behind on emigrating to America. (What became of her husband we are not told.) Lately that son, now fourteen, had showed up at her apartment. It had been an especially bad time for him to do so because she was about to have a baby. She gave the lad $100 and sent him back to Russia.

Another typical streetwalker was Jennie Silver. She was pretty too: she stood five feet, six inches, weighed about 140 pounds and had blonde hair. One of Shoenfeld's men picked her up and accompanied her to her second floor place overlooking East Houston Street. She "opened the door," Shoenfeld writes, "and there were two men drinking a pint of beer. The woman said to [one of the men], 'Come on Jake, get out of here for a few minutes. I have a John.' There was a little girl of about two years lying on a couch. This was Jennie's child, and Jake, whose name is Jacob Silver, is Jennie's husband-mack. She has been living with him for the past ten years. He never works. If she does not make enough money for him, he kicks and beats her. . . ."

---

* See, for instance, the astonishing letters, full of pathos and intelligence, that a one-time Philadelphia Jewish prostitute, Maimie Pinzer, wrote to an upper-class Boston philanthropist, Fanny Quincy Howe, over a twelve-year period, 1910 to 1922. Pinzer after many setbacks finally married the man of her choice and gracefully settled into middle-aged respectability.

Hundreds of such case studies were compiled by Shoenfeld's vigilantes; they differ from each other only in detail and setting.

Occasionally prostitutes used the back rooms of stores, or "weisbierstubes" (literally, "white beer parlors"), leading in from the streets and cordoned off by a curtain, or they sublet space from families. A survey of the "social evil" published in 1910 described how one family, consisting of man and wife and three small children, made ends meet by subletting to a prostitute. "The other member of the household was an immoral woman who received men both night and day in one of the two rooms in which the family lived. Occasionally, another prostitute from a neighboring tenement came to the house and assisted in receiving company. There was no door between the two rooms, and when men came in the daytime the mother with the baby in her arms offered to leave the place if desired. At night, when the other children were home from school, the whole family remained in one room while the other was being used by this immoral woman."

This inescapable mixture of depravity and normal everyday life, this shameless promiscuity, especially offended visitors to the Lower East Side. One of them described what he saw: "hideous women swarming on the streets, lolling out of the windows, and sitting on stoops, making wanton exhibitions, inviting customers, and indulging in their peculiar methods of speech and action, in full view of hundreds of children, who romped about the streets, looking curiously at the women betimes, and noting well all of the degrading commerce."*

The effect of the "degrading commerce" on children of course consituted the most serious problem of all. "Almost any child on the East Side in New York," a famous report on prostitution observed in passing, "will tell you what a 'nafke bias' [whorehouse] is." The effect on young girls in particular may be judged from Lincoln Steffens' recollection of a poignant moment, one of the many he wit-

---

* Benjamin Antin remembered well the whores of Allen Street: "A hundred women on every . . . corner. Tall women, short women. Fair women. Ugly women. Powdered women, looking at an immigrant boy who stood by in amazement while they jerked their heads in a beckoning welcome, who wondered what it was all about."

nessed during the years he covered the Lower East Side as a crime reporter. The example is admittedly an unusual one. " 'Oh, Meester Report!' an old woman wailed one evening. 'Come to my house and see my children, my little girls.' She seized and pulled me in ... up the stairs, weeping, into her clean, dark room, one room, where her three little girls were huddled at the one rear window, from which they—and we—could see a prostitute serving a customer. '*Da, sehen Sie*, there they are watching, always they watch.' As the children rose at the sight of us and ran away, the old woman told us how her children had always to see that beastly sight. 'They count the men who come of a night,' she said. 'Ninety-three one night.' (I shall never forget that number.) 'My oldest girl says that she will go into that business when she grows up; she says it's a good business, easy, and you can dress and eat and live.' "

Steffens' account is corroborated in a more general way by the Headworker of the University Settlement Society. He wrote in 1900: "The worst sin is the sin against the children in the tenement houses, whose eyes are forced to behold sights which they never ought to witness; the youth whose moral sense is blunted; the girls who ceased to be shocked by the sight of vice and come to envy the vicious women, who appear to lead an easy and comfortable existence. . . ."

The growth of the community brought corresponding changes to the institution. Some buildings were converted into fancy houses of assignation, comparable to those flourishing in the better quarters, where prettier and younger women, the pick of the crop, as well as superior entertainment and food and drink, were available for those who could afford them. At the more pedestrian level there sprang up the "Raines Law hotels," threadbare establishments consisting of several rooms and a saloon, a favorite place for a relaxed evening. (They were called Raines Law hotels after an 1896 New York State ordinance which forbade the sale of alcohol on Sunday except in hotels, a hotel being defined as anything with at least ten bedrooms, a dining room, and a kitchen. By 1905 there were a thousand such places in Manhattan and the Bronx alone; no estimate has been made on how many the Lower East Side had.) "The average citizen goes there," a group of reformers wrote in 1902, "to drink his glass of beer and listen to the bad music and worse jokes that play so important a part in summer entertainment. When there, he becomes subject to solicitations which have the appearance of a mere flirtation; if he yields it is with the least possible shock to his moral sensibilities; he may feel he did not seek vice, but he was overcome by circumstances." But despite these changes, despite the increasing professionalism of their trade, most Jewish prostitutes continued to solicit on the streets and use the tenement apartment as their workshop.

Then, of course, there were the pimps, or "cadets" as they were called (why remains a mystery, the dictionaries and lexicons telling us nothing about the origin of the word), who as always announced their presence on the Lower East Side at exactly the same time the prostitutes did and were as ubiquitous and as easily identifiable. The typical Jewish cadet, in the words of an official report, "is a young man averaging from eighteen to twenty-five years of age who, after having served a short apprenticeship as a 'lighthouse' [an employee of a brothel], secures a staff of girls and lives upon their earnings. He dresses better than the ordinary neighborhood boy, wears an abundance of cheap jewelry, and he usually cultivates a limited amount of gentlemanly demeanor." How often Marcus E. Ravage, author of a fine memoir, *An American in the Making*, would encounter on the Lower East Side streets of his youth "a young gentleman with piercing, relentless eyes, faultlessly attired in modish clothes, high collar, and patent leather boots" who "painted me a dark picture of the fate of the fool who thought he could succeed in America with the antiquated notions he had brought with him from the old country." That young gentleman had come to terms with America.

No one was more reviled and hated in the community at large than the cadet, for his stock in trade was seduction and false promises. No scheme or deception was too outrageous for him to perpetrate. Aside from his personal charm he freely used marriage brokers and employment agencies to snare his victims—the young, the lonely, the innocent, the weak, the alienated, the oppressed. He sometimes showed up at the immigrants' processing center to catch the girls as soon as they landed. ("Beware," advised a Yiddish-language leaflet distributed to women who had just arrived, "beware of those who give you addresses, offer you easy, well-paid work, or even marriage. There are many evil men and some who have in their way led girls to destruction.")

Nor was it unheard of for cadets to recruit women in the old country, going back there themselves or working through marriage brokers. The United States Immigration Commission detailed one such case, that of a seventeen-year-old Polish-Jewish girl who was picked up by her bogus fiancé at Ellis Island: "He took the girl directly from New York to Montana and broke her into the life there. He put her in a crib [a bordello], and forced her to lead the life of a prostitute. They stayed in —— about six weeks, and he then took her to Seattle, Wash., and put her in the crib house of which ——, a Japanese, is the proprietor, and in which there are Japanese, Jewish, and French women as inmates. He kept her there about a month, and then moved her to the —— House, a house of prostitution of French and Jewish inmates. At the time he placed her in the —— House the girl was about two and a half months pregnant. Up to this time she had hoped the man would marry her. When he found that she was pregnant he refused to marry her, but made her work as an inmate in the house of prostitution daily, and collected all her money; he refused to give her any street clothes, and made her continue to work during her pregnancy and up to the time she went to the hospital. She did not go to the hospital until the day before her child was born. She was forced to continue her work when she was too ill to walk, and suffered terrible pain. The man refused to give her any money, and she went to a charitable hospital. While she was in the hospital, the man took another prostitute and left Washington for Butte, Mont."

The cadet as villain, as the sum of iniquity—that would be an egregious oversimplification.* And it flies in the face of everything already said about prostitutes. For by and large they were his willing

---

* Cadets were human too and they often helped women—for a price, to be sure—toward whom society, life, had turned a cruel face. In *Jews Without Money* Michael Gold tells the story of one such:

"[Rosie] worked for years in the sweatshops saving money to bring her parents from Europe. Then she fell sick. Her savings melted. She went to a hospital. She came

accomplices, and we include many of those he deceived, seduced, gulled into submission. The cadet typically drew his "victim" from women who had spent time in this country, who had become somewhat acculturated, who were prepared for the choice he represented and held out to them. That so-and-so was a cadet on the prowl was hardly a secret; his carriage and clothes and air were his badge of identity. He did his recruiting, he sought out the susceptible, accordingly, wherever women gathered: on the streets, in factories and workshops,* and in places of entertainment. Especially the dance halls.

As early as the 1880s Jacob Riis, a fairly perceptive reporter, noticed that the "young people in Jewtown [his term for the Lower East Side] are inordinately fond of dancing." Riis went on to describe how these dances often erupted into free-for-alls; at which point the "police come in, as usual, and ring down the curtain." And yet what choice did young people have? For as little as a nickel men and women—those with enough energy to do so—could enjoy a whole evening's fun, make new friends, in any event escape the tedium and thrall of the twelve-hour workday. By 1900 dance halls abounded; one or two could be found on every block. "If you walk along Grand Street on any night in the week during the winter months," wrote the great social worker and reformer Belle Lindner Israels (later Moscowitz), "the glare of lights and the blare of music strikes you on every side. It might be an esplanade at Dreamland instead of a busi-

---

out and could not find a job. She was hungry, feeble, and alone. No one cared whether she lived or died.

"She was ready for the river. A pimp met her. He took her to a restaurant and fed her her first solid meal. He made her a practical offer. Rosie accepted. She never regretted her choice; it was easier than being in a sweatshop. She saved money to send for her parents, and she was never sick with asthma again."

* Here is what the Committee of Fifteen wrote in 1912 in *The Social Evil*: "By occasional visits he [the cadet] succeeds in securing the friendship of some attractive shopgirl. By apparently kind and generous treatment, and by giving the young girl glimpses of a standard of living which she never had dared hope to attain, their friendship rapidly ripens into infatuation. The Raines Law hotel ... is soon visited for refreshments. After a drugged drink, the girl weakens and finds herself at the mercy of her supposed friend. Through fear and promises of marriage she casts her fortune with her companion and goes to live with him. The companion disappears and the shopgirl finds herself an inmate of a house of prostitution."

ness street. Columbia Street, Delancey Street, Stanton Street, Allen Street, Houston Street all have their quota of places, good, bad and indifferent." Most, by her reckoning, were bad and indifferent. Popular too were the dancing academies, where women learned the art and in the process learned how to socialize American-style. Cadets liked the academies because they attracted so many recently arrived immigrant girls and they often enjoyed the cooperation of the dance teacher or "spieler" (an untranslatable word meaning someone who plays). Reformers like Belle Lindner Israels judged the dance halls and academies by severe moral criteria. "You cannot dance night after night, held in the closest of sensual embraces, with every effort made in the style of dancing to appeal to the worst in you and remain unshaken by it. No matter how wary or wise a girl may be—and she has enough things in her daily life in factory and store to teach her— she is not always able to keep up the good fight. It is always a matter of pursuit and capture."

Reformers generally favored shutting down the dance halls and academies, treating them as if they were so many Raines Law hotels, "gathering places," as one settlement-house worker put it, for the "moral degenerates of the neighborhood." Some like Mrs. Israels realized, however, that this solution, even if desirable, would have been impossible to carry out, and they proposed more modest reform: the regulation of the dancing establishments—licensing them, for one thing—so that they might become decent and wholesome; or, better yet, the creation of alternative places, run by social work agencies and settlement houses. ("In one you see an instrument for the uplifting of the community; in the other an influence that certainly lowers the standard of morality.") Little came of these proposals, however, for young Jews had their own notions of what was decent and wholesome and pleasurable. And they were right. Rough-hewn and ungenteel and unsupervised as they were, and despite the lurking presence of cadets, the dance halls and academies, taking them all in all, did an admirable job in helping maintain the equipoise of the hard-pressed masses, in seeing them through the travails of those ghetto years.

With the passage of time cadets become more professionalized, more entrepreneurial. The successful ones came to dominate the industry, success being measured by the number of women in one's stable, the number of houses one owned, the weight one carried among one's peers. A distinction thus emerged between the petty entrepreneur, who had one or two or at most a handful of women in his employ, and the large-scale middleman, the procurer, who had many.

Some were large-scale indeed. Motche Goldberg ("King of the Vice Trust") had started out in the 1890s with one girl; by 1912 he had a controlling interest in eight whorehouses and 114 women and was earning $4,000 a month, an incalculable amount by today's standards. Capitalists like Goldberg, furthermore, possessed resources that enabled them to go far afield in pursuit of business, to ship their women wherever the traffic was most profitable—out west, even to the remotest mining towns, and abroad as well.*

This propensity of New York cadet-capitalists for traveling gave rise to a more general fear (to be taken up later in detail) that there indeed existed a "vice trust," a network of Jewish white slavers headquartered in the notorious Jewish ghetto of lower Manhattan. Those who made the charge pointed to a legally incorporated outfit called the New York Independent Benevolent Association, a huge ring, so it was assumed, of procurers, cadets, madams, prostitutes, and their upperworld political and economic helpmates. On closer examination, however, the Benevolent Association proved to be only that: a burial and mutual-aid society for people whom the Jewish community had anathematized and disinherited. As to the charge of a specific Jewish monopoly or conspiracy in the sale of vice, the Immigration Commission repeated what all the authorities who studied the subject had: "There are large numbers of Jews scattered throughout the U.S., although mainly located in New York and Chicago, who seduce and keep girls. Some of these are engaged in importation, but apparently they prey rather upon the young girls

---

* It was around this time that the myth of the passionate, hence desirable, Jewish redheaded prostitute gained currency around the country. Nell Kimball, a prostitute and madam, describes in her memoirs what happened when the procurers and their women came to San Francisco at the turn of the century: "[The] rage for redheaded Jew girls took on in the town. Most of the Jew girls were snappy but willing, and a great many of them soon became madams. They learned quickly and they gave a john the act he was impressing them, driving them mad with his abilities as a man."

whom they find on the streets, in the dancehalls and similar places and whom, by the methods already indicated ... they deceive and ruin." And that, in the end, was all there was to it.

Cadets naturally enjoyed the protection of the Tammany political system. This was the sine qua non of their political existence. But cadets needed more help than their political friends, however well paid, could supply. The politicians did not care how cadets handled their own affairs, worked out their intramural relations, so long as they upheld their part of the bargain. Cadets, then, had little guarantee that they would not be the quarry of other predators, of those who could seize their means of production, their territories. And since they could scarcely ask the law to step in, there being no legal claim, no rights, in the underworld, they had to defend themselves in the accustomed manner: hire their own enforcers; that is, pay a second tribute. In self-defense, the use of hoodlums or gangsters to secure one's illicit livelihood thus became inseparable from prostitution, became its logical corollary, on the Lower East Side and everywhere else in the city. One can argue that respectable society was mainly responsible for this marriage of vice and crime.* By outlawing prostitution society gave it over *tout court* to the most violent segment of the underworld. That was the supremely immoral act; and the Jewish community in particular paid dearly for it.

• • •

m

Whether Jews gambled more than other people, or gambled much at all, is an open question. That they did gamble at least to some extent, and from the moment they landed on the Lower

---

* By the first decade of the twentieth century the "social evil" had grown so rampant that the leading citizens who comprised New York City's Committee of Fourteen were urging the legalization of prostitution and its removal from the tenement districts to carefully assigned red-light areas. What the folks at large thought of this proposal, born of desperation, can be imagined. Except in whispered conversations behind closed doors it was never taken seriously.

East Side in 1881, is not in question. Now friends playing cards for money—common among Jews and everyone else—is one thing. Men playing against a house in the hope that a tiny investment might yield an astronomical return is quite another. The player who takes on the house thus assumes a double burden: he bets against the laws of probability, and he does so on terms laid down by his adversary, an expert in his line of work whose honesty is inversely proportional to the player's credulity and innocence. No gambler, in short, will hesitate to cheat if he can get away with it. (For good reason, then, the unswerving rule of the profession is and always has been "never give a sucker an even break," a sucker being defined tautologically as anyone who tries his luck against a professional.) To the extent that they gambled at all the earlier Jewish immigrants obviously did so for tiny stakes. The neighborhood houses they frequented were run by German or Irish or American proprietors. The Jews learned fast though, as is their wont, and in gambling as in prostitution they soon had their own proprietors and establishments.

Above all other games Jews favored *stuss*, a Yiddish word meaning "joke, jest, nonsense, a bit of foolishness." Stuss was a variation of faro, which took Europe and the United States (where it was also called "bucking the tiger") by storm in the nineteenth century and which citified Jews in the old country may have once played.

To get a more precise idea of the game, which eventually disappeared and remains only as a curio of the past, let us imagine a typical Lower East Side stuss parlor of the 1880s or 1890s, carved out of a tenement apartment or storefront or cellar. The players face a table on which are painted or glued cards representing each of the deck's thirteen denominations. If protocol is observed the first row (seen from right to left) shows a king, queen, jack, ten, nine, and eight; the second row an ace, two, three, four, five, and six; in between, on the extreme left, is the seven. Using chips of diverse colors, or simply coins, the players bet on the denomination of their choice. The dealer turns up two cards at a time. Those who have bet the number shown on the first card lose; those who have bet the second win; if both cards turn up the same number (a "split") the house takes everything. On the face of it stuss, like faro, was rather fair to the players, the odds of winning being just under fifty-fifty. But the professionals, the "bankers," true to their calling, usually tilted the odds to their advantage by cheating, seeing to it that the heavily bet numbers won less often than they otherwise might have.* Presumably the players were aware of the cheating, certainly of the strong possibility of it. Yet that hardly deterred them from playing. Then as now nothing discourages the habitual gambler.

At any rate, stuss parlors multiplied, the more prosperous ones becoming in time larger and fancier and offering their patrons poker and pinochle and twenty-one and any other game they might like to play, and for stakes that would have been deemed unthinkable once. The stuss parlor had evolved into the casino.

The poolroom was another favorite institution. The poolroom of old New York should not be confused with today's variant, really only its namesake, the billiard parlor. In the nineteenth and early twentieth century pool meant betting on horses, and one went to a poolroom then much as one might go today to a bookmaker (or in New York City to an OTB—Offtrack Betting—store), with this difference: the poolroom was also where one often spent a day among friends watching the "dope sheet" posted on the bulletin board to see how the horses fared at the various tracks (the information being conveyed via telegraph and telephone) or reading the latest issue of the *Morning Telegraph* and one also whiled away the time talking shop, playing cards, or shooting billiards. Hence the invidious association of pool and billiards; hence the taint of evil attaching to poolrooms for decades after they had ceased to be horse-betting establishments. Because poolrooms required more capital than stuss parlors, it took longer for Jews to gain entrée into this lucrative business. Eventually it became as much theirs on the Lower East Side as the stuss parlors.†

---

* "To justify the expenditure," R. F. Foster, perhaps the best authority on the subject, wrote in 1914, the banker "must have some permanent advantage, and if no such advantage or 'percentage' is inherent in the principle of the game, any person playing against such a banker is probably being cheated."

† Abe Shoenfeld describes one such poolroom, Harry Green's place at 267 Rivington Street. "Harry Green is an ex-pickpocket. . . . He is about 28 years old—5 ft. 6 inches—135 lbs.—blonde hair. He has a reputation as a pugilist and also a prison record trailing in his wake. . . . This place is consequently patronized by thieves, yegmen,

About the time they moved in, anti-vice crusaders had begun to mount a great assault on the poolrooms. The muckraking press was full of articles exposing and condemning them, especially those in New York City, as sinks of depravity and corruption. Reform judges and district attorneys would periodically order them raided and shut down. Some skeptics even then wondered why betting at the track should be legitimate while betting in a poolroom ("a horse race without horses") should not. One New York City police captain in charge of conducting the raids let out the truth when he asserted: "The man who goes to a race-track to gamble is presumably a man of leisure, and, therefore, possessed of means which he can afford to lose. The poolrooms are an invasion of neighborhoods in which wage-earners, salaried men and boys, are likely to be tempted. . . . That tends to produce destitution. It also tends to destroy character and take away the incentive to individual effort by holding out a constant hope of making money without work." But the crusaders' zeal would invariably peter out and the poolrooms would open again and prosper as before. Nothing could extinguish them.

By the turn of the century Jewish gamblers were important members of the Lower East Side political fraternity. They had paid their dues to Tammany Hall in return for the right to stay in business. (An informal "Gambling Commission" made up of Tammany chieftains met weekly to grant or renew licenses to applicants, the size of the "tax" depending on the volume of profits. In one year alone, 1899, the Commission received $3,095,000 in gambling payments.*) The Lower East Side's presiding monarch, Timothy D. "Big Tim" Sullivan, worked closely with its gambling elite, investing in its houses and inviting their investments in his. He was pleased to launch "smart young Jewboys"—the likes of Herman Rosenthal,

---

guns, second story men, macks and others in similar fields of enterprise. . . . [It] is patronized by young boys. After school they come in here and learn how to play pool. Inves. found these young boys playing pool during school hours, and from their talk gathered that they were playing 'hookey.'"
* Gambling houses were also expected to supply jobs for the faithful; each customarily hired at least one ward heeler for a "no-show" position at the going rate of five dollars a day.

Louis "Bridgey" Webber, Sam Paul, and Arnold Rothstein—on their way to the big time. With Sullivan's help they opened such large, opulent neighborhood casinos as Sam Paul's resort, the Hesper's Club on Second Avenue, and the Sans Souci on Fourteenth Street. And they also went into cognate fields of endeavor: loan-sharking, insurance-selling, bail-bonding—anything to do with money, for they were, in effect, all-around bankers. And like bankers the top gamblers wore their new-won status proudly, ostentatiously. They could hardly be mistaken for lowly cadets or the petty hustlers and toughs operating on every block. They were shining exemplars of the American promise.

No Lower East Side gambler, none of Big Tim Sullivan's Jewish darlings, was destined to travel further and attain greater fame than Arnold Rothstein. From the outset Rothstein was an anomaly: fear of poverty had never been the spur to his ambition. He was born in 1882 into a fairly well-off family, so well-off it could afford to live in a fine uptown house and send its children to the best schools. But as a boy Arnold was drawn to the Lower East Side underworld, its poolrooms and stuss parlors and street life in general, as to a magnet; there was no denying him. (His wife tells of the extraordinary lengths he would go to to "borrow" money. His father, a pious man, would put his money and valuables away in a drawer as the Sabbath approached. Young Rothstein would rifle the drawer, gamble through the following day, and replace the amount before sundown. "Sometimes he even took his father's watch, pawned it, gambled with the proceeds, redeemed the watch, and slipped it back in the drawer, undetected.") Rothstein many years later explained his passion: "I always gambled. I can't remember when I didn't. Maybe I gambled just to show my father that he couldn't tell me what to do, but I don't think so. I think I gambled because I loved the excitement. When I gambled nothing else mattered. I could play for hours and not know how much time had passed." Not, he added, that he was "different from the other kids. Everyone gambled."

Sullivan recognized Rothstein's talents and asked him to manage his gambling concession in the Metropole Hotel on Forty-third Street. This was the break Rothstein had hoped for; it brought him into the thick of the uptown crowd, the universe of wealth and notoriety. Soon, with Sullivan's approval, he had opened his own place a few blocks away. Mastering the art of public relations, practicing every subtlety of self-advertisement, using women as "steerers," Rothstein attracted more and more of the "high-rolling" players of the day to his casino, among them such men as Charles Gates (son of John W. "Bet-a-Million" Gates), Julius Fleischmann (the yeast king), Joseph Seagram (the Canadian whiskey baron), Harry Sinclair (the oil magnate), and Percival H. Hill (of the American Tobacco Company), taking them for astronomical amounts of money. Hill, for example, lost a cool $250,000 to Rothstein in a single night of play. The rich, he discovered, were only suckers on a larger scale.

Rothstein's uptown colleagues, all non-Jews, were scarcely pleased by his triumphs. Anti-Semites or not, they feared that he would be only the first of many, that the coming of the Lower East Side gamblers would change the character of their fashionable district—the meatiest part of the Tenderloin—and in due course drive them out.* But Rothstein demonstrated that the district's character had already changed, or was ready for the change he brought. The significant fact was that the high-rollers and playboys, whatever they thought of arriviste Jewish entrepreneurs like Rothstein (he was no cultured gentleman-gambler in the tradition of Richard Canfield, Frank Farrell, and Tim Churchill), were willing to patronize his casino because they enjoyed his dash and bravado, his type of play, his unlimited stakes. They at least did not especially care that he might be the first of many Jews to make his mark in the neighborhood. And so he was. The direst prophecies of Arnold Rothstein's detractors were to come true.

---

* This animosity against Rothstein forms the background of a celebrated incident that occurred shortly after he had opened his own house. Rothstein happened to be a first-rate pocket-billiard player, a skill he perfected in his poolroom years. His colleagues, taunting him without letup, got him at last to bet that he could beat the player of their choice. Their aim was to embarrass and discredit him, perhaps send him back to the fleshpots of the Lower East Side. They produced a Philadelphia shark named Jack Conway. The game, which took place at John McGraw's billiard parlor (yes, *the* John McGraw, fabled manager of the New York Giants), lasted thirty-four straight hours, becoming a highly publicized marathon, tensely watched by hundreds of Broadway cognoscenti. Thanks to a spectacular "run" Rothstein finally devoured the shark and turned what should have been a debacle into a personal victory. The papers made much of this New York "sportsman."

Like cadets and procurers, gamblers discovered that Tammany protection was insufficient. Against present and future enemies, competitors, hoodlums, and thieves who lurked in every crevice of their society, who were a constant menace to their lives and properties, gamblers had to rely on their own praetorian guard. And, moreover, how else but through such enforcers could they ever collect their debts? Outside the law it is fear of injury that alone validates the obligations of contract. So we note again how the satisfaction of an illicit pleasure became a major source of criminal venality, how, ramifying endlessly, it sustained the most sordid part of the underworld culture. And we note again where vice truly lay: with those who in the name of virtue declared that pleasure illicit and shrouded it in darkness.

w

The agents of "vice" might be a bothersome presence, a moral affliction, at the least a reproach to the community. But they did not force their attentions on customers; they only offered to service their forbidden desires. Criminals belonged to a more lethal underworld species. The capacity to deliver violence was their métier, terror was the service they sold or inflicted on others.

It would be interesting to know when the first certified Jewish criminal showed up on the Lower East Side; also, who he was, where he came from in the old country, why he took to this particular vocation. Unanswerable questions, of course. All the chronicler knows is that just as social need called forth the Jewish prostitute, the Jewish cadet, and the Jewish gambler, so it called forth the Jewish criminal, the practitioner of violent deeds.

Like his counterparts in every other poor neighborhood the Jewish criminal exploited the opportunities that lay close at hand. He shook down peddlers and pushcart vendors and storeowners, anyone with property vulnerable to assault, anyone whose livelihood could be easily impeded. He was occasionally a burglar or thief or "fagin." One such fagin, Harry Joblinsky, had fifteen nimble pickpockets under his wing; another, Abe Greenthal, commanded the notorious Sheeny Gang. More often, the criminal was a fence, a receiver and mover of stolen goods. For years the untitled queen of the fences was "Mother" Fredrika Mandelbaum, squat and corpulent, whose Clinton Street notions store concealed a gigantic operation, citywide, indeed nationwide if the accounts about her are true, complete with a battery of defense lawyers and a whole communications network.* Common too, and especially loathsome for obvious reasons, was the arsonist who would gut a house or store for the insurance it brought him or his employer. In the early 1890s, after an epidemic of neighborhood fires, the authorities sent eighteen of the worst arsonists to jail, some for life. The most fiendish of them, Isaac Zucker, had a ring of "mechanics," each of whom he paid $25 for burning down a building or store which he, Zucker, had insured.

Yet, all in all, these were random, episodic crimes carried out by "lone-wolf" individuals and rings and routinely dealt with by the police. Very rarely, it should be pointed out, were Jews ever muggers or rapists or holdup men, nor did they indulge in the sort of anomic and senseless violence that we who live in the inner city are familiar with today. The Lower East Side ghetto was a horror, but its streets were safe even at night. Fear of physical harm was absent in the community.†

Another kind of criminal eventually arose, less crude and more insidious, one who served society even as he preyed on it, one who it could be said performed a quasi-legitimate function. We refer to the

---

* Here is how Lewis E. Lawes, onetime warden of Sing Sing, describes Mother Mandelbaum: "The energy of her character seemed to be all drawn down into the capacious thick blubbered reservoir of her body, quiescent in reserve for things more vital than a handshake: and some of it welled up and shone forth in the rich geniality of her smile. 'They call me Ma,' she said expansively, 'but I ain't their mother. Not the real one. But I'm a real mother too. Four, Gott bless them. But to them,' she waved her hand toward Mr. Pitney [one of her business associates], 'I am Ma because I give them what a mother cannot sometimes give—money and horses and diamonds. When they call me Ma I know they are happy.'"

† But we must not be carried away. Robbery on the Lower East Side was all too common and merchants regularly cried out for police protection. One day in April 1911 hundreds of Lower East Side storekeepers stormed the Criminal Court Building to testify before the grand jury on the problem. *The New York Times* reported: "[M]any of the 400 told remarkable stories of robberies. Several had had their homes or places of business plundered half a dozen times since the first of the year. One man said that his loss through robberies amounted to more than his profits for the entire year. Others told of moving to other parts of the city to escape the depradations of gangs which operated without police molestation in their neighborhood."

member of those organized gangs that emerged around the turn of the century and that came to dominate the neighborhood's underworld culture. By organized gang we mean more than just a group or association of criminals; we mean a group or association of criminals who sold their labor power, their specific skills—their ability to get things done through violence—on the open market and to the highest bidder, much as any business did, and with the consent of the authorities. Violence, like vice, had its uses. A closer look at the first of the major Jewish gangs, Monk Eastman's, illustrates the point.

Monk Eastman, born Edward Osterman, "began life with a bullet-shaped head, and during his turbulent career acquired a broken nose and a pair of cauliflower ears, which were not calculated to increase his beauty. He had heavily veined, sagging jowls, and a short bullneck, plentifully scarred with battle marks, as were his cheeks. He seemed always to need a haircut, and he accentuated his ferocious and unusual appearance by affecting a derby hat several sizes too small, which perched precariously atop his shock of bristly, unruly hair." That is how Herbert Asbury, the most entertaining historian of New York gangs, pictures Monk Eastman as one might have seen him in his heyday, 1901 say, strutting down Lower East Side streets with his henchmen at his side. Asbury draws on earlier accounts of the gangster, all of which describe him as a brute who loved violence for its own sake, who carried an assortment of weapons—brass knucks, blackjack, pistol—that he used with pleasure. (It is said, however, that he never used them when slugging a woman.) The newspapers were full of his gang's escapades, its brawls and intramural killings, all done with perfect impunity: for what witness would foolishly step forward to testify against them?* To his con-

---

* Much is made of Monk Eastman's interminable feud with another fabled thug of the times, Paul Kelly (originally Paulo Antonio Vaccarelli), boss of the Five Pointers, an Italian outfit whose most famous graduates would later be John Torrio and Alphonse Capone. The Eastman-Kelly feud erupted into an extraordinary gun battle one day in August 1903: scores of bandits—the police estimated a hundred—shot at each other from behind the pillars of the Second Avenue El. When the smoke cleared, three lay dead and seven wounded. A truce was called after the supreme Tammany sachems marked out a buffer zone between the two gangs, the warring Italians and Jews. The truce, it goes without saying, did not last very long.

temporaries Monk Eastman was as frightening as he looked, malevolence incarnate.

But to emphasize this side of his career, the side displayed by "his ferocious and unusual appearance," is to lose sight of what made Eastman what he was, what distinguished him from the run-of-the-mill criminal who might have been just as unlovely as he. In fact, Eastman's career was on the whole quite prosaic and businesslike. Early on in life he was part of the Lower East Side, or Tenth Ward, clubhouse organization, an organic part of the system that controlled the city. He worked as a bouncer in "Silver Dollar Smith's" famous saloon—the floor of which was inlaid with silver dollars—situated, not accidentally, across from the Essex Market Courthouse, the organization's home base and source of power. Silver Dollar Smith, a Jew whose real name was Charles Solomon (or was it Finkelstein? or Goldschmidt? no one knew for sure), was one of its high-ranking members, a status conferred upon him and them by their ability to round up votes.

Of Smith, Abraham Cahan writes: "Once I saw him making a campaign speech from the rear of a wagon parked diagonally across from his saloon. After talking for about five minutes, he growled: 'Boys, you know I deliver a better speech in my place than out here in the street. Let's go, boys!' The entire crowd followed him into his saloon. He set up drinks for everybody—on the house! That was the kind of speech he made." Tammany, meaning Big Tim Sullivan above all, depended on the likes of Silver Dollar Smith to get out the votes—for without them nothing was possible, with them everything—and Smith in turn depended on such men as Monk Eastman. So Eastman formed his own strong-arm cadres, paying them well to ensure that the citizens of the neighborhood voted, and voted often. Once mobilized, his gang hardly limited itself to this one activity; it branched out into or usurped other fields of enforcement and intimidation, serving local cadets and gamblers (among them the fast-rising Arnold Rothstein) along with music and dance halls and manufacturers wishing to protect scabs from striking trade unionists or, conversely, trade unionists wishing to protect themselves from employers. The accompanying violence, then, was directed mainly against professional opponents, rivals competing for the same or contiguous territories.

Not that Monk Eastman's men were averse to individual acts of thievery, extortion, and other conventional predacities; only they had to perform them within the limits set by the gang, the collective will as interpreted by its leader. And indeed it was precisely such buccaneering gangsterism that finally brought down Eastman himself. One day in February 1904 he shot a Pinkerton detective while attempting to rob someone; he had gone too far this time and Tammany could no longer protect him. After a speedy trial and conviction he received ten years at Sing Sing. Eastman was finished as a gang leader and he dropped out of sight.*

The portrait of the man is thus more complex than one is at first led to believe. Bad as he was, Eastman obviously knew how to conduct himself with local politicians and businessmen and vice lords. Whatever impression he gave, or affected, he was at bottom a shrewd and seasoned operator. It was that ability to deal with the outside world, with the customers who bought the services his gang offered, that defined his role as its boss. We can say, further, that Eastman (and for that matter any gang leader) continued to play his role only as long as he was successful in those dealings with the outside, success being measured by the enlargement of territories and membership and, not to be minimized, by deferences received from friend and foe. With good cause the gang could regard itself as the visible church, the ghetto's elect.

Monk Eastman's torch was picked up by one of his lieutenants, Max Zweibach, a talented killer who adopted, or was given, the nom de guerre of Kid Twist. Little is known about Kid Twist's past, where he or his parents came from, or how he developed from juvenile delinquent to professional gunman. What is known is that he seized power only after considerable struggle. His main rival within the gang was one Richie Fitzpatrick (a pseudonym obviously). After

---

* Eastman returned to the Lower East Side after serving most of his term, but there was no longer any place for him and he drifted about for years. In 1917, soon after war was declared, he joined the army and fought valorously in France. (New York's governor honored him by giving him back his rights as a citizen.) Again he tried to reestablish himself on the streets. Prohibition gave him the chance, but rival bootleggers cut this short by gunning him down on December 26, 1920. This headlined event suddenly brought back memories of the distant past; it seemed the resurrection of a very ancient ghost.

much blood was spilled between their factions the two men agreed to settle their differences amicably in a Chrystie Street bar.

Fitzpatrick arrived there first. Just then the lights went out and a shot was fired. When the lights returned Fitzpatrick lay stone dead on the floor.

Asbury and others cite this and similar incidents to prove Kid Twist's duplicity and cunning; not for nothing was he also called Kid Sly Fox. But these were classic virtues in the underworld culture, and Twist was undoubtedly right to assume that Fitzpatrick had a similar trick up his own sleeve. At any rate, Kid Twist carried on where Eastman left off, furnishing protection to various Lower East Side institutions, some illicit and some not, from brothels and casinos and stuss parlors to manufacturers, while keeping an army of "repeaters" (those who voted more than once) for Tammany Hall.

Twist was also reputed to have established his own lucrative celery tonic monopoly in the neighborhood, celery tonic—a mixture of syrup and carbonated water—having been a favorite soft drink among Jews. Candy stores, cafes, and restaurants found Twist an extremely persuasive salesman. In smoothness and finesse he represented a definite advance over Monk Eastman. He resolved that henceforth "no 'wop' and no 'mick'" would "rule over the Lower East Side of New York."

But Kid Twist got his comeuppance, too. On May 14, 1908, he and a bodyguard, Samuel Teitsch, a circus strong man who went by the stage name of "Cyclone Lewis" (his specialty was bending iron bars around his, or an opponent's, neck) were both shot to death outside a Coney Island bar. Their assassin, Louis "Louie the Lump" Pioggi, did the deed—so it was alleged—for personal revenge, because he and Kid Twist were in love with the same woman, Carroll Terry, a music-hall singer. That may have been the motive, yet it should be said that Louie the Lump belonged to the Five Pointers, whose war with the reigning Jewish gang had never let up, and that a horse-drawn carload of Five Pointers was present at the scene of the murder. It would not be amiss to believe that Louie took the rap for the gang (no huge sacrifice: he got only a few months for it).

Next in line of descent was William Alberts, or Big Jack Zelig to the underworld at large and to the citizens of New York City. Zelig beat back every other aspirant for gang leadership thanks to his three close comrades-in-arms, each a notable "life-taker": Jacob "Whitey Lewis" Seidenschnier, Louis "Lefty Louie" Rosenberg, and, worst of all, Harry "Gyp the Blood" Horowitz, an unusually vicious brute whose strength, belied by his modest size and weight, enabled him to break a man's back, a skill he would demonstrate from time to time, and the very mention of whose name produced a tremor of fear.

Zelig was born on the Lower East Side in 1882 of parents who were middle class by the standards of the day. In his early teens he ran away from home to become a pickpocket, graduating to the status of fagin. He seems to have been a fetching lad, with large innocent brown eyes, his appearance giving him an advantage in his run-ins with the law. Still, he served his share of time in reformatories and prisons and when barely twenty was already one of Monk Eastman's prize gunmen.

As gang leader, Zelig exhibited the same duplex, even schizophrenic character that his predecessors had. On the one hand he managed the protection business splendidly, expanding and systematizing it, offering his clients fixed rates for services performed: up to $10 for a knife slash on the cheeks; up to $25 for a bullet in the leg or arm; up to $50 for throwing a bomb; up to $100 for a murder. Numerous cadets, dance- and music-hall owners, operators of stuss parlors and poolrooms and casinos, and employers in the garment trades paid him handsomely to keep order (which often enough meant to be left alone by him). He consorted with politicians and banker-gamblers, uptown as well as on the Lower East Side, his home base. There was no containing Big Jack Zelig.

On the other hand he, even more than his predecessors, was forever engaged in open and highly publicized feuds and jurisdictional disputes with his enemies. There was the time, for example, when his three comrades struck down the famous desperado "Spanish Louie," a Sephardic Jew easily recognized by his black clothes and sombrero; or when—as he lay in the hospital with a bullet wound in the head—his gang shot up Chick Trickster's Bowery headquarters, the Fleabag, in a massive display of force; or when he himself slew the gunman Julius Morrello who had been commissioned to kill him, the shootout taking place before a large crowd at the Stuyvesant Casino, a fancy Second Avenue ballroom. (Morrello, it was said, had shouted as he walked through the door, "Where's that big Yid Zelig? I gotta cook that big Yid!") And while all this was going on his gang's battle with the Five Pointers, now headed by Jack Sirocco, was continuing unabated, from one generation of gangsters to another.

The crescendo of assaults and counterassaults on Lower East Side streets and establishments finally had their effect on public opinion. The police were compelled to go after Zelig; he had become too hot. Responding to public outcry, a few years earlier the state legislature had passed the Sullivan Act (sponsored by Tammany boss Big Tim Sullivan to prove that he and his organization were no friends of the gangsters) which outlawed the possession of unlicensed weapons. So now, to avoid arrest, or rather harassment—naturally he had others carry his gun for him—Zelig sewed his pockets tight. Not that that helped either, for he was jailed repeatedly on manufactured charges. But his troubles came to an abrupt end on October 5, 1912, the day a petty hoodlum with a grudge, Phillip "Red Phil" Davidson, killed him on a Lower East Side trolley car. Found on his body was a packet of letters from his three comrades, Gyp the Blood, Whitey Lewis, and Lefty Louie, all of whom were, along with a fourth man, behind bars waiting to be tried for murder*

Taking over Zelig's gang, or what remained of it, was one of his coadjutors, Benjamin "Dopey Benny" Fein, specialist nonpareil in "labor" or "industrial relations." Born in 1889 into a typically penurious Lower East Side family, Benny was a prodigy of the streets, where he acquired his nickname, a reference to his unusually heavy eyelids; by his early teens he was leading a gang of pickpockets and wagon thieves. Then came successive terms in Elmira Reformatory

---

* The reasons for their trial will be discussed in Chapter Two. Here we might note that their letters are a touching evocation of simple friendship and solidarity, giving us an impression of gangsters wholly different from the one drawn in the press or in the history books. Typical were Whitey Lewis' remarks: "I want you to stop worrying about us, as we have everything that we wish for, and we are having the best of times up here. We are here on a very short vacation to have a good rest and fatten us up. So if we hear that you are taking things to heart we will be very angry with you. So cheer up and be good. That is all we ask for."

and Sing Sing for various offenses, including armed robbery. In 1910, having just emerged from a three-and-a-half-year stretch, he joined Zelig's gang and immediately found himself involved in the burgeoning conflict between the unions and the manufacturers. That was when he mastered his trade in the field of labor and industrial relations. The enormous significance of Benny's rise must be seen against the backdrop of those larger events.

For years, under the very noses of Eastman and his epigones, the neighborhood had been experiencing a radical economic transformation. Sweatshops were giving way to factories. The garment industry was learning to meet the demands of a national market. Production grew by leaps, as did the number of workers and the amount of capital invested. Meanwhile, the workers in all the major facets of the industry—women's and men's apparel, furs and hats—were becoming increasingly restive. A new crop of militant, class-conscious men and women, many of them tempered by the Russian and Polish and Austrian Socialist and trade union movements, were providing more of the leadership now, emboldening the rank and file to organize and resist as never before. And so in 1909, twenty thousand female shirtwaist workers rose up and struck and stayed out for six months, a miraculous show of solidarity and courage; then the cloakmakers went out, followed by the furriers in 1912, and the men's clothing workers in 1913–14. The manufacturers obviously were not about to yield to upstart unions which, once recognized, would insist on yet more and more for their members, cutting into profits and reducing the possibility of further expansion; the unions had to be nipped in the bud no matter what the cost. When the strikes broke out the manufacturers, as was their historic wont, brought in other workers, scabs. But bringing them in was harder to carry off than in the old days when there had been such a huge surplus of labor, when unions were so pathetically weak and so poorly led. Many employers—not all but many, including the largest—hired strong-armers (guerillas or "schlammers" or "bolagulas") as never before to terrorize the rank and file and above all punish the leaders as only professionals knew how. Under the exigent circumstances the unions had little choice but go to the same source, hiring gangsters in turn as protection for their organizers and strikers.

Now Eastman, Twist, Zelig, and many other gangsters of lesser note had all earned money in past years serving both sides of the class struggle, beating up workers one day, scabs the next. Compared to Dopey Benny's operation, though, theirs was primitive and amateurish. Benny's specific genius lay in rationalizing the Lower East Side labor protection market. Like Zelig—but much more ruthlessly—he worked according to a fee schedule, the contractual arrangements for which were actually drawn up by lawyers and formally ratified by his clients. The fee varied with the job: for injuring or maiming a person—for "clipping his ear off," as the saying went—it ranged from a low of $50 to a high of $600, depending on the victim and the length of the desired incapacitation; injuring a foreman, for example, cost $200; so did a "complete knockout" of an ordinary scab. ("One job," said Benny, "concerned a forelady in an underwear shop. My employer said to me, 'The forelady in that shop knows the boss too well. He tells her everything. She has to get a good licking, and the best thing for you to do is to get somebody to throw her down the cellar.' ... We followed the woman till she was passing a saloon with an open cellar door. We threw her down the cellar and got away.... I got [only] $50 for the job.")

Benny charged $150 for wrecking a small firm, much more of course for a large one. And he was just as rational when it came to breaking down the fees within his organization. He took $12 a day for himself and paid each of his mobsters $7.50 exclusive of bonuses and other emoluments. Though he worked by the job he demanded regular salaried payments for himself and his men as insurance against the hazards common to his occupation, he himself having once been stabbed in the line of union duty and laid up for four months without income. Gangsters, he argued, also needed protection.

Benny even instituted a sort of due process—a kangaroo court more exactly—to guarantee that the orders and contractual obligations were observed, that justice was done. If a gang member violated internal rules or if a client broke his agreement, the gang, acting as a "General Sessions Court," decided how he should be punished: whether his thumb or arm or leg should be broken, his ear clipped, or worse. From these decisions there was no appeal.

It should be pointed out that Benny treated both sexes alike, giving equal pay for equal work. This was only right since women were indispensable to him, and he was smart enough to realize it. Some women served as the gang's "gun-toters," concealing the weapons in mufflers or wigs or a special hairdo popular in those days called a "Mikado tuck-up." Their primary duty, though, was to infiltrate the garment factories and make certain that a strike order was observed when it came down. Hat pins and weighted umbrellas were their favorite weapons of attack against scabs, recalcitrant rank-and-filers, employers, and occasionally the police as well. By all accounts Benny's women were terribly effective.

Benny gave further evidence of his genius by working out an elaborate system of territorial jurisdictions. Under his hegemony lesser gangs were free to service some of the unions on their own. Furriers and bakers, for instance, went to Joseph "Joe the Greaser" Rosenzweig and his band of toughs, among them Hyman "Little Hymie" Bernstein, Benjamin "Nigger Benny" Snyder, and Jacob "Tough Jake" Heiseman. To Joseph "Yoski Nigger" Toblinsky's horse thieves and poisoners, known as the "Jewish Black Hand Association," went control over the teamsters, Yoski and his top confederates each concentrating on a particular subdivision of the industry, Yoski himself taking livery stables, Charles "Charley the Cripple" Vitoffsky soda and seltzer deliveries, Jacob "Johnny" Levinsky ice cream deliveries, and so on. Yoski had his fee schedule too: for stealing a horse and rig, $25; for poisoning a single horse, $35; for poisoning a team, $50. Later he admitted that he personally had dispatched at least two hundred animals, each of them worth on the average between $300 and $500.

Benny's system also embraced the non-Jewish gangs in other neighborhoods. He drew up a treaty—that is what it amounted to—according to which the Hudson Dusters to the west and the Car Barn and Gas House gangs uptown would confine their activities to their own realms and would cooperate with each other in matters of mutual concern and always on the principle of reciprocity. If, say, the Hudson Dusters of Greenwich Village were offered a contract to demolish a Lower East Side shop, they would turn it over to Dopey Benny; he would of course do the same for them. In this complex of quid pro quos, this exchange of courtesies and favors, this attempt to impose a cartel on neighborhood crime, we have the crude precedent on which gangsterdom would one day build its mansion of national wealth and power. As yet it was only a gleam in a lonely prophet's eye.

Benny himself was something of a prophet. The system of territorial limits he tried to establish was still a distant ideal; its realization depended on whether he could eliminate his remaining opponents, those who resisted his hegemony within the neighborhood or, like the Five Pointers, refused to join the gang alliance outside it. Benny's failure would in time be his undoing and would have many far-reaching consequences to boot. But until then his gang came to occupy the summit of the Lower East Side underworld.

v

One rarely comes across Jewish gangsters, gamblers, cadets, and prostitutes who were in their thirties, hardly any who were in their forties. The Lower East Side underworld was a culture of young people. What the criminologist E. H. Sutherland wrote years later, generalizing from the Chicago experience with which he was familiar, certainly applied to New York's ghetto: "The age of maximum criminality lies ... in the young adult period of life. This period is not clearly defined, for delinquency or criminality increases from the age of ten to about nineteen, where it remains nearly constant until the age of twenty-seven, after which it decreases sharply with advancing age."* But what is also true is that the underworld had no trouble filling the places left vacant by the young men who dropped out by their mid- to late-twenties. It kept renewing itself; it kept bringing in fresh blood. That capacity to continually attract and sustain the young, to nurture successive generations, was the abiding measure of its triumph.

---

* This was borne out by a survey based on the names of New York criminals conducted in 1908. Of the 460 Jews convicted of felonies the year before, 259 were between fifteen and twenty-one and 143 between twenty-one and thirty, leaving only 58 (or 12.6 percent) who were over thirty. The survey is incomplete though because it omits those Jews—and there were many—who went by non-Jewish names, and also omits offenders under fifteen, an enormous group.

Youth gangs sprang up on the streets almost from the time the immigrants moved into the neighborhood. Youth gangs had been a feature of New York City lower-class life for decades, and they formed an institution in their own right. They represented another kind of response to the hammer blows of poverty and deracination that the urban proletariat suffered. Jewish (and Italian) families, like the Irish and German before them, often collapsed under the strain and yielded up their children to the nurturing warmth of the streets. At best the conflict between home and streets was a standoff, a tense modus vivendi. At worst it was a war, the outcome of which hung in the balance until the children reached late adolescence. This conflict of the generations, writes Morris Raphael Cohen, the great teacher and philosopher, was "so fraught with heart-rending consequences ... [that] the unity of life, nurtured by pride in the achievement of children, was broken. There was scarcely a Jewish home on the East Side that was free from the friction between parents and children. This explosive tension made it possible for the same family to produce saints and sinners, philosophers and gunmen."*

Boys joined gangs as a matter of course,† though not always voluntarily. There was hardly any way a boy could avoid answering to them; he certainly could not challenge their suzerainty. Here, for example, is what happened to a ten-year-old boy who with his mother

---

* Lincoln Steffens is an eloquent witness to this "tragic" struggle. "We saw it everywhere all the time," he writes in his *Autobiography*. "Responding to a reported suicide, we would pass a synagogue where a score or more of boys were sitting hatless in their old clothes, smoking cigarettes on the steps outside, and their fathers, all dressed in black, with their high hats, uncut beards and temple curls, were going into the synagogue, tearing their hair and rending their garments.... Their sons were rebels against the law of Moses; they were lost souls, lost to God, the family, and to Israel of old."

† We omit girls from these pages even though as time went on, as more and more children were born and reared in the ghetto, girls became gang members too—of a sort. "Often some of the more adventuresome girls of the same age in the district are taken into the secrets of the 'gang,'" the citizens' Committee of Fourteen reported in 1910. "The boy and girl chums soon become very intimate, and the strange loyalty begins which afterward astounds judges when they seek to secure evidence against the boys appearing before them as 'cadets.'" Such examples of boy-girl chumminess within gangs were frequent, but the fact remains that they were dominated by boys completely, that they were a boys' institution through and through.

and younger sister and another family had recently moved into a three-room tenement flat. "The boy's mother went out to work each day and left him to lead the life of the streets. He was a 'greenhorn' and hardly knew what it was to steal. A 'gang' set upon him, realizing his unprotected circumstances, and practically beat and bullied him into stealing from pushcart peddlars. He was finally caught, but let go by a kindhearted peddlar, who in turn tried to protect him from his tormentors. The boy, however, continued to receive their attention as long as he remained in the neighborhood."

The gang, willy-nilly, was the average boy's rite of passage to manhood. It was where he discovered solidarity, purpose, a hierarchy of values, loyalties, duties, a moral authority superior to society's and beyond the reach of his family. In this respect the Jewish boys' gang of the early 1900s resembles every other gang—Irish, Italian, Puerto Rican, black—that has laid claim before or since to its share of New York City streets.

And just as the gang gave meaning and sanctuary to its members, so it was at war, actively or potentially, with other gangs in the vicinity, whatever their ethnic composition (Irish to the west, Italian to the south). The most intense combat was fought with the nearest rivals, those gangs made up of fellow Jews. "If Division Street was at war with Henry Street," recalls Eddie Cantor, a prototypical child of Lower East Side streets, "and you tried to run an errand across Division, you'd get backed in a corner by the Division Street boys. They'd threaten to kill. What's more, they meant it." (In one of these fights young Cantor almost lost his life; he lay in a hospital for three months with a fractured skull.) Youth gangs reflected the neighborhood ethos of competition and conflict; it was their way of telling adults that they had evolved their own techniques for coping with the vicissitudes that would envelop them soon enough.

Youth gangs, then, went in for mischief, pranks, high jinks, fun usually at someone else's expense or suffering. Mainly they introduced kids to the forbidden mysteries of adulthood, the more forbidden and *outré* the more seductive. And of course nothing was more seductive, because nothing was more forbidden and *outré*, than the pervasive underworld culture that confronted them at every turn. If parents warned their children to stay away from the underworld, the

gangs to which they belonged exerted countervailing moral authority by experimenting with it. Through gangs children learned to
gamble—shooting craps and betting pool when they were old enough
were their favorite pastimes—consort with whores and cadets, hang
around the casinos and cafes and clubs (like Segal's) where underworld characters met, and in general imitate the lingo and dress and
carriage and manners of these "role models." The underworld characters were so fascinating because on top of everything else they exemplified the cynical truth behind the American dream, the incon-
trovertible fact that vice and crime were escape routes to freedom
and that all the preachings at home and in school and in the press
were so many lies and deceptions.* Success taught its own lessons.

It was the "rough gang," so-called, that took boys beyond the
thrill of breaking taboos, the limits of occasional vice and mischief. It
took them, perhaps by easy stages, to the exotic realm of crime, to a
whole gamut of crimes endemic to the neighborhood, as we have had
occasion to note: pickpocketing, stealing and extorting from storeowners and street vendors and pushcart dealers and ragpickers—
from anyone sufficiently marginal and defenseless to be at their mercy—to furnishing hoods for employers, and even burglarizing from
time to time.† As a lad Eddie Cantor belonged to "Pork-faced Sam's"
outfit which had its specific modus operandi. "The distracted storekeeper knew who had committed the theft, and the next day the leader came down to see him and sold him back his own stock of
bicycles." Pork-faced Sam's boys also served as scabs, each of them
receiving the sum, princely then, of three dollars a day. "I pulled a
cap down over my eyes, donned a big red sweater and flourished a

---

* "Thousands of children are growing up today with the belief—firmly rooted by
personal experience—that vice is not entirely incidental to life; it is the most comfortable and luxurious form of life they know; but also, that is the fact in their lives most
closely allied to, and most protected by, the only force of law and restraint they
know." So states a writer in the University Settlement Society of New York *Yearbook*
for 1900.

† Concerning the "rough gang" Frederick A. King wrote: "Jewish boys of this class
have a strong tendency toward playing the petty thief much more than toward drinking or committing an occasional misdemeanor, as is characteristic of youthful
offenders of other nationalities."

bat, looking for all the world like the chief of a gashouse gang, when in reality I was flat-chested, underweight, frightened at my own bluff, and ready to be blown over by a breath."* In thus accustoming boys to the use of violence, in going beyond mere cynicism and the practice of mere vice, the "rough gang" acted as the preparatory school for adult criminality; it was the transition to full-throated gangsterism.

It is possible to describe the prototype of the Lower East Side boy who step by step drifts into the underworld. He grows up in a broken home, at all odds a home ground down by poverty, confusion, ill fortune, defeat. As a member of his local "rough gang" he does the usual things, spending his days and nights in gambling joints, roaming the streets in search of anyone he can victimize (for kicks and money both), breaking the law—which he deems a piece of hypocrisy—with less and less compunction. He is, it should be added, quick, intrepid, energetic, resourceful. He earns the respect of his peers and perhaps also of the demimonde adults on whom he has modeled himself. Their respect for him increases greatly when he gets sent away to the reformatory as a certified juvenile delinquent. He is now something of a hero on the block. And by now, aged fifteen or so, he has acquired his vocation; he has earned his journeyman's card. He will be a gangster.

Now this ideal type in actual life took in many variations and exceptions. Arnold Rothstein and Big Jack Zelig, for example, came out of good solid middle-class homes; others completely circumvented youth gangs in arriving at their criminal vocations. What is more, few Lower East Side kids even of the roughest kind ended up as he, our prototype above, did. They may have done outrageous things, committed wrongs, violated the law, were caught and punished, but as adults and paterfamilias they usually led conventional lives, earn-

---

* Other gangs employed other techniques. Police Commissioner William McAdoo describes one: "A group of women in one of the Ghetto streets are marketing; along comes a boy about sixteen years of age apparently trying to ride a bicycle; he is stumbling and falling, mounting and dismounting. All at once he gets into the midst of the group of women, who have their satchels open, and down he goes, wheels and all, in among them. He clutches awkwardly here and there at them. In the meantime confederates have been busy picking pockets and snatching pocket-books right and left. The young thief is on his wheels in a jiffy; the plunder is slipped to him and he is off."

ing the little they had by the sweat of their brow. And for that matter it was far from certain that our ideal type of nascent gangster remained one, and if he did, for how long. In short, it was hard to be a Jewish gangster even if one had all the credentials. We have in mind the rara avis, the man who graduated from the streets and became a professional. But on the Lower East Side these rare birds comprised a multitude.

What did the Jewish community do—what could it do—about these delinquent and pre-delinquent boys? Very little, in fact. The Jewish Protectory and Aid Society, an uptown–sponsored philanthropy, was launched in 1902 and opened the Hawthorne School in Westchester County five years later. Its six cottages held nearly two hundred boys (and some girls later on), all of them sent there by New York Children's Court for an indefinite term—until, that is, the School decided to release them. Since the alternative was the reformatory the handful of Jewish kids selected to go to Hawthorne were lucky indeed. But they were all too few.[*]

The settlement houses, those financed by wealthy Jews (the Educational Alliance, the Henry Street Settlement) and Christians, did attempt, often valiantly, to accomplish something; and posterity owes them its gratitude. If they had any single mission it was to rescue children from the horror surrounding them—as many children as they could, at any rate. There, however, lies the nub of the problem. At best the settlement houses might rescue a token few youngsters, bringing them along nicely, even putting one or two of them through college. (Some of these youngsters were known as "SEI Boys," or graduates of the "SEI Club," SEI standing for Social and Educational Improvement.) But the settlement houses and charity organizations could scarcely touch the more than fifty thousand Jewish school-age children who lived on the Lower East Side at the time.

And the outsiders, for all their good intentions and noblesse oblige and accomplishments—nothing to be despised—often failed

---

[*] In one year, 1909, three thousand Jewish youngsters appeared before Juvenile Court.

the few children they did manage to attract. We have a bitter and devastating critique of these outside institutions, Jewish and gentile alike, written in 1904 by a local journalist for the Yiddish press, A. H. Fromenson, who saw the problem from the viewpoint of the child, the recipient of their ministrations. "True, these institutions have their clientele," Fromenson wrote. "A certain number of people visit them a certain number of times a year, a month, or a week. Some more, some less. A certain very inconsiderable minority of the great mass of human beings take advantage of the opportunities offered by the Settlements and the Education Alliance. When all is said and done, however, when every claim made for them by their most enthusiastic admirers and workers is conceded, it is as if these institutions did not exist at all. Worse even than that, they are regarded by a very large number with absolute antipathy and by another very large number with distrust."

Fromenson faults them especially for having failed to check the rise of criminality among the Jewish young. Instead of appreciating the Jewish boy for what he is—"a virile, healthy animal, with an exuberance of spirits which finds its natural outlets only in physical expression and boyish pastime"—the settlements "expected him to take advantage of classes for the study of Homer and Shakespeare, to read Plutarch's Lives and absorb the philosophy of Aurelius and Epictetus, and to play chess, checkers, fishing-pong, and other lady-like games." The street boys, the average gang members, were deprived of their "inalienable right to play"—with the result that too many of them fell in with the rough gangs described above, criminal types, fulfilling in this way their "craving for excitement," the "privilege of basking in the presence of an adult 'Fagin' and accompanying him to some vile burlesque theater," this being "the whole of the young criminal's reward."

Lower East Side Jews themselves, in the extremity of their situation, were finally led to believe that there was only one answer to the problem of raising their children. That answer was to get out and leave Gehenna behind altogether.* While social reformers performed

---

* In his preface to Hutchins Hapgood's marvelous book *Spirit of the Ghetto*, Harry Golden writes of his own childhood on the Lower East Side: "This was the greatest challenge—to get out."

heroically in bringing to the benighted masses better housing (particularly with the Tenement Reform Act of 1901), more parks, improved health and sanitary and working conditions and the like, these palliatives, valuable as they were, rested on the assumption that the ghetto would prevail generation after generation, no other possibility being then conceivable.* The Jews knew better. None of the changes, however salutary, not all the neighborhood improvements in the world, could induce them to remain one second longer than necessary, and they fled the ghetto as soon as they could, settling wherever they found breathing space, above all for their children, wherever—so they prayed—there were no gangs and no underworld, no Segal's Cafes.†

That was for the future. In the meantime the underworld culture offered its young votaries what it always had: destiny, style, excitement, the feel of advantage, the prospect of money, hence freedom. For, morally speaking, the aspiring neighborhood vice lord and gangster hardly differed from the aspiring neighborhood capitalist: both accepted the premise assumed to be quintessentially American, that life was a war between competing exploiters for dominion over the exploited, dumb, passive, anonymous. The underworld culture was a culture of privilege and exclusivity. That was the mystique on which it prided itself. And that was its appeal to youth, those who grew up on Lower East Side streets and who therefore confronted it as an everyday choice, a constant temptation.

---

* On March 5, 1910, the New York City Park Commissioner, Charles B. Storer, assured the University Settlement trustees: "Why should it not be the purpose of this institution to render the Lower East Side a desirable place of residence? The people have been here for the past two centuries, and I think they will remain here for the next two centuries." And according to the members of the Tenement Reform Commission, "The new races coming in are, besides, distinctly gregarious in their habits." Inducing emigration from neighborhood and city therefore "probably never will succeed on a large scale."

† The exodus began full-scale with the completion of the Williamsburg and Manhattan bridges in 1903 and 1909 respectively, both connecting the Lower East Side to Brooklyn, and with the expansion around the same time of subways into the other boroughs. It should be remembered, however, that while the exodus was going on immigrants kept streaming into the neighborhood, 1904–6 being in fact the years of heaviest departure from Czarist Russia, years of war, revolution, and pogroms.

TWO

THE MUGWUMPS
AND THE JEWS

i

The Reverend Doctor Charles H. Parkhurst, minister of the Madison Square Presbyterian Church, learned one day in 1890 that several of his young parishioners were frequenting brothels and gambling houses and saloons. Here was a problem he had never before confronted. He knew that vice abounded in other neighborhoods, the great Lower East Side ghetto and the Tenderloin being only a few blocks away from his church. And he was a grown man, intelligent and worldly; he was aware of what was going on in the streets and tenements of New York. What disturbed him was the fact that his parish, which served some of the most affluent families in the city, was no privileged enclave after all, that iniquity and vice and disease, issuing up from the surrounding slums, threatened the "manliness" of even the best of the young.

Parkhurst acquired an interest in the broader question of vice: where and how it was available and what effects it had on those who indulged in it. He quietly made inquiries, conducted his own research. And what he discovered shook him to his depths. He discovered the System. In his "rustic innocence," he tells us, he thought the police "existed for the purpose of repressing crime." It "now began to dawn" on him that "the principal object" of the police was "to protect and foster crime and make capital out of it." Nor was this all. Probing further, he came to realize that the betrayals reached higher and higher, embracing even the mayor, Hugh J. Grant. But the mayor was himself only a creature of the Tammany organization, which was led by boss Richard C. Croker.

These revelations changed the Reverend Dr. Parkhurst. For ten years he had been a conventional pastor who had rarely strayed from the orthodox tenets of the faith: it was the severe Calvinism of his "rustic" Massachusetts youth, his schooling at Amherst and Williston Seminary and pastorate in Lenox that had recommended him to the elders of the Madison Square Presbyterian Church in the first place. Now, the blindfold having fallen from his eyes, he enlisted in the crusade against Tammany. He joined the Society for the Prevention of Crime and soon after, in April 1891, was elected its president. He accepted on condition that the Society adopt tactics as "radical" as the evil itself, that instead of going after occasional and quite petty wrongdoers—a brothel, a poolroom, a saloon that sold to minors—the Society go after the System as a whole and without concern for niceties and good manners.

The Society's members had long been familiar with Tammany's litany of evils. They were "Mugwumps" of high standing. Citizens of the better class, therefore Protestant and Republican, these Mugwumps had never let up in the struggle for good government. Some, going back a generation or more, had fought the valiant fight against Boss Tweed and had helped bring him and his ring down. But then along had come Tweed's successors, first "Honest" John Kelly and now Croker, probably the most formidable, certainly the craftiest chieftain of them all. Mugwumps favored political reforms—a civil service without patronage, a clean, non-partisan government resting on the votes of an intelligent, informed public—which were laudable enough in themselves but which meant little to the poor, more and more of them newly arrived immigrants; they needed bread and the Mugwumps offered them a stone.

Few Mugwumps for that matter interested themselves in the everyday life of the masses except when it impinged on them, Parkhurst's experience being typical: it took him a decade to learn what was going on and then only by accident. So it was with the other members of the Society for the Prevention of Crime and with Mugwumps in general. The contrast between them and Tammany was put very well by Croker himself in the course of a rare interview given to an English reporter. "There is no such organization [as Tammany] for taking hold of the untrained friendless man and converting him into a citizen. Who else would do it if we did not? Think of the hundreds of thousands of foreigners dumped into our city. They are too old to go to school. There is not a mugwump in the city would shake hands with them. They are alone, ignorant strangers, a prey to all manner of anarchical and wild notions. . . . Yes, and they are of value to Tammany. And Tammany looks after them for the sake of their vote, grafts them upon the Republic, makes citizens of them in short; and although you may not like our motives or our methods what other agency is there by which so long a row could have been hoed so quickly or so well? If we go down into the gutter it is because there are men in the gutter, and you have got to go down where they are if you are to do anything with them." So far as Parkhurst and his Society and the rest of the Mugwumps were concerned, the gutter was where Tammany belonged—not at the commanding heights of municipal power.

On Sunday morning, February 14, 1892, Parkhurst startled his congregation. They had not expected the sermon he delivered to them, nothing less than a full-scale denunciation of the city's politicians and police. He called them all, from Mayor Grant and Boss Croker down to the lowliest worker on the payroll, "lying, perjured, rum-soaked and libidinous" and accused them of protecting "every building in this town in which gambling and prostitution or the illicit sale of liquor is carried on." He demanded their extirpation root and branch lest the city suffer the fate of Sodom and Gomorrah, this being the inescapable choice Providence was imposing on his congregation, on Christian New Yorkers at large. "Ye Are the Salt of the Earth" was the title of his jeremiad.

It had its intended effect. It made the newspaper headlines the next day. Editorials commented on it extensively. All of them, pro- and anti-Tammany both, called on Parkhurst to prove his charges, chapter and verse. A grand jury, called into action, did likewise and even invited him to testify behind its locked doors. He had no choice but to accept. He drew a blank: the fact was he possessed no exact information, could cite no names, places, incidents. And so with a broadly advertised flourish the grand jury (itself part of the System, as he of course knew) dismissed him as a gossip and crank who willfully sowed "distrust in the mind of the community." The pro-Tammany press, as one can imagine, said worse things about him. ("The best employment to which the Reverend Dr. Parkhurst can now devote himself," wrote the *Sun*, "is prolonged prayer and repentance to atone for the grievous sin of which he has been guilty. An appropriate place wherein to give him the opportunity to subject himself to such spiritual mortification would be a penitentiary cell.") Not only was he personally reviled and humiliated; he had let down the cause of reform. The skirmish had gone to the devil's party.

Parkhurst was a stubborn and pertinacious man, however, a loyal child of his ancient New England forebears. If anything, the defeat was his spur. To gather the evidence on which the outcome turned he took a brave chance—brave because failure would have ruined him completely. He hired a toughened, street-wise private detective, one Charles W. Gardner, to chaperone him and a Mugwump companion through the city's lowest dives, to immerse them in the squalor, every detail of it. (Gardner wrote a very funny description of the tour, *The Doctor and the Devil*, on which much of this account relies.)

Together, night after night, this improbable trio, two of them disguised as pleasure-seeking gentlemen from the hinterlands, went looking for sin in general, and especially sin leagued with and sanctioned by authority, sin as political corruption, sin as the fuel of the Tammany machine. While they found it everywhere on Manhattan Island, nowhere did they find it more shamelessly displayed and available and depraved than in the Tenth and Eleventh Precincts on the Lower East Side, where immigrant Jews and Italians lived, and in adjoining neighborhoods, mainly Irish and black, such as Greenwich Village, the Tenderloin, and Chinatown. In Hattie Adams' downtown bordello, for example, Gardner had several of the girls put on the standard performance: they came out in Mother Hubbards, then stripped bare (except for stockings and garters), danced a can-can, and ended up by playing leapfrog, Gardner happily serving as the frog. Throughout the show, Gardner writes, "the doctor sat in the corner with an unmoved face . . . watching us and slowly sipping at a glass of beer." They attended a "French Circus" at Marie Andrea's place, the ultimate in erotic display (we are not told what it was) during which Parkhurst "sat in a corner with his feet curled under his chair and blankly smiled." He continually pressed

Gardner for "something worse"; he "really went at his slumming work as if his heart were in this town."*

By Sunday March 13 Parkhurst was ready to present another sermon on municipal corruption. Expecting a bombshell, reporters and Mugwumps and curiosity-seekers filled the Madison Square Presbyterian Church to its last pew. Nor were they disappointed. Calmly, dispassionately, he allowed the shocking truth to unfold of its own accord. He recounted one experience after another, among them an hour spent in a whorehouse only three blocks "from where I am now standing." And clinching his case he announced that he held in his hands 284 affidavits laying bare his charges and proving beyond cavil that the police, the politicians, and the underworld were the inseparable partners of a single despotic System and that the people of New York, all appearances to the contrary, were in bondage to it. He flung down the challenge directly to Tammany: "This morning I have given you the particulars.... Now what are you going to do with them?"

The answer of course was nothing. The pro-Tammany papers held up Parkhurst as nothing more than a dirty middle-aged man, a Pecksniff, a charlatan. The leapfrogging episode at Hattie Adams' came in for special censure and reproof. Did the girls fondle the minister as they sat on his lap? Was Gardner the only frog? The music halls invented a ditty sung to a familiar tune:

> *Doctor Parkhurst on the floor*
> *Playing leapfrog with a whore,*
> *Ta-ra-ra-Boom-de-ay*
> *Ta-ra-ra-Boom-de-ay.*

---

* Yet some kinds of experience, it seems, were out of bounds even for Parkhurst. One night, for example, the two men visited the Golden Rule Pleasure Club, the basement of which consisted of a series of thinly partitioned stalls, each with bed, table, and chairs. Also, a young man [in Gardner's words] "whose face was painted, eyebrows blackened, and whose airs were those of a young girl. Each person talked in a high falsetto voice, and called the others by women's names." Parkhurst may or may not have guessed where he was; he may not have wanted to know. At any rate when Gardner told him he "instantly turned on his heel and fled from the house at top speed. 'Why, I wouldn't stay in that house,' he gasped, 'for all the money in the world.'"

His detractors got nowhere. They might ridicule him, exploiting the comicality of the whole affair, the laughter it provoked; they might try to impugn his integrity, otherwise solid as oak. What they could not dismiss was the evidence he had sedulously gathered, the signed affidavits, the recitations of names and places. His case was overwhelming, and it threw the System, or those who spoke for it, on the defensive.

Parkhurst's crusade rapidly became the movement for political reform that he always intended it to be. Its immediate goal was the ouster of the Democratic regime in the 1894 election. Bending every resource to that end Parkhurst and the Mugwumps persuaded the Republican-run state senate to establish a special committee to investigate corruption in the New York City police department. That committee, headed by Senator Clarence Lexow of Westchester, was staffed by lawyers drawn from the Mugwump community and associated particularly with the Society for the Prevention of Crime. Who knew more about such corruption than they?

The Lexow Committee met regularly for the better part of 1894, its testimony filling more than 6,000 densely packed pages, much of it as sensational as anything Parkhurst had brought forth, and the press had another field day. A never-ending procession of witnesses—prostitutes, madams, pimps, the dregs of society—told of payoffs to policemen high and low and to political functionaries who worked with and through them. The public, though inured to so much, was surprised to learn how Tammany arranged the promotions, appointments, and transfers of policemen, each transaction therefore constituting the debt which subsequent payoffs from illicit enterprises would redeem. The Lexow Committee unraveled some of the arcane features of the System—the diabolic marriage between municipal government and the underworld. Never had there been such revelations, such insights into the cloaca of the city's night life. The Reverend Dr. Parkhurst had actually seen very little of it, though what he had seen had forced the gates of perdition to open all the way.

In the course of its inquiry the Lexow Committee revealed the existence of the cabal of vice overlords and Tammany bosses operating in the Jewish quarter of New York's Lower East Side. Testimony day after day brought out the names of such ward heelers as Max Hochstim and Martin Engel and the flamboyant Silver Dollar Smith (for whom Monk Eastman and other strong-armers had worked), members of the infamous "Essex Market Courthouse gang" who in return for guaranteeing that the district went massively Democratic received the right, with the cooperation of the police, the courts, and the government apparatus in general, to exploit the community as if it were their fiefdom.

This very Lower East Side crowd, Hochstim, Engel, and Silver Dollar Smith and their cohorts, also gave the interminably long Lexow investigation its most dramatic moment. A poor, desperate immigrant widow, Mrs. Caela Urchittel, accused them of fiendishly attempting to destroy her and her three young children because she had refused to submit to the System; she had committed lese majesty. Her story, which took many hours on the witness stand to tell, went as follows.

Mrs. Urchittel and her children had arrived in New York in 1891, her husband having died in Hamburg en route from Russia. The Hebrew Charities lent her enough money to start a boarding house. She scrimped and saved and bought a tiny restaurant in Brownsville, Brooklyn. After losing one of her children and suffering other misfortunes she returned to the Lower East Side and opened a tiny cigar store. That was when her troubles really began. A man entered the store one day and ordered her to pay "a designated person" fifty dollars; if she refused, she was told, her children would be taken from her and placed in an orphanage. "Not knowing to have done anything wrong" (to quote from the translator's rendering of her Yiddish) "I laughed at the man and told him I wouldn't give a cent to anybody, and if that man should come again I will chase him out with a broom." Two men returned, both detectives, stating that they had evidence she was running a "dishonest business" and demanding fifty dollars for "protection." "I opposed to his assertion and protested against his wanting money of me, saying that I ever made a living by honest business, but he wouldn't listen to me, and in spite of my protesting and the crying of my children, I was forced to leave the store and follow him."

Mrs. Urchittel then met Max Hochstim, the ward heeler, who advised her to pay up as ordered. The twenty-five dollars she happened to have with her she handed over to the detectives who promptly divided it with Hochstim. She was then hauled before the Essex Street court on the charge of soliciting for immoral purposes. Witnesses were trotted out to testify against her, each claiming to have paid her for "gratifying his pleasure." Pronounced guilty and unable to hand over the fifty-dollar fine or raise bail, Mrs. Urchittel was sent to the Tombs, the dreadful municipal jail. Her brother-in-law paid the fine, securing her release. "I ran then crazy for my children, for I didn't know where they were." It took five weeks to learn where (and only because one of her children sent her a postal card): a Hebrew orphanage way uptown at 151st Street and Eleventh Avenue. She begged the orphanage to return them to her. It refused. "Grieved at the depth of my heart, seeing me bereaved of my dear children, I fell sick, and was laying six months in the Sixty-sixth Street Hospital, and had to undergo a great operation by Professor Mundy. After I left the hospital, I had the good chance to find a place in 558 Broadway, where I fixed up a stand by which I am enabled to make a nice living, to support and educate my children.... My heart craves to have my children with me. I have nothing else in the world, only them. I want to live and die for them." The crowning moment came when Mrs. Urchittel addressed Senator Lexow personally: "I lay my supplication before you, Honorable Sir, father of family, whose heart beats for your children, and feels what children are to a faithful mother. Help me to get my children. Let me be mother to them. Grant me my holy wish, and I will always pray for your happiness, and will never forget your kind and benevolent act toward me."

There was a vast outpouring of public sympathy for Mrs. Urchittel. The return of her children became a cause célèbre. But enormous roadblocks stood in her way. Under the law, the authorities, including the courts, found it very hard to compel orphanages to yield up the children in their charge, especially to a mother convicted of prostitution. But suddenly, in the late afternoon of October 19, 1894, six weeks after Mrs. Urchittel had testified, the Committee's chief counsel, John W. Goff, interrupted a black prostitute (who was reciting the familiar tale of payoffs and other favors granted the police) to announce, "We have a very pleasant duty to perform ... we have the children of Mrs. Urchittel here in court." The charity organization which ran the orphanage had concluded "that all that had been testified to against her was absolutely false." "I think," Goff said, visibly moved, "while we have had many harrowing scenes here, and listened to many harrowing stories upon this witness stand during our [many] months' investigation, there is at least one silver lining to the black cloud, and that came here tonight; and it affords me pleasure, in your names, to give these children to their mother, and here is the mother to take them." The *New York World* wrote that Mrs. Urchittel took them in her arms "like a bunch of flowers."

By the time the Lexow hearings ended the Croker machine had been voted out of office by an indignant public and a reform or "fusion" administration voted in.* The Mugwump mayor, William L. Strong, did bring more efficiency to the government, did fire supererogatory personnel, did let out contracts honestly, did introduce changes in the old and corrupt Police Board (to which he appointed young Theodore Roosevelt). But the reform impulse quickly ran its course. "These movements," said an authority on the subject—a local underworld leader—"are like queen hornets. They sting you once and then they die." And so after the next election Tammany was back in power as if nothing had happened in the interval, an inconvenience perhaps, little more. Croker's machine seemed as invincible as ever. And intact as ever was the monstrous alliance, on the Lower East Side and in every other slum, of the government, the police, and the merchants of illicit ware who returned to their stands with the old accustomed brio and confidence.

The public had stopped listening to the Reverend Doctor Parkhurst. Or rather it had become indurated to descriptions of vice; it had learned to assimilate them, and was surfeited for the time being. And while he remained an active Mugwump, never ceasing to speak

---

* It was an administration that, incidentally, included several of the people who had participated in the Lexow hearings and otherwise made their reputations as enemies of Tammany Hall. This pattern was well established and would endure far into the twentieth century—using demonstrable opposition to the political machine as a lever to achieve personal success. Not that there was anything wrong in securing the material or spiritual rewards of virtue. The question is how well-earned were those rewards, how truly effective the combating of evil; i.e., how soon after the reformer's departure from the battlefield, complete with honors and the trappings of victory, did the evil return.

out against wrongdoing (he would go on practicing his vocation until his dying breath three decades later), Parkhurst's moment in history had fled. He would always be remembered for the time he spent observing the brothels and dives of New York City and for the impetus he gave to municipal reform.

ii

The defeated Mugwumps easily explained their dashed hopes and Tammany's resurgence. It was the immigrants who were to blame: it was their vote after all that provided the raw nutriment of conquest, that fed the pullulating evil. In 1890 the Lower East Side was already overcrowded beyond comprehension; by 1900 the Jewish population alone had doubled to over a half million, and the Lower East Side was probably, acre for acre, the most thickly packed area on earth. Reformers counted it no accident that Tammany headquarters, the "Wigwam," now stood on Fourteenth Street, facing the northern extremity of the Jewish district. Nor did they count it an accident that the man who ruled over that district, Big Tim Sullivan, had become Tammany's main chieftain, *primus inter pares*, eclipsing even the mighty Croker, who was devoting his energies to his race horses and would soon (in 1901) retire altogether to his green and lovely English estate.

From his Broome Street saloon, the Occidental, Sullivan held court like a lord of the manor, handing out food and clothing to the needy, settling disputes, apportioning benefices to the faithful (e.g., the Essex Market gang), receiving tribute—reckoned in the millions—and the votes of the masses, always that, quintessentially that.* He often went out among the people, attending their weddings

---

* Sullivan offered this famous piece of advice to neophyte politicians: "Whenever they vote with their whiskers on, you take 'em to a barber and scrape off their chin fringe. Then you vote 'em again with sideburns and moustache. Then to the barber again, off come the sides and you vote 'em a third time with just a moustache. If that ain't enough, and the box can stand a few more ballots, clear off the moustache and vote 'em plain-face. This makes every one of 'em good for four votes." How well Sullivan brought out the vote may be judged by this anecdote. In the 1892 presidential election, his Lower East Side assembly district went 395 to 4 for Grover Cleveland. Sullivan then apologized to Croker: "Harrison got one more vote than I expected, but I'll find that feller."

and bar mitzvahs and funerals, honoring their holidays (or creating them: Columbus Day, a gesture to his Italian constituents, was his doing), learning some of their languages, and in general judged them not their pleasures and vices and idiosyncrasies that he be not judged his. He exemplified all that the reformers found reprehensible in New York City politics, the more so since he embraced the evils over which he presided, declaring them in fact no evils at all, thus flinging them back, as it were, into the teeth of virtue. "I was born in poverty," Sullivan would say, replying to his Mugwump critics, invariably bringing his audience to tears, "one of six children, four boys and two girls. The boys used to sleep on a three-quarters bed, not big enough for two, and the girls on a shakedown on the floor. Some nights there was enough to eat and some nights there wasn't. And our old mother used to sing to us at night and maybe it would be the next day before we would think she had been singing but that she had gone to bed without anything to eat. That's the kind of people we come from and that's the kind of mother that bore us down here. If we can help some boy or some father to another chance, we're going to give it to them. The thieves we have down here ain't thieves from choice, they are thieves from necessity and necessity don't know any law. . . ."

There was a discernible change of attitude among reformers toward Eastern European Jews. No longer were the Jews regarded simply as victims of circumstances, as patient, hard-working, deserving poor whose suffering should be relieved and lives improved or morally uplifted by the ministrations of assorted philanthropists, charity and social workers. Now, and to an increasing extent, Jews were also being regarded as practitioners of crime, willing accomplices of Big Tim Sullivan and the other Tammany hierarchs.

The volumes of settlement-house reports plainly reflect the note of resentment and hostility, the rising animus. Jews were turning out to be more refractory than anyone had once thought, leading to the widespread view that there might be something after all in their "racial" heritage predisposing them to the vice that seemed to issue from every orifice of their community. "The habits and modes of living of the East Side residents (except in isolated cases)," the 1897 report of the University Settlement Society of New York informed its readers, "are obnoxious in the extreme, the same having a tendency to immorality of every phase. Male and female mingle together without the slightest regard of sex and common decency." And again: "It is not possible to hold up before the East Sider the Anglo-Saxon home ideal, with its individual privacy, its cosiness, and the general meeting and social enjoyment of all around the family hearthstone. Such an ideal is impossible of attainment in a tenement house...." Invidious comparisons between the habits of Eastern European Jews (and Southern Italians too) and Anglo-Saxons became a favorite theme of the reform and settlement literature: to be sure, one must help these benighted "races," at least so far as they can be helped, but without illusions or false expectations; "race" was everything.

Resentment and hostility toward Jews certainly defines the most celebrated exposé of New York corruption at the time, a massive three-volume tome, *American Metropolis*, whose author, Frank Moss, was one of Parkhurst's brethren in the Society for the Prevention of Crime and a counsel to the Lexow Committee; a paladin, in short, of the anti-Tammany crusade. Moss lengthily details the complexities of the System, the nexus of vice and politics and vote-mongering, notably on the Lower East Side—or "New Israel," as he calls it. Moss is out of patience with the Jews, and he cannot contain his bigotries toward them. He writes: "Ignorance, prejudice, stubborn refusal to yield to American ideas, religious habits and requirements, clannishness, and hatred and distrust of the Christian; these combine to hinder any device for raising the condition of the poor of this great Jewish district.... There is no part of the world in which human parasites have greater feeding and can be found in more overpowering numbers." It does not surprise him that Jews are congenitally attracted to crime. "The criminal instincts that are so often found naturally in the Russian and Polish Jews come to the surface in such ways as to warrant the opinion that these people are the worst element in the entire make-up of New York City." Moss expatiates on New Israel's dominant vice, prostitution, which is peddled on the streets conspicuously and without fear of community censure, such being the moral degradation to which the Jews have sunk, to which their "criminal instincts" have reduced them. Moss goes on flogging the Jews page after page and sums them up in a sentence: "a large proportion of the people of New Israel are addicted to vice." He is generous enough not to say all of them.

What is to be done? Moss has no answer, only the vaguely formulated hope that unrelenting opposition to the System by the decent enlightened citizenry—we are back to Mugwumpery—will bring about its destruction and usher in the reign of good clean government. The Jews could then be safely left to their own devices, their own "criminal instincts."

Events conspired for a season to vindicate that expectation. Moss himself was appointed chief counsel to another Republican legislative committee investigating New York City debauchery, this one headed by upstate Assemblyman Robert Mazet. And though the Mazet hearings, held in 1899, went over pretty much the same ground that the Lexow Committee hearings did and heard the same kinds of witnesses—madams, streetwalkers, pimps, police officials—they were sensational enough (thanks mainly to Boss Croker's candid testimony) to help cause Tammany's defeat a year later. Again the good citizens rejoiced, especially since their prospects had suddenly brightened. Brooklyn, city of churches, with a population the size of Philadelphia, had been incorporated into New York. Would this tip the balance permanently in favor of reform? Mugwumps could now seriously entertain such a question.

But Tammany, supple as always, its genius for organization unimpaired, recaptured the government in the next election (1903).*

Under a new chief, Charles F. Murphy, who as everyone knew owed his election to Big Tim Sullivan (Sullivan having turned down the chance to be the boss of bosses, which he was in any event, whatever the formal titles and accouterments of honor), Tammany advanced with seven-league boots, winning election after election in

---

* The election sequence is itself a story, confusing to all but the cognoscenti. Ordinarily, the mayoral term was three years. But because the reformers won the 1894 election the Republican state government assumed they would win again in 1897 and decreed that the mayoral term should thereupon run for four years. Then to everyone's surprise Tammany won. Piqued, the Republicans in Albany decreed that the next term should last only *two* years. And so when the reformers took the 1901 election they served only until 1903 when Tammany restored its ancient rule—and kept it for ten straight years.

Manhattan and the boroughs and eventually taking over the state government as well. Boss Murphy, speaking for New York's millions and its huge bloc of electoral votes, emerged as one of the arbiters of the national Democratic Party. Tammany Hall had come a distance since Tweed and Croker.

Mugwumps were aghast. They contemplated a logic grotesque beyond imagining—a logic that even *American Metropolis*, their recent guidebook through dark and mephitic swamps, failed to properly grasp, the swamps having grown prodigiously in the meantime. Ten years had passed and Tammany was reigning supreme, expanding in every direction, drawing its great strength mainly from Sullivan's Lower East Side appanage, the most populous and best organized in the city (no one could out-perform its repeaters); also the richest in vice and crime, therefore in illicitly gotten revenue. So New York's destiny, perhaps America's—for the Presidency itself now lay within Tammany's reach—turned ultimately on, of all places in God's universe, "New Israel." Satan himself, cruel jokester that he was, could not have contrived a more fantastic game of chance.

⋯ *m*

In the September 1908 issue of the *North American Review*, that stodgiest and most ancient of American magazines, there appeared a mildly interesting article. "Foreign Criminals in New York" was its title, and its author must have known what he was talking about because he was the city's highly respected police commissioner, Theodore A. Bingham. Bingham's point was innocent enough: that the size of New York's immigrant communities, Jewish and Italian in particular, and the number of gangs they spawned, warranted the creation of a special detective force drawn from these communities and speaking their languages who could infiltrate the "criminal organizations."

Police Commissioner Bingham's proposal would have elicited scant notice but for the following obiter dictum. "Wherefore it is not astonishing that with a million Hebrews, mostly Russian, in the city (one quarter of the population), perhaps half the criminals should be of that race, when we consider that ignorance of the language, particularly among men not physically fit for hard labor, is conducive to crime; nor is it strange that the precinct [the Lower East Side], where there are not four native-born heads of families in every hundred families, the percentage of criminality is high." These "Hebrews," Bingham went on, tend to commit crimes against property, not against life and limb. "They are burglars, firebugs, pickpockets and highway robbers." And worse yet, "among the most expert of all the street thieves are Hebrew boys under sixteen who are brought up to lives of crime." Bingham found that the "juvenile Hebrew emulates the adult in the matter of crime percentage."

Bingham presented these statistical proofs in a casual and offhanded way, as backup for his argument. He failed to say where he got them from, nor did he break them down to indicate magnitude, felonies and misdemeanors being lumped together under the same rubric. And suffusing the piece is the odor of Mugwump anti-Semitism (and dislike of Italians too)—the silly and illogical generalization, for example, about the character of the Jews, how their ignorance of the language, reinforced by their aversion to "hard labor" (a remark no one who had spent any time on the Lower East Side would even have made) somehow led them to lives of crime.

Still, even these insults probably would have passed unnoticed if they had not appeared when they did. Jews by 1908 had come to be extremely concerned about their fate. The Dreyfus affair, dragging on year after year until a much-disputed acquittal in 1906, had had a traumatic effect on European Jewry (serving as the midwife of modern Zionism). The wave of anti-Semitism throughout the Czarist Empire was sending more Jews to America than ever before: over a hundred thousand a year since the 1903 Kishinev Massacre. Meanwhile, sentiment was growing in the States to restrict or eliminate such immigration—sentiment that was feeding into the broader stream of nativism and racism. So Lower East Siders were justifiably sensitive to anything that might be construed as an attack on them by well-placed officials; experience had taught them to fear the worst. That sensitivity, that fear, explains their response to Police Commissioner Bingham's article: it seemed to them that no less a personage than the police commissioner of New York was raising the familiar standard. Throwing caution aside, they rose to their own defense.

The instant they learned of the article, Jewish newspapers and organizations demanded Bingham's resignation or ouster. The clamor was so loud, so insistent, that the German-Jewish community was forced into battle. Until now the Germans had had little to do with their downtown kinsmen; they inhabited a different universe, constituted a race apart. Lower East Siders knew them contemptuously as the "Jewish 400" because among their families could be counted some of the leading investment bankers and merchants and lawyers and publishers in the city and nation (e.g., the Schiffs, the Ochses, the Sulzbergers, the Adlers, the Lehmans, the Strausses, and the Guggenheims). At the very least the downtowners embarrassed them. The outrageous behavior, the vice and crime, might somehow taint them too, might undermine their hard-won status. How long, after all, would their tolerant Christian hosts go on drawing distinctions between one sort of Jew and another? The uptown leaders, then, had no choice but to join in the criticism of Police Commissioner Bingham: the one thing they did not want was to let the matter get out of control and fall into the hands of the downtown demagogues and radicals and religious fanatics. The tense cooperation between the Eastern Europeans and the Germans did lead to results. On September 16, 1908, Bingham withdrew the offending statement "frankly and without reservation." That ended the affair.

But it had alerted the Jews, uptown and downtown alike, to a problem. For vice and crime did pervade the Lower East Side, and no one knew it more keenly than its residents. The better part of wisdom, so far as they were concerned, was to keep the disgrace quiet, to avoid publicizing it. An open discussion, with the whole world listening in, would only give the nativists further encouragement. Besides, how would such a discussion improve anything? Yet the fact to which Bingham had called attention could not be gainsaid. And if his statistics were doubtful, if actually there were fewer Jewish criminals than he maintained—a lively and inconclusive debate swirled around this very question*—there were nonetheless plenty of them

---

* Before Bingham's article appeared, *The Federation Review*, organ of the Jewish Federation of Philanthropies, published what seemed to be a thoroughgoing study of Lower East Side criminality. Using the New York County Court of General Sessions for 1907 as its basis, the study showed that Jews accounted for only 16.1 percent of

however one reckoned their numbers, and the rate of juvenile delinquency was appalling. The enormity of the problem required that the cooperation go beyond ad hoc emergencies and turn into something permanent. The stakes were too high for everyone.

And so early in 1909 delegates representing 222 organizations formed a "Kehillah," Hebrew for communal body, the term having been borrowed from the Kehilloth that once presided over the public lives of Eastern European Jews. Here is not the place to detail the history of the New York City Kehillah; that has been brilliantly done by Arthur A. Goren. What can be said is that it represented the only attempt of its sort ever undertaken in the United States and that it was the first time uptowners and downtowners belonged to the same institution, though the uptowners financed and led it. The Jewish underworld and the anxieties it engendered had made it all possible.

Though Bingham might not have realized it, his article turned out to be the opening salvo in the Mugwump offensive, the most ambitious one since the Reverend Doctor Parkhurst had delivered his sermon

---

the convictions; for the population as a whole the rate was only 6.1 percent. But as Arthur A. Goren points out, other Jews privately found the study "totally misleading." For one thing, "the estimate of Jewish population was too crude for statistical purposes"; for another, the sound of names was a poor index of ethnicity, many Jews having adopted gentile names. For still another, legal convictions gave an inadequate measure of real criminality. And finally, such convictions "did not take into consideration the misdemeanor and vagrancy cases handled by lower courts where the proportion of Jews tried rose sharply."

The United States Immigration Commission tried its hand at statistical analysis and came up with similarly inconclusive results. Its 1911 report, *Immigration and Crime*, relied on data taken from the New York City Magistrate Court between January 1901 and January 1909. Under the category of "gainful offenses" the Commission found Russian—that is, Jewish—immigrants to be the greatest culprits: 8.3 percent of them were convicted as against 7.7 percent of the Germans, 6.4 percent of the Italians, 4.4 percent of the Irish, and 4.3 percent of the French. In the subcategories of "gainful offenses" Jews (Russians) ranked as follows: first in burglary, third in larceny and receiving stolen property, sixth in robbery, fourth in forgery and fraud, and fifth in blackmail and extortion. When it came to "offenses of personal violence" Jews were far down on the list: 3.3 percent compared with 7.3 percent of the Italians, 4.3 percent of the Germans, and 3.7 percent of the Irish; only the French, with 1.6 percent, were lower. The great fallacy of these statistics, of course, is that they say nothing about the degree of the offense; felonies and misdemeanors are thrown together.

seventeen years before. It was no accident therefore that *McClure's* magazine, the premier muckraking publication of the day, should feature two articles in 1909 which together constituted the most startling revelation of the New York System yet to appear in print. Nor was it accidental that the main protagonist in the unfolding spectacle was Lower East Side Jewry. For it was the standard Mugwump case that *McClure's* was presenting to America—to the hundreds of thousands of small-town and rural and middle-class folk who eagerly devoured news of the big city moral pollution, the more sordid and sensational and grotesque the better. Both pieces were written by George Kibbe Turner, *McClure's* specialist on the subject and a muckraker par excellence.

The first, conspicuously leading off the June number, details the story of "Tammany's Control of New York by Professional Criminals." To anyone reasonably familiar with the ancient struggle it said nothing new. But for the typical American to whom it was addressed it must have been a wild, eye-opening bit of exotica, a candid glimpse of native life in a far-off land.

Turner begins with Big Tim Sullivan and the society that produced him decades ago, namely the Five Points and Cherry Hill sections of Manhattan, "Irish slums . . . as foul as any in the world." How foul is made clear in the next sentence, a descent into hell. "Scores of tenement saloons, reeking 'dead house' groggeries beneath the level of the sidewalks, and sailors' dance-halls, with names unspeakable, lined the streets; in every shadow bands of soft-fleshed young thieves—good, strong Irish peasant stock, rotted by the unhealthy city life—whistled and watched and waited for the drunken laborer reeling home by night." Sullivan, a gifted street brawler and organizer, rose to leadership of the notorious Whyo gang of thieves and repeaters. He therefore made his mark in Tammany circles and at Boss Croker's behest became sachem of the Assembly District in 1892, the position he still held.

Turner then gives a good and accurate account of the neighborhood changes to which Tammany was forced to respond. While Sullivan was taking charge of the district its population was shifting drastically. The Jews and Italians were replacing the Irish and Germans on whose electoral support the politicians had always depended. The newcomers were not so dependable. And this, according to Turner, was a major cause for Tammany's 1894 defeat. The stage was set for Sullivan's conquest of power. To him fell the task of converting the heathen to the true faith. "These people, especially the acute and intelligent Jew, could not be handled by the old-time, brutal, saloon-keeping Irish politician." Tammany had to "resort to an entirely artificial method of control." And that method was the use of criminal repeaters. The use of criminals was of course not new to Tammany Hall. What was new, Turner contends, was the *extent* of their use; in the old days every Irish and German voter was "naturally" Democratic. Now more forceful measures had to be employed to bring out the Jewish and Italian voters. And those measures, Turner argues, already lay at hand.

While gangsters abound in every poor neighborhood, and Turner does discuss them too, he is interested primarily in the Jewish gangsters of the Lower East Side. The logic is self-evident. It is the Lower East Side vote that explains Sullivan's incredible success, that has made the difference in Tammany's fortunes, its triumph in every city election but one since 1894. "Fifty-cent prostitution" has been the Jewish underworld's continuing source of wealth, according to Turner. By the late 1890s, he estimates, "at least three or four thousand men and women were engaged" in Lower East Side prostitution. Thanks to "Jewish commercial acumen" the Lower East Side became "notorious across the world as the Red Light district." That is the picture Turner draws for his audience. He says nothing about the community, nothing about the extraordinary civilization that flourishes there. Like Moss and other Mugwumps he reduces it to a charnel house of vice and crime, the world's brothel. He does concede that "the Jew makes the most alert and intelligent citizen of all the great immigrant races that have populated New York. He [the Jew] was a city-dweller before the hairy Anglo-Saxon came up out of the woods. . . ."

But the effect of these generous statements is to make the Jew seem even more sinister, someone capable of the most heinous evils. And so Turner arrives at another familiar landmark: the Essex Street Courthouse ring of Max Hochstim Associates, headed by Silver Dollar Smith and Martin Engel, "a society of politicians, pimps and thieves." It was from the Essex Market Courthouse gang that something much worse emerged: the professional gangster.

Enter Monk Eastman, who has gotten his start as a repeater and roughneck of all work. Even though he takes considerable space bringing out Eastman's colorful life and appearance, Turner sees him for exactly what he was: a leader of hoodlums who offered his services to anyone who was willing to pay for them, a "sort of licensed bandit on the East Side." But Tammany was Eastman's most important client and furnished his gang with legal protection in return for getting out the vote by hook or crook. By now the gangsters had become an independent force. "The time had come, as an old criminal expressed it, when 'the gang needed the politician and the politician must have the gang.' " Turner then traces the further growth of the Eastman outfit following upon Kid Twist's accession. Being Jewish, Twist not only had a more effective and ruthless gang, murdering opponents right and left; he easily doubled the number of repeaters that Eastman had once mustered, each repeater "being good for from five to ten votes at election time, and from ten to twenty at primaries." Turner asserts without qualification: "Under Twist the East Side gang assumed its present position—the strongest in New York." And so it has remained, despite Twist's own death by Louie the Lump's gun, up to the time of Turner's writing.

What Eastman and Twist and lesser criminals have done, then, is tragically clear: they enable Tammany to hold New York City in "absolute control" (returning to Turner's central theme). "The government of the second largest city in the world, when the system is in full working order, depends at bottom upon the will of the criminal population—principally thieves and pimps. The eighteenth century governments founded on mercenary troops offer mild examples of social decadence compared with this." And by criminal population Turner means chiefly the Jews. But it should be said to Turner's credit that, unlike Frank Moss, he avoids the gratuitous asides on Jewish character or "instincts," at least here. Shrewdly, he lets the dark, horrific facts speak for themselves.

Once he takes leave of the Lower East Side and dilates on other matters of general interest to reformers (i.e., the rivalry between Tammany bosses and their criminal allies), Turner's pace slackens, he grows dull, our minds wander, and we hasten to his conclusion, his unabashed support for the Mugwumps in the mayoral election that fall, his plea to deprive Tammany and its "mercenaries" of "the most tremendous political prize on the continent—the handling of a municipal expenditure of $150,000,000 and the control of millions more in semi-public expenditures." The outcome, we are left to infer, is more significant even than the recent presidential election.

Turner's second article, "The Daughters of the Poor" (subtitled "A Plain Story of the Development of New York City as a Leading Center of the White Slave Trade of the World Under Tammany Hall"), expands on the previous discussion of Jewish criminality. But nothing in that discussion or elsewhere could have prepared the reader for what follows. *McClure's* saved it for the November issue.

We encounter a lurid and bizarre history, full of astonishments. In the late nineteenth century, says Turner, an enormous traffic in prostitutes emanated from the impoverished Jewish settlements of Poland and Austria. Many found their way to the pestholes of India and the Asian subcontinent. He quotes Kipling's "Ballad of Fisher's Boarding House" which describes one such prostitute, "Anne of Austria":

> *From Tarnau in Galicia*
> *to Juan Bazar she came,*
> *To eat the bread of infamy*
> *And take the wages of shame.*

Leading this migration was the "Jewish Kaftan," a sort of super-pimp who sold his goods wholesale. Turner tells us little about this strange creature, only that "the Jewish church" fought him in vain and that he "comes out of Galicia and Russian Poland, with his white face and his long beard,—the badge of his ancient faith—and wanders across the face of the earth." How does Turner know this remarkable facet of Jewish history, hitherto concealed or neglected by every reputable study? He does not say; one is expected to take his word on authority, but his word is nothing more than the pose of omniscience.

For some reason (unexplained) the Kaftan did not go to the United States. It was to Buenos Aires, another great Jewish immigration center, that he transported his women (who then set up houses of their own). Not that New York needed the Kaftan. It had his equivalent, Turner claims, among the "large number of criminals" who had been emigrating from Eastern Europe since the early 1880s. Here he seems to contradict himself; in his previous essay he made a point of showing that the Jews had not been criminals on their arrival, that the Irish had "carefully trained" the boys to be pickpockets, "and little girls of thirteen and fifteen to be prostitutes." In any event "homeless Jewish men" were pouring into the Lower East Side, creating an illimitable market "for the sale of women." A tremendous business thus grew up, a whole industry involving, as he has already told us, thousands of men and women, not including politicians, police, and landlords.

Turner leads the shocked reader through the Lower East Side nether world, the great red-light district. He begins by demonstrating how the poor Jewish working girls drift into prostitution, an account that reveals the all too familiar bigotries and must have made exciting copy. "The odds in life," he writes, "are from birth strongly against the Jewish-American girl." And that, he informs us, is because most Jewish families favor the sons, sending them to schools, conferring every other privilege and kindness upon them. The girls are condemned to toil and suffer. "There is no more striking sight in the city than the mass of women that flood east through the narrow streets on a winter's twilight, returning to their homes in the East Side tenements. The exploitation of young women as money earning machines has reached a development on the East Side of New York probably not equaled anywhere else in the world.... Thousands of women have sacrificed themselves uselessly to give the boys of the family an education."

Now how Turner arrived at this preposterous notion—that Jewish girls were sent out to slave for the boys—he withheld from the reader. This charge could have been checked out; all Turner had to do was go to the neighborhood and keep his eyes and ears open, to do his homework. He would have seen precious few Jewish boys living the life he describes. And he would have noticed the thousands of Italian girls working in the local shops and factories, side by side with their Jewish sisters. Could anyone claim that they, the Italian girls, did so in order to send the boys in their family to school? It hardly occurs to Turner that the survival of the immigrant family often depended on its children's labor, male and female alike. In other words, Turner finds it easy to understand why Jewish girls more than any other became the targets of, and offered themselves to, cadets and procurers: not the poverty, dirt, hopelessness, anomie that surrounded them; it was their parents, their culture. The fault lay with the Jews as a people.

To reveal in detail how the Moloch of prostitution devours its victims Turner takes us to the dance halls and academies. It is a brief Cook's tour. "On Saturdays and Sundays the whole East Side dances after nightfall, and every night of the week there are tens of thousands of dancers within the limits of New York. . . . To these places, plastered across their front with the weird Oriental hieroglyphics of Yiddish posters, the new Jewish immigrant girl—having found a job—is led by her sister domestics or shop-mates to take her first steps in the intricacies of American life. She cannot talk the language, but rigid social custom demands that she be able to dance." And with the dancing establishments come the army of cadets, now grown so large and powerful in the neighborhood's gang culture they hold their own balls, even own their own places. Successful cadets are "local heroes" and Jewish girls regard them "exactly as . . . the girls in a college town" regard "football captains."

Turner has given his readers an idea of how Lower East Side prostitution comes about, how the women are recruited and put to work as white slaves. And we know that in sheer quantity the number of prostitutes, cadets, and other sycophants and profiteers is enormous, several thousand at a minimum. Inevitably, he goes on, the business of prostitution gets rationalized: it even resembles the trusts, imposing order and empire where once unlimited free enterprise prevailed, and—as trusts are wont to—branching out in every direction.

Here Turner plunges into a quite amazing area of research. He discloses how the Lower East Side exports its vile commodity to the rest of the country ("about one half of all the women now in the business throughout the United States started their career . . . in New York"), and to the entire world for that matter. Wherever a demand for cheap low women arises, especially in remote frontier outposts, there, he explains, the New York dealers in flesh, latter-day Kaftans, are suddenly on the spot: in the gold and diamond mines of South Africa, the Australian outback, the Panama Canal zone, the Alaskan Klondike, Shanghai, Eastern Siberia (scene of the recent Russo-Japanese war), and so on throughout the world. Above all, and most dangerously, they have spread to the American cities at large, from nearby Philadelphia and Newark to Chicago, where a thousand or so New York prostitutes "who could scarcely speak the language" have struck permanent root, and further west and south to St. Louis, New Orleans, San Francisco, Seattle, Los Angeles, and the mining regions of the Rockies. White slavery is a virulent fungus—this is what Turner would have us believe—emanating from New York and of distinctly Jewish origin and inspiration that is infecting the other cities of America, helping to transform their governments into so many versions of Tammany Hall.

The conspiracy of evil, the System—that unity of Irish politicians and immigrant prostitutes and gangsters and voters—is rampant in the land. And unless something is done, America is headed for a moral apocalypse. "There is little doubt that from now on the larger part of the procuring and marketing of women for the United States will be carried on by the system of political procurers developed in New York," a system, moreover, which tends increasingly "to hold the balance of power in city elections." America's very destiny might depend on the results of the trial of strength that is to take place within a few weeks of the magazine's appearance on the newsstands.

George Kibbe Turner's two articles drew a hysterical response—an understatement—from his boss, the pioneer of the muckrakers, S. S. McClure himself. They so upset McClure that he wrote his own piece in the same issue, more exactly, a long editorial or open letter to his countrymen, on the "Tammanyizing of a Civilization," by which he meant the imminent danger that the foreign-born, the Jews above all, would pull American down to their depraved state of morality and, as Turner prophesied, turn every city into a replica of the Lower East Side. The opening lines of this long philippic convey its entire argument: "For a thousand years the Germanic races have built up, slowly and laboriously, the present civilization of the West, the great and complicated structure that now lifts the whole race above barbarism and bestiality, and gives the individual the guarantees of security and justice and decency that make civilized life more worth living than savagery. The three leading nations in which this development has come about have been England, Germany, and the United States. The United States had every prospect, from the traditions and motives and stock of its founders, of carrying this development to its highest point. But for at least half a century strong reactionary forces have been continuously at work in this country to drag its inheritance of civilization down again to barbarism. The lowest point that they have yet attained is their nation-wide organization for the sale of the bodies of women. . . . The deep-seated and instinctive disgust of every normal person for this transaction proves beyond my demonstration its essential nature. It is not a mere attack on individual morals. It aims at the disintegration and degradation of civilization, and the social training of centuries—set in the bone and marrow of the race—revolts against it."

We might in passing take note of McClure's "remedy." It is the Mugwump formula borne to its absolute extreme. He would replace the present local governments by a commission made up of the best men in the community. His model is the well-run corporation, where the directors are answerable to the stockholders when they fail to perform efficiently. As for New York, America's greatest city, it should be governed by the nation's five "ablest" citizens, among them Theodore Roosevelt as mayor; J. P. Morgan, commissioner of finance; and General Leonard Wood, commissioner of police. It would be a government of the good, the virtuous, and the wise; it would be unerringly beneficent in its concern for the welfare of the people and the strongest of parents in getting its way and securing obedience. "Only by the most thorough and revolutionary reforms along this line," McClure asserts, "is there hope for the future of democracy." To which one can only reply, paraphrasing the army officer who put the torch to a Vietnam village: To save democracy the reformer must destroy it.

Turner's prostitution article brought fresh consternation to the Jewish community. It amounted in some ways to a more serious indict-

ment than Bingham's remarks because it attributed so much of the
"social evil," the scourge of prostitution, to alleged wholesale de-
fects in the Jewish character, specifically the insistence that girls
sacrifice their happiness for their brothers' freedom. Jewish spokesmen were not slow to condemn Turner and McClure for this palpable
slander and also for the description of the Kaftan ("with his white
face . . ."), implying that bearded Jews in general were suspect, the
patriarchal aspect being a cover for a professional white slaver. But
to whom could the protesting Jews complain? Turner was no official;
he held no power. And was it prudent to challenge him aggressively,
carry on a public debate? All that the Yiddish press and the Kehillah
could do was cry out within their own community against the way
the issue had been presented, the way prostitution was seen as a
Jewish phenomenon. How could one deal with this tissue of misrepresentation?*

Politics further complicated the situation. Some Lower East Side
groups were pro-Tammany, and they seized on the Turner article as
evidence that the Mugwumps, meaning the Mugwump candidate for
mayor in 1909, could not be trusted, that in the end the Jews should
stick with their traditional friends and patrons, Big Tim Sullivan
above all. The uptown Jews, Mugwumps themselves, were in a quan-
dary. They could not openly agree with Turner; neither could they re-
pudiate him, not if Tammany stood to be the beneficiary. And then
there was an extremely large group of downtown Jews, perhaps the
largest, for whom the Socialist *Forward* spoke, who were willing to
accept much of what Turner wrote, despite the hyperbolic language,
the sensationalism, the hint of bigotry, for, after all, he was only
verifying what every Lower East Sider experienced, so long as the

---

* One Yiddish-language paper did try to refute the charges by conducting an investigation of its own. On three straight days the *Warheit* published the names of prostitutes brought to book in Manhattan night court. The *Warheit* concluded that only a
little more than a quarter of them was Jewish, though Jews comprised a third of Manhattan's population. The survey was unscientific, to say the least. The important question of course is what percentage of the prostitutes brought to book were Jewish. (For
that matter, the *Warheit's* findings were less than a smashing refutation of the
Turner thesis, if we can call it that.) The Lower East Side may not have been the red-
light district of the world, as Turner maintained, but it was a great red-light district
nonetheless and no statistic-mongering could alter that fact.

blame went where it belonged—namely, to the system of wage slavery, the root cause of every social evil. But no more than any other group did the *Forward* have any answers or suggestions (beyond the ultimate one of a socialist commonwealth). What to do *hic et nunc*: that was the burning question.

Turner's piece, like Bingham's the year before, compelled Jews in general to acknowledge the existence of an intolerable fact. And it was becoming more and more difficult to contain that fact, to prevent the attendant publicity from getting out of hand, Turner being a model of restraint compared to the virulent anti-Semitism waiting to be called up. Only a few months earlier all of Chicago had learned the extent of Jewish prostitution in that city during a police inspector's trial for corruption, specifically for taking graft from brothel owners. Even the *Forward* had had to admit: "The facts that were uncovered at the trial of Inspector McCann are horrifying. Seventy-five percent of the white slave trade in Chicago is in Jewish hands. The owners of most of the immoral resorts on the West Side are Jews. Even in Gentile neighborhoods Jews stand out prominently in the nefarious business." This was what Turner had been saying.

So great, so universal, was the concern of the Jews that several of their more famous representatives from the United States, Germany, Great Britain, and France gathered in London in April 1910 to deal with "The Suppression of the Traffic in Girls and Women" (as the conference was called). While it would be an exaggeration to say that the delegates deliberately kept news of the proceedings from the press, they conspicuously avoided advertising them, and the world scarcely knew the meeting had been held at all. That may have been the reason the talk was so frank and critical. And it may have been why the main speaker, Arthur R. Moro of London, in effect corroborated one of Turner's more speculative contentions—that Jewish white slavery was international in scope and to a scandalous degree.

"I wish I had time to tell you all we know, which goes to show that the traffic of Jewesses is almost worldwide," said Moro. "But I must restrict myself to a few . . . incidents to prove that an extensive traffic does exist. . . . In 1901, a Rabbi came from the Transvaal and told me that the amount of Jewish prostitution and traffic in Johannesburg, Pretoria, Lourenço Marques, Beira and Salisbury are appalling. In later years the same story came from another Rabbi regarding Capetown. . . . In 1903 a Jewish schoolmaster who had spent some time in Egypt said that the traffic by Jews of Jewesses to Alexandria, Cairo and Port Said was an absolute scandal.

"There were Greek, Italian and French prostitutes, but they were far outnumbered by the Jewesses. . . . We have received, and have correspondence to show that this awful condition of affairs exists in Calcutta to a large extent, and also all along the free ports of China. . . .

"From the Chief Rabbi of Constantinople, from a distinguished Jewish-American scholar, from a prominent London gentleman, and from a schoolmistress in Galata we have had letters during the past six months describing an outrageous condition of affairs in Constantinople where traffic in prostitutes is carried on openly and shamelessly, and where the traffickers have their own Synagogue. . . . They say that in Damascus things are even worse."

Such statements, private and confidential though they were, are open to the same criticisms as Turner's comments. Much of the data was impressionistic, derived from second and third hand or from random observations. No solid, quantitative or statistical evidence was offered or sources cited. (Except for a reference to Argentinian authorities who revealed that of the 199 licensed whorehouses in Buenos Aires in 1909, 102 were kept by Jewish madams and that of the 537 women working in these establishments 264, or about half, were Jewish.) But even if hard, impeccably reliable information had been secured, it is doubtful that the Jewish International Conference on the Suppression of the Traffic in Girls and Women could have done anything with it. Like the Jews of New York, the delegates were not going to broadcast the results and give their enemies a further boost, making it harder yet for emigrating Russian Jews to find a haven in the West. So no recommendations came out of the Conference and no other conference of the kind was ever held.

In America the prevailing hysteria soon died down even though Tammany's mayoral candidate won the 1909 election. The danger of course had been egregiously overblown. A plethora of public and private commissions and citizens' groups looking into New York prostitution—it became quite the rage to do so—concluded that there was no trust, no ring, no cabal, no international organization, nothing to justify the transcendent fears Turner and McClure and the Mugwumps had raised. They also found that though the social evil was prospering unabated, especially on the Lower East Side, it was not "Tammanyizing" the rest of the country. These findings had a sobering effect, for the nonce anyway, and as the election receded into the distance, as life under Tammany stewardship went on as ever, the threat of Anglo-Saxon civilization collapsing receded into the distance too.

But the image of the System was now graven in the public mind. To that extent the reformers from Parkhurst through Turner had accomplished their mission. They had established the existence of a tight arrangement between the squalid, criminalized immigrants and the political machine, so that to think of one was to think reflexively of the other. They had created in the collective imagination an ironbound stereotype of a dreadful foe, bearer of contagious evils. The assumption of such a conspiracy explained everything. The more improbable the facts the more likely it was that they were true and consistent with each other, for by definition a conspiracy is never what it seems to be and always what it seems not to be.

w

Few Mugwumps could have dreamt that within a few years their stereotypical view of the System—at least the Jewish component of it—would be so dramatically, so richly borne out and that they would then be so fulsomely rewarded by the electorate. No one, that is, could have predicted anything like the Rosenthal-Becker affair.

It began with a rather puzzling newspaper story. On Sunday, July 14, 1912, Pulitzer's *New York World*, which had been producing sensations before there was ever a muckraking press, printed in full a rambling, disordered, innuendo-laden statement by Herman Rosenthal, proprietor of a midtown Manhattan gambling house, and (as we noted in the last chapter) one of Big Tim Sullivan's "Jewboy" protégés. Rosenthal claimed that Police Lieutenant Charles Becker—whose reputation around town for ruthlessness was well known—had once been his partner in a gambling concern but was now harassing him without letup. Why? Because Rosenthal had decided to tell the truth and by now did not care where the chips might fall.

"I have repeatedly sent persons to Becker to ask him to take the policeman out of my house and he told them to tell me that as long as he was in the police department he would see that the copper was not taken out. And he did also say that I would be driven from New York . . . because I have not hesitated to tell anybody the truth regarding my own experience with Lieutenant Becker, as representing the police." The scoop was less interesting for what it said—who could make sense of such a confession?—than for its devastating potential. What more did Rosenthal have in store? What would be Becker's response? What would be the police department's and the city government's? How far beyond the two protagonists would the issue ramify?

The public soon received answers to these questions and to others no one could conceivably have asked. Two days after the story appeared Rosenthal was shot dead in front of the Metropole Hotel, on Forty-third Street just off Broadway, where gamblers and Broadway high-steppers often gathered in the early morning hours. The murder had a seismic effect. The Manhattan District Attorney, Charles S. Whitman, a Mugwump Republican of the Parkhurst school who had been elected the year before (thanks to a split among Democrats), immediately and off the top of his head accused the police department, "or certain members of it," of complicity in the crime. "And the time and place selected," Whitman continued, "were such to inspire terror in the hearts of those the system had most to fear. It was intended to be a lesson to anyone who might have thought of exposing the alliance between the police and crime."

The public also learned that Big Tim Sullivan had recently lent Rosenthal some money and that Rosenthal had expressed his undying devotion to the boss. "I knew him as a boy," Rosenthal was heard to say shortly before the assassination. "I would lay down my life for him. . . . He is the only man who could call me off, and he told me I am doing right in trying to protect myself and my home." (What

Sullivan really thought of Rosenthal could not be ascertained because Sullivan was by the summer of 1912 literally out of his mind, institutionalized for insanity.) So the impression conveyed and broadcast far and wide in boldest headlines was that a mysterious and illicit connection existed between a petty Lower East Side gambler, a high-ranking police officer, and the city's leading Tammany sachem, the presiding monarch of the whole System, that the gambler was dispatched because he was going to expose the connection, and that fresh revelations were about to break.

And so they did. Someone had spotted the getaway car which the police traced to a Lower East Side automobile rental service. One of the owners of the service then named a gambler, opium-den keeper, and all-around underworld character, "Bald Jack Rose" (born Jacob Rosenzweig) or "Billiard Ball Jack"—he had a very shiny pate—as the man who had rented a car on the night of the murder. Arrested with Rose were several other Lower East Side gambler-hoodlums, some prominent in the neighborhood, some rivals and enemies of Herman Rosenthal: Louis "Bridgey" Webber, Harry Vallon (né Valinsky), Samuel Shepps, and "Jack Sullivan" (originally Jacob Reich), notorious in the neighborhood as "king of the Newsboys."

The case then burst open. In exchange for immunity from prosecution these men readily confessed everything, and gave D.A. Whitman the information he was seeking: namely, that Lieutenant Becker had threatened to have them jailed on trumped-up charges if they failed to do his bidding and murder Rosenthal; that on Becker's orders Bald Jack Rose got in touch with the infamous bandit Big Jack Zelig, who happened to be in the Tombs just then on a transparently false charge; that after raising a large sum to bail out Zelig, Rose and his friends hired four of Zelig's most trusted henchmen to do the deed—who else but "Whitey Lewis," "Lefty Louie," and "Gyp the Blood," along with Francesco Cirofici, known as "Dago Frank," a sometime member of the gang. The four, picked up in their various hideouts during the summer of 1912, were charged with slaying Rosenthal. So of course was Charles Becker.

This amazing rapid-fire sequence of events seemed to provide striking confirmation of the historic Mugwump argument. Everything that Parkhurst and his epigone had been warning against had now come out into the open. An editorial in *The Outlook* (Theodore Roosevelt's journal) expressed the universally held view, bodied forth in every newspaper and magazine and implicit in every account of the affair: "One thing is clear now as it ever can be—that Herman Rosenthal was killed by the 'System'. His death was a byproduct of that hideous combination of vice and crime with politics and misgovernment which is probably the most powerful force in New York." This view was further confirmed, indeed given a final seal of validity, when Big Jack Zelig was slain on the eve of the trial. Nothing conspiratorial could be pinned on the killer, Red Phil Davidson, but few failed to draw the same inference: the System had struck again. According to D.A. Whitman, who kept up a running commentary on the case he was prosecuting, receiving unlimited space in the press, and who was in fact already running for higher office (no one yet knew which one), Zelig was scheduled to be one of his star witnesses and would sustain Bald Jack Rose in every particular.* And Rose himself was quoted—after the fact—as having predicted all along that "Zelig will never see the trial start. Watch. He'll be the next one they get." "They" meaning of course the ineffable forces that had silenced Rosenthal.

This much was certain as the miserable scandal unraveled. Nothing like it before had so defiled the Jewish community. The underside of Lower East Side life was exposed to the whole world; few events in recent history had elicited such enormous and persistent interest from newspapers throughout the country and abroad—especially after the trial got under way and an army of Jewish gangsters and hustlers were brought to the witness box. They painted a horribly detailed landscape of the neighborhood. More accurately, they filled in the one that Parkhurst, the state investigating committees, Frank Moss's *American Metropolis*, Commissioner Bingham, the various studies of the "social evil," and George Kibbe Turner and others had chalked in. And now some of the figures in the landscape,

---

* The most authoritative study of the Rosenthal-Becker affair, Andy Logan's *Against the Evidence*, argues that on the contrary Zelig was probably going to be a witness for the defense or at least deny Rose's allegations.

hitherto indistinguishable, were present in the flesh, on the stand and in the dock, for the world to see and hear, exemplifying by their very appearance—for with the exception of Lieutenant Becker, who was and looked every inch a WASP and who tried to keep an absolute distance between himself and the others, they were all short and dark, were immigrants or the children of immigrants—the "barbarism" of which S. S. McClure, echoing the nativist passions of the moment, had warned the American people.

Nor did the anti-Semitism have to be overt. The implications were sufficient, as they were, for example, in Richard Harding Davis' widely read report of the trial for *Collier's*. Davis was America's most sought after, most highly paid, and most frequently emulated journalist; only the important stories were worthy of his attention, and this story certainly qualified. "The New York gunman," he wrote, "is a dandy, exquisitely scented, wearing silk socks, silk ties to his tan shoes, with rings on his well-kept fingers and a gold watch on his well-kept clothes.... If the murder of Herman Rosenthal brought about no other good it served to force into the limelight these Morlocks of the lower world. It convinced an incredulous public of the real existence of these armed degenerates." And so on and on in this vein.

These episodes in the long summer of 1912 stunned New York Jews, all of them, rich and poor, German and Eastern European. Compared to the Rosenthal-Becker affair every previous reference to a specifically Jewish vice and crime was a trifle. Here, presented to humanity, was no mere interpretation of an assumed evil, the factual basis of which could be disputed, the motives called into question. The exposure of the Lower East Side underworld rendered any interpretation superfluous. The daily headlines week after week, month after month, required no further comment. "American Hebrew" was how the press described Zelig, Gyp the Blood, Lefty Louie, Whitey Lewis and the others, causing the editor of a Yiddish-language newspaper to observe, "The divine word, 'I choose you among the people of the earth,' ends up this way." And so the Jewish community turned in on itself, confronting itself as never before. One can imagine how Jews pondered and discussed the subject wherever they gathered. The Rosenthal-Becker affair had brought a long-simmering issue to a boil.

In the end each faction in the community came up with a different analysis; each regarded the affair as confirmation of its viewpoint. They all agreed that a dangerous pathology afflicted the Lower East Side; the disagreements as always lay over causes and answers. Religious leaders thought that too many Jews had lost their soul, abandoning the faith of their fathers to materialism and success and greed, passing these profane values on to their children who then carried them one step further. Unbelief and cynicism, sapping the roots of morality, disintegrated family and society, destroyed the willingness to work, and encouraged disobedience to all institutions, secular as well as religious. Return to tradition, to the synagogue and the *cheder* (religious school)—that was the answer to prostitution, gambling, delinquency, and gangsterism.

The Socialists, who stood at the other pole, held that religious values, false in themselves, simply did not apply to a modern industrial and urban and scientific world divided into capitalists and proletariat. Thus only Socialism, embodying as it did the highest ethic of humanist and working-class solidarity, could banish the irresistible effects of capitalism, poverty, acquisitiveness, anti-social behavior of every kind. Capitalism, and in its most extreme form at that, was ultimately responsible for the breakdown of family and community, the vice and crime, particularly among youth. And that was why Jews should seek alliances with the working class at large and join the burgeoning Socialist movement abroad in the land rather than pursue retrograde and fruitless religious and national formulae. Redemption would be found by turning outward, not inward.

Between these opposing schools stood the middle class and those with middle-class pretensions who felt that the Socialists were correct in their attacks on orthodox religiosity* and narrow provincial-

---

* Louis Marshall wrote a scathing letter (which he may not have mailed) to New York's orthodox rabbis accusing them of closing their "eyes to the departure of the children of a race that justly prided itself on the purity of its moral life, to adopt the career of gamblers, thugs, gangsters, thieves and prostitutes, and to become a byword and a hissing. You have remained silent witnesses to the degradation of Judaism, to the alienation from it of the new generation."

ism but wrong in rejecting capitalism, liberal capitalism American style. They contended that too many Jewish children became either delinquents or revolutionaries precisely because they were not Americanized enough, had not learned the ideals of the new land and its democratic values, and were not introduced to a form of Judaism that was up-to-date and compatible with those values. This certainly was the uptowners' argument, their own lives being conclusive proof of its validity. Was there any reason why Russian Jews, if they set their minds to it, could not follow their example, become like them? So the debate raged on in the Jewish press.

Now whatever value the debate might have had in itself the conditions which called it forth had to be attended to at once; whatever the causes, the symptoms had to be treated. Jewish community representatives could not passively allow events to simply take their adventitious course. A remedy had to be devised, at the least an attempt made, to check the malignancy of Jewish vice and crime. As it happened the possibility of one lay at hand.

Since its creation in 1909 the Kehillah had been floundering. Though it did good work in fields such as charity and education and labor relations—achievements worthy of notice—and brought a deal of German-Jewish money and talent into the ghetto, as an institution it never caught fire. Much of the Lower East Side remained aloof from it if not downright hostile, and even its participants were riven by factional differences, uptowners versus downtowners, religionists versus secularists, and so forth. Forming a Kehillah in New York City on the Eastern European model proved an awesomely difficult task, in the long run an impossible one (it would expire in 1922).

Beyond question the Kehillah's ornament was its chairman, Judah P. Magnes. Magnes was a remarkable man. He had come to New York from San Francisco via Cincinnati and Germany, where he had done advanced study in religion and philosophy, and had made his mark as an eloquent spokesman for liberal Judaism and as a civic leader in general. He was only twenty-nine when the "Jewish 400," into one of whose families he had married, selected him to be chief rabbi of Temple Emanu-El, their spiritual center. The Lower East Side happened to fascinate Magnes; he spent considerable time down there learning Yiddish, exploring its culture in depth, the high and the low of it, its upper and nether worlds. No one but he could have brought the two branches of New York Jewry together. He was the Kehillah's guiding force from its inception. The Rosenthal-Becker case gave Magnes the chance to restore it to life, or rather give it the life it never had.

At his urging the Kehillah set up a special "Bureau of Social Morals" to "stir the conscience of the citizenship of the city to the realization of the political and moral corruption of which the Rosenthal case is but a symptom."* Behind the fluffy generalities lay something definite, something novel and daring. We refer to the spy and surveillance operation that Mr. Abe Shoenfeld headed up. His assignment, it will be remembered (pace Segal's Cafe and the Boston brothers and their wives), was to find out exactly and in detail who the Jewish criminals and practitioners of vice were, what they did, where they stayed and "hung out," what relations they had to each other and to the System as a whole. Magnes was to receive the data Shoenfeld and his assistants compiled and pass it on to the highest authorities, the mayor and the police commissioner, who would ensure that it was properly used, that it would help crush the evil at its source. The authorities promised their complete support. And the uptown Jews, led by Jacob Schiff, the great investment banker, agreed to finance it. All was in place.†

From the start the drastic remedy encountered obstacles. Armed with information and sometimes people supplied by Magnes, police raids would be conducted on bawdyhouses and stuss parlors

---

* Magnes' accompanying statement was more to the point: "[Almost] all these young men were born and brought up right here under American institutions. Where does the foreigner cease and the native begin? Is it not when he learns the lesson of corrupt American politics and forgets the teachings of his foreign-born father, who never was, and is not now, a gambler and corruptionist.... Heaven help us from this kind of Americanization."

† We might note the irony here. Magnes' plan was just what Commissioner Bingham had suggested in his 1908 article, otherwise so objectionable. In Bingham's exact words: "With the civilian branch of a detective service, the members of which should be engaged and dismissed entirely at the will of the Police Commissioner and who should be known to two or three officials, wonderful results could be accomplished in the breaking up of [Jewish and Italian] criminal organizations."

and poolrooms and opium dens, and criminals would be watched and harassed and occasionally brought to heel. There were even convictions. But the results as a whole were disappointing. Precious few establishments were closed for long and those that were managed to reopen elsewhere. It is a law as unvarying as gravitation that illicit establishments survive raids and usually the reform impulse that engenders them. So it was then. What was more, the operation met police resistance at every level but the top. The police were understandably hostile to vigilantes, outsiders who trod dangerously close to their interests: the collaboration between vice and local law enforcers, which had evolved organically and was almost as old as the city itself, was not going to be broken so easily. And to make matters worse, ill will arose between Magnes and the new reform mayor, John Purroy Mitchel, and the new police commissioner. So that by the end of 1914, two years after its launching, the spy and surveillance operation was failing and the money to sustain it was drying up too.

Yet Shoenfeld was untiring and continued to send in his reports or "stories" on disreputable places and individuals, from the grubbiest gamblers and macks to the most infamous life-takers and guerillas. By the time Magnes officially ended the operation in 1917 a vast *oeuvre* had been accumulated, nothing less than a documentary portrait of the Lower East Side's sprawling subculture, a rich source— this only incidentally—for the further understanding of the Jewish experience in New York and America. This treasure Magnes kept in his personal file and took with him to Palestine in 1922, where, starting over, he became a man of international standing as a philosopher and teacher and founder of Hebrew University. And there, in Jerusalem, his archive on the Jewish underworld remains to this day.

The Rosenthal-Becker affair meanwhile dragged on to its inexorable close. The trials, first of Zelig's comrades, then of Becker, were a formality, a mere procedure. The outcome had already been decided in the papers, the defendants' guilt affirmed beyond the particle of a doubt. Should anything go askew—for everyone knew how quickly and effectively the System would exploit the slightest advantage—

the presiding judge foreclosed the possibility. That judge was none other than John W. Goff, Parkhurst's onetime associate and chief counsel for the Lexow Committee. It might also be mentioned that the Assistant District Attorney, the man who mostly handled the trials, was another of Parkhurst's children, namely Frank Moss, author of *The American Metropolis.* Judge Goff acted as though it were the defendants' burden to prove their innocence, as though, to put it bluntly, he were the judicial arm of the prosecutor's office. At the very least Goff was unerringly loyal to the Mugwump cause.

The predictability of their outcome scarcely affected the public's fascination with the trials. For months, day after day, they seized the headlines, and not only in New York to judge by the number of correspondents from other papers, European as well as American, who jammed the courtroom to witness the spectacle and tell the readers back home what New York (at least the immigrant and ethnic part of it) was really like. It was this prurient sense of anticipation more than the fate of the defendants that invested the trials with their drama. But no surprises were sprung, no other people named and held culpable. So that in the end the case was what it had been in the beginning—the state versus five men indicted for murder. The jury found them all guilty as charged. All went to the electric chair, the four Lower East Side comrades routinely, Becker after a grueling second trial (the appeals court having overturned his conviction) that was much less celebrated than the first. By then—it was now July 1915—the scandal had long been over and done with.

By then too the Mugwumps had won their case decisively, where it mattered most to them: in the court of public opinion. The scandal had triggered yet another Republican-led inquiry into Tammany and police corruption, a replay of past inquiries and featuring the same cast of character types—madams of bawdyhouses, cadets, prostitutes, peccant officers and politicians. The reform movement swept the boards clean, taking over City Hall in 1914 (with Mayor John Purroy Mitchel at its head) and the state capitol a year later. The name of the governor? Who else but former district attorney Charles S. Whitman. The movement that Parkhurst had inaugurated decades ago in Madison Square Presbyterian Church was completely triumphant. Or so it seemed.

v

Lower East Side gangs had particular cause to feel unhappy about the Rosenthal-Becker affair. The heat of public opinion was on them; more exactly, it was on the police to demonstrate their trustworthiness as New York's "finest." And so the police went after the gangs with a vengeance. They scored a breakthrough in 1913 (with the help of Kehillah vigilantes) when they arrested Yoski Nigger and his gang of horse thieves and poisoners, the Jewish Blackhand Association, and persuaded Yoski himself to admit everything, including the identities of the livery owners he serviced and protected.

Not long afterwards, "Joe the Greaser" Rosenzweig and his sidekicks "Little Hymie" Bernstein and "Tough Jake" Heiseman were apprehended for their part in the slaying of Philip "Pinchy" Paul, another of Joe the Greaser's men, "Nigger Benny" Snyder (or Schneider) having blown the whistle on them. According to Nigger Benny, one day in May 1914 Joe the Greaser had asked him to undertake a special job. "I said, 'I always took your orders. You're supposed to be smarter than I am. Anything you say I will do.' He said to me, 'We've got to do away with this guy [Pinchy Paul] because he's always in my way. He goes around and knocks me. He's knocking me with the Furrier's Union, and he's trying to get the furriers away from me.' " Now Joe the Greaser was not that important. What was important was the fact that he also confessed to everything, and in doing so brought into the picture the Lower East Side's commanding gangster, the legatee of Eastman and Twist and Zelig—namely, Dopey Benny Fein. But the picture is complex and requires a closer look.

We have already seen that Dopey Benny tried to give a measure of order and coherence to the Lower East Side underworld. It was a valiant effort and met with a good deal of success, certainly with gangs from other neighborhoods. But some intrepid, or foolhardy, enforcers, such as the late Pinchy Paul, would have no part of Dopey Benny's order, would accept no limits on their right to pursue the main chance. Neither would the nearby Five Pointers, the powerful Italian mob headed by Jack Sirocco. Sirocco categorically rejected the alliance system Benny had worked out with other gangs. The hatred Benny and Sirocco felt for each other was all the fiercer because Sirocco tended to side with the manufacturers while Benny sided with the unions. (We should emphasize that commercial, not ideological, motives determined which side they chose.) Shootouts between these two gangs became increasingly violent. One such battle, in October 1913, fought at the entrance to the struck Feldman Hat Factory, took the life of Benny's old comrade Max Greenwalt and he vowed reprisal at any cost.

The struggle came to a head a few months later. The occasion was a ball given at the Arlington Dance Hall on St. Marks Place and Second Avenue, very near Segal's Cafe, which members of Sirocco's gang were known to be attending. Benny's carefully positioned troops attacked them as they left the ball. In the melee that followed an innocent man was slain. That man, Frederick Straus, happened to be a city official and well-known in the neighborhood. The public was outraged anew—the Rosenthal-Becker affair still being fresh in its mind—and demanded action. Mayor Mitchel promised to destroy the "organized gangs and gangsters" and the police cracked down harder than ever. Benny and several of his accomplices were arrested for the murder of Straus, but in the absence of corroborative evidence, had to be released.

The police then embarked on a campaign of systematic harassment, jailing Dopey Benny on any pretext. On one occasion he received five years for suddenly and without evident provocation assaulting a policeman on the beat. From the depths of the Tombs he smuggled out a letter of despair that was widely published: "Last July it was an open rumor in police circles, which eventually came to my ears, that I was to be 'framed up' before long. For that reason I took particular care not to have disputes of any kind, even at times when it seemed as though they were trying to lead me into a trap. Since my release from Sing Sing [on a previous rap] I have tried my best to be a good boy and avoid trouble, but the police would not have it that way. I am not without heart. I am human, even though the police think otherwise." Benny was evidently right, for the Appellate Court threw out the charge and the conviction, arguing that the wounds he ostensibly inflicted on the policeman were too superficial to warrant the indictment. He had already served four months.

We now come back, circuitously, to Joe the Greaser. He confessed not only to the specific crime for which he was in jail, the dispatch of Pinchy Paul; he also obliged the authorities by asserting that he was present when Frederick Straus was accidentally shot and that he could name the guilty parties: Isidore "Jew Murphy" Cohen, Abraham "Little Abie" Beckerman, Irving Wexler (later familiar to the world as Waxey Gordon), Julius "Little Yutch" Eisenberg, Morris "the Mock" Kaplan, David "Battleship Dave" Sanders, Harry "Shorty" Gordon, Joseph "Brownie" Brown, and August "Augie the Wop" DelGrasio—these along with Dopey Benny, of course. Benny therefore found himself in the Tombs again, and with no end of his troubles in sight, the likelihood being that all his gangster friends would talk to save their skins.

As it turned out they did not talk. Only two of them, Waxey Gordon and Jew Murphy, were tried for the murder; after very lengthy trials both were acquitted.

In February 1915 Dopey Benny broke, too. He admitted everything, omitted nothing, offering as evidence a diary in which—exemplary businessman that he was—he had recorded his commercial transactions over the years. The reason he was talking, the reason he could no longer hold out, he claimed, was that the unions had ceased to need his services and now regarded him as an albatross, that they had in fact cooperated in his entrapment. "They knew I knew too much and they thought they had better get me out of the way." Now there is no way of knowing if Benny told the truth: Had the unions abandoned him? Indeed, had they conspired to get him? Or did he make this startling accusation in order to justify his own confession, the deal that would save *his* skin? In any event he now belonged body and spirit to the city prosecutor's office.

The Manhattan District Attorney, Charles A. Perkins, and his assistant L. S. Breckenridge—both certified Mugwumps who had also been swept into office in the landslide occasioned by the Rosenthal-Becker affair—ordered the arrest of eleven gangsters and twenty-three trade union officials, all Jewish, among them the general secretary-treasurer of the International Ladies Garment Workers Union, the president of the United Hebrew Trades, and the general manager of the Cloak and Suitmaker's Union, for their alleged complicity in the murder of a man named Max Liebowitz who had acted as a scab during the tempestuous cloakmakers' strike five years before. Conviction carried the possibility of a death sentence.

The New York left, the Jewish left especially, saw the case in strictly class terms. In a series of mass protests the trade union and socialist organizations and press denounced the arrests as a shameless attempt by "reactionary" forces, using the city government and New York's worst gangsters, chiefly Dopey Benny, to undo with one blow the progress made after years, decades, of struggle. Remarks by Perkins and Breckenridge lent credence to the accusation. Questioned by reporters, the prosecutors denied that employers, solid men of property, ever "hired guards [*sic*] except when driven to desperation by the unions" and that "they hired to protect their plant [only] licensed private detectives." Everyone involved—the unions, the gangsters, the employers—must have smiled grimly at these innocent words.

The trial of seven of the leading trade unionists (the others were to be tried later) opened with great publicity on September 23, 1915. District Attorney Perkins amassed overwhelming evidence to show that during the heated days of the 1910 strike the defendants had plotted to attack Liebowitz, a comrade turned renegade, and had gone after him en masse, clubbing him to the ground, kicking and beating him to death. Their case seemed hopeless. Now the chief defense lawyer was the socialist writer and speaker and party theoretician Morris Hillquit. Hillquit realized that he could not possibly win if he tried to refute the state's argument point by point, that he must pursue a different strategy, one pioneered by the great radical lawyer Clarence Darrow—namely, to place the deed in its social context, explaining how it came about and why its perpetrators should not be found guilty, the question of guilt being precisely the wrong question to ask.

Hillquit re-creates the scene for us in his autobiography. The trial was in its last day. Its outcome, he felt, depended on his summing-up. "I was not interrupted," he writes, "and for the next three hours I had my first seminar with the jury on the social, economic and psychological aspects of the labor movement. I took them back to the wretched houses and shops of the cloakmakers before 1910 to explain the reasons and causes of the general strike of that year, I summarized the principal demands of the strikers and pointed out what they meant to them in terms of food and shelter, of health and human dignity, of opportunity for rearing and educating their children." The strategy worked to perfection: the jury cleared all the defendants.

It was not yet time to rejoice however. Many more union officials remained to be tried, and they might find it considerably harder to employ the Hillquit-Darrow strategy of defense. But before the district attorney could get around to them Providence intervened, in the form once again of the electorate: the district attorney was voted out of office. Voted in was a loyal and true Tammany man, ex-judge Edward Swann, who promptly asked the court to dismiss the complaint against the remaining defendants, in effect to grant them amnesty, the gangsters and the trade unionists both. This of course provoked another cry of outrage. L. S. Breckenridge, speaking for Mugwumps and reformers, pointed his finger at a "disreputable Tammany plot . . . part of a pre-election promise which gained for Judge Swann the support of the East Side labor leaders."

Breckenridge was undoubtedly right. A deal must have been made or simply taken for granted as the normal give-and-take of politics. Yet most people, Republicans as well as Democrats and Socialists, were relieved that the episode, divisive and charged with emotion, had been disposed of. It was time for the dead to bury the dead. Tammany as usual had performed the morally opprobrious dirty work, doing what had to be done but what respectable folk would never stoop to do. Though the judge of the General Sessions Court denounced Swann's conduct and recommended that the governor discipline him, he, the judge, agreed to drop the charges. And though Governor Whitman also deplored Swann's conduct he did nothing to countermand it; he certainly was not going to alienate the Jewish vote.

As for the man who set off the whole contretemps, he had had enough of the criminal life; or, rather, the criminal life had had enough of him. Dopey Benny Fein finally went straight at the age of twenty-six, becoming a garment manufacturer (thereby turning his insider's knowledge of the industry to productive account), and apparently a prosperous one at that. It is the last we ever hear of him.

Dopey Benny's demise was no lone, anomalous event. It exemplified a much larger phenomenon: the demise of the Lower East Side underworld in general, the end of the epoch that had begun in the 1880s. The demise of the underworld could be attributed in part to the stabilizing effect that the new institutions, the trade unions and the Socialist and Zionist movements chief among them, were exercising in the neighborhood. An ethic of community and social solidarity had emerged as a powerful corrective to the ethic of raw competition and predacity which had hitherto held sway and from which the underworld culture had drawn its strength and justification. And as these new institutions grew and increasingly claimed the loyalties of Lower East Side Jews so the dependence on Tammany's services—the basis at bottom of the System (however one construes the meaning of that all-inclusive term)—was broken irreparably. The neighborhood, and for that matter the city, would never again see the likes of Big Tim Sullivan.

Above all, the demise of the Lower East Side underworld could be attributed to the advent of the World War and therefore to the undreamed-of prosperity that struck the garment industry and the other Jewish trades. With the steady rise in incomes and expectations the flight from the great ghetto swelled to a mass exodus. Immigration, meanwhile, was slowing to a trickle and soon would end altogether. The statistics tell much of the story: at its height around the turn of the century and through its first decade the Lower East Side contained over 500,000 Jews; by 1916 it was down to 313,000; by 1925, to 264,000 and declining swiftly. (A further breakdown would be useful, one that would show the age distribution and the size of families. Our guess is that the average age of Lower East Side residents rose appreciably, that more and more of those who stayed behind were old.) The prostitutes and cadets and gamblers and gangsters—many, perhaps most of them—were swept along on this cataract of redemption; they too settled into anonymous respectability in the newer habitations of the Bronx and upper Manhattan and Brooklyn and elsewhere, leaving only the ghosts of their wayward past to walk the streets of the old neighborhood.

And because the character of the Lower East Side had changed so markedly and because so many of its voters were departing its precincts for the outlands—because, in a word, it was no longer Tammany Hall's reliable bastion—the Mugwumps and reformers would henceforward cease to single it out for special notice and obloquy; they would cease to condemn it in particular, as they had since Parkhurst's day, for its vice and crimes, real and exaggerated. Mugwumps would leave the Lower East Side alone, regardless of how the remaining underworld Jews down there behaved. (We certainly are not done with them.) They would look for and find other enemies, other conspiracies, other reasons to explain Tammany's astonishing vitality.

THREE

BREAKING OUT

i

A seasoned observer of the Lower East Side at the end of World War I would have had reason to feel optimistic about the future. Though aging whores and pimps and gamblers and thugs and enforcers and hustlers could still be seen on familiar streets and in familiar hangouts, the underworld culture was not what it used to be. The quite obvious fact was that it was no longer renewing itself, that youth, bearer of its ancient tradition, was becoming scarce. The culture was dying. But what about the intermediate generation that had grown up when the underworld throve and glittered, the generation born around the turn of the century, roughly between 1895 and 1905, and just now coming of age, the generation that had already produced so many delinquents—their role models having been Zelig and Yoski Nigger and Dopey Benny and their ilk—and so many purveyors of vice and crime? That generation would have given our observer some cause for apprehension, no doubt of it. Yet even here the prognosis would have been a happy one. For if precedent was any guide, almost all of those criminals now reaching manhood could be expected to go straight by their mid- to late-twenties, just as the previous generation of criminals had done. In other words, our imaginary observer would have been correct to assume back in 1918–19 that within ten years or so Jewish gangsterism, the community's deepest reproach and most awful

' out. It would have been as much a relic
'shops and tenements and unrelieved

ver East Side was also true, and in
, ery other large Jewish community in
,eing well-informed, would not have been
..arities. Except in scale the Lower East Side
.rom the other thickly packed ghettos, the various
..nat had sprung up in every major northern city since

Chicago's Westside, with its 200,000 inhabitants, was an almost
exact replica of the New York ghetto. Had the observer visited Chicago before World War I he would have noticed the rickety buildings, the pushcarts, the garment sweatshops, the ragpickers and junk dealers, the settlement houses (Jane Addams founded Hull House, the first and greatest of them in the festering Jewish quarter), the local representatives of the Irish-dominated System, and of course the surrounding neighbors, all fellow ethnics and quite as poor. He certainly would have noticed the Westside's Jewish underworld, which had become rather famous too, a prairie empire of vice and crime. Its ward was known as the "Bloody Twentieth," and its main thoroughfare, Maxwell Street, was known as "Bloody Maxwell." A description of Bloody Maxwell written in 1906 will give some idea of its reputation: "Murderers, robbers and thieves of the worst kind are here born, reared and grow to maturity in numbers that far exceed the record of any similar district anywhere on the face of the globe. Reveling in the freedom which comes from inadequate police control, inspired by the traditions of the criminals that have gone before in the district, living in many instances more like beasts than like human beings, hundreds and thousands of boys and men follow day after day and year after year in the bloody ways of crime. . . . From Maxwell come some of the worst murderers, if not actually the worst, that Chicago has ever seen. From Maxwell come the smoothest robbers, burglars and thieves of all kinds, from Maxwell come the worst 'tough-gangs.' In general, it may be safely said that no police district in the world turns out such skilled and successful criminals."

And so it was in every pullulating ghetto: in Philadelphia's ramshackle southeast wards, where the authorities "concentrated the gambling, prostitution and speakeasies of the city"; in Cleveland's noisome and brutal Woodland section, just east of the Cuyahoga; in Boston's Chelsea quarter, and then (after a fire that ravaged its wooden frame houses) Dorchester across the Mystic, "with its dreary massed tenement blocks, its narrow purulent streets and swarming waterfront"; in Detroit's slum-ridden eastside, the Hastings area south of Grand Boulevard, a center of mayhem and violence; and in Newark's fierce Third Ward, a running sore in the heart of the city. Chicago, Philadelphia, Cleveland, Boston, Detroit, Newark—these held the worst, that is most criminalized, of the Jewish neighborhoods in America, the ones calling forth underworld cultures that most closely approximated the Lower East Side's.

Now the observer who bore witness to this spectacle might have wondered why some very substantial ghettos, chief among them Pittsburgh's and Baltimore's, each with 50,000 inhabitants, failed to produce underworlds comparable to those listed above. Or why a relatively small Jewish community in the southside of Minneapolis was a nursery for youth gangs and criminals. Only the minutest of studies might have disclosed what "variables," apart from sheer size, went into the making of a Jewish underworld culture—what weight to give a city's particular ethnic mix, i.e., the relation between its Jews and other groups and between its assimilated and established German Jews and its Eastern European newcomers, the extent and virulence of its anti-Semitism (all cities being more or less anti-Semitic), the degree of its poverty and the density of its population, its occupations and industries, its corruptibility (all cities being more or less corrupt), and, not least, the force of accident or chance, the random presence among the Jews of exceptionally gifted gangsters and illicit entrepreneurs. No such study was done. Each Jewish community regarded its underworld as a wound, the pain of which had to be quietly endured and overcome. In this respect, too, they all resembled the Lower East Side.

But our observer, in his post–World War I survey, would have been no less optimistic about their future than he was about the Lower East Side's. Nor, as we said, would he have been surprised, for the pattern everywhere was the same: Jews everywhere were moving up and out, leaving the old immigrant neighborhoods behind them as rapidly as possible. Which meant that their respective under-world cultures were dying of inanition too and would soon be only memories. The age that began in 1881 with the arrival of the first boatloads of Eastern European Jews and that had seen almost two million of them settle in the great metropolises since then—that age, the observer would have assumed, was at last drawing to a close, and with it the age of Jewish criminality.

But he failed to reckon with the unpredictability of circum-stances, the accidents of history. Not that he or anyone else could be blamed for failing to take the Eighteenth Amendment seriously until it was too late. It happened so quickly. Only a year earlier, on Decem-ber 18, 1917, to be exact, Congress approved the Amendment and gave it to the states for ratification. And ratify it they did, in pitiless-ly short order. It was on January 29, 1919, that the Constitution pro-hibited (though no sooner than a year) "the manufacture, sale, or transportation of intoxicating liquors ... for beverage purposes." And it was six months later that Congress passed the Volstead Act enforcing the Amendment, defining the permissible limits of the alco-holic beverages that could be manufactured, sold, or transported in the United States and its territories—nothing with more than one-half of one percent of alcohol (which is to say nothing at all)—setting the precise date, January 16, 1920, the ban was to go into effect, and specifying what jail terms and other penalties would be meted out for what offenses. To judge from the speed with which Prohibition went through there could be no question it was what the majority of Americans wanted; a majority, it should be added, that was almost entirely WASP, small-town and rural, and that held disproportionate power in the state legislatures, none of which came close to the one-man one-vote principle. Nor was there much debate about a measure that affected people's lives so greatly. For one thing city politicians simply did not put up much of a fight, and the issue lacked the bite and attention it deserved. For another the public had other matters to worry about: the progress of the war, the peace talks, the Ver-sailles Treaty, the incapacitation of President Wilson, the great flu epidemic (which claimed ten times as many lives as the battlefield), and much else as well. These the people, and our observer, took seriously, and rightly so. Meanwhile Prohibition was stealthily advancing ahead with seven-league boots.

Jews had scant interest in it one way or another. Unlike other groups Jews would experience no overwhelming hardship by the denial of alcoholic beverages. Drink happened not to be one of their needs or vices. They drank moderately, rarely turning to it in pleasure or sorrow, though there were occasional Jewish drunks—an anomaly if not a disgrace—and here and there a Jewish derelict could even be found on Skid Row. All in all, they regarded Prohibition as a piece of silliness and immaturity to which Americans were susceptible and which was bound to meet the same fate (as they, the Jews, knew too well by now) that every other attempt to outlaw and thus redeem a putative vice had met.

Yet Prohibition was a disaster for the Jews. Not for the community as a whole but for that part of it comprising the underworld. Or, more specifically, that part of the underworld already spoken of, the generation of delinquents and aspiring criminals just then coming into its own, the generation which, had normality prevailed, had precedent held up, would have gone straight by the end of the decade at the latest and never been heard of again. By breaking the historic continuum when it did, at that delicate instant, Prohibition could be likened to a *deus ex machina*: an unseen, unanticipated force that suddenly reverses the action and brings something calamitously new in its train. If on that fateful day of its arrival, January 16, 1920, the *deus ex machina* had apostrophized the inhabitants of America's underworld cultures (just as it did on the Greek stage), it would, we believe, have said the following:

"Wait! Do not give up your criminal vocations. What you have learned on the streets and in reformatories and prisons will stand you in good stead; it will give you every advantage. The alcohol industry, profitable beyond reckoning, will eventually be yours. Not in the dreamiest days of your delinquent youth could you have imagined that such miraculous opportunities for gain—at such negligible risk—would be yours for the asking. In your defiance of this absurd law, you will discover a resounding affirmation of the life you were about to or would soon abandon. And further, you will enjoy a status never enjoyed by criminals before. In defying the authorities (and growing rich if you do it successfully) you will be serving your community, not merely exploiting it. You will be contributing your bit in the general resistance to the *kulturkampf*—for it is no less than that—which the nativists are attempting to impose on city folk, Jews and Catholics alike. There is a crusade under way in this land to reduce your people to second-class citizens: witness the spectacular rise of the Ku Klux Klan and the movement to restrict immigration. You represent the advance guard of a countercrusade and deserve the gratitude of all who participate in it."

Consider, for example, how the *deus ex machina* of Prohibition suddenly changed the life of one notably undistinguished Lower East Side gangster: Waxey Gordon.

We are no stranger to the likes of Waxey Gordon. His biography, or police file, is a familiar study. Born Irving Wexler in 1886 to a large, wretchedly poor Polish-Jewish immigrant family, he had by early adolescence left public school for good to spend all his time on Lower East Side streets where he excelled as a pickpocket, acquiring the nickname "Waxey," meaning light-fingered. He graduated from the youth gangs in the customary way, serving stretches in reformatories and penitentiaries for committing a multitude of misdemeanors and felonies, using many aliases during his odyssey, one of which, Gordon, stuck fast to him. He was a gruff, powerful, thickset man, with a particular talent for "schlamming": he could be depended on to break a jaw or arm, or take a life if necessary. As such he rose to a high position in Dopey Benny's outfit and, as we may recall, was once unsuccessfully tried for murder during a shootout with the Five Pointers gang. After Benny's demise Waxey worked for one or another of the gangs that still roamed the neighborhood streets, variously as a labor goon, strikebreaker, dope peddler, burglar, extortionist, etc. Prohibition enabled him to add booze to his repertoire.

Then one day in the fall of 1920 a miracle entered his life. It was in the person of Max "Big Maxey" Greenberg. How they knew each other, where and when their paths had crossed, has never been ascertained, and since all the parties are dead and have left behind no written evidence, it never will be. We do know something about Greenberg, however, and what brought him to New York. He had been a member of a dreadful St. Louis mob named "Egan's Rats" after its leader William Egan, a gangster-politician of local renown. Originally Irish, Egan's Rats had adapted to the changing times and admitted to its ranks young Eastern European Jews and Southern Italians who had fought their way out of their respective ghettos in the traditional manner, Big Maxey Greenberg being one of these upwardly mobile thugs. Egan must have been particularly fond of him. How often does a United States President pardon a man who has served only two years of a ten-year sentence for grand larceny? Yet that is exactly what Egan, through the St. Louis Democratic machine, got Woodrow Wilson to do for Big Maxey in 1919. From St. Louis Big Maxey emigrated to Detroit, which was then establishing its preeminence as a thoroughfare in the bootlegging trade. A few months later, he knocked on Waxey Gordon's door.

The reason Greenberg visited New York, simply put, was that he needed cash, plenty of it, in order to mount his own bootlegging business. He estimated that it would require $175,000 to pay for the boats, warehouses, trucks, bribes, gunmen and other functionaries, not to mention the alcohol itself. And he needed the money at once. Entrepreneurs from all over the country were pouring into Detroit, situated happily just across the river from Windsor, Ontario. Whether Greenberg expected Waxey to try to raise the money himself or put him, Greenberg, in touch with others who could is unclear. In any case, Waxey was able to introduce Greenberg to the one man who might help him, who could help him if anyone on earth could—the fabled Arnold Rothstein.

Rothstein had vaulted far beyond the stuss parlors and pool halls and political clubhouses of his Lower East side youth and was now America's premier gambler, certainly its cleverest, best known, and most daring gambler. It was no surprise that Rothstein's name had recently surfaced as the evil genius behind the 1919 "Black Sox" scandal, the worst, or the only serious, scandal in baseball history. And though Rothstein denied having had anything to do with the fix, and was never brought up on charges, he bore the inescapable presumption of guilt: only he could have inspired such a heinous deed, the corruption of the great American pastime (and the World Series at that!). Nor was gambling his only claim to notoriety. The press also referred to him as a "sportsman and man about town" who consorted with the rich (even as he fleeced them) in Saratoga and Long Island and elsewhere, who had his own stable of fine race horses and belonged to the exclusive New York Jockey Club.

But Waxey Gordon was privy to a side of Rothstein's life that the dazzling gambler-sportsman image artfully concealed from public view. Waxey knew that Rothstein would bankroll any underworld venture which promised a fair return, that he had financed or otherwise had been on intimate terms with the most flagrant of the old neighborhood gangs from Monk Eastman's to Dopey Benny's, that he always kept enforcers on his secret payroll (Waxey had been one of them), that beneath his elaborately wrought persona Rothstein met Waxey as a kindred soul, one gangster to another.*

So it was on an October day that Rothstein heard Greenberg out (on a Central Park bench, Waxey attending) and soon after announced his decision. It was the decision one would have expected of him. Yes, he was definitely interested and would put up the $175,000, more if necessary. He had several conditions, however: first, he, Rothstein, must be the senior partner and overall director of the operation, not merely its banker; second, it must be a New York operation and rely entirely on Rothstein's network of friends and contacts; and third, if he wished to be included Greenberg must mortgage to him, Rothstein, all his personal property and take out an expensive life-insurance policy from Rothstein's insurance firm. One can only imagine what went through Big Maxey Greenberg's head as

---

* F. Scott Fitzgerald's thumbnail sketch of Rothstein in *The Great Gatsby* catches intimations of this darker self. Meyer Wolfsheim, Gatsby's mysterious business associate, defines himself by his "gonnections" (though Rothstein of course spoke impeccable English). These "gonnections" are unexplained, but the word is precisely right. Rothstein's connections with gangsters—among them the most murderous in the land, engaged in some of the foulest misdeeds (heroin smuggling, for instance)—enabled him to perform his popular role as the reigning gambler-sportsman of the age.

Rothstein's wife claimed that he kept his gangster connections concealed from her too. She "might have as dinner guests judges, lawyers, or a bucket shop proprietor or two, but no crook with a police record ever was introduced to her by her husband."

he pondered this breathtaking counterproposal. He must have felt under some constraint, his choices being so limited. If he refused to go along with Rothstein to whom else could he turn? Could he doubt that Rothstein would not proceed with the plan or counterproposal in any event? Greenberg, then, could return to Detroit empty-handed, or he could acquiesce and become part of Rothstein's team. The choice was of course no choice, and he acquiesced.

With Greenberg and Gordon each receiving a share of the profits corresponding to his own investment the smuggling venture was launched without delay. Rothstein instructed his agent in Great Britain, a Lower East Side crook named Harry Mather, to buy 20,000 cases of Scotch whiskey and hire a cargo ship to bring them over. Speedboats were rented to meet the ship off Montauk Point, Long Island, a region Rothstein knew very well. A fleet of trucks was to meet the speedboats at special landing sites and carry the goods to warehouses in Queens. Money of course was to be lavishly distributed at every stage; i.e., to the Coast Guard patrolling the waters and to the local and county police forces from Suffolk County to New York City. And, indeed, everything went off smoothly. Ship after ship crossed the Atlantic; the booze was transported by boats and trucks and sold to the street gangs. The profits were immense and repaid many times over the initial and all subsequent investments. There was vindication enough for all three of them, Greenberg for his original idea, Rothstein for his boldness and system and capital, Gordon for serving as broker. They were the pioneers, and every subsequent bootlegger or rumrunner would be in their debt, whether he realized it or not.

It was while the eleventh voyage was making its way across the Atlantic that the weakest link in the elaborate chain snapped. The Coast Guard had discovered the corruption in its ranks, and a fresh patrol lay in wait off Montauk Point for the ship. Rothstein, however, learned of the trap—he was never without a fallback position—and by radio diverted the vessel to Cuba where the cargo was safely unloaded. With federal authorities closing in, Rothstein decided that bootlegging, however lucrative, was simply not worth the risks now; the famous gambler-sportsman could hardly afford to be unmasked and shown for what he was. And so late in 1921, a year after establishing the business, Rothstein "walked away" from it, giving it over to his junior partners, each of whom had by now accumulated a tidy nest egg.

While Big Maxey Greenberg returned to St. Louis, Waxey Gordon used his capital and considerable experience to set up his own outfit comprised of associates drawn from the old neighborhood (Samuel Rappoport, Albert Ross, Charles Kramer), all penny-ante bootleggers who had worked the streets much as he had done before that fateful knock on the door. Waxey's gang would procure the booze from "Rum Row"—the fleet of alcohol-laden ships brazenly anchored off the New York and New Jersey coasts just outside the three-mile limit (later extended to twelve)—and sell it to restaurants and clubs and bootleggers at large in the New York metropolitan region. That Waxey and his men tailored the product to suit the particularities of the market went without saying: the best clientele received the "real McCoy"; the rest, or the most gullible, received the ersatz stuff, regardless of the name on the label. Alcohol-cutting had become an art and Waxey's gang was as proficient in it as any.

At his headquarters disguised as a realty company, in the Knickerbocker Hotel on Forty-second Street and Broadway, Waxey maintained a complex system of passwords, codes, maps, and radio communications to handle the expanding volume of business. And as it expanded so Waxey moved further and further toward the model conceived by his mentor Rothstein: to be independent of the middlemen; to assume control over the various stages of the operation, from production to consumption. Cargo ships contracted to him alone were plying the waters between New York and the French-owned islands off Newfoundland, St. Pierre and Miquelon, an enormously fecund source of alcohol for the American market. Overnight Waxey Gordon had become a captain of the bootleg industry.

Success was also bringing out new facets of his character. Gone was the schlammer and gunsel of yore. He was reborn Irving Wexler, free-spending New York businessman, owner of real estate and stocks and other properties of a vaguer nature, Broadway angel (with hits to his credit), a gentleman about town conspicuous by his fancy dress and limousine and companions. He too cultivated a persona. And while he could not yet be a Rothstein—he was still too grubby and coarse and arriviste-looking—he was definitely cutting his own swath of respectability. The transformation was startling.

Federal alcohol agents, however, were unimpressed. They had been carefully watching Waxey's progress for some time, waiting for a chance to pounce on him. They were under heavy pressure to come up with results—to get important rumrunners, not the small fry who worked on the streets. They saw their chance when one of Waxey's ship captains, Hans Fuhrman, who was unhappy over his negligible share of the loot, decided to blow the whistle. Fuhrman informed the alcohol agents that the steamer *Nantisco*, bound for Astoria, Queens, with a cargo of Canadian lumber and other building supplies, carried a large cache of Scotch whiskey on order to Waxey. Here was the concrete proof the agents needed. On September 23, 1925, they raided Waxey's Knickerbocker Hotel headquarters and caught everyone but Waxey who was with his family just then aboard a luxury liner headed for Europe.

Among the suspects rounded up was none other than Big Maxey Greenberg, now Gordon's helpmate. Things had not gone very well for Greenberg in St. Louis. He had had an altercation with his one-time boss William Egan. Egan, it seems, had paid him to transport four thousand cases of whiskey up the Mississippi River, but the whiskey somehow never arrived at its destination. Maxey claimed he had been hijacked. Egan accused Maxey of being the hijacker. Warfare broke out between them, in the course of which Egan was slain and Maxey ran for his life.

The government also captured the incriminating maps, charts, radio codes, and the names and addresses of the customers. With Captain Fuhrman as its star witness the government appeared to have an open and shut case.

Again Waxey's luck, or skill, came to his rescue. Before the trial began Fuhrman was found dead in his ostensibly well-guarded New York hotel room. The police called it suicide. So it might have been, there being no evidence to the contrary, though his wife insisted it was murder and many others assumed it as well. Whatever it was, suicide or murder, his death destroyed the case against Waxey and company, the material evidence alone being insufficient to persuade a jury of their guilt, especially since juries in bootlegging trials were notoriously hard to persuade under the best of circumstances.

Yet Waxey had been set back, no doubt of it. His losses were prohibitive and his dream of a vertical combine had been shattered.

But he was as resourceful as ever, and he still had his lieutenants, chief among them Big Maxey, and a good deal of capital. Would he fail to explore other criminal possibilities, other fields of alcoholic endeavor? His response was not long in coming. He next showed up comfortably settled within the fastnesses of Hudson County, New Jersey, across the river from New York, over which Jersey City's Mayor Frank "I Am the Law" Hague ruled with a mailed fist. Waxey must have paid Hague and his satraps handsomely indeed. Supported by county and municipal judges, politicians, district attorneys, and police (all cogs in the Hague machine), Waxey was able to operate a host of breweries, each officially licensed to produce "near-beer," i.e., beer that could be legitimately made and sold because its alcohol content did not exceed one half of one percent. One such brewery (it may serve as our example) went under the name of the Eureka Cereal Beverage Company. Its real purpose of course was to turn out the heady, potable stuff. And this it did through underground pipes leading to another building several blocks away where the barreling and bottling and truck-loading went on under cover of night.

By 1930, thanks to Eureka and his other companies, Waxey was supplying beer to much of northern New Jersey and eastern Pennsylvania. In that year alone, according to government accountants, he earned $1,427,531.42, on which sum, incidentally, he paid a grand total of ten dollars in taxes. And by then he had deposited over two million dollars in local New Jersey banks, this apart from the cash he kept under personal lock and key. None of the banks asked him any questions. Why should they? Waxey Gordon and his ubiquitous mob were enriching the whole community. If the wealth trickled down in continuous flow who wanted to know its source, or, since everyone did know, make an issue of it?* To one and all in Hudson County and environs he was Irving Wexler of New York City, businessman and benefactor.

---

* With the depression going strong bankers went out of their way "to accommodate the hoodlums," writes Elmer L. Irey who was a chief Treasury agent for many years. Bankers "were destroying records, perjuring themselves, and doing all sorts of things with deposits to make them difficult to trace."

Now Waxey Gordon is admittedly an imperfect example. He was no youngster when Prohibition appeared; he was in fact a holdover from the previous criminal generation, most of his erstwhile comrades (e.g., Dopey Benny) having long since opted for the straight and narrow. Waxey might have been one of the few gangsters who in the teeth of every rebuff and all the accumulating responsibilities (he had a wife and three children) persisted in his vocation to the end. Any conjecture on what he might have done with his life is pointless. The point is that the *deus ex machina* found him ready. Miracles save only those who are prepared for them.

Waxey is an imperfect example in another respect—in his having leaped to success in a single bound, thanks to the intervention of that second *deus ex machina*, Arnold Rothstein. Even as a minor partner in Rothstein's enterprise Waxey began with an unparalleled advantage. This is not to minimize Waxey's native talents; it was he, after all, who grasped the main chance when it came his way and exploited it for what it was worth. But we know of nothing in the history of Prohibition to compare with the extraordinary run of good luck that he enjoyed, that made him what he was in the space of a few years.

The typical neighborhood gangster, by way of contrast, was in his late teens or early twenties and started out modestly, accepting his opportunities as they arose, carefully measuring his possibilities by his own experience, his daily encounters on the streets. He was quick to notice that soon after Prohibition went into effect a seller's market in alcoholic beverages had opened up, that those who could supply the market would be handsomely rewarded. And so everywhere hustlers bought and sold booze, acting as middlemen between customers and producers. The hustlers often became producers themselves, distilling or fermenting or brewing in their own apartments or buying from fellow producers in other apartments and stores. The ethnic communities of America were full of them.* For

---

* "They tell me," a New York official reported, "that in each of these districts you can find from one hundred to one hundred and fifty, and in some of them, two hundred stills. And these stills are not operated alone in cigar stores, delicatessen stores, and all sorts of places, but they are operated also in the houses of people in the tenements. You open the door of the tenement and walk in, and the first thing you get is a whiff of liquor or some kind of alcohol. . . ."

all we know Waxey Gordon may have been running such stills and cookers before Greenberg showed up. Or, like his counterparts everywhere, he may have been involved in a more sinister aspect of the trade: stealing or hijacking, or even worse. He, like them, was capable of anything.

Ordinarily, where market conditions are unfettered, competition creates its own order, its own rough balance; an "invisible hand" establishes itself. But where the market is underground and illicit, the hand is visible indeed. Competition then also means the capacity to inflict violence, there being no other way to determine who survives and who fails, no other principle of order. And so it was above all in these chaotic early days of Prohibition. The carnage that accompanied the struggle for local territories and markets was appalling, a continuation on the homefront, in old neighborhoods, of the war recently fought on foreign battlefields. (These street wars, it might be added, also required the most up-to-date weapons and vehicles and professional training and other military skills.) Success, it follows, went to those who could best organize muscle. The lone individual, however tough and intelligent, had no chance. Resources had to be pooled, territories consolidated, alliances or gangs formed and led by men who could make decisions for the gang as a whole, who could treat with the outside world, namely politicians, customers in the trade, other gangs.

Now these were not the same gangs that had grown up in the old ghetto enclaves, the ones Eastman and Kid Twist and Zelig had headed in the old days. The neighborhood bootlegging gang represented a more advanced state of development. It would increasingly supply the capital for "the stills and the raw materials and employed the tenement dwellers to handle the details of manufacturing, to barrel and bottle the alcohol, and to have it ready for shipment when the collecting trucks made their periodic calls." The stakes were vastly higher now than in the old days and so therefore was the magnitude of the violence and the degree of professionalization required of gang members.

In some ways the Jewish gangs that emerged from the hecatombs of early Prohibition were tougher than the non-Jewish ones. The reason very simply was that Jewish communities, being negligible consumers of alcohol, furnished them with no huge market of their own. To capture their main chance Jewish gangsters had to secure a foothold elsewhere, in gentile neighborhoods. Their task, as we can imagine, was especially difficult and their accomplishments therefore were especially notable. A few illustrations will do.

Arthur Flegenheimer is an improbable name for an aspiring gangster. So this child of Austrian-Jewish parents, brought up in the sinkholes of the South Bronx, chose as his *nom de guerre* Dutch Schultz. "The Dutchman" demonstrated his exemplary gifts at an early age: he was smart and quick and demonically cruel, and he had no trouble becoming the leader of his local street gang. After serving as a free-lance gunman with several bootlegging and hijacking outfits the Dutchman struck out on his own. His South Bronx gang, a grab bag of Jewish, Italian, and Irish hoods, a ruthless assemblage if there ever was one, beat down, muscled in on, or co-opted one neighborhood rival after another, supplying beer and liquor to speakeasies, restaurants, and clubs as far away as Manhattan's Upper West Side and Harlem. It was a foolhardy adventurer who dared challenge the Dutchman's expanding fiefdom.

Detroit's Hastings Street quarter, "Little Jerusalem," spawned a farrago of teen-age Jewish street gangs before the Great War. None compared to the gang which the Fleishers, Harry and Louis, and the Bernsteins, Joseph and Benjamin, presided over. How they acquired the name that would one day make them nationally famous—the Purples—is a matter of some dispute. One writer contends that the folks in Little Jerusalem, storeowners especially, called them "tainted," "off-color," in a word, "purple," the epithet that was invoked whenever they showed up. Another writer traces its origin to an early leader, Samuel "Sammy Purple" Cohen. And a third traces it to a new member, Eddie Fletcher, who wore a purple jersey while working out at the local gym, the others soon following suit. In any event, when Prohibition arrived the Purples had the rudiments of an organization, a preestablished network. From their original base in the downtown ghetto they radiated out in a steadily widening arc of appropriation and control. And like every bootlegging street gang they went on to acquire whatever illicit operations lay within reach—gambling, prostitution, extortion, loan-sharking, rackets of every kind. To be sovereign over a territory was to embrace every profit-making activity within it.

Different from the Dutchman's gang or the Purples were the Cleveland Four, an astonishing quartet by any standard. Louis Rothkopf, Morris Kleinman, Morris Dalitz, and Samuel Tucker formed their historic alliance after each of them had climbed a cubit or two up from the streets (Cleveland's Woodland ghetto being inch for inch the equal of New York's Lower East Side or Chicago's Westside at their most brutal), one of them, Moe Dalitz, having previously done so in Detroit as a member in high standing of the Purple gang. And though a good deal has been written on the Cleveland Four we know precious little about them personally: what their early lives were like, how they met, what strengths and weaknesses each of them brought to the partnership. It would be especially valuable to know the secret of how they worked so well together and for so long, death alone dissolving (in old age and in bed) their ancient bond, leading one to conclude that it must have been forged in heaven.

Then there was the Minneapolis gang led by Isadore Blumenfeld, alias Kid Cann, and his brothers Yiddy and Harry Bloom. Tempered by constant struggle, for their neighborhood was enclosed by a particularly vicious anti-Semitism (on which more later), they and their confederates rose aggressively to the challenge of Prohibition, as though the *deus ex machina* had addressed them specifically, becoming the most successful bootleggers in town. Minneapolis, gateway to the Far West, was an ideal entrepôt in the alcohol trade, and it was not long before Kid Cann was a power to reckon with throughout the upper Mississippi region and beyond.

And so it was that Jewish gangs formed and prospered in one city after another. In St. Paul it was Leon Gleckman and his boys; in Kansas City, Missouri, it was Solomon "Cutcher-Head-Off" Weissman; in Boston Charles "King" Solomon, with Joseph Linsey, Hyman Abrams, and Louis Fox ("the wealthiest liquor syndicate ever built up in New England"); in Newark Joseph Reinfeld and Abner "Longy" Zwillman and their exemplary mob; in Philadelphia Max "Boo Boo" Hoff, aided and then displaced by Harry Stromberg, better known as Nig Rosen (an expatriate from the Lower East Side), and their terrible myrmidons: Willie Weisberg, Max "Chinkie" Rothman, Samuel "Cappie" Hoffman, Joseph "Little Kirssy" Herman, and the rest. There is no need to list every single Jewish gang that crystallized in the 1920s; we have enumerated the major ones. What should be emphasized again is that their presence constituted a tragic reversal for the Jewish community at large. Our observer friend would have ceased feeling so optimistic about the future. He would by now have seen thousands of Jews, almost all in their early to mid-twenties, returned to the underworld, justified and lionized as none of their ghetto forebears had ever been or could have envisioned being, with every prospect that their numbers would grow and their commitment to the criminal life deepen, for there was no end to Prohibition in sight.

Where a thriving Jewish underworld culture existed, as in Boston, Cleveland, Detroit, and Philadelphia, there generally emerged at least one important gang. It does not follow though that a thriving underworld culture necessarily produced an important gang on the order of Dutch Schultz's, the Cleveland Four's, the Purple's, and the like. What happened in Chicago is a case in point.

Out of the Gehenna of the Westside had come the Jewish "Twentieth Ward Group," whose members—Benjamin "Buddy" and Samuel "the Greener" Jacobson, Hershel and Max Miller, Max Eisen, Isadore "Nigger" Goldberg, David Edelman, and Samuel "Nails" Morton—were man for man as ferocious as any in the country. Yet the Group as a body could not compete with the neighboring mobs, so much larger and more affluent and therefore so much better organized and connected politically: on one side the forces commanded by Dion O'Bannion and Bugs Moran and Hymie Weiss (who was Polish, not Jewish); on the other those commanded by Johnny Torrio and Al Capone. The protracted war between these two massed armies during much of the decade has been the most highly publicized event of its sort in American history, the source of a whole literature and folklore and apocrypha. Being no match for either, ground between two gigantic millstones, the Twentieth Ward gangsters came to terms as well as they could with both of them, some joining one or the other and some dropping out altogether. By the end of the 1920s the Group had completely disappeared. Why it failed whereas far lesser Jewish gangs made good elsewhere in America is an intriguing question, but it is not one that can be dealt with here, if it can be dealt with at all. For it may turn on too many imponderables, leadership for example (Nails Morton, probably the Group's most talented gangster, was killed in 1921, just as his career was getting started), and requires a large-scale study of its own. The history of organized crime, Jewish and other, is still *terra incognita.*

Gradually, inexorably, the expanding street gang reached the stage from which Waxey Gordon had been launched in 1921 on Rothstein's departure. What Rothstein possessed at the start, namely capital, is what the bootlegging gang achieved after years of scrimping and saving and beating down violent opposition. But once it accumulated the capital it could do what Waxey had done (what Greenberg had sought to do earlier): take leave of the streets and move to the wholesale end of the industry. In gangsterdom as in business enterprise money and brains go where the profits are higher and the risks are lower. This was the logic of Prohibition capitalism, and the successful Jewish gang was its exemplar.

Reporter Hank Messick has written a book, *The Silent Syndicate,* that allows us to observe closely, even microscopically (for it is detailed to a fault), one such gang, the Cleveland Four, as it made the transition from the streets to the commanding heights of the industry. That Rothkopf, Kleinman, Dalitz, and Tucker were talented gangsters goes without saying. They were as violent and duplicitous as they had to be, and how they brought the alcohol from Canada across Lake Erie, eluded the Coast Guard and the Treasury agents, and overcame their numerous competitors and adversaries is a fascinating story that Messick tells well. But they mainly owed their success over the long haul to their genius as businessmen, their willingness to invest their earnings with a free hand, sparing no outlay. Early on in the game the Four realized—and here is where they, like Arnold Rothstein and Waxey Gordon, demonstrated their superiority—that if they were to engage in rumrunning on a grand scale they must buy the best, most up-to-date equipment (boats, vehicles, weapons, radios) and, more important yet, that they must buy the best people, those occupying the highest places. That meant financing candidates and parties, bribing city and state officials, especially judges, prosecutors, and police, and retaining the finest legal talent available. The System, to borrow the old Mugwump-Progressive term, was their indispensable carapace of security.

Equally indispensable to them was the alliance they established at the opposite stratum of society—the alliance with Cleveland's street gangs, notably the Italian "Mayfield Road" mob, headed by the remarkable Alfred "Big Al" Polizzi, which had been gaining control of more and more of the neighborhoods and which therefore could be relied on to guard, insure, and dispose of the merchandise that they, the Four, were smuggling in from abroad. An ethnic community of interests thus developed, one destined to last long after Prohibition ran its course.* Acting in concert these allies extended their territory throughout the populous Lake Erie region, from Toledo to Buffalo, using the carrot and the stick as circumstances demanded to impose their wholesale-retail hegemony, corrupting every locality in which they won a foothold and drawing local gangs into their nexus.

The magnitude of the Four's success, the profits realized from the capital they kept plowing back into the business, may be gauged by their income: over $800,000 a year for each of them by decade's end,† an income comparable to that of only the very richest Ameri-

---

* Besides Big Al Polizzi many in the Mayfield Road gang went on to become rich and famous in their own right, among them Charles "Chuck" Polizzi and the Angersola (alias the King) brothers, John, Fred, and George. An interesting sidelight may be mentioned here; Messick makes much of it. Chuck Polizzi, once believed to be Big Al's brother, had actually been born a Jew (to parents named Berkowitz), had been orphaned as a youngster and adopted by the Polizzis. Messick takes this familial oddity to mean—so we cannot help but infer—that Chuck Polizzi's Jewish blood fastened the ethnic ties, that he, in effect half Jewish and half Italian, mediated between the two gangs, the Four and the Mayfield Roaders.

† We know the amount because Morris Kleinman admitted it (at least regarding his own income) in 1932, when the federal government was prosecuting him for tax evasion. He admitted it on the assumption that the fix was in on his behalf, that the government would go easy on him in return for a guilty plea. A correct assumption, says Messick: President Hoover's Republican administration was routinely about to follow the Cleveland mayor's recommendation for leniency toward this otherwise excellent citizen. But alas, Franklin D. Roosevelt, a Democrat, took office in 1933. So the fix was off, and Kleinman had to serve a forty-month sentence. He was the only member of the partnership ever to suffer such a humiliation. The ending was happy though. When he returned home in 1937, Kleinman found everything as it had been; his comrades had kept his place intact.

cans even in that era of high-flying prosperity and easy fortune. Yet only a few years before, Rothkopf, Kleinman, Dalitz, and Tucker, like Waxey Gordon, like the other gang leaders across the nation, only a few of whom have been mentioned here, were small-time hustlers just coming of age. America was indeed the land of infinite miracles.

This wholesale-retail arrangement, this union of capitalist gangsters at one end of the spectrum and street gangsters at the other, poses a question of definition. The organization that evolved so haphazardly over the years was more than a gang, at least in the conventional sense. What had once been considered a gang was now, by the end of the 1920s, a consolidated body of individuals who carried out their social function (bootlegging: satisfying the appetites of a multitude of customers) in defiance of or in cooperation with other organized bodies, including the state. The gang had also become a syndicate.

Though usually applied to criminals, the term "syndicate" is, or can be for the purpose of analysis and understanding, a perfectly neutral one. Too often authorities on organized crime mean by it a group of sinister men acting conspiratorially and with unerring efficiency to work their evil will, that is, to manipulate and dominate the rest of society, the hard-working, tax-paying, law-abiding citizenry. By syndicate we mean, simply, an extensive gang on the order of, say, the Cleveland Four, the Purples, Kid Cann's outfit, King Solomon's, Dutch Schultz's, Waxey Gordon's and the others, that exercised hegemony over a large area or region around the city from which it arose, therefore over many smaller gangs, each with its own territory and source of income. The gang/syndicate was to the gang what the gang was to the solitary gangster.* The criminal economy of the 1920s had called a new criminal institution into existence.

---

* In his classic study *The Gang* Frederick M. Thrasher has defined the incipient criminal syndicate as follows: It "represents a multiplication of units under a more or less centralized control. . . . The multiplication of units is brought about by the necessity of covering a larger territory or carrying on an increased amount of business, which may be local, regional or national in scope. It usually has political linkages which afford protection."

Style and appearance followed function. The emergence of the gang/syndicate saw the emergence of new gangsters. Wealth and respectability reshaped their character. Other gang leaders underwent the same change Waxey Gordon underwent when he prospered as a rumrunner, emulating Rothstein in demeanor, taking on the trappings of status and class. And they too copied the great Rothstein: they made themselves over, taught themselves to talk, eat, dress, gesture properly, and generally to comport themselves in keeping with their place as gentlemen.* These leaders, it is true, assumed the Rothstein persona for tactical reasons, so that they could deal confidently, from a position of strength if not equality, with their well-bred and well-educated coadjutors—governors, mayors, judges, prosecutors, lawyers, corporate executives, others public and private—whose cooperation they required and whom they paid off handsomely by way of quid pro quo. Reducing their actions to a tactical ploy, however, fails to do them justice; it misses a vital dimension of their lives. Dalitz and Solomon and Dutch Schultz and Waxey and the rest sought to break down the barriers still excluding them from so-called legitimate society, barriers which they regarded as hypocritical and spurious in any case, where moneyed success received the approbation and entitlements and deferences that were its due. By changing their appearance and style they were affirming their faith in the System—which they of course defined in their own image, property and status resting in their view on theft, guile, and mendacity—their belief that it would eventually accept, even embrace, them.

At one level, let it be called the Broadway level (for want of a better term), the System did accept and embrace them with open arms. Gang leaders had no trouble finding their place among the throng of politicians, gamblers, hustlers, playboys, prostitutes, show-biz performers, newspaper columnists, gossip-mongers, press

---

* Even literally so. Rothstein, writes Lucky Luciano in his memoirs, "taught me how to dress, how not to wear loud things but to have good taste. . . . If Arnold had lived longer [he was gunned down in 1928], he could've made me pretty elegant; he was the best etiquette teacher a guy could have—real smooth."

agents, and assorted sycophants who converged on Broadway in the 1920s. (Broadway should be taken also as a metaphor: every American city had its version of it.) New-fashioned gangsters lived in the best hotels, especially the Waldorf-Astoria, where each of them it seems had a suite or a *pied-à-terre* and were entertained by the classiest women in the most desirable restaurants, nightclubs, speakeasies, gambling and sports palaces, were driven about in the fanciest cars. And not content to enjoy the Great White Way they endeavored to appropriate it. They underwrote Broadway shows, especially musicals, and bought into theaters and hotels and nightclubs. Above all, the nightclubs, which consummately expressed the spirit of the era, its gay, carefree pleasures, its insouciance, its love of consumption. None were more popular than Larry Fay's several resorts, chief among them El Fay, where the legendary Texas Guinan ("Hello sucker . . .") established her extraordinary fame, Dutch Schultz's Embassy Club, where the great Helen Morgan sang before overflow crowds, the enormously successful Hotsy Totsy Club (until Legs Diamond one day in July 1929 slew its owners on the dance floor), the Casablanca, the Silver Slipper, the Rendez Vous, the Jungle Club, Les Ambassadeurs, or in Harlem, the Excelsior and Cotton clubs (the latter owned by Owney Madden and featuring the finest jazz musicians of the time, including Duke Ellington, Count Basie, and Cab Calloway). Broadway was the gangsters' ideal cultural milieu; its very existence served as their vindication.

These remarks should be qualified. Yes, Broadway was wide open; it was receptive to anyone who could satisfy its voracious Babylonian appetite for novelty and fun. And, yes, if Jewish gangsters took advantage of it so did Jewish entertainers and artists for their own worthy and legitimate ends. Broadway was one of the few places in America outside the underworld where ethnics and minorities could offer their talents, gain acceptance, become successful and celebrated. Broadway indiscriminately welcomed all the children and grandchildren of the ghetto, Waxey and the Dutchman and their like as well as George Gershwin, Irving Berlin, Al Jolson, Eddie Cantor, George Burns, Fanny Brice, and others. Broadway was where they converged, mingled, and fused in those venally innocent years.

Here is the place perhaps to take up an obvious question: What response did the Jewish Prohibition gangsters elicit, especially as they became better known in their respective cities? Or phrased more pointedly: To what extent did they exacerbate the prevailing anti-Semitism? That American anti-Semitism was pervasive and deep in the 1920s is beyond argument, as witness the immense appeal of the Ku Klux Klan in the cities as well as the countryside and the overwhelming support for the new laws that practically eliminated further emigration to the United States from Southern and Eastern Europe, instituting what amounted to a *numerus clausus* against undesirable ethnic and racial groups. This anti-Semitism had nothing to do with Jewish gangsters, and would have existed if no Jew had ever committed a felony or gone to jail, if Jews were perfect, in which case their very virtue would have been held against them. So that turning the question around, one might ask: To what extent was Jewish gangsterism itself a response to the anti-Semitism?

Yet it is true that Prohibition gangsters did give anti-Semites another reason to justify attacking Jews. For now Jews could be accused of criminality along with all the other vices and flaws of character imputed to them. A distinguished Washington, D.C., judge, Nathan Cayton, saw the country inundated by "a Jewish crime wave" and concluded, not surprisingly, that "the Jews of America have produced far more than their share of criminals." And while this, as we have seen in the previous chapters on the Lower East Side, was an old accusation, now, in the heated climate of the 1920s, with the names of Jewish gangs visible to every eye,* it took on ominous meaning; it bore dangerous consequences. One example may be cited if only because it came to be so well known and so well documented.

The setting was Minneapolis where Kid Cann and his gang/syn-

---

* The Cleveland police force kept a "black-list" of "persons whom the most experienced officers believe to be criminals of a dangerous character" and broke it down by ethnic groups. Of the seventy-four native whites of foreign parentage on the black-list—this in 1930—twenty-seven were "Hebrew," comprising by far the largest group; Germans were next with fifteen, thirteen were Italian, and nine Irish. Of thirty foreign-born whites on the list thirteen were Italian and twelve Jewish.

dicate was establishing its primacy. By the mid-1920s a popular revulsion against the city government had set in, and what everyone suspected was openly and explicitly bruited about, namely that important officials, from the mayor on down, were tied or beholden to bootlegging gangsters, most of them Jews. The attack took an extremely anti-Semitic turn. One muckraking publication, *The Saturday Press*, charged in 1927, and at inordinate length, that Jewish gangsters were paying off the police chief and his men, that the mayor was derelict if not worse, that the county prosecutor knew everything but did nothing (the implication being clear), and that the grand jury itself was tainted with corruption. An excerpt from the November 19, 1927, number of *The Saturday Press* will give an idea of the story's tone and language. The *Press* is quoting a local non-Jewish gangster:

> Practically every vendor of vile hooch, every owner of a moonshine still, every snake-faced gangster and embryonic yegg in the Twin Cities is a JEW.
>
> Having these examples before me, I feel that I am justified in my refusal to take orders from a Jew who boasts that he is a "bosom friend" of Mr. Olson [the county prosecutor].
>
> I find in the mail at least twice per week, letters from gentlemen of Jewish faith who advise me against "launching an attack on the Jewish people." These gentlemen have the cart before the horse. I am launching . . . no attack against any race, BUT;
>
> When I find men of certain race banding themselves together for the purpose of preying upon Gentile or Jew; gunmen, KILLERS, roaming our streets shooting down men against whom they have no personal grudge (or happen to have); defying OUR laws; corrupting OUR officials; assaulting business men; beating up unarmed citizens; spreading a reign of terror through every walk of life, then I say to you in all sincerity, that I refuse to back up a single step from that "issue"—if they choose to make it so.
>
> If the people of Jewish faith in Minneapolis wish to avoid criticism of these vermin whom I rightfully call "Jews" they can easily do so BY THEMSELVES CLEANING HOUSE.

I'm not out to cleanse Israel of the filth that clings to Israel's skirts. I'm out to "hew to the line," let the chips fly where they may!

I simply state a fact when I say that ninety percent of the crimes committed against society in this city are committed by Jew gangsters.

It was a Jew who employed JEWS to shoot down Mr. Guilford. It was a Jew who employed a Jew to intimidate Mr. Shapiro, and a Jew who employed JEWS to assault that gentleman when he refused to yield to their threats. It was a JEW who wheedled or employed Jews to manipulate the election records and returns in the Third Ward in flagrant violation of law. It was a Jew who left two hundred dollars with another Jew to pay our chief of police just before the last election, and:

It is Jew, Jew, Jew, as long as one cares to comb over the records.

I am launching no attack against the Jewish people AS A RACE. I am merely calling attention to a FACT. And if the people of that race and faith wish to rid themselves of the odium and stigma THE RODENTS OF THEIR OWN RACE HAVE BROUGHT UPON THEM they need only step to the front and help the decent citizens of Minneapolis rid the city of these criminal Jews. . . .

The incident would very likely have passed into limbo as such incidents—so numerous then—ordinarily did, but for the fact that it was caught up in an issue of vastly larger moment. The county prosecutor, Floyd Olson (later a famous liberal governor), indicted the publisher of *The Saturday Press*, a man named J. H. Near, under a state law that forbade the printing of "a malicious, scandalous and defamatory newspaper, magazine or other periodical," Olson maintaining that Near had defamed several persons and "the Jewish race." Near was duly tried and found guilty. Years later, his appeal reached the Supreme Court. In its landmark decision the Court threw out the Minnesota statute as a violation of liberty of the press inscribed in the First Amendment and guaranteed by the Fourteenth Amendment—the first time the Fourteenth Amendment was invoked against a state government in behalf of civil liberties. But by then (1931) Minneapolis Jews could look upon the case with some dispassion, for the particular crisis that had engendered it was over. The authorities, however, were far from done with the notorious Kid Cann. And Minneapolis was far from done with anti-Semitism.*

ü

The success of the gang/syndicates produced a serious problem: how to secure the territories they spent so much time and blood carving out for themselves; how to avoid the ruinous conflicts, a repetition on the wholesale or regional level of the wars that the street gangs had been fighting since Prohibition began and that gave such a bad name to criminal enterprise in general. This kind of problem is faced by any large-scale business, and the gang leaders dealt with it as any large-scale businessmen would—by attempting to reach mutually advantageous agreements on prices and markets and inventories. "Cartel" is the conventional word for such an arrangement. The rise of the gang/syndicate had as its corollary the rise of the gang/syndicate cartel.

Now the argument is often given that Johnny Torrio, one of the authentic geniuses of modern crime, was largely responsible for persuading the gang/syndicate chiefs to get together and in effect form a cartel. On the strength of his Chicago experience (he had fashioned the great Southside mob before turning it over to Al Capone, whom he had imported from New York's Little Italy, his own nurturing ground) Torrio had concluded that cooperation, even with one's most despised enemies, was the better part of wisdom, that unless gangsters restrained their imperial greed and their predisposition to violence they must fall either by each other's hands or by the public's.†

---

* Some authorities have claimed that Minneapolis was unusually anti-Semitic and continued to be so into the 1940s (as late as 1946 Carey McWilliams wrote that "Minneapolis is the capital of anti-Semitism in the United States"), but this would be hard to prove objectively. It could also be argued that Minneapolis produced more liberal opponents of anti-Semitism than other cities, Hubert Humphrey for example.
† Elmer L. Irey calls Torrio "the father of modern American gangsterdom." He was "the original exponent of 'leave us out of the shooting, boys, there's enough here for

Torrio's advice had gone unheeded in Chicago, forcing him to fly for his life, and he returned to New York where the underworld gave him a more sympathetic ear. Torrio's influence no doubt was considerable. But it was economic need rather than any one man's sagacity that brought about the desired change. Even in Chicago's steaming jungle an uneasy modus vivendi came to prevail by the late 1920s. The giant bootleggers would have seen the virtue of the cartel whether or not Johnny Torrio had pointed it out to them.

By the end of the decade the major gang/syndicate bosses were convening regularly to hammer out strategies of cartelization. Their most notable achievement was the creation of the "Big Seven," a consortium of rumrunners and street gangs centered in the East Coast corridor from Boston to Newark, from King Solomon's bailiwick to Joe Reinfeld's and Longy Zwillman's, whose control was "so complete," according to Hank Messick, "that it was possible to determine the exact amount of liquor to be permitted a member at a given time. Prices were fixed and no one was allowed to undercut those prices. Central offices were set up where customers could place their orders. Graft was centralized as well." The Big Seven drew up a series of "cooperative alliances" with numerous mobs from "Maine to Florida and west to the Mississippi River." And while this cartel "was clearly a violation of the Sherman Anti-Trust Act . . . no prosecutions were reported."

The most spectacular of the gang/syndicate meetings was held in May 1929 at the President Hotel in Atlantic City, New Jersey, then one of America's premier resort communities. It was also one of the most wide open and debauched communities, thanks in no small measure to its larger-than-life political boss, Enoch "Nucky" Johnson, whose needs for women, clothes, gambling, and all the other good things matched his stupendous income. It was fitting that Nucky Johnson should be the proud host to what must rank as the most disreputable assemblage since Satan gathered up his army after the

---

everybody.' . . . In time every city in America where gangsters flourished adopted the Torrio policy of 'territorial assignments.' "

Fall.* Present from Chicago was the "Big Fellow" himself, Al Capone, accompanied by his sidekick and financial adviser Jacob "Greasy Thumb" Guzik, one of Maxwell Street's ornaments who years earlier, as a proprietor of whorehouses, had joined forces with Torrio; from Detroit came Joe Bernstein and other Purples; from Cleveland Moe Dalitz, Lou Rothkopf, and Chuck Polizzi; from Kansas City Cutcher-Head-Off Weissman and John Lazia, both mainstays of boss Tom Pendergast's political machine; from Philadelphia Boo Boo Hoff, Nig Rosen, and comrades; from Newark Longy Zwillman; and from New York a bevy of crooks: Francesco Castiglia, or rather Frank Costello; Salvatore Lucania, or Lucky Luciano; Joseph Doto, or Broadway Joe Adonis; along with Larry Fay, Owney "The Killer" Madden, Frank Erickson, and, not least, Meyer Lansky of the intrepid "Bugs and Meyer" gang. (Combining his pleasures, Lansky was also in Atlantic City on his honeymoon.) There is no record of what these hierarchs discussed; the government wiretaps caught nothing of substance. The meeting itself was the event, ratifying and legitimating as it did present and future cartels and, more significantly, the general principle of a social contract among the gang/syndicates.

According to Capone a contract was actually drawn up and signed by the participants. It "was time to stop all the killings," Capone asserted, "and look on our business as other men look on theirs, as something to work at and forget when we go home at night. It wasn't an easy matter for men who had been fighting for years to agree on a peaceful program. But we finally decided to forget the past and begin all over again and we drew up a written agreement and each man signed on the dotted line." No evidence of such a written agreement has been found.

One other agreement appears to have been approved at Atlantic

---

* The reader will catch the historic jest here. Atlantic City went into an apparently hopeless decline after World War II, and only the surviving boardwalk hotels testified to the elegance and glory of the old days. But in the last few years the resort has had a resurgence, to say the least, attracting millions to its newly established gambling casinos every year. Without elaborating on the subject further we can assume that the gangsters have returned to Atlantic City, many at any rate, and not to attend conventions.

City and deserves more than a passing mention. It concerned a burgeoning phenomenon of the 1920s, bookmaking, i.e., gambling on
horse races. The growth of bookmaking, reflected in the number of
"handbook" parlors that sprang up, usually several in every neighborhood, some 15,000 in the country by the decade's end, called forth
two demands. First, for bookies with enough capital to handle
"layoffs," or bets placed by financially strapped bookies unable to
cover sudden and catastrophic losses, and hence requiring a form of
insurance. This afforded a perfect opportunity for the prosperous
gang/ syndicates; they had the requisite capital and muscle to handle
such layoffs. Many lower-order bookies already had to pay those
same gangs for the "protection" they enjoyed. The second demand
was for an efficient and reliable service that could inform bookies of
the racing results at once, in any event earlier than anyone else could
learn of them. And so emerged an institution as remarkable as any in
the history of the American underworld, namely the racing news industry, and with it a man as remarkable as any encountered in these
pages.

Moses Annenberg had fought his way up from Chicago newsboy
to high executive positions in William Randolph Hearst's empire on
the strength of his performance in the interminable "circulation
wars" between competing newspapers and magazines.* Then, step
by step, he bought out first the daily racing journals and, soon after,
the wire service company that had been supplying the results to
those journals. Singlehandedly he had created his own racing news
monopoly, the Trans-National. He had pulled off this mighty feat,
seizing control of a service on which every bookie depended, with the
help of the gang/syndicates, Al Capone's in particular, Chicago being Annenberg's or Trans-National's headquarters.

That Annenberg and the Prohibition and gambling mobs had interests in common is indisputable. An information monopoly, nomi-

---

* "Reporters might compete as gentlemen for scoops and editors blast one another
in high-flown language, but on the streets of America hired goons battled with iron
pipes, brass knuckles, and steel knives for choice locations from which papers could be
sold for three cents each. Many of the gangsters who became rich during Prohibition
owed their success to the training in violence they received working for newspaper
'circulators.' " Moses Annenberg was such a "circulator."

nally independent, gave the mobs the wherewithal to police the complex, sprawling kingdom of book; it was an instrument of their sovereignty. In return Annenberg was allowed to reap inordinate profits and become one of the richest men in the land, the founder of one of its singular dynasties. This happy quid pro quo, this exemplary arrangement, received its official imprimatur at that Atlantic City convention.

Now it would be an error to assume that the gang/syndicates succeeded altogether in their joint undertakings, their elaborate plans and consultations. Much of the literature on them would lead us to assume their invincibility. That they definitely were not. Intending to form a cartel is one thing, accomplishing it another. A cartel, as we know, requires as the condition of its success effective control over the market (much as Annenberg controlled the racing news market). Such control the syndicates never had. Only over their own limited areas of jurisdiction did they exercise command, and imperfectly at that. There were simply too many bootleggers around, most of them small-fry distillers and runners who were beyond anyone's reach. But it would be an even greater error to assume therefore that the gang/syndicates failed. For the decisive fact, the historic fact, which underlay all those meetings and confabulations by the end of the decade was that the gang/syndicates had come to acknowledge a sense of community transcending any specific task or problem confronting them. Cartels might come and go; Prohibition might not last forever; but the new community would endure as long as gangsters engaged in large-scale or corporate business enterprise.

It would be well to remember, though, that the subject is gangsterism, not capitalism; the political economy of the underworld, not the upperworld of legal rights and immunities. A member of the gang/syndicate community could expect no protection if he lacked the ability—the force of arms—to secure his own interests. On that ability, that power, rested the community's principle of justice, such as it was. The sad fate of Samuel Bloom gives us an insight into the brute, irreducible reality of the gang/syndicate compact, no matter how closely it otherwise followed accepted business practices.

Bloom, a hoodlum out of Chicago's Twentieth Ward and now associated loosely with the Capone empire, had built up a lucrative smuggling operation as an importer of booze from the Bahamas via Charleston, South Carolina. Capone thought Bloom should join the Eastern consortium, based at that time in New York's fancy Claridge Hotel, and so he did. An agreement was set: Bloom would sell the Big Seven 10,000 cases of liquor a month. The responsibility for protecting the convoys from Charleston to a Brooklyn warehouse was given to "Bugs and Meyer," leaders of a Lower East Side "group of killers so tough even the Dutchman shied away." Bugs and Meyer were Benjamin "Bugsy" Siegel and Meyer Lansky, long-time partners in crime (they began as adolescents) and now specialists without peer in guarding trucks, riding shotgun as it were. They were very much in demand and were rising fast in the underworld establishment.*

Somehow, though no mishap occurred, part of the first shipment disappeared en route. Bloom, liable for the loss, took his case to the Big Seven, insisting that the contract be honored, that the consortium pay him for the missing cargo—half a million dollars' worth. That insistence, which he could not back by the threat of retaliation, was his undoing. Sam Bloom disappeared one night—it must have been shortly after leaving his West Fifty-seventh Street apartment house—and was never seen again. His removal scarcely affected the flow of commerce, however. Lansky and Siegel promptly visited Charleston and the Bahamas and brought back "bills of lading for future shipments of booze." Their coup de grâce, Messick tells us, marked their ascent to stardom, their admission as full-fledged members to the gang/syndicate community.

Recall who met at Atlantic City. With the exception of a handful of Irish and WASP gentlemen (none consequential any longer, not even

---

* Successful shotgun riders were highly appreciated. Not only did they have to fend off hijackers—a very risky endeavor, since hijackers often left no witnesses—they also had to be adept in dealing with any contingency that might turn up on the road. That was why successful shotgun riders did so well. Along with Siegel and Lansky the most famous of them was Longy Zwillman. He started out in his late teens transporting booze from Boston to Newark for Joe Reinfeld. Eventually he became Reinfeld's partner and, still later, one of America's chief gang/syndicate leaders.

the master bookie Frank Erickson or the once vaunted Owney the Killer Madden) all were Jews and Italians, roughly of the same age and drawn, therefore, from the generation about which we have already remarked at some length, who had come up from their ghetto streets at the same time and in the same way.* Here then was something extraordinary: Italian and Jewish gang leaders collaborating, acting in concert within their respective gangs, at the street level.

Let the proposition be put differently: Among the many Italian and Jewish gangsters raised and nurtured in their respective underworld cultures were those few who, for whatever reason, sought out and developed contacts, relations, friendships with each other. They were the few who dared to cross the abyss between two traditionally alien, hostile tribes. To the extent that they did so these few bore the germ of future "rationality": they embodied the conviction that a world of criminal possibilities lay beyond their own inbred parochialisms, the constraints of their elders and most of their peers, and that to grasp these possibilities it was necessary to work with outsiders, members of the other tribe, however feared and despised, and even to unite with them.

Because we know so much about Lucky Luciano and Frank Costello (prime movers of the Atlantic City convention), they provide an insight into the genesis of this new gangster type, the vanguard of his class. Growing up in their Italian ghettos both of them were attracted to Jews. Luciano, reared in Little Italy, was almost a son to the man for whom he worked, Max Goodman, owner of a hat company; he fondly remembers the kindnesses and favors Goodman showed him, the Friday night meals and prayers over lit candles. And Luciano in his memoirs takes special pride in having helped forge the Italian-Jewish alliance, in speaking a language that Waxey

---

* Humbert S. Nelli writes of Italian criminals at this time: "Manpower for the syndicates came from a number of sources: some 'graduated' from Black Hand and Italiancolony Mafia gangs; others had served as whorehouse proprietors, gambling-house operators, labor goons, counterfeiters, narcotics dealers, and a wide range of petty crooks and thieves. Former juvenile-gang members . . . grew up to maturity in time to participate in the scramble for wealth made possible by the enactment of the Eighteenth Amendment. . . ." These words could just as well apply to the Lower East Side and to the Jewish neighborhoods of all the large cities.

Gordon and Longy Zwillman and "Bugs and Meyer" and Dutch Schultz and Louis "Lepke" Buchalter could understand and reciprocate. Time after time his Italian compatriots chided him for his ecumenism. "When I first started hanging around with Jewish guys like Meyer and Bugsy and Dutch, the old guys Masseria and Maranzano and lots of my friends used to beef to me about it. They always said that some day the Jews was gonna make me turn and join the synagogue." Costello, who spent his youth in the East Harlem slum, had similar experiences. Almost from the start of his career he was the friend or partner of Jewish gangsters. He also married his Jewish childhood sweetheart. Some of his Italian confreres resented this intimacy with Jews, even suspecting a betrayal of loyalties.

Luciano recounts a telling incident. One day, at the Claridge Hotel, Meyer Lansky introduced Luciano and members of Luciano's gang to Lepke Buchalter, who had been doing quite well as a union racketeer. Costello meanwhile had brought along Dutch Schultz. Vito Genovese, years later an enormously powerful gang leader in his own right, could take it no longer: " 'What the hell is this!' [Genovese shouted.] 'What're you trying to do, load us with a bunch of Hebes?' Before Benny Bugsy Siegel and Meyer could open their mouths, Frank [Costello] almost swung on him, and he said, very quiet, 'Take it easy, Don Vitone, you're nothin' but a fuckin' foreigner yourself.' " That effectively silenced Genovese, a Neapolitan and therefore almost as much an outsider among the clannish Sicilians as the "Hebes."

The Lucianos and Costellos were to be found in the Italian gangster communities of every city. (These lay cheek by jowl with the Jewish communities, the pauperized immigrants of both having arrived at the same moment and been compelled to occupy adjoining space.) None stood out more conspicuously than the great Al Capone, himself a Neapolitan, whose gang was a model of ethnic pluralism, though it was dominated by Italians of course; but in business matters no one stood closer to the Big Fellow than Greasy Thumb Guzik. By the same token Italians were assimilated into or joined up with predominantly Jewish gang/syndicates. Dutch Schultz's murderous Bronx legion was, like Capone's, a veritable League of Nations (though his chief lieutenants were Jews). And we have had occasion to observe how trans-ethnic solidarity worked to excellent effect in Cleveland where the Four (Rothkopf, Kleinman, Dalitz, and Tucker) and the Mayfield Road Gang (led by Al and Chuck Polizzi and the Angersola brothers) held sway. By the late 1920s Detroit's Purple gang had become a thoroughly mixed bag of Jews and Italians, the latter consisting of novices such as Peter and James Licavoli, Joseph Zerilli, Joseph Massei, and Vincent and Frank Camerata, all of whom in later life would distinguish themselves as high aristocrats of American crime. The Boo Boo Hoff–Nig Rosen mob now included the Matteo brothers, Francesco, Salvatore, and Nicholas, and Marco Reginelli, or "The Little Guy," the Italian "czar" of South Jersey. Mario Ingraffia was among the founding fathers of King Solomon's Boston gang. Among Waxey Gordon's best operatives in northern New Jersey were the notorious Moretti brothers, Salvatore and William, both of whom would also come into their own years later, long after Waxey was gone. And so it was with every Jewish or Italian gang/syndicate—the examples could be multiplied—that willingly entered the consortium, that embraced the principle of a rational sense of community, of enlightened self-interest. Their opinion of themselves and each other is summed up by Luciano: "To me, the whole thing was a matter of organizin' a business."

These young leaders were demonstrating how far they had come in placing their ambition ahead of ethnocentrism or any other kind of insular loyalty. They represented the completion of the metamorphosis begun a decade earlier when the Eighteenth Amendment and the Volstead Act were only portents and foreshadowings.

The new syndicated gangsterism also produced tensions and conflicts of its own. This was especially so in the Italian community where traditional values, rural and semifeudal in origin, were slow to yield to the forces of modernity. The opposition that Luciano and Costello encountered for consorting with Jews only emphasized the conflict that had already been germinating for some time between them and the older generation of gangsters. And as the younger generation, or rather its avant-garde (Luciano and Costello being archetypes here), came into its own, as it adopted a rational businesslike approach to crime, developing the sense of community discussed above, so it looked upon the older generation with increasing contempt and disdain. The new-fashioned gangsters labeled the old-fashioned ones "Mustache Petes," the thick handlebar mustache symbolizing everything that they, the Young Turks, had labored to leave behind in the course of their rise. What could be more incongruous or embarrassing than a Mustache Pete meeting a silver-haired WASP judge on vital business affairs at the Claridge Hotel? The incongruity, the embarrassment, would have brought back bitter memories of the old days when mustachioed immigrant fathers, hat in hand, head bowed, pleaded before that very judge, or his equivalent, in some other punitive agency of the government for mercy toward his errant child or perhaps himself. To wipe out these humiliations it was necessary to remove the Mustache Pete and all he stood for. This burgeoning conflict between generations of Italian gangsters was not an intramural one: it certainly involved Jews. And it involved them as active and violent participants.

We are referring specifically to the "Castellammarese War" (named for a Sicilian region southwest of Palermo, birthplace of one of the warring factions), a historic event by now deeply embedded in myth and fancy. The accounts that have come down to us are heavily exaggerated and full of false drama. This much though cannot be doubted: the Castellammarese War—or whatever one wishes to call the struggle that took place and that claimed so many lives—announced the triumph of the Young Turks. And what cannot be doubted too was that their Jewish friends and allies had a good deal to do with the outcome.

Joseph "the Boss" Masseria was a squat porcine killer who operated out of New York's downtown Italian ghetto. Luck, cunning, and murderous skill enabled his gang in the 1920s to win the "war of the curb exchange," a war fought for dominion over Italian neighborhood streets where drugs and alcohol and other such commodities were bought and sold. Masseria might have made his mark on the future, risen to Al Capone's heights if he had not been a Mustache Pete (though he shaved clean), if like Capone he had been willing to co-opt nearby Jewish and Irish and American gangsters. He relied on his underling Luciano to establish the necessary connections with other gangs, a talent, as we have noted, for which Luciano was uniquely equipped, and with the wholesale importers and distributors. Masseria (as we noted also) had divided feelings about Luciano's relations with the Jews, feelings that may have reflected his own inability to make the leap from the old neighborhood gangster to the new-fashioned kind, his inability to adapt and metamorphose.

Just then an extraordinary band of criminals showed up. These were the "Twenties Group": young Sicilians, many from Castellammarese, who fled when Mussolini's Fascisti cracked down on the Mafia, there being no room in Italy for two sets of gangsters. Among this group of newcomers were names America would one day have to reckon with, alas, names such as Joseph Bonnano, Stefano and Antonio Meggadino, Joseph Profaci, Joseph Magliocca, Michael Coppola, and Salvatore Maranzano.

Maranzano, who arrived late (1927), had been a leading Mafioso in Sicily and was determined to be one in New York. He seems to have been a throwback to the more traditional Sicilian bandit who ruled by terror and personal authority and brooked no concession to ethnic pluralism and rationality, to whom America was alien territory. One fellow gangster later wrote: "When we arrived it was very dark. We were brought before Maranzano who seemed absolutely majestic, what with his two pistols stuck in his waist and about ninety boys who were also armed to the teeth surrounding him. . . . I thought I was in the presence of Pancho Villa." In a very short time Maranzano had organized his *paisanos* and Masseria's enemies into a powerful gang indeed, and it openly challenged Joe the Boss's hegemony over the Italian neighborhoods.

War between gangsters brings out their basest qualities. The attribute they value most, without which their calling would be impossible, namely personal loyalty, is now called into question: no one and nothing can be taken for granted; treachery becomes a fact of life. And so it was in this conflict to the death.

Maranzano, who was gaining the upper hand, got a message through to Lucky Luciano asking him to betray Joe the Boss. Luciano hesitated, but not for long: he was taken for a ride, tortured, and left half dead in far-off Staten Island. Luciano was persuaded; and as proof of his new-won loyalty to Maranzano he promised to arrange Masseria's assassination himself. On April 15, 1931, he met Joe the Boss for lunch at Scarpata's in Coney Island. After eating they played cards, as was customary. The killers struck the moment Luciano retired to the toilet. Joey Adonis, Albert "the Executioner" Anastasia, Vito Genovese, and Bugsy Siegel were the members of the high-ranking squad who shot Masseria as he sat, waiting for his betrayer to return.

Luciano and his friends realized, or soon learned, that their troubles were far from over—that with Joe the Boss gone, Maranzano would now go after them. Maranzano was well on the way to becoming the Mussolini—he modestly liked to think of himself as the Caesar—of the Italian-American underworld, at least the greater New York segment of it. Quite an achievement for someone who had arrived in the United States less than five years before.

So far as the Jewish underworld was concerned Maranzano's triumph would be a disaster. All the meetings, all the attempts to form a community of interests between like-minded, rationally disposed gang/syndicates would be for naught or set back indefinitely. They had an investment in keeping Luciano and the other young Italian Turks alive and well.* Meyer Lansky and Bugsy Siegel, who were especially close to Luciano and especially strong apostles of the new criminality, worked out a daring plan of attack. They hand-picked six of the best Jewish gunsels in the business, chief among them one Samuel "Red" Levine, a Toledo-born professional (he was strictly Orthodox: wore a skullcap and never slaughtered on the Sabbath if he could help it), none of whom were known to Maranzano and his bodyguards. The killers were carefully coached down to the most exacting detail of their scenario. Failure was unthinkable both for the Young Turks and the Jews, Lansky and Siegel and the others, who had conspired with them.

On the afternoon of September 10, 1931, five men knocked on the door of Maranzano's midtown New York office. They were let in and

---

* It was imperative, one scholar has recently written, "to rid the Italian underworld of those who refused to reach a peaceful accommodation with non-Italian gangs such as the Jewish organization."

of course surrounded by his bodyguards. The men showed their badges which were duly inspected: it seemed to be a routine raid by federal alcohol agents. So when the bogus agents ordered the gangsters in the office to raise their hands and face the wall they meekly complied. Maranzano stepped forward and protested his innocence, claiming he had no contraband and challenging the agents to search the premises. He led a few of them into his inner office. There he was slain after putting up a fierce struggle. His bodyguards, who were still being covered, were powerless to do anything. The killers ran down the stairs and leaped into waiting cars. It had been a perfect job.

There followed, we are told, the "Slaughter of the Sicilian Vespers," as it has been called, the swift, merciless purge of Maranzano's men in cities all across the country. Whether such a "slaughter" took place on the scale alleged is problematic. We have only the vaguest idea of what happened. Who directed and carried out the "slaughter"? How many were killed? Who were they? Who took their places? Here the literature, otherwise so omniscient, fails us. And one authority even denies the purge ever happened. Moreover, we discover that Maranzano's most trusted lieutenants or "capos" managed to survive the slaughter quite nicely. They seem to have had no difficulty transferring their allegiance to Luciano and the Young Turks, leading us to surmise that perhaps they were also in on the conspiracy, that they had their own reasons for favoring the overthrow of the despot. The undisputed fact is that Maranzano's death marked the vindication of the new order, of the rational and pluralistic and cooperative gangsterism that had been gestating for years. The Mustache Petes had joined their Jewish counterparts of an earlier time, the Eastmans and Twists and Zeligs of the old neighborhood, once and for all in the mausoleum of bygone heroes.*

---

*   Some students of the Mafia ascribe great historic significance to the Castellammarese War. The triumph of Luciano and the Young Turks, they argue, brought organization to the underworld, a tightly regulated administrative and bureaucratic structure, national in scope, with its own hierarchical authority—councils, families, captains, lieutenants, soldiers, etc.—and a system of enforcement, a state within a state. This thesis (best argued by criminologist Donald R. Cressey) is overdrawn; it falls victim to the social scientists' passion for symmetry, for clearly defined models, and, at a more

A few weeks later Lansky and Siegel and Moe Dalitz and Nig Rosen and Dutch Schultz, Luciano and Costello and Adonis and Torrio and their entourages were Al Capone's honored guests at Chicago's Congress Hotel. They had come obviously to celebrate the recent triumph. But they had also come to discuss new business, or rather new problems looming in the near distance. The most ominous of these was the fact that the urban masses were no longer amused by the bootleggers, were increasingly apprehensive about crime. Politicians were getting elected—even in Chicago!—on the law-and-order issue. Prosecutors were developing sophisticated tactics in their exploitation of that issue. The Big Fellow himself would soon be tried for tax evasion, of all things. Not that he was or seemed especially concerned, not with his battalions of lawyers, his connections at the top, his mastery of the whole recondite system of corruption. Yet . . . yet the federal government might just pull it off—and if it did, then every other gang/syndicate boss would be on notice. The heat would be applied as never before.

The future was insecure in a more nebulous way. Prohibition was clearly doomed. The *deus ex machina*, by now creaking and broken, would soon be trundled off the stage. Exactly how soon was the only uncertainty. The Democrats, the party of Repeal, were obviously going to win the presidential election next year, there being no sign that the Depression would let up by then. To judge from the country's mood, Repeal would have little trouble getting support from the required thirty-six states. And when that happened what would they, the gangsters, do? What preparations should they make

---

superficial level, to the need of investigative reporters, novelists, and moviemakers for easy and convenient answers. The thesis is therefore the ideal target of those—and they are social scientists too—who deny that the Mafia exists at all, who contend that it is mostly a myth, an imaginary construct resting on a generalized and diffuse anxiety, a feeling, as Daniel Bell writes, "that 'somewhere, somebody' is pulling all the complicated strings to which this jumbled world dances." But in our view neither of these schools of thought is correct. To assume that there is a Mafia is not necessarily to assume a vast and sinister conspiracy or a government of the sort Cressey and others describe. If a political term applies it would be *confederation*, and a confederation of the loosest kind at that: a series of sub-confederations brought together for a common purpose. We have tried to show in this chapter that the confederation of gang/syndicates took shape in the 1920s, that it embraced both Italians and Jews from the outset (and even earlier, the friendships having been formed at the street level), and that on the Italian side it received its final ratification in the Castellammarese War.

for the eventuality? How they took up these questions at the Congress Hotel we do not know. Nothing concrete was or could have been decided. Given their profession, the servicing of illicit needs, they might anticipate things to come; they could not plan for them. Meanwhile Prohibition, the source of their wealth, was still on the books, and they, the honored guests, still had their work to do, their cartel to maintain.

They might also have reminisced about the past, actually the recent past, hardly more than eleven years ago, when as youngsters they had trod the ghetto streets, their horizons extending no further than the outer limits of the old neighborhood. Now they were millionaires and were only in their late twenties or early thirties. And so, whatever their futures held in store for them, with Al Capone as their host, with the best food and drink and entertainment at their disposal, nothing could prevent them from having the grandest of times.

FOUR

LEPKE'S RISE: THE CHRONICLES OF LABOR

i

The Buchalters were typical of the penniless Russian-Jewish immigrant families who settled on New York's Lower East Side in the 1890s. Except in one notable respect: there were thirteen of them, each parent, Barnet and Rose, having been widowed before and left with young children. So the Buchalters were condemned to suffer more than their share of adversity, more than their share of crowding, toil, exhaustion, the relentless everyday lot of their tenement neighbors and co-workers. Yet they endured, defiantly and heroically. Barnet Buchalter managed to open a little hardware store while Rose singlehandedly oversaw raising the children, an awesome accomplishment in itself, a miracle of tenacity and faith. By the time Barnet died in 1909 she had seen the worst of the travails pass. The older children were married and departed. The younger were approaching adulthood and could begin to take care of themselves. Rose, tired and worn, went to Colorado to live out her days with a married son. The family epic was over.

Before she left Rose Buchalter placed her fourteen-year-old son Louis, affectionately called "Lepkele" or "Lepke," in the care of a married daughter who lived in the Williamsburg section of Brooklyn. He was still going to school, a good student; Rose had reason to assume he would do as well as her other children and like them redeem the hope that had brought her and Barnet to the New World. She may or may not have known that Louis, or Lepke (as we shall refer to him from now on), was already a very tough and mischievous kid, that he was, to put it candidly, a delinquent—an audacious and ruthless one, according to the sparse accounts we have—who spent most of his time across the river on the Lower East Side where he committed petty thefts and extortions and other random acts of violence.

She may or may not have known—she must have had some intimation—of Lepke's delinquencies; but even if she did know of them she still would have been justified to assume that they were at most ephemeral incidents, that he would emerge morally intact. Youth gangs, and what we today would regard as delinquent behavior, were conventional aspects of Lower East Side life then, one more discomfort for harried parents to suffer through. And we might imagine that Rose Buchalter's older boys, who mercifully did turn out well, had also sown their wild oats in familiar style and given her more than occasional tremors of anxiety. As a mother of healthy, bumptious boys no one was better aware than she of the snares and traps of the urban wilderness. The underworld culture was the omnipresent danger—and attraction. But the older children had passed through it and were, in retrospect, none the worse for the experience. Her beloved Lepke would assuredly pass through it too, though she would not be on hand to witness the triumph of his maturity.

But Lepke broke family precedent; he disappointed his mother's faith in him. We cannot even speculate on why he alone among the Buchalters went "wrong," why he alone chose the criminal life. Practically nothing is known about his infancy and youth, his relations with his parents and siblings, and nothing at all about what drove him to become what he was, to rebel against—and simultaneously embrace—authority the way he did. The dry facts tell us that in his teens he began to consort with the local stars of gangsterdom, themselves graduates of previous generations of youth gangs, the likes of Jack Zelig's boys, Dopey Benny's, Yoski Nigger's, and others, that he liked to hang around with them in their favorite clubs and cafes and casinos (so numerous, so abundantly documented by Abe Shoenfeld and his squad of investigators), that he took on occasional tasks at their behest, increasingly won their confidence, and gained grudging admission into their inner circles—that, in short, he had become a journeyman member of the elect.

Now Lepke's life choices depended on a certain interpretation of the world, one he never ceased to affirm. He saw the world through the gangster's eye, an eye educated by long, arduous training, through the assumption of a whole value system according to which mankind consists of two distinct species, wolves and lambs, predators and victims, winners and losers, deceivers and deceived—the elect and the rabble. It is the elected few, of course, who grasp the truth of this irreparable division, who possess the courage and energy to act on it. And what distinguishes gangsters, so-called, from the rest of the elect—capitalists, politicians, law-enforcers, and all the others who are successful in their putatively legitimate vocations—is that they, the gangsters, are open, aboveboard, and transparently honest with themselves, i.e., free of illusion, self-deception, and hypocrisy. So, by their own perverted logic, they, the gangsters, define themselves as the most virtuous of the elect. Lepke assumed that logic as a matter of course—he need not have articulated it, though he probably did—in becoming one of them, in ascending to their exalted ranks.

It was a while before the world acknowledged him in turn, bestowing on him its seal of confirmation. Officially, Louis Buchalter's criminal career began in 1915, the year of his first arrest and conviction on a felony charge (for stealing luggage in Bridgeport, Connecticut, where he had gone to work for an uncle). From then on he was true to his calling. One arrest followed another, and he shuttled back and forth between the various punitive, retributive, and rehabilitative agencies—station houses and courts and prisons and parole boards—and the Lower East Side streets, the *fons et origo* of his creative energies. By the time he completed his longest stretch, two years for burglarizing a downtown New York loft, he was a seasoned gangster. He was twenty-five years old.

Yet nothing was impossible. In fact, though he was getting on in years, and precisely because he was getting on, Lepke might still have vindicated his mother Rose's faith in him. He still might have gone straight. He had seen most of the heroes or role models of his youth drop out by the time they had reached his age and join the great trek to happier environs. He had seen the underworld culture decline, most of the prostitutes, pimps, gamblers, and hustlers having dropped out too. And his own career was hardly a smashing success. How long would he, tough and resourceful as he was, remain a scavenging crook, inveterate jailbird, the target of every cop on the beat? The likelihood is that he too would have followed the pattern drawn by past generations of criminals and chosen the straight and narrow, settling down in security with spouse and family. But as we have observed, that historic pattern had been broken. Prohibition had come along, the *deus ex machina* that had changed everything. We observed the effects of the change: how the Waxey Gordons of America had been raised from obscurity to wealth and power, how that generation of Jewish (and Italian) gangsters had been granted a startling new lease on life. Prohibition recommitted them to criminality by the amplitude of its rewards, the promise it held out of high status and recognition. Our emphasis earlier was on the economics of Prohibition—on the fact that America had gratuitously turned over to them, the Waxey Gordons, control of a huge industry supplying the wants of millions of otherwise conscientious citizens. But there was much more to Prohibition than economic gain. Broadly speaking, Prohibition broke down the distinction, always fragile in a wide-open capitalist society, between the legitimate and the illegitimate, the proper and the improper, the permissible and the impermissible.

The climate of amorality enveloping the country encouraged, or rather sanctioned, criminality, and not only the main form of it, bootlegging. There was a recrudescence of old-fashioned street gangsterism, a return to antique practices such as extortion, racketeering, gambling, drug purveying—these alongside of and inseparable from the extraordinary possibilities suddenly opened up by the manufacture, sale, and transportation of alcoholic beverages. And that enveloping climate of amorality gave rise to violence such as the country had never before experienced, as though gangsters had lost whatever limits and self-restraints they had once possessed. Even at their worst, the Monk Eastmans, Kid Twists, Jack Zeligs, and Dopey Bennys were triflers and amateurs compared to the killers who now stalked each other on the streets of the old neighborhoods. This, then, was the world Lepke entered in 1922 after serving his last and lengthiest term ("fully reformed," said his parole board).

Undoubtedly the first thing Lepke did on coming back to the Lower East Side was rejoin his comrade-in-arms Jacob Shapiro. We have no exact idea of when and how these two men struck up their incredible friendship, as intimate as any in the annals of gangsterism—so intimate that people who dealt with them in later years would usually mention their names or initials together, as one would a well-known company, Sears, Roebuck or A & P for example, often as not accompanied by a shudder of fear. Shapiro, born in Odessa and brought here as an adolescent, was two years older than Lepke and had traveled the route from Lower East Side youth gang to small-time professional hood, interspersed by varying terms in state prisons. Along the way he picked up his famous nickname "Gurrah," derived apparently from one of his favorite expressions, "get outta here," which he would ejaculate in a guttural Yiddish accent. The two made a striking pair, the contrast between them heightening their effect. Lepke was a short, dark-skinned man of average build, soft-spoken, reflective, a brooding presence who kept his own counsel. Gurrah was large and gross, a notable schlammer or bolagula in the Waxey Gordon mold who would explode into violence at the merest provocation. Lepke clearly dominated the partnership, but it would be fair to say that each without the other would not have become what he was.

When Lepke and Gurrah were reunited in 1922–23, two gangs were fighting for primacy over the Jewish Lower East Side, one led by Kid Dropper, the other by Little Augie. In his interesting memoir *Behind the Green Lights*, the police captain of the district, Cornelius Willemse, attributes at least twenty-three murders to their feud, the "bloodiest," he claims, "New York has known." One would be hard put to say who among these bandits was the most vicious. Kid Dropper, born Nathan Kaplan (one of seven brothers), was indisputably a brave and talented performer: in 1911, at the age of sixteen, he fought a highly publicized duel with and nearly killed the legendary "Johnny Spanish." After spending eight years in Sing Sing for robbery Dropper formed a mob that was the equal of any in New York. He swaggered through the old neighborhood like a reigning popinjay. Herbert Asbury writes how he "appeared along Broadway and throughout the East Side in a belted check suit of extreme cut, narrow, pointed shoes, and shirts and neckties of weird designs and color combinations, while his pudgy face, pasty-grey from long imprisonment, was surmounted by a stylish derby pulled rakishly over one eye." Different in appearance was Little Augie, or Jacob Orgen, like the others the sole black sheep in a respectable immigrant family. He was "a good looking young man, except for a scar across his cheek, a souvenir from his early teens as a master knife-wielder and gunman"—he had been one of Dopey Benny's bodyguards or "gun-toters"—who had single-handedly "shot his way to the top." Between Augie's mob and Dropper's no accommodation was possible; the enmity was too deep. As the number of bodies attest, they neither gave nor asked for any quarter.

Lepke and Gurrah threw in their lot with Little Augie, quickly rising in the gang hierarchy as Augie assigned them the job—entrusted only to the best operatives—of assassinating the Dropper in his own lair. This they almost accomplished. One day in August 1923 they drew a bead on the Dropper outside his Lower East Side headquarters. He managed to escape injury in the exchange of fire (even though two people, one a bystander, were killed), while Gurrah was hit badly enough to spend several weeks in a hospital. It was soon after this shootout that the Dropper was brought down, though not by Lepke and Gurrah. How that feat was pulled off is worth recounting.

The police of course had been following the rivalry with some interest and, using the familiar tactic of harassment, had tried repeatedly to "get" Dropper and Augie and their men; or, at the least, drive them out of the city. The police would regularly pick them up and throw them in jail, charging them with loitering or concealing weapons or resisting arrest; the charges would rarely stick. On one occasion—it was right after Gurrah's abortive assassination attempt—the police rounded up Dropper and fourteen of his men for violating the Sullivan Law and sent them to the Tombs. This time the tactic worked. Kid Dropper announced that he had had enough: he was ready to call it quits.

According to Captain Willemse, Dropper agreed to the following arrangement: he would proceed from the Essex Market Courthouse (the same one that had governed the neighborhood since the era of Max Hochstim and Silver Dollar Smith) to Pennsylvania Station where, in the company of his brother, he would board a train for the West, never to return; he would start a new life, presumably a straight one (not that the police cared), as Nathan Kaplan, Esquire. And so on August 28, the appointed day, Dropper emerged from the Courthouse, guarded by an army of policemen and detectives. Their task was to keep the throng of onlookers at a safe distance. Under the plan the police, led by Willemse himself, would escort Dropper to a waiting taxi and take him to Penn Station and see him off. Flanked by Willemse and a detective, the Dropper slid into the car. Just then a young, nondescript boyish-looking man appeared from nowhere and fired the pistol he had hidden in his rolled-up newspaper into the rear seat, killing Dropper and missing Willemse by a hair's breadth. The arrangement, as it happened, worked excellently to the killer's advantage: Dropper had been left with no defense but the one the police furnished. Penetrating that defense evidently proved no great obstacle.

To make matters worse, Willemse tells us unashamedly how he took personal revenge on the dying man who had given the authorities so much trouble, whispering in his ear: "Well, you ——, you had it coming to you. What do you think of it? You gave it to a lot of other guys yourself. How do you like it yourself?" "These," Willemse assures us, "were the last words the Dropper ever heard. He went into a coma and died soon afterwards." Proof again that gangsters and police are often opposite sides of the same coin, practitioners of a common ethic, united by bonds of sadism and cruelty.

The murder of Kid Dropper raises questions. The killer, Louis Cohen, alias Louis Kushner, claimed at first that he did the deed for personal revenge, because Dropper had been extorting large sums from his laundry store. This was a fabrication; Cohen owned no laundry store. Captain Willemse presents a more plausible motive. Cohen, he says, was a naïve, easily gulled youngster (though he was in his twenties and had already served time) who badly wanted to prove to Little Augie and the gang that he could be one of them, that he would do anything they asked. This may have been so, but his cool professional behavior at the scene of the execution and later in court hardly suggests the kind of simpleton who would willingly give his life for the gang. His mission, in fact, was not quite so hazardous as one might have thought. We learn that Cohen's lawyer was none other than James "Dandy Jim" Walker, Tammany's darling and soon to be mayor of New York, and that, predictably enough, the district attorney, himself a Tammany hack, reduced the charge to manslaughter, enabling Cohen to escape with a light sentence. We should further note that years later, when he returned to the Lower East Side, Cohen immediately resumed his place as a soldier in the same gang, causing us to doubt if the person Captain Willemse and Jimmy Walker and the newspapers described ever existed.

With Kid Dropper's passing, Little Augie was finally able to embark on the great mission of his life: to become the underworld proconsul over the field of "labor relations," Dopey Benny's sole successor.

Earlier we said that the labor violence characteristic of the Lower East Side in the old days had subsided and by the end of World War I seemed, along with so much else, the prostitution, gambling, and so forth, to be a thing of the past. The deadly conflicts between garment unions and manufacturers which had persisted generation after generation, which had given rise to the likes of Joe the Greaser, Pinchy Paul, and Dopey Benny, seemed to be resolved. Continued prosperity made it easier for manufacturers to recognize the unions as the workers' bargaining agents and grant them comparatively generous concessions, such concessions being a fair price for the stability the unions provided. But by 1921 ominous changes could be discerned. The long prosperity had run its course. The recession of that year brought special hardships to the garment industry. As profits fell, more and more manufacturers, beginning with marginal ones, lengthened the work week (which in good times had been reduced to forty-four hours), increased production schedules, restored the contracting-out system. They were declaring war on the unions; the progress made since the massive uprising of 1909–13 was coming apart.

As the conflict deepened the gangsters were brought in again. Who was initially responsible for bringing them in is an academic question, and in any case too complicated to answer satisfactorily. There were, after all, four major components of the garment industry—women's clothing, men's clothing, furs, and hats—hence four unions, each with problems of its own. And to complicate matters further each of the unions was riven into two sharply hostile factions, one led by the Socialists, the other by the Communists (or left-wingers). Now a reasonably cool, disinterested understanding of what happened is difficult to come by because the accounts are so inflamed, so shamelessly apologetic on one side or the other: the Socialists claim that the Communists used gangsters while denying that they themselves employed any; the Communists claim the Socialists employed them while denying that they used any; and both accuse the manufacturers of using them. As for the manufacturers, they have left us no official account, but if they had we can assume it would deny their guilt and cast the entire blame on both union factions. What are we to make of these fierce recriminations that have echoed through the decades down to the present (for some of the participants still live)? The safest bet is that they all used gangsters and that once the gangsters were introduced—and does it matter who was the first to do so?—the others had to follow. So it had been in the old Lower East Side days and so it was now. It is an equally safe assumption that the gangsters hired themselves out to every faction, working now for one, now another, depending on who paid the most. In this respect, too, little had changed since Dopey Benny held sway.

The situation was made to order for Little Augie and his men. They happily found themselves in a seller's market; their services—as goons or schlammers or bolagulas, as experts in the arts of blackjacking, acid and bomb throwing, bone-breaking and the like—commanded a higher and higher price, higher than bootlegging (taking everything into account, the risk of death or bodily injury along with the possible rewards), to judge from the increasing number of gangsters attracted to the field of "labor relations." The field was so lucrative that even the big men were drawn to it before long—big enough, that is, to take on Little Augie and compete with him for hegemony. No less a hero than the fabled Legs Diamond (John T. Nolan), a vicious, intrepid gunsel if ever there was one, offered his services to anyone in the garment industry who would buy them.

Conditions were set for a fresh round of gang warfare, this time with New York's garment manufacturing district, one of the most densely packed areas on earth, as its battlefield.

By the fall of 1926 such a war was on the verge of breaking out. For that was when the festering three-way conflict, at once economic and ideological, came to a head, most notably in women's clothing.

For years the General Executive Board of the International Ladies Garment Workers Union (ILGWU) had been attempting to purge local Communist or left-wing leaders (this in clear violation of due process, these leaders having been voted in legally). The purge, however, was least successful where it was most desirable from the International's point of view, namely in New York City, where by far the single largest body of workers was concentrated, where the Communists effectively controlled the union's decision-making body, the Joint Board. Resisting the purge, the New York Joint Board created its own semi-autonomous organization, collecting dues, handing out cards, bargaining with employers, without, however, formally breaking with the International. Meanwhile the cloak and suit manufacturers, the biggest group in the industry, were exploiting the factional conflict and presenting a hard line to the union. So hard, all the workers, Socialist and Communist alike, threatened to go on strike.

Governor Alfred E. Smith then intervened, appointing a commission to recommend the basis of a fair settlement. The strike was put off. In June 1926 the Commission handed down its recommendations (the details of which cannot concern us here). The manufacturers reluctantly accepted them, the marginal ones holding out longest. And so, after acrimonious debate, did the International. The Communist-led New York Joint Board rejected them as retrograde and humiliating. It then took the next fateful step and called a strike. For half a year some 50,000 men and women stayed away from their shops; the strike committee spent three and a half million dollars, a staggering amount in those days. But the union, or rather the Joint Board, finally had to throw in the towel, settling for less than the Commission's original recommendations. The Communists accused the Socialists of sabotaging the strike; the Socialists accused the Communists of incompetence and misleadership. Both were probably correct. In any case, the Communists lost the argument because they lost the strike and therefore most of the rank-and-file support. Depleted and reduced, the union now rested safely in Socialist hands. The strike had accomplished what the purge could not.

It was during the strike that the gang war in question nearly erupted. Representing the manufacturers were Legs Diamond's banditti; their assignment was to protect the manufacturers and the scabs and terrorize the pickets and union cadre. Representing the Joint Board were Little Augie's banditti; their assignment, to protect the pickets and union cadre and terrorize the manufacturers and scabs. If the Socialists had their underworld representatives, as seems likely, they were hardly to be seen; it was not exactly their affair. That there would have been bloodshed on Seventh Avenue—or more bloodshed than actually took place—is fairly certain if the strike had not been called off when it was. And it was called off only because the two gathering armies had agreed to do so. In short, the greatest struggle in the clothing industry's history depended ultimately on the acquiescence of two infamous gangsters. How that agreement or acquiescence came about is itself an astounding tale.

It is no secret. Many books have revealed the gangsters' role in the great strike. None, however, disclose as much as the most recent book dealing with it, David Dubinsky's autobiography, in which he recalls a triumphant life, rising from the Czarist prisons of his youth to head of the International Ladies Garment Workers Union, becoming for decades a confidant of Presidents, a revered labor statesman. Dubinsky, witness and prime mover of the 1926 events, enables us to fill in some of the gaps. Some, not all.

When the Communists who ran the New York Joint Board decided to sue for peace, Dubinsky writes, they appealed to someone on the manufacturers' side whom they trusted, whom everyone trusted. He was Abraham Rothstein, a retired cloth merchant, universally respected for his piety and even-handedness. (Governor Al Smith knighted him "Abe the Just.") But Rothstein said he could do nothing; the combatants were too far apart. On his suggestion the Communists approached another manufacturer who shrewdly advised them to try another Rothstein, Abraham's cursed son Arnold, the very Arnold Rothstein encountered repeatedly in these pages, America's premier sportsman-gambler and, underneath the cleverly done-up visage, all-around criminal.

They tried Arnold Rothstein. He was receptive; he promised he would do his best. Here we can pick up Dubinsky's narrative. "Rothstein's first assignment was to persuade the Legs Diamond gang to stop working for the employers in helping to smash picket lines and intimidate the union members. A telephone call took care of that. With the industry's goons gone, the Joint Board decided it would stop paying Little Augie's mob. But Little Augie had other ideas, until he too got a phone call from Rothstein. That took all the mobsters out of the picture. At that point Rothstein demonstrated that he had a lot of muscle not only with the hoodlums but with the employer associations as well. He got the bosses and the Joint Board together, and in a short time the essence of a settlement had been worked out."

And that, according to Dubinsky, was the end of it. The gangsters—Rothstein, Legs Diamond, Little Augie—depart from his pages now that the strike is over, now that the Communists have lost and his Socialist faction has won. We must infer from the veil of silence that closes over the issue that these particular gangsters ceased to exert further influence in the union or the industry. And yet Dubinsky compels us to wonder about the details he has omitted, the questions he avoids addressing. Why, for example, did Rothstein respond to the Communists' appeal? Some would have us believe that for once he acted charitably because he had always sought his father's approval. We can dismiss this as a piece of nonsense. Even Dubinsky does: "More probably this astute manipulator saw a chance to muscle in on the garment industry." Also, how did Rothstein manage to end the strikes? What was the quid pro quo behind those telephone calls? We know for one thing that Little Augie's gang continued its association with the industry, with unions and manufacturers both, long after the strike. We know for another that Legs Diamond joined forces with Augie, indeed becoming his close confederate and companion. The best guess, then, is that Arnold Rothstein arranged *two* settlements simultaneously, one between the Joint Board and the bosses, and the other—on which the first rested—between the rival gangs, under which terms they all shared the spoils, that is, retained their footholds, their steady source of income, in the ladies' garment industry. To imagine Legs and Augie obeying Rothstein's phone calls simply because he was Rothstein is ludicrous. Rothstein was the mediator of the *gangsters'* interests, not the unions' or the manufacturers'.

The ILGWU suit and cloak strike, the most dramatic strike in that tempestuous era, pointedly illustrates how Little Augie and his compeers entered the garment trades. Once invited in by employers and unions in times of conflict, when the hammer was on the anvil, the gangsters could not be invited out after the settlement, especially when they had proved indispensable in bringing about that settlement. So it was in men's clothing too. So it was in furs. So it was in hats.

Now the extent of gangster penetration varied from one of these industries to another, from one union (or faction of a union) and set of manufacturers to another, as we will soon learn in intricately sordid detail. And we should add that what occurred in the garment trades as a whole occurred elsewhere as well, and usually in the same way. No industry was immune. Or, rather, every industry which employed gangsters to resolve its labor disputes—always on the mistaken assumption that they could be dispensed with when no longer needed—was vulnerable to their assault.

From all appearances Little Augie was by 1927 one of New York's outstanding mob leaders. He had eliminated or co-opted his chief rivals. The steady lucrative income from his "labor relations" business he was investing in uptown nightclubs and cabarets, enabling him to make his mark also as a man-about-town, as one of the intriguing underworld figures who graced the Broadway landscape.

But appearances dissemble. Little Augie was not quite so powerful as he seemed to be, his very success revealing his limitations as a leader. No gang, not even Al Capone's, was a tightly structured organization on the order, say, of a well-disciplined army, or corporation, or church, with their hierarchies of super- and subordinate ranks. The gang or gang/syndicate (this we tried to emphasize in the previous chapter) was typically an ensemble of partnerships and alliances, each claiming its own territory, its own source of illicit revenues, all formed around the leader; he served as the juncture, the terminus, the meeting place of their common interests. What drew them together was the presence of an enemy, a common threat to life and property. And so, it follows, the gang cohered most solidly, the leader was most secure, when the rank and file felt most threatened.

The converse also follows: the leader's problems became acute when the external threat ceased or diminished. He then ran the risk of insurgent groups rising up, of internal conflict. His survival depended on the amount of violence he could bring to bear, his ability to substitute his threat for the external one. That explains why leaders surrounded themselves only with lieutenants they could trust (family relations, close chums) and with janissaries, professional killers brought in from the outside. It is hardly an accident that these are the devices which political despots have always used to protect themselves from domestic, even household, enemies. Gangs were small despotisms and gang leaders were despots whose legitimacy rested on might, who commanded obedience primarily through terror and fear and the accompanying mystique of invincibility.

Little Augie's despotism was being challenged by insurgents— by Lepke and Gurrah—who had been relentlessly consolidating their positions in the gang, expanding their network of alliances, even as they faithfully carried out their assignments for him, expecially during the 1926 strike. And further, Augie had brought in Legs Diamond in order to add that necessary component of terror, in order to extinguish such acts of disobedience or insurgency as Lepke and Gurrah and their friends were contemplating.

It should not surprise us that Lepke and Gurrah struck out on their own the instant Little Augie and Legs Diamond coalesced. To go from open breach to open warfare required only a single step, a single provocative act, however trivial in itself. And what could be more trivial than a strike by a Brooklyn painters' local?

Years earlier a petty gangster, Jacob "Jake the Bum" Wellner, took over Local 102 of the International Brotherhood of Painters, Decorators and Paperhangers, his immediate predecessor having been beaten senseless and forced to quit. Wellner prospered by this usurpation. The local's area of jurisdiction, Brooklyn's Flatbush section, was filling up with Jews and other ghetto émigrés seeking decent space and shelter; the boom was on and Wellner was able to extort princely sums from builders and contractors. Nor did his success go unnoticed. One of Lepke's cohorts, a monstrously cruel roughneck named Hyman "Little Hymie" or "Curly" Holtz—garment circles knew him all too well—muscled in on the racket, becoming Jake the Bum's superior, in effect absorbing him. Meanwhile a group of contractors balked at paying the agreed-upon union wage, a portion of which was kicked back to the racketeers Wellner-Holtz-Lepke. So the union struck.

Now these contractors obviously were as defiant as they were because they had hired their own formidable gangsters—who else but Little Augie and Legs Diamond and their combined mob? And for a price worthy of their talents: $30,000 down and $20,000 more when the job was done, i.e., when the gangster-led union was defeated. In the summer and fall of 1927, pitched battles broke out on Brooklyn streets and in unfinished buildings between Lepke's men and Little Augie's, between those attacking the contractors and nonunion workers and those defending them.

The real fight of course was between the leaders, not the troops in the field. And here, at that level, Lepke's gang demonstrated how much better organized and how much more audacious it was, resembling in this respect Little Augie's outfit back when it was doing battle with Kid Dropper's. And like Kid Dropper, Augie and Legs adopted a defensive strategy, retreating to their well-guarded Lower East Side citadel (Delancey and Norfolk streets to be exact). It was there, in that citadel on the evening of October 15, 1927, that Lepke and Gurrah and Little Hymie found them and struck them down in a barrage of gunfire. Little Augie died at once. Legs Diamond recovered after a long hospital siege. And it must be said for once he learned his lesson: never again would he try his hand at "labor relations."

(The strike, incidentally, came to an abrupt end when the contractors, out $30,000, sued for peace and settled on Jake the Bum's original terms.)

Little Augie's funeral, to complete the saga, was itself an event; certainly the press treated it as such. His parents and brothers and sisters all attended, prompting the newspapers to draw the predictable contrast between these model Jewish immigrants and the errant son lying in his closed casket, symbol of his inglorious life. The papers also delighted in reporting who among Augie's Lower East Side associates had come to pay their last respects: "Moocher" Ravine and his Chrystie Street boys, "Little Sammy" and his Goerck Street gang, "Cocaine Manny" and "Red" Miller and others, all of whose names, so fearful to the public at the time, have sunk into oblivion and mean nothing to us today.

As for Lepke and Gurrah and Little Hymie, they were out of sight, hiding from the police. When they were satisfied that no solid evidence would be forthcoming, that no witnesses to the deed would testify against them, Lepke and Gurrah humbly turned themselves in. (Little Hymie, less confident, was later apprehended but quickly let go.) The judge who signed their release warned them: "When you get out of here you'd better look out." And the deputy inspector added: "If they're wise, they'll keep away from the Lower East Side." Lepke and Gurrah must have smiled, for the Lower East Side was precisely where they were headed.

ü Lepke was to "labor relations" what the bootlegging syndicate leaders were to the Mustache Petes. Compared to Lepke, Little Augie (and of course Kid Dropper) was nothing more than the old-fashioned neighborhood gangster incarnate. Lepke avoided all flamboyance and displays of bravado. He was reserved in speech, manner, and dress, and while he occasionally gambled, drank, and womanized he was rarely seen in the popular haunts. He lived with his wife and stepson in a nicely furnished Central Park West apartment. He kept a "low profile," in short—so low the authorities, along with the press and the celebrity-mongers at large, hardly recognized him; or if they did, regarded him and his sidekick Gurrah (who lived quietly with his family in the Flatbush section of Brooklyn) to be mere Lower East Side gunsels on the make, between gangs as it were.

Methodical is the term that best characterizes Lepke's modus operandi, that best measures the distance separating him from the past. He was methodical in everything he did. He was methodical in establishing a gang of top-flight Jewish criminals, the most brutal

The Reverend Doctor Charles W. Parkhurst in 1895, a year after the defeat of Tammany Hall. COURTESY OF THE NEW-YORK HISTORICAL SOCIETY, NEW YORK CITY.

Monk Eastman, a model of respectability here as he posed for photographs during his 1904 trial for attempted robbery and felonious assault. NEW YORK POLICE DEPARTMENT.

Kid Twist dressed in the fashionable attire of the day as he appeared in a police lineup. NEW YORK POLICE DEPARTMENT.

A portrait of Big Jack Zelig looking his dapper best. UNITED PRESS INTERNATIONAL PHOTO.

Lefty Louie (left) and Gyp the Blood, two of Big Jack Zelig's comrades, during their 1912 trial for the murder of Herman Rosenthal. NEW YORK POLICE DEPARTMENT.

A police mug shot of Dopey Benny. Note the droopy right eye, the source of his nickname. NEW YORK POLICE DEPARTMENT.

The Lower East Side powerhouse Kid Dropper in a photograph taken during one of the numerous police pickups. NEW YORK POLICE DEPARTMENT.

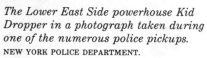

Little Augie shortly after his gang disposed of his blood enemy Kid Dropper. NEW YORK POLICE DEPARTMENT.

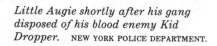

Arnold Rothstein photographed on familiar turf: the race track. N.Y. DAILY NEWS PHOTO.

Waxey Gordon (right), accompanied by a U.S. marshall, appearing in federal court in early 1933. UNITED PRESS INTERNATIONAL PHOTO.

Early in 1933 New York detectives learned that a bevy of gangsters was holding a conference at the Hotel Franconia on Broadway and Seventy-second Street. The raid came up with this group of notables. From left to right: Joseph "Doc" Stacher, Bugsy Siegel, Harry Teitelbaum, Lepke Buchalter (unaccountably wearing an eye patch), Big Greenie Greenberg, Louis "Shadows" Kravitz, Gurrah Shapiro, Philip "Little Farfel" Kavolick, and Little Hymie Holtz.   LOS ANGELES HERALD EXAMINER.

Thomas E. Dewey, in a rare show of informality, shortly after he was appointed special prosecutor in 1935.   N.Y. DAILY NEWS PHOTO.

Looking doleful, Dutch Schultz sits in a room of the New York County Courthouse one day in August 1935. BETTMANN ARCHIVE, INC.

Dutch Schultz on his deathbed in a Newark hospital. It was here, in moments of semiconsciousness, that he mumbled his famous soliloquy. N.Y. DAILY NEWS PHOTO.

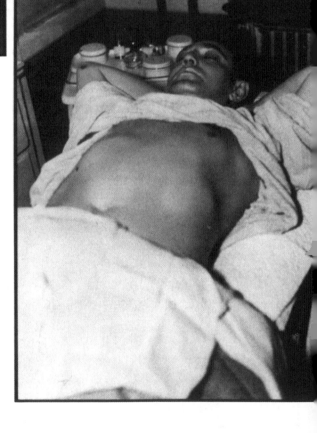

Gurrah Shapiro as he looked when he turned himself in on April 14, 1938. He would spend the rest of his life in jail. N.Y. DAILY NEWS PHOTO.

DETECTIVE DIVISION
CIRCULAR NO. 11
AUGUST 8, 1939

POLICE DEPARTMENT
CITY OF NEW YORK

CLASSIFICATION

$25,000 REWARD

DEAD OR ALIVE

TWENTY-FIVE THOUSAND DOLLARS will be paid by the City of New York for information leading to the capture of "LEPKE" BUCHALTER, aliases LOUIS BUCHALTER, LOUIS BUCKHOUSE, LOUIS KAWAR, LOUIS KAUVAR, LOUIS COHEN, LOUIS SAFFER, LOUIS BRODSKY.

WANTED FOR CONSPIRACY AND EXTORTION

The Person or Persons who give Information Leading to the Arrest of "LEPKE" will be fully protected, his or her identity will never be revealed. The Information will be received in absolute confidence.

RIGHT HAND

LEFT HAND

DESCRIPTION — Age, 42 years; white; Jewish; height, 5 feet, 5½ inches; weight, 170 pounds; build, medium; black hair; brown eyes; complexion dark; married, one son Harold, age about 18 years.

PECULARITIES—Eyes, piercing and shifting; nose, large, somewhat blunt at nostrils; ears, prominent and close to head; mouth, large, slight dimple left side; right-handed; suffering from kidney ailment.

Frequents baseball games.

Is wealthy; has connections with all important mobs in the United States. Involved in racketeering in Unions and Fur Industry, uses Strong-arm methods. Influential.

This Department holds indictment warrant charging Conspiracy and Extortion, issued by the Supreme Court, Extraordinary Special and Trial Terms, New York County.

Kindly search your Prison Records as this man may be serving a Prison sentence for some minor offense.

If located, arrest and hold as a fugitive and advise the THE DETECTIVE DIVISION, POLICE DEPARTMENT, NEW

The last of the wanted circulars on Lepke distributed to the nation by the New York Police on August 8, 1939. Two weeks and two days later he surrendered to J. Edgar Hoover. N.Y. DAILY NEWS PHOTO.

Abe "Kid Twist" Reles enjoying a light moment—
he prided himself on his wit and badinage—while
in protective custody as the State's chief witness
against his former Murder Inc. comrades.   UNITED
PRESS INTERNATIONAL PHOTO.

Brooklyn District Attorney—later Mayor—O'Dwyer (left) and his
assistant Burton Turkus during their prosecution of Murder Inc. in
1940.   N.Y. DAILY NEWS PHOTO.

A grim-faced Moses Annenberg in 1939 a few minutes after he pleaded guilty to the charge of feloniously evading federal income taxes. He had by then given up his racing wire business. WIDE WORLD PHOTOS.

ugsy Siegel (left) and his pal eorge Raft, both looking as content nd prosperous as they in fact were ı the summer of 1944. WIDE WORLD ʜOTOS.

ugsy Siegel as the world saw him ▶ *ɔon after his execution on June 20, 947* WIDE WORLD PHOTOS.

New Jersey's gang/syndicate boss, Longy Zwillman, at the height of his prestige and power, testifying before the Kefauver Committee in March 1951. WIDE WORLD PHOTOS.

Moe Dalitz, last of the Cleveland Four, as he looked in 1966, while still proprietor of the Desert Inn. Before long he would be declared persona non grata in Las Vegas. WIDE WORLD PHOTOS.

The Chicago police picked up this group of suspicious characters outside a hotel in April 1932 and took this picture before releasing them. Meyer Lansky (4) stands to the left of Lucky Luciano (3). The others are Capone mob chieftains Paul "the Waiter" Ricca (1) and Rocco Fischetti (5) and two lesser known gangsters, Sylvester Agoglia (2) and Harry Brown (6). CHICAGO POLICE DEPARTMENT.

Meyer Lansky in 1950, when he presided over the Florida Gold Coast on behalf of the gang/syndicate community. N.Y. DAILY NEWS PHOTO.

Meyer Lansky in a Jerusalem court in June 1971, during his struggle to remain in Israel. The man on his right is the official interpreter. WIDE WORLD PHOTOS.

and talented of their breed. He built an apparatus of violence which was loyal to him alone, which he was able to mobilize and dispatch at will, by means of which he subdued even the most implacable foes. He deployed his forces methodically, seeking out, probing, testing his foes' or his victims' weaknesses, and when he found them he moved in decisively, with minimum violence (eventually his name was worth battalions)—with just enough violence at any rate to secure the well-mapped objective.

These military similes may convey the wrong idea. Lepke attained his phenomenal success without heroics, by a grimly unspectacular process. The blood and melodrama emerged later, when his universe was collapsing and he had become the most widely hunted villain on earth. The history of his rise is and will forever remain incomplete, though we have enough documentary proof—above all we have the end results, the startling achievements—to outline it industry by industry, racket by racket.

We begin with furs, about which a good deal is known, thanks to the FBI and the trial records.

During the fur industry's time of troubles, which lasted through the 1920s, the manufacturers and the warring union factions, Communist and other, all freely employed gangsters. By the early 1930s the Communist faction, masterfully led by Ben Gold, had become the dominant one, and so no longer needed Lepke's help or any other gangster's. The union was cleaner than it had ever been; it was indeed a model of cleanliness. But by then Lepke's interests shifted; he had reached another plateau of his ambitions: he now was involved with the manufacturers, specifically the producers of dyed and dressed furs, those who specialized in making furs seem what they were not, changing the colors and textures of the skins so that a cheap garment, rabbit above all, was scarcely distinguishable from an expensive one. This technique of treating skins had revolutionized the industry around World War I, giving rise overnight to an immense new market and countless new producers, almost all situated in New York's fur district on or near Seventh Avenue between Twenty-sixth and Thirtieth streets, most of them small and of course sharply competitive. It was the dynamics of the marketplace that brought Lepke into the picture.

During the prosperous 1920s the competition could be tolerated; if the industry kept expanding the savagery could be confined to the margins, the very tiniest producers. The onset of the Depression changed that. The demand for fur coats collapsed, and the larger manufacturers began going under too. Self-defense required that the leaders of the industry join together to control the market, to bring order and stability in place of unbridled competition. They accordingly organized themselves into two groups, the Protective Fur Dressers' Association, comprising the largest rabbit-skin dressers, and the Fur Dressers' Factor Corporation, comprising the main producers of non-rabbit skins. How could these protective associations police themselves and so maintain the integrity of the cartel? The question answers itself. One of their organizers asked Lepke and Gurrah if they could administer the "rough stuff." He could hardly have been surprised by their response. But the price was high: a penny or two for each skin, plus a straight fee from each member. And the price rose as Lepke consolidated his power, as he methodically gained dominion over the protectives.

For the occasional offender who failed to keep up his payments (every Friday afternoon on the barrelhead) or violated policies laid down in the industry's name there were the usual retributions: the bombed-out shop, the beatings, or if the recusant was especially uncooperative, the acid thrown in the face. The procedure was routine.* How much did Lepke and Gurrah and the mob receive for their extraordinary services? An astronomical amount, says Philip Foner, official historian of the Fur and Leather Workers' Union: almost ten million dollars a year *from rabbit skins alone.* How much of this

---

* Lepke worked closely with other gang/syndicates. We have a grisly instance of their collaboration in his struggle against one large recalcitrant rabbit-skin dresser, J. Joseph Inc. Some of J. Joseph's work was farmed out to the Waverly Fur Dressing Company of Newark, New Jersey. Newark happened to be Longy Zwillman's bailiwick. Lepke thereupon farmed out the violence to him. Zwillman several times tried to persuade Waverly's manager to join the protective. To no avail. In 1932 the shop was bombed and wrecked. Even this failed to move the courageous Mr. Joseph. A few weeks later a vial of acid was thrown in his face. He capitulated.

went to Lepke and Gurrah personally—for they had quite a payroll to disburse—would be impossible to estimate.

That the Fur and Leather Workers' Union would have preferred a cartel without gangsters goes without saying. But a cartel with gangsters, even one run by gangsters, was better than no cartel at all. For workers no less than manufacturers profited from the "stabilization" that the protectives brought. The union played an important part in upholding the new arrangement. The protectives wanted the union to organize the smaller shops, if necessary drive them out of business. To that end the protectives gave the union thirty thousand dollars toward an "unemployment fund," in reality an organizing fund. At any rate the violence, once so endemic to the industry, declined perceptibly; or rather it became selective and rational, incorporated as it was in the order of things as administered by Lepke and his henchmen.

With the industry brought in line, the protectives could begin to take a tougher stand toward the union. Harmony and class collaboration was well and good when manufacturers and union faced a common threat in minuscule, cutthroat producers. But as the Depression deepened the protectives, backed or represented by Lepke and his indestructible legions, refused to honor commitments given in previous contracts. When contract negotiations broke down early in 1933 the violence followed in due course.* Expecting the worst, the union formed its own paramilitary cadre. The attacks grew more frequent and intense. The gangster invasion of union headquarters on April 24, 1933, was the single bloodiest encounter, one that involved

---

* Philip Foner claims that the union leaders had no idea of Lepke's role among the employers, at least not until the negotiations got under way. The union's secretary-treasurer, Irving Potash, was shocked one day (this is Foner's version) when Gurrah walked into the bargaining room with the Protective Fur Dressers' Association president, Samuel Mittleman. What was Gurrah doing there, Potash asked in horror. "Well, we'll be together," Mittleman replied matter-of-factly. The union, Potash insisted, would "have nothing to do with Shapiro. My dealing is with you." Gurrah, said Mittleman, "is the Protective." Now all of this is transparently disingenuous. Yes, Potash undoubtedly wanted Gurrah out of the room, certainly out of sight, but he obviously knew all along what everyone in the industry knew, that Gurrah (or rather Lepke) "[was] the Protective." Others contend that both Gold and Potash had dealings with "L and G" but this has not been proved.

Lepke's schlammers, the union's "red guards" (if we can call them that), and the police, both plainclothes and uniformed. In the melee a gangster and a fur worker were killed on the spot and many were wounded, including policemen. While it was going on thousands of fur workers streamed out of their Seventh Avenue buildings and joined in. But for the police they would have drawn and quartered the gangsters on the spot. When it was over only one of Lepke's schlammers, Samuel "the Dove" Turtletaub, was indicted, and that for shooting a comrade. (The Dove, incidentally, jumped bail; seven years later he was captured in Phoenix, Arizona; he was extradited, tried and convicted, and received twenty years to life.) The union had proved too tough and well organized, and Lepke settled for a truce, a restoration in effect of the status quo ante. Not that this lasted long either. And when the time was propitious, as we shall see, his adversaries, the Communist furriers, would contribute mightily to his own downfall.

The fur industry may serve as our paradigm of all the others that succumbed in greater or lesser degree to Lepke's charms. The particularities of each industry determined what tactic he brought to bear upon it.

In the case of men's clothing (about which we also have considerable data) Lepke's strength lay in his possession of New York Cutters' Local No. 4, with its thousand or so members, a small but critically important part of the union and industry. Nothing was possible without the cutters, the most highly skilled and best paid workers in the trade. Generally speaking, the takeover occurred during the years when men's clothing, like all the garment trades, was ravaged by conflict and violence, by the widespread use and counteruse of gangsters. Lepke's genius was to perceive that control of this one local would be sufficient for his purpose, his helpmates being cutters themselves, gangster-cutters so to say, who expected to line their pockets and then, having saved enough capital, go into business for themselves.

Control of the local gave Lepke a double advantage. It kicked back to him and his men a portion of the rank-and-file dues and it enabled him to manipulate employer protective associations, the Textile Finishers Association and the Coat Front Makers' Association among others, in much the same way as he was doing in furs. If anything, he had an easier time of it because there were fewer men's clothing firms; they tended to be larger, more profitable, better established. Also he and Gurrah had their own companies (e.g., Raleigh Manufacturing, The Pioneer Coat Front, Greenberg and Shapiro). How much tribute each firm paid its protective association we cannot say—one of them, Hammonton Park, a fairly large manufacturer, gave $7,500 a year—nor can we say precisely how many firms belonged to them. One of Lepke's prosecutors has argued that he "virtually 'owned'" men's clothing "in the Metropolitan area." And even if we allow for exaggeration and are properly skeptical about the meaning of "owned," the fact remains that Lepke's power in the men's clothing industry was astonishing.

To these nefarious developments the union, the Amalgamated Clothing Workers of America, gave an ambiguous response. Its leaders, from president Sidney Hillman on down, were men of high integrity. Schooled in Socialist ideals, they were willing to struggle selflessly and without end to improve the workers' lot in life and the welfare of society as a whole. The vexing problem that faced them, as it did the other unions, was how to deal with the competition of the manufacturers, how to establish order and stability in their own industry. And so the Amalgamated Clothing Workers tolerated, if it did not condone, such order and stability as Lepke was able to impose, mainly through force to be sure and with all the cancerous possibilities let loose by his presence. As in furs so in men's clothing the controlling question was whether a reasonable balance among competing interests could be struck—among Hillman, Lepke, and the manufacturers. When that balance was upset, trouble inevitably resulted.

Circumstances again upset the balance. Manufacturers desperately needed to reduce their costs, i.e., wages; and Lepke, through his man, Local 4's executive secretary Philip Orlovsky, was willing to oblige them. This put him or Orlovsky in conflict with the union's authority. The situation became so grave Sidney Hillman decided he must act at once, any further delay being fatal to his leadership. In early June 1931, before a routine gathering of shop stewards and union officials Hillman announced (catching his audience by surprise): "We might as well be frank here and say out in the open what we have been saying to each other in private. What the New York market is suffering from more than anything else is the racketeering evil." He went on to promise a fight to the death over "who is to run the union." Hillman, who knew his enemy, planned his campaign with great care. He ordered the union to go out on strike against a firm that had been consorting with Lepke. In the brief skirmish that ensued Lepke's hoods, as expected, bloodied the pickets. (Where were the police? In Lepke's pocket, to put it bluntly; the "industrial squad," which ostensibly handled labor violence, was corrupt through and through.)

Here was the outrage Hillman sought. The next day he called a monster rally and parade through the garment district. Hundreds of New York's leading citizens joined the tens of thousands of workers who participated in it. Mayor Jimmy Walker (himself a monument of corruption) publicly announced his support of Hillman. Hillman was now in the position to launch his major assault—on the gangsters' bastion, Local 4. Mobilizing all his forces he called a general strike. Battle-toughened workers picketed the pro-Lepke shops. New York's garment center reverberated with the sounds of clashing armies. And as the strike continued week after week, as the toll of broken heads and limbs mounted, one man (Guido Ferrari, a manufacturer) being killed in a shootout, Hillman moved relentlessly toward his goal; the violence served as his counterpoint and justification. He officially accused Orlovsky and the others of Local 4 of stealing $149,000 from its treasury and demanded that Orlovsky appear before the Amalgamated's General Executive Board. When Orlovsky refused, he was tried in absentia and dismissed. But how to physically remove him and his gangster cohorts from the premises? Hillman got a special police detachment (not drawn from the industrial squad) to join the union in its attack on Local 4. There was no resistance however. Orlovsky had absconded. Curiously, no charges were brought against him and the others. With Lepke's ignominious defeat the strike ended. The Amalgamated Clothing Workers could again turn its attention to the real business of its life, to the question of social justice and the well-being of its members.

Now all of the foregoing is the union's version of what transpired. It is the generally accepted account. It is the account that Matthew Josephson, a fine writer and historian, bodied forth in his influential biography on Sidney Hillman. And on its face it is correct. Local 4 *was* cleansed and redeemed. Hillman and the Amalgamated *did* go on to accomplish wondrous things for the men's clothing workers, for the union movement at large. Hillman himself, like Dubinsky, became a national statesman, among other things serving as President Franklin D. Roosevelt's political confidant during World War II. A happy conclusion, in short, to a nasty, demeaning episode.

But we also have another side of the story, one that reaches a less happy conclusion. It is the side presented by several authorities on crime, chief among them Lepke's prosecutor, who in turn drew on the confessions and testimonies of Lepke's top assistants. It goes as follows.

The Amalgamated and Lepke did fall out in 1931, the primary irritant between them being Orlovsky's crooked local. And the falling out did lead to violent conflict in the manner already described. Here the accounts diverge. According to Lepke's cohorts, the prosecutor, and Lucky Luciano's biographers, while the general strike was going on and growing more violent by the day, the Amalgamated's general organizer (Hillman's "efficient expediter"), a man named Bruno Belea, went to Luciano and appealed for help. So far as we know Belea did this on his own; at least we have no proof that he acted at the union's behest. Luciano turned him down flat, asserting that the garment industry belonged to Lepke under arrangements worked out between the gang/syndicates; it was Lepke's territory and that was that. Belea then did a rash and foolhardy thing: he involved himself, perhaps unwittingly, in the emergent conflict of New York's leading Italian gangsters, the so-called Castellammarese War: specifically, he asked Salvatore Maranzano to help the Amalgamated get rid of Lepke.

Maranzano grabbed at the chance; he needed all the money he could get to furbish and expand his army for the showdown ahead. And it was indeed the presence of Maranzano's men during the strike that caused blood to flow, that brought death to Guido Ferrari, a businessman friendly to Lepke. Here was a mortal danger to Lepke's interests, not to say to Lepke himself.

Lepke handled it with tact, finesse, and wisdom. Instead of taking on Maranzano directly he persuaded Luciano to do so. He argued that if Maranzano succeeded in destroying him, then Luciano and his friends would be next. Maranzano must be stopped in his tracks. Luciano's biographers even supply us with Lepke's conversation (though they do not bother to explain how they overheard it or where they saw a copy of it): "You think this is a clothing business fight only it ain't. Maranzano is out to take over the 'family' again. He knows you and me are pals—right! He figures hitting me is the same as hitting you." Obviously Luciano did not need much urging, and if this provocation had not been the *casus belli* it would have been another. And as we know, he and his friends saw to it that Maranzano, the aspiring boss of bosses, was slain in his office on September 10, 1931—shortly before the strike ended—by a handful of brave Jewish gunmen disguised as revenue agents.

Having disposed of Maranzano, Lepke could deal with the Amalgamated from a position of strength. Bruno Belea, who had made a dreadful mistake, saved his skin by promising Lepke his full cooperation and support, enabling Lepke to advance surreptitiously into the union's very headquarters, its executive board. Lepke also struck a bargain. In exchange for surrendering the local and throwing out Orlovsky (who received a year's severance pay!) Lepke was allowed to keep and enlarge his grip on the manufacturing side of the industry, making certain that the market was regulated and stabilized and that the members of the protective associations under his auspices came to terms with the union. Furthermore, Lepke was encouraged by the union to pursue the elusive "runaway shops," those firms that fled the city for nearby small towns where labor was cheap and compliant, that is, unorganized. And in this he proved as good as his reputation. He muscled his way into the trucking local whose rank and file serviced the runaways in New Jersey and Pennsylvania. So that truckers and manufacturers who refused to go along with him and the union suffered the usual consequences: stoppages, terror, bodily harm, or worse. In the end everything had turned out for the best. The old balance of power between Lepke, Hillman, and the bosses had been placed on a new footing, a more solid one at that because better concealed from public view.

We arrive, then, at a consensus, a resolution of the two apparently divergent or contradictory accounts. We can agree that Lepke maintained his considerable strength in the men's clothing industry and his extensive connections with the Amalgamated Clothing Workers, even with its leadership. We can also agree that there was nothing devilishly sinister in those connections (though the one between Lepke and Belea came close), nothing sinister in the fact that the manufacturers and the union both had to acknowledge the enormity of Lepke's presence and in so doing turn it to their own best advantage. Lepke, we repeat, was more a creature of the anarchic competitive system than anyone's conscious malevolence.

At least as far-reaching and profound was Lepke's success in women's clothing. And again he exploited a situation made to order for him. Again he helped introduce a modicum of stability—through the ubiquitous protective associations—where it was most needed, where conditions were most volatile, as in dresses say, where runaways were most apt to threaten the larger manufacturers and the International Ladies Garment Workers Union. For his troubles Lepke earned $2.5 million dollars from women's clothing manufacturers, according to Benjamin Levine, a highly placed member of the organization. (A typical case: to discipline the cutthroat producers, keep prices and wages uniform, et cetera, the owner of the Blue Comet Dress Company, one of the largest, paid Lepke and Gurrah a total of $44,000 over the years, this by its own admission.)

One of Lepke's levers of power was the Five Borough Truckmen's Association, a mostly Italian gangster outfit consisting of such thugs as Johnny Dio, Jimmy Doyle, and Dick Terry—John Dioguardi, James Plumeri, and Domenick Didato respectively—all Luciano's henchmen, leading one to surmise that they came into women's garments as part of the package deal which the two hierarchs, Lepke and Luciano, had made in disposing of Maranzano. The Five Borough Truckmen's Association* brought the runaways—or dragged them kicking—into the protectives, hence into the union-management nexus. No one justified this crooked arrangement, the racketeer's vocation, more eloquently than Johnny Dio himself some

---

* To be strictly accurate the Five Borough Truckmen ceased to exist in 1934 following a fight between two of its partners, Doyle and Terry (Terry was slain). But the operation continued as ever under another name, even after Johnny Dio was tried and convicted and sent away in 1937 for a brief stretch.

years later: "What did I do that J. P. Morgan didn't do? . . . It's all a racket. Isn't Wall Street a racket where the strong take advantage of the weak? Every industry needs a strong man. After you put us in jail, another strong man will come up to keep the industry from becoming a jungle."

As for the hat industry (to complete the garment circuit), it seems to have been the only one which kept Lepke at bay. Not that the manufacturers in the madly competitive hat industry were unwilling to have him just as they had a succession of small-fry gangsters on their payroll. The best informed guess is that he decided the potential rewards of involvement were simply not worth the risks it might incur, especially the risk of taking on the tough and resourceful United Hatters, Cap and Millinery Workers union, whose few thousand members, all concentrated in two blocks of lower Manhattan, could be called out en masse in an emergency, as the fur workers were, and wreak terrible revenge upon their enemies, however fierce. Still, Lepke might have tried harder and, given his ingenuity, might have even succeeded if the millinery trade as a whole was not so marginal, if its pickings were not so slim.*

With the garment industry as his base of operations, as the primary and most fecund source of his wealth and power, Lepke was able to reach out further and further, tracing a wider and wider arc of usurpation. Consider what he wrought in two other entirely disparate industries, baking and movies, each a marvelous object lesson of his ruthlessness and tactical skill.

A brief review of the history of the baking industry in New York City discloses a pattern already familiar to us. The manufacture and delivery of baked goods had been transformed over the years, so

---

* According to Donald B. Robinson, who has written the best history of the union, one of its dissident and corrupt locals did ask Lepke—for $25,000—to intervene in its behalf and make war on both the manufacturers and the union. One of the union's leaders then visited Lepke and warned him of a fight to the death if he took up the offer. Lepke rejected the offer, though it is not clear that he did so because of the warning.

that by the mid-1920s much of the bread, pastries, and pies which had once been made and sold exclusively in neighborhood bakeries was now being made in plants on the outskirts of the city and trucked to groceries or "commission bakeries." The competition at all levels intensified; price wars erupted, often accompanied by violence. Enter the gangsters.

Exactly when Lepke appeared on the scene is unclear. What is clear is that he eventually seized the industry by the throat. The procedure was self-defining: his men captured Teamster Local 138, which brought the flour to the baking companies and conveyed the bread and pastry and pies to stores throughout the city. The nominal union chief was William Snyder, and he was assisted by William "Wolfie" Goldis. Meanwhile, Lepke's men were also capturing the Flour Truckmen's Association, the wholesalers who provided the flour for the bakeries. His agent in this, the head of the Association, one Max Silverman, was a thug whose underworld genealogy went far back to prewar days. Through work stoppages, or through more forceful measures when necessary—the destruction of goods and vehicles, intimidation and beatings—the bakeries were brought in line, that is, incorporated into the protectives: Max Silverman's Flour Truckmen along with the United Pie, Cake and Pastry Bakers, run by Silverman's son Harold. Each member of course contributed an initiation fee plus weekly fees, the size of which depended on the volume of business, plus such other emoluments or bonuses along the way as Lepke might require to meet his pressing obligations.* The large concerns—e.g., the California Pie and Baking Company, Fink, Gottfried, Rockwell, Dugan's, and Levy's—paid the elder Silverman as much as $3,000 a week (apart from special favors). On one occasion Lepke demanded $25,000 from the Gottfried Baking Company. When the owner protested, Local 138 promptly called a strike. A

---

* The head of the United Flour Trucking Company, a large concern, held out for a long time despite the strikes and the sabotage. Finally, unable to get help from the authorities, he submitted and joined the Flour Truckmen's Association. Nonetheless, Lepke's men dumped one of his trucks into the river. Why, the owner of the company asked Silverman, did they do this? "You're marked lousy with the boys," Silverman said, "and we had to do something to show you that we mean business."

compromise was reached. Gottfried got away with paying Lepke $9,000 in cash and promising $5,000 later. Of this $9,000 Lepke kept $4,000 for himself; the rest went to his lieutenants who divided it among themselves according to a sliding scale.

Now what was unusual was that the transaction took place in the office of a Tammany leader, William Solomon, and for good reason; he had worked out the compromise. This commonplace episode suggests the breadth of Lepke's network, and incidentally, the proportion of his own average take. The authorities estimated that he and Gurrah received above one million dollars a year in tribute from the bakery racket. In return, the industry, the large concerns in particular, received again what they could not obtain by other means; the regulation of prices and wages. Which explains why the union rank and file, despite the kickbacks to Lepke's henchmen, raised no demonstrable fuss—not as long as they also drew benefits from the protective associations.

Once a fuss did get raised, and by, of all people, the president of Local 138, William Snyder. Why he did so has not been established. Some say that he was an ambitious mobster who resented being treated as a tool or figurehead; others that he had a change of heart and tried to be a conscientious union leader. In any case his gangster comrades concluded that he was a threat to all of them. And that was Lepke's conclusion too.

The predictable event happened on the evening of September 13, 1934. Snyder was meeting with members of the Flour Truckmen's Association in the banquet room of Gurfein's Restaurant on the Lower East Side. The Silvermans and other racketeers were present. Snyder may or may not have seen the man who approached his table; that he knew the man well went without saying, for he was Morris Goldis, the secretary-treasurer's brother and a frontline soldier in Lepke's army. Morris Goldis in any event greeted Snyder by drawing out a gun and shooting him point-blank; then he turned and unhurriedly left the restaurant. The patrons denied having seen anything, or having seen enough to identify the assassin; the place they claimed was poorly lit, the lights had gone out, they dove for cover, the confusion overwhelmed them, and so on—they hardly lacked pretexts.

Though the police knew everything, and indeed they detained Morris Goldis for a while, they could prove nothing. (We know what happened because years later, as we will see, the whole story unraveled.) Wolfie Goldis took over the local, and put his brother the killer on the payroll into the bargain. Lepke had demonstrated anew what lay in store for any of his subordinates in any of the rackets who dared cross him. Obedience had to be exacted from time to time with the blood of apostates.

Lepke's method of assault on the movie industry was entirely different. He was an important link in a chain of events over which finally he had no control. It is the extraordinary end result that gives significance to the part he played.

Lepke's quarry this time was New York Local 306 of the Motion Picture Operators' Union, affiliated with IATSE, the International Alliance of Theater and Stagehand Employees. Without motion picture operators no movie theater could function. The union was therefore able to make good its featherbedding demand that two projectionists be on hand in each theater at all times. Despite the featherbedding there was a good deal of discontent among the rank and file because too few jobs were available in those desperate years. Quickly exploiting that discontent, Lepke set up his own projectionists' local and offered theater owners a "sweetheart" deal: more men at lower cost, far lower than the rival union permitted. His aim of course was to destroy Local 306, giving him monopoly status; then he would proceed to organize the New York movie houses into a protective association. Whether he also envisioned other, more ambitious possibilities at this moment we do not know. Others did envision them.

The scene shifts to Chicago. There the business agent of Local 2 of the Motion Picture Operators' Union was one George E. Browne. Browne was acquainted with William Bioff, a lowly stringer in the ubiquitous Capone mob, who made his living variously as a pimp and petty thief and racketeer (kosher meats was his specialty). Bioff was also very clever, for when Browne one day in 1932 told him about his, Browne's, setup, Bioff immediately smelled a racket in the making.

He persuaded Browne of it and the two men teamed up. Success swiftly followed. They shook down Chicago's major theater owners, chief among them Barney Balaban of the Balaban and Katz chain, for huge sums. Now Bioff could be seen around town with classy women, high-rolling in expensive gambling houses; he was quite unlike the contemptible hustler of old. His Capone mob friends assumed he was on to something and it was not long before he disclosed to them—under duress—what it was. And it was not long before the Big Fellow's successors (he was in Alcatraz) moved in, reducing Bioff and Browne to proper subservience.

The gang had indeed stumbled onto something immense. The large movie theater chains, such as Balaban and Katz, had become the financial bulwark of the movie industry; the Hollywood studios depended increasingly on them and were, or soon would be, in all but name their mere instruments of production, the important decisions being made in New York where the theater chains had their headquarters. From the Capone gang's point of view, then, the whole industry could be theirs provided the whole union, the International Alliance of Theater and Stagehand Employees, which embraced the movie projectionists, was theirs as well. And so capturing IATSE was what the gang systematically set out to do.

The scheme, in brief, was to put Browne forward as candidate for president of the International at the upcoming 1934 convention and use all the power at their command to ensure that he won. That meant asking Lepke's cooperation, for Lepke had some influence in New York and environs. Early in 1934 Capone's legatees asked Lepke to come to Chicago posthaste for a crucial meeting. There at Frank "the Enforcer" Nitti's house with Lepke was the mob's general staff—Philip D'Andrea, Charles "Cherry Nose" Gioe, Paul "the Waiter" Ricca, and Louis "Little New York" Campagna—and listening in, waiting for instructions, Browne and Bioff. With Lepke promising indispensable Eastern support, the assembled gangsters, among them the most powerful in the land, plotted their course of action: winning over enough of the delegates to IATSE's June convention in Louisville, Kentucky, to elect their man. Suffice it to say that Lepke did come through at the convention, that Browne did become president of the International, and that the Capone mob was now or shortly would be in the position to challenge the great movie moguls themselves.

(It should be borne in mind that while the Chicago gang took the lead in this attack, it was allied with, and to that extent beholden to, the other gang/syndicates abroad in the land. It was a cooperative endeavor.)

By 1937 Willie Bioff was conferring with the moguls in their Hollywood and New York executive suites and homes. He must have been unusually persuasive, for they proved as diffident and obliging as Barney Balaban (himself one of the top moguls by now) had been three years earlier in Chicago. For starters Bioff induced them to hand over to him—to IATSE—the 10,000 Hollywood studio workers, as yet unorganized but threatening to form their own militant union. This privilege of belonging to the gangster-run Alliance, this sweetheart arrangement granted by the stroke of a pen, cost each member two percent of his wages—a multimillion-dollar bonanza right there for Bioff and Browne, or rather their gang/syndicate sponsors. The moguls were furthermore required to draw heavily from their own exchequers as the price of industrial peace, if they wanted their films made and shown on schedule. The responsibility for seeing to it that the movie companies scrupulously obeyed Bioff's orders fell to two of the most exalted of the moguls, the Schenck brothers, Joseph and Nicholas, themselves alumni of the Lower East Side streets and now the chiefs respectively of Twentieth Century-Fox and Loew's Theaters. Through them Bioff received tribute of $50,000 a year from each of the large studios and $25,000 from each of the small ones—this in addition to sizable bonuses and gratuities on demand. And it was only the beginning, there being no limit to what the great American dream factory was expected to yield.

How much of this spectacular largesse, millions upon millions, reached Lepke? It would be impossible to say. None perhaps, for by the time his Chicago gangster friends had subjugated the movies and were ready to honor their debt to him in full, he and Gurrah were "on the lam." They had already embarked on their last—and fatal—journey.

m

It would be tedious to go on describing Lepke's infiltration and conquest of local industries.* We have by now a fair idea of how, once he had eliminated Little Augie, the last of the Jewish Mustache Petes so to speak, Lepke constructed his empire methodically, systematically: how he stabilized or rationalized "industrial relations," raising it to the level of large-scale criminal enterprise, emulating in this the gang/syndicates of Prohibition, learning from their experience and mistakes. Racketeering had replaced bootlegging as quite the rage by the early 1930s, and other reputable gangsters were gathering fortunes from restaurants, dry cleaners, wet wash laundries, poultry and fish and artichokes and other produce, milk deliveries, the numerous construction trades (painters, bricklayers, laborers), teamsters, longshoremen, and so on. In fact, every highly competitive industry lay at their mercy. But of the racketeer-gangsters Lepke was far and away the biggest and best organized and most aggressive and feared. And what further distinguished him from the rest was that he specialized in exploiting the *mainly Jewish* industries, all of them subject in extreme degree to the pitiless laws of the open market, or rather jungle, all susceptible to the lure of quick deliverance. Lepke and his victims and accomplices shared the same ethic; he was only its pathological expression, its malignant form.†

---

* Pocketbooks, for example. In 1929 Lepke and Gurrah muscled into the International Pocketbook Makers Union and proceeded to conduct a "reign of terror" against non-union manufacturers. One of the manufacturers, Hyman Leder by name, ran away to Poughkeepsie, though Lepke had warned him not to leave the city. One day in May 1929 Leder was struck on the head by a lead pipe and died. Thirteen years later the two assailants were arrested; one of them, Harry Epstein, served on the union's executive board.

† Harold Seidman, who nicely chronicles the misdeeds of the labor racketeers, has framed the issue very well. He writes: "For them [the tiny capitalists] unrestricted competition with its concomitant evil of ruinous pricecutting has not resulted in the survival of the fittest but in the destruction of all. Instinctively, they have sought to bring order out of a chaotic economic system. Prohibited by the anti-trust laws from legally regulating competition by joint action, they, too, have invited labor racketeers to organize their industries. Again we find labor-capital trusts springing up, and the

At the apogee of his power in the mid-1930s Lepke was one of America's paramount gangsters. The estimates vary but the generally held view is that he and Gurrah commanded above two hundred and fifty men—a tremendous organization, including experts in accounting, management, trade unions, influence peddling, not to mention the experts in schlamming and murdering—and that he and Gurrah each cleared between one and five million dollars a year. And what was more and perhaps quintessential, Lepke had close working relations with his fellow gang leaders (this we saw on several occasions), those whose sense of community transcended their ethnic and regional and occupational parochialisms, those who valued rationality and cooperation enough to refrain from violating each other's territories and, in a crisis, even to protect them. Lepke lent his burgeoning prestige to that community of gang/syndicates all of whose conferences from 1929 onward he dutifully attended, whose policies he helped shape and whose full-throated support, as we shall soon note in every gory detail, he received when he needed it. Until, that is, his time was up.

Lepke's success brought him exactly the notoriety he had tried assiduously to avoid. Those who dealt with him through his surrogates and intermediaries, for few were privileged to lay eyes on him, found his secretiveness and obscurity, his ghostly omnipresence, all the more intimidating. The invocation of his name—and Gurrah's by way of contrast—came to exert its own effect, as though one tempted fate simply by uttering them. The sound of "Lepke" can easily call up onomatopoeic images of a wolf—*lupus, lupo*—creeping up on unsuspecting prey for the kill; "Gurrah" suggests, perhaps, a huge growling beast.

---

dishonest union boss becomes the policeman to enforce regulations in regard to competition. If corrupt unionists are not available, outright criminals are called upon to perform the same function. The result has been that many associations, established to counteract abuses engendered by the competitive system, have degenerated into out-and-out rackets. In the end the businessman usually becomes the victim of his own racket and is compelled to pay tribute to the racketeers whom he has hired."

We are taking liberties here perhaps, associating visual images with the sounds of words. But by all contemporary accounts the sound of their names did chill the bones, did paralyze the will, did lend themselves to metaphors of assault, enslavement, destruction. And the mystique that surrounded them, it should not be forgotten, had its basis in hard truth, in the fact that they were as ferocious and cunning and indefatigable as their reputations made them out to be.

And what the public learned only whetted its appetite for more information about these fearful gangsters, their extraordinary rackets, their enormous empire. In this as in all things the public was destined to be served.

FIVE

LEPKE'S FALL: THE CHRONICLES OF THOMAS E. DEWEY

i

Leaving behind the familiar ghettos and garment factories and Jewish underworld let us turn briefly to another part of the country, another way of life, another kind of upbringing.

In 1902 Thomas E. Dewey was born in Owosso, Michigan, population 8,000, of solidly middle-class parents, descendants of pioneer New Englanders who had emigrated across the continent, reproducing their communities and life habits wherever they had settled. And like almost all their neighbors and all such small towns in the upper Midwest the Deweys had been invincibly Republican. Tom's grandfather had been a founder of the Grand Old Party in 1854 and the Deweys had been active in party affairs ever since, often at a high level. Republicanism was bred in the lad's bones. A Republicanism, it should be emphasized, that feared and loathed Tammany Hall as the universal symbol of the boss-ruled city machine, the alliance of politics and vice, the festering Babylonian enclaves inhabited by strange disreputable peoples—now or soon to be voters!—who had recently emigrated from far-off lands. To the Deweys of Owosso, Tammany had replaced the slave power of the South as the sum of human wickedness, the abiding threat to God and nation.*

Tom Dewey was a model child and adolescent and young man. He rarely took a false step (though for a while he hoped to be a singer, for he had a splendid voice) and always did what was expected of him. From the University of Michigan he went directly to Columbia Law School and then on to a good New York City law firm, marrying his fiancée when it was clear he had a future in corporate law. So he found himself living in the heart of Babylon itself (in its fashionable quarter to be sure), and at a time when Tammany was riding high as ever—as high as in the halcyon days of Tweed and Croker and Sullivan and Murphy—under the irresistible and completely corrupt stewardship of Mayor Jimmy Walker. True to his heritage and in the furtherance of his career, Dewey actively participated in local Republican affairs, associating with the upper-class businessmen and professionals who carried on the ancient Mugwump tradition (though it should also be understood that most Republican Party regulars—a corporal's guard—were furthest from being Mugwumps and in fact enjoyed Tammany patronage themselves, thereby carrying on another tradition, and one just as ancient). Dewey was soon noticed. He was diligent, reliable, judicious, and smart. His coolness and reserve and iron self-discipline kept people at a distance but inspired confidence. And he had a lovely wife, was a practicing Episcopalian, and otherwise bore the most desirable credentials.

One of the men Dewey impressed was George Z. Medalie, a prominent lawyer and leader of the New York City Republican organization. Medalie was himself a fascinating character. Son of a rabbi and brought up on the Lower East Side, he had as a young man thrown in his lot with the Republicans. Advancing rapidly on the strength of his legal talent Medalie served as mediator between the genteel class and the party regulars at the precinct level. Early in 1931 President Hoover appointed Medalie United States attorney for the Southern District, which took in New York and environs.

---

* In Dewey's own words: "I did bring with me an inborn conviction that the Tammany Hall political machine was the epitome of corruption and oppression, and that the Republican Party was the only worthy instrument of government."

Now for an ambitious Republican this was the best of times to be a federal prosecutor. Tammany Democrats suddenly found themselves in grave trouble. The investigation into municipal wrongdoing headed by Judge Samuel Seabury (a Mugwump of the old school, a disciple of the Reverend Dr. Parkhurst) was dredging up one sensational scandal after another, each leading closer to the mayor's office. The Democratic order was coming apart and Medalie was bent on making the most of his and his party's opportunity. He chose Tom Dewey, who was not yet twenty-nine, as his chief assistant and gave Dewey free rein to handle the office as he saw fit. Nothing more could have been done to launch the young man's political career.

But the corruption of the city machine paled into insignificance compared to the suffering brought on by the Great Depression and therefore to the discredit into which the national Republican Party had fallen. Its defeat in 1932 was catastrophic, amounting to a revolution in American politics. As a federal prosecutor representing a lame-duck administration, Dewey had little chance to draw much attention to himself, though he demonstrated repeatedly just how able and efficient he was; his brief tenure was about to end uneventfully, in a whimper, as soon as Franklin D. Roosevelt, who replaced Hoover in March 1933, got around to appointing a Democratic district attorney. Before this happened, however, Dewey got his big break.

In 1931, at about the time Dewey was appointed assistant U.S. attorney, the federal government proved in Chicago that it was possible to convict the gang/syndicate leaders, even the largest and most notorious among them, namely the Big Fellow himself. The government brought off this remarkable coup by hard work, its various intelligence and investigative agencies, its legal staff and accountants cooperating to establish by the sheer volume of the evidence adduced—all documented and therefore incapable of being silenced—that Al Capone had evaded paying his income taxes, that anyone who spent as much as he on food, clothes, homes, not to mention other amenities such as gambling, necessarily earned much more money than he had reported. The government prosecutors treated the great Capone on his own terms, as a businessman (they did not concern themselves with how he acquired his fortune, one source of income being as worthy as the next) who happened to be delinquent and thus needed to be taught a lesson in social ethics. For his delinquencies, he received eleven years, effectively finishing him off. That the Capone syndicate went on functioning, and for many more years at that, is another matter; at least he, the arch villain of the era, was in jail. The public was propitiated, its faith in the laws buoyed up. And prosecutors were given a magnificent chance to make their names: gangsterdom offered them an embarrassment of riches.

It is hardly surprising, therefore, to find Dewey enlarging on the Chicago experience. The same team of federal treasury men who had performed so well on the Capone case came to New York and joined Dewey's organization, or rather machine. Scores of lawyers, FBI and Narcotics Squad agents—specialists in wiretaps and surveillance and infiltration—postal inspectors (who opened mail with impunity), accountants, and others all worked together under his vigilant eye and strict standards. Beyond everything else Dewey was a masterful, and very demanding, administrator and executive.*

This huge, finely tuned apparatus Dewey employed against the best-known New York area gangsters of the time, namely Waxey Gordon and Dutch Schultz. Both flaunted their ill-gotten riches and fame; both were celebrities, owners of nightclubs or other such properties on the Great White Way, men who dared the authorities to take them on. And in taking them on Dewey knew exactly what was at stake for him, how much his future depended on his performance. He therefore spared nothing, neither expense nor manpower nor time to prepare his cases against these master criminals. Hundreds of thousands of calls were tapped, thousands of people interviewed, the files of hundreds of companies and scores of bank records carefully examined. (In gathering evidence, we might note in passing, Dewey and his staff strayed far from the bounds of civil liberties, their assumption being that gangsters deserved no such liberties, not outside the courtroom at any rate. Prosecutors in general and of

---

* "Dewey," writes Elmer L. Irey, chief Treasury Department investigator, "was the perfectionist to end all perfectionists. His thoroughness is beyond description, although some of my boys made some handsome efforts to describe it in exquisite flights of profanity. He never varied in his working customs."

course the police shared this assumption, and the courts rarely challenged it.) Two years after Dewey turned his machine on Waxey and the Dutchman he was ready to try them. By then Medalie had quit and Dewey was chief attorney.

Dewey had to move quickly because the two gangsters were just then locked in a ferocious death struggle. Each had always been a lone operator, maintaining only the loosest connection, and only as necessity required, with the emergent community of gang/syndicates. Neither respected the other's territories and they personally despised each other. Small conflicts led to large ones; in time war broke out along the coastal strips on either side of the lower Hudson River, their respective appanages. By 1933 Dutch Schultz's mob was definitely gaining the upper hand; it was seizing more and more of Waxey Gordon's northern New Jersey subsidiaries, systematically decimating his army, forcing his customers to change their beer distributorships.

Waxey himself came within a hair's breadth of assassination. On April 12, 1933, he and his closest associates, Big Maxey Greenberg (who, we remember, had begun it all back in 1920 and had traveled a circuitous route before ending up as Waxey's lieutenant) and one Mandel Gassell, familiar to police and gangsterdom as Max Hassell, were staying at the Carteret Hotel in Elizabeth, New Jersey, on routine business. Dutch Schultz's gunmen arrived in the middle of the night and caught Greenberg and Gassell in their beds, killing them instantly. Waxey, ever alert, climbed out the window of his adjoining room when he heard the shots and bolted for his life. On Gassell's body the authorities found a key to a local bank's safe-deposit box; in the box was $213,500 in cash and a $50,000 promissory note, all of which the federal government confiscated in partial payment for the taxes the dead man owed.

Waxey and his surviving lieutenants went into hiding. Posing as William Palinski he rented a hunting lodge on White Lake in the Catskills. By then Dewey's office was chasing him too, hoping to apprehend him before the Dutchman finished the job. The decision, to quote the chief treasury investigator, was coldbloodedly simple: "It is extremely difficult to collect back taxes from gangsters' estates." Receiving an anonymous tip, federal marshals on May 21 went straight to Waxey's hideout.* He claimed he was William Palinski, but when the marshals pointed out to him that his silk underwear bore the initials "I.W." (Irving Wexler) he gave up the pretense. At least he had eluded Dutch Schultz.

The trial, held six months later in New York City's federal courthouse before a vast audience—the entire newspaper-reading public—was a splendid triumph for U.S. Attorney Thomas E. Dewey. The one hundred fifty witnesses he called proved beyond doubt, by the quantity of evidence they presented or confirmed, by the number of breweries, warehouses, and trucks Waxey owned, by the customers he supplied, by the banks he kept accounts in, that he had earned vastly more than he had declared in his tax returns. They also described in embarrassingly fulsome detail how he and his family lived—how much he paid for the cars (a Pierce Arrow, a Lincoln, a Buick), the luxurious West End Avenue apartment and furniture, the help (a cook, a maid, a chauffeur), the private schools his three children attended, the expensive clothes he wore, as well as the other accouterments of wealth duly noted and recorded. Dewey throughout delighted in ridiculing Waxey's vulgar *parvenu* taste, making much of the fact that Waxey filled the apartment bookshelves with the collected works of Scott, Thackeray, and Dickens, every volume bound in fine leather, many in "full levant," and not a single one of them opened(!); or that Waxey wore the finest silk shirts and underwear (they were practically put on display) and had hundreds of suits and jackets made to order by Al Capone's tailor. Dewey's purpose, we must infer from our reading of the trial proceedings, was not only to build up an open-and-shut case against Waxey Gordon; this went without saying. It was also to humiliate the man, strip him to the bone, reduce him to what he really was, always had been, and always would be, no matter what money might buy, namely the vile, crude

---

* Luciano (if his testament-memoir is to be believed) tells us that Meyer Lansky may have been the informer. Lansky, it seems, had long been having his own feud with Waxey, each accusing the other of the most atrocious misdeeds, and had been feeding Dewey leads on Waxey's many illicit operations. Without Lansky's information, Luciano continues—and here he strains all credulity—it is doubtful if Dewey could have prosecuted Waxey.

Lower East Side schlammer and jailbird. Dewey was assuring the world, certainly his world, that such a hoodlum could not after all purchase respectability and class, could never really transform himself.

Waxey tried to help his cause by testifying in his own defense. He represented himself as a poor boy from the ghetto who had aspired to the American dream and, thanks to good fortune and certain modest talents as a businessman, was on the way to realizing it, though of late he had suffered grave financial losses, hence his low income for the years in question, hence his admittedly low taxes. He did admit to "only two vices. One is for beautiful clothes and the other is for a beautiful home"—vices which scarcely merited the punishment that the government now sought to visit upon him. In his cross-examination Dewey toyed with poor Waxey, easily drawing out his mendacities, encouraging him to drone on and on, the very sound of his words, his very language, betraying his underworld origins and life, strengthening the impression that he, Dewey, sought to put across. The contrast between these two men, the district attorney from Owosso, Michigan, and the defendant, an expatriate from the fleshpots of the Lower East Side, was itself a central part of the well-advertised drama. It was a contrast the public would long remember.

The jury took exactly fifty-one minutes to find Gordon guilty. The judge warmly applauded the decision, congratulated Dewey and his staff, and gave Waxey ten years. Waxey Gordon went off to prison—could the irony be crueler?—a few days before Prohibition ended. His rise and fall had been circumscribed by the fate of the Eighteenth Amendment.*

Waxey was the curtain raiser for Dewey's major event: the prosecution of Arthur Flegenheimer, known far and wide as Dutch Schultz or the Dutchman, who had come to be regarded as public enemy

---

* Nor did the gods who ordained Waxey's fall show him any mercy. Soon after his conviction he learned that his elder son had died in a car accident while driving up from Duke University to visit him.

number one (though such a designation had not yet been invented). He was so feared that the Secretary of the Treasury himself, Henry Morgenthau, Jr., made a special point of going after him, enlisting everyone, from the mayor of New York to J. Edgar Hoover, in the posse comitatus.*

These fears were amply justified: the Dutchman's exploits were incredible by any standard. With his inner circle of gunmen—a savage crew, which included the likes of Abraham "Bo" Weinberg, Martin Krompier, Solomon "Solly" Girsch, Abraham Landau, and Bernard "Lulu" Rosenkrantz—he cut a wide swath that extended from the central Bronx to upper Manhattan and across the river to New Jersey, having displaced Waxey Gordon and lesser rivals in the process. The Dutchman had all the attributes of a successful gang leader: he was smart, decisive, unsentimental, and he could deal easily with others outside his own gang and neighborhood—with politicians and other gang leaders, for example. Like the younger Turks of gangdom he was soft-spoken and polished. (One of his intimate associates later wrote: "His murderous reputation had led me to expect a ruffian, but he was not at all that way. He was a small but well-set man with good features. The girls used to say he looked like Bing Crosby with his nose bashed in.") And he was as quick as any of his coevals—Lepke, Lansky, Luciano—in perceiving an opportunity and leaping over obstacles to seize it.

---

* We have transcripts of the telephone conversations Morgenthau had with Mayor LaGuardia and the FBI boss. Here are some excerpts:

Morgenthau: "Mr. Mayor, I think you and I have got a common interest in Dutch Schultz."
La Guardia: "Yes."
Morgenthau: " . . . Well now the point is the Treasury wants this fellow."
LaGuardia: "Yes."
Morgenthau: "And he's the last of the big gangsters that are out [sic]."

Morgenthau: " . . . I just wanted to tell you personally that as far as Treasury is concerned that that's the last of the big income tax gangsters who are out and I am particularly interested in it myself."
Hoover: "Oh, I am very glad to hear that. We haven't been making any first—what they might call first-line drive on trying to find him because we thought that naturally it was a matter the Treasury would give its first attention to, but if you would like to have us do so, I would be very glad indeed to instruct our New York office to just bring all pressure to bear on that."

Which leads us to his conquest of the numbers racket, by all odds his outstanding achievement and, as far as the authorities were concerned, the cause of deepest apprehension. Here we can only hint at its complexity and magnitude.

Numbers, or policy gambling, was an old story, predating Dutch Schultz's birth by many years. It was, and is, a mode of gambling especially congenial to the poor, the bet being exceedingly small, the odds exceedingly high—meaning, therefore, a rich return to the bettor in the unlikely event of a hit. It worked this way: a bettor would put down a dime, say (he could have put down as little as a nickel), and choose any three numbers. The odds against his winning were accordingly 999 to 1; if he hit he received 600 to 1, or $60. Now the winning number had to be drawn from an objectively valid and trustworthy source, accessible to anyone. That source happened to be the daily reports of the New York City Clearing House printed in the financial pages of newspapers.

Every poor neighborhood in New York had its policy makers or bankers, each assisted by a farrago of runners and collectors and other hangers-on. Reliability was of course critically important. The only question in the bettor's mind was whether the banker could pay him if—as sometimes happened—enough people won at the same time. A banker who proved his reliability attracted business and enlarged his clientele. And so we come to Harlem, that vast area of upper Manhattan which mainly Jews had tenanted until Blacks began moving in en masse during World War I.

By the end of the 1920s Harlem had become the largest black ghetto in the country. The poor there, like the poor Italians to the east and the poor Irish to the north and west, played the numbers of course, and before long several enterprising bankers had sprung up in their midst. We know with some exactitude what profits these entrepreneurs were reaping. One of them, a West Indian named Adolph Brunder, was worth, or had saved, $1,753,342; a second, José Enrique Miro, a Puerto Rican, had $1,215,556 in his possession; and so on. All in all, Harlemites were betting around $35,000 a day on the numbers; and of this stupendous amount (each dollar then being worth at least ten today) the bankers and their retinues kept on the average four fifths, a good part of which obviously went to police, politicians, and lawyers. And if anything the numbers industry was growing. For with the Depression setting in more and more people were betting, praying for the redemptive miracle, everything else having failed them.

Dutch Schultz had been watching the Harlem situation rapaciously and carefully, waiting for the right moment to strike. It came when the bankers found themselves in a bit of a fix. With local and federal authorities in hot pursuit, two of the largest, Brunder and Miro, fled to their respective homelands in 1931 after giving their businesses over to an associate, Joseph Matthias Ison, for safekeeping until their return. One day, according to the most authoritative account, Bo Weinberg and Abe Landau, gunsels nonpareil, took Ison for a ride and informed him that Dutch Schultz wanted to protect him. Was he amenable? Ison thought it over and agreed in every particular to their terms. And thus by the inexorable logic of the racket (a logic completely familiar to us by now), Ison was reduced to a functionary, a member of the apparatus, a glorified collector. As were several other erstwhile Harlem bankers, including Miro and Brunder who, returning to their old haunts, discovered they had two choices in life: obey Schultz or leave Harlem; the third choice, resistance, was out of the question. The Dutchman had muscled into the biggest policy racket of all.

If he forced the Harlem bankers to become his hired hands he also provided the betting community with the benefits of organization. The Dutchman did not bother with cops on the beat or ward-heeling politicians. He went to the top, to Tammany chieftain James J. Hines, an ex-blacksmith who had risen through the hierarchy in orthodox fashion and was now boss of upper Manhattan and therefore of countless judges, prosecutors, and police officials. The Dutchman paid Hines extravagantly, between $500 and $1,000 a week, for seeing to it that the operation was left alone. These arrangements, incidentally, were worked out by the Dutchman's main adviser, a smooth and cunning lawyer well versed in policy matters—he had represented Ison and Miro and other Harlem bankers before being himself co-opted into the syndicate—who went under the name of J. Richard Davis, "Dixie" to his friends, once Julius to his Rumanian-Jewish parents. "I soon learned," Davis would later write, "that to run an organized mob you've got to have a politician. You have heard about the suspected link between organized crime and politics. Well, I became the missing link."

With great resources at his disposal Dutch Schultz, like the best of the racketeers, had brought order and rationality into the numbers industry. Black neighborhood spokesmen were forced to admit this even as they deplored the white takeover, the blatant colonialism. But, at least, in the words of *Harlem Age*, "it ensures the players of getting paid off when they hit. Formerly, when the bankers were too hard hit on any one day or succeeding days they either had to welch on payments . . . or else go out of business. Now, it is said, with Schultz money behind the game the players are assured of payment."

What the *Harlem Age* could not have known was that the Dutchman had rigged the game in his favor, pulling off one of the grander deceptions in the history of American crime. In a word, he developed a system of organized welching. It was ingenious. What he did, first of all, was alter the basis for selecting the winning number; he derived it now from the daily pari-mutuel race-track "handle" rather than from the New York Clearing House reports. Assume, for instance, that the winning horses of the first three races paid a total of $297.28, those of the first five paid a total of $550.98, and the first seven $886.06. Taking the third digits of each total we arrive at the number: 706. This method, on the face of it, and however complicated it seems to the novice or outsider, was perfectly legitimate, perfectly objective, and anyone with a newspaper could check it for himself in a trice. The newspaper, however, neglected to mention one important fact: that the race track—Cincinnati's Coney Island (since renamed River Downs)—was owned by . . . Dutch Schultz.

The rest of the scheme falls into place. The Dutchman hired a legendary mathematical wizard, a human computer named Otto Biederman, Abbadabba Berman to the cognoscenti, to go through the thousands of policy slips by the time the first seven races were run at Coney Island and decide which number must not win—the one, that is, on which the most money had been bet. That information was relayed to a Coney Island race-track operative who then made the necessary adjustment in the pari-mutuel handle. How much the Harlem bettors were cheated may be gathered from the size of the Dutchman's earnings from numbers alone—a staggering twenty million dollars a year according to government lawyers, much of it, to be sure, distributed to the mob, the middlemen, and the politicians.

The riches drawn from Harlem's proletariat enlarged Schultz's power tremendously, enabling him to undertake other ventures, to extend his imperial realm in every direction. He was the rogue elephant of gangsterdom. His easy destruction of Waxey Gordon sent shock waves through the underworld community. So did his success in the industrial rackets, a field of endeavor he had not hitherto exploited. After capturing the strategically important locals of both the Hotel and Restaurant Employees International and the Delicatessen, Countermen and Cafeteria Workers, the Dutchman established his own protective, the Metropolitan Restaurant and Cafeteria Association, whose contributions added millions more to his treasury or war chest. That he would treat the other industrial racketeers—even the great Lepke perhaps—as his fair game was all too clear. It was only a question of time, for his appetite was boundless.

We can appreciate, then, why Thomas E. Dewey was so eager to try him. We can also appreciate why the Dutchman was less than eager to be tried by Dewey, no ordinary prosecutor, and why, unlike Waxey, he made good his flight. Wisely, he hid out in the most insulated and secure refuge of all—New York City—the heart of midtown Manhattan at that, openly frequenting the familiar haunts, including his Château Madrid nightclub, taking over for his gang, his clients, his political associates, as occasion demanded, one of the plushest whorehouses in Babylon, Polly Adler's famous Fifty-fourth Street salon, and by and large carrying on as usual. The failure of the police to apprehend him for over a year, though flyers on him had been broadcast by the thousands, might be attributed to the Dutchman's splendid good luck; more likely though it was because he had so many well-placed friends, none of whom sympathized with Dewey's crusade, none of whom wished to see their benefactor removed from circulation.

It was after Dewey had been replaced (the Roosevelt administration having waited until he completed the Waxey Gordon case to appoint a successor) that the Dutchman gave himself up. And he gave himself up not in New York City but in Albany. So the trial was held in another part of the Southern District, in Syracuse, where presumably the case would be treated on its merits and without prejudice. Here the Dutchman proved just how shrewd and lucky he was. The jury simply could not make up its mind that he was guilty of the charges and the case was retried, this time in the pleasant, remote little North Country community of Malone, New York. And this time he beat the rap altogether, the jury acquitting him on all counts. One could only conclude that he was a wonder-worker and that he would go on indefinitely as public enemy number one.

An incident that took place during his upstate interregnum illustrates the man's unconscionable brutality. It is told by his mouthpiece, Dixie Davis, who witnessed it; there is no reason to doubt Davis' veracity. Needing cash at once, the Dutchman sent for his functionary in charge of the restaurant racket, a hulking roughneck named Jules "the Commissar" Martin (born Julius Modgilewsky). The Dutchman had suspected Martin of shortchanging him in his absence, and while they were arguing he took his pistol from his belt, shoved it into Martin's mouth, and fired. "It was as simple and undramatic as that—just one quick motion of the hand. The Dutchman did that murder as casually as if he were picking his teeth." The Commissar was buried without ceremony somewhere outside Troy, New York.

But the Dutchman's troubles were far from over. No sooner did he escape from one danger than another and potentially worse one rose up to confront him. It was as though the Furies were after him, in the form of his old enemy, Thomas E. Dewey. There was something strange and inexplicable in Dewey's reemergence or reincarnation, in the succession of events that brought him back to scourge the gangsters. On May 13, 1935, a Manhattan grand jury did the rarest of things: it actually rebelled against the district attorney, William C. Dodge, a Tammany creature whom Jimmy Hines, the Dutchman's comrade, in particular had helped to select the year before. Finding Dodge hopelessly incompetent the jury demanded that a special district attorney be appointed to clean up the gangsterism, above all the racketeering, which held the city in its thrall.

Mugwumps and businessmen and the press and the mayor, Fiorello LaGuardia, added their voices to the cry. The movement was irresistible. Governor Herbert H. Lehman, himself a reform Democrat, acquiesced, agreeing to appoint a Republican as Special District Attorney for New York County who would be independent in his sphere—racketeering and such crimes—and answerable to none but the governor. He offered the job to one prominent Republican after another; each refused, each maintaining that Dewey was the only man who could do it justice. And again the Mugwumps and the press and the others joined the chorus, and again Lehman submitted, this time very reluctantly, for he was as apprehensive as the rest of the Democrats that the young knight-errant might in the end slay them along with the gangsters. And so in July 1935, a few weeks after the Dutchman's acquittal in Malone, Dewey set up shop, forming his own staff of prosecutors, many of whom had assisted him before, and his own team of investigators and policemen, the latter carefully screened and rigidly segregated from their brethren on the force. They owed their entire loyalty to Dewey.

The Dutchman of course knew what was in store for him. He knew how much depended on Dewey's putting him away after humiliating him, as he had Waxey, in a spectacular show trial. The Dutchman then made his move; it was as bold as one would expect of him. He tried to persuade New York's gang/syndicate leaders— Lepke, Luciano, Lansky, Adonis, Costello, et al.—to officially approve the assassination of Thomas E. Dewey. He argued lengthily that Dewey was as much a threat to them as to him, that once he went they would surely follow one by one until Dewey had reached his goal, high political office, perhaps the highest in the land. He insisted that a crisis situation required crisis measures, however unpalatable, for he, Dutch Schultz, was no less aware than they how dangerous it was to kill a prosecutor, especially a popular one—but, in short, it was Dewey or them.

The Dutchman forced these gangster-statesmen, these architects of a new rational order of crime, to face the crisis that did in fact exist, that did pose exactly the threat he had pointed out to them. What were they to do? If they refused to go along with the Dutchman he might, he *would* (the meaning of his words could not be misinterpreted) send his own boys after Dewey. This act, successful or not, would willy-nilly implicate them, all of them. So they undertook what might be called a feasibility study of how Dewey would be slain should they decide to go ahead with the Dutchman's proposal. They assigned the task to one of their most experienced killers, Albert "the Executioner" Anastasia of Brooklyn, a man destined for high fame in the years ahead.

Posing as the father of a young child whom he had borrowed for the occasion, Anastasia and an accomplice walked back and forth on the sidewalk near Dewey's Fifth Avenue apartment house. Having learned the man's habits, they outlined a plan of attack: in a nutshell, the assassin would follow Dewey into the corner drugstore, where he stopped every morning at seven-thirty before heading for work, and gun down everyone in sight, the proprietor and the customers, if there were any, as well as Dewey. A silencer would have to be used so as not to alert Dewey's two bodyguards who always waited outside the store for him.

The gang/syndicate leaders studied the plan and turned it down flat. They decided against departing from their established policy, great as the provocation was. For while Dewey was a menace, no question of it, to depart from that policy even this one time was to bring down upon themselves the vials of public wrath. Of that they were certain. Frank Hogan, one of Dewey's prosecutors at the time, later said, "I suppose they figured that the National Guard would have been called out, or something like that, if Dewey had been killed, and I guess they wouldn't have been far wrong."

That decision to forbear gave rise to other decisions almost as momentous. In the first place the Dutchman had to be prevented from doing what they had rejected: the public would not distinguish between gangster-statesmen and gangster-outlaws; his rash deed would sink them as well. Now prevailing on the Dutchman to do or refrain from doing anything was no simple matter. He had always been a loner, had always kept his distance from the other syndicates. Moreover, he and they distrusted each other. He had reason to believe that they had been conspiring behind his back with his chief lieutenant, Bo Weinberg, to seize and divide his territories while he was sweating out his trials upstate. (We should say his erstwhile chief lieutenant, for Weinberg disappeared after he had met with the syndicate leaders and was never heard of again, the story being that Schultz's men took him on a boat up the East River, encased his feet in concrete, and after waiting for it to dry—he was conscious throughout—heaved him off the boat.) Nor were the syndicate leaders averse to the unfortunate Bo Weinberg's suggestion. Lepke and Luciano and the others coveted the Dutchman's rich possessions, and they justifiably feared his designs on them. They were as disappointed as the authorities that he had beaten his rap. And then, not to be dismissed either, was the possibility that he would do a volte-face and talk to Dewey, for the mob had betrayed him, and in exchange for his freedom he would feel no compunction in betraying them. In other words, every argument arrived at the same conclusion: the Dutchman had to die. The responsibility for carrying out the execution was entrusted to Lepke, an expert without peer in this delicate art, and the Dutchman's co-religionist to boot.*

Lepke chose the finest, most experienced killers in his employ: Emmanuel "Mendy" Weiss, a loyal subordinate of long standing, and Charles "the Bug" Workman, an artisan of the highest reputation, at once coldly professional and recklessly brave (hence the nickname), who had free-lanced for many gangs, including Dutch Schultz's, and given them complete satisfaction. On the night of October 23, 1935, the two men were driven to the Dutchman's present hangout, the Palace Chop House in Newark, New Jersey. There he and his henchmen customarily went over the day's receipts, calculating how much they had won and lost, waiting for Abbadabba Berman to wind up

---

* It should be pointed out here that Dutch Schultz dabbled in several different religions, and it has never been established what he became, if he became anything. We have Lucky Luciano's word that he was more interested in Catholicism than anything else and would have converted to it. "And then I'll be damned," Luciano is quoted as saying, "if he didn't start to talk about the Catholic religion; he wanted to know what it was like to be a Catholic; whether Vito Genovese and me ever went to confession, if we knew what a guy had to do to switch into Catholicism from bein' a Jew. . . . It's funny. When I first started hangin' around Jewish guys like Meyer and Bugsy and Dutch, the old guys Masseria and Maranzano and lots of my friends used to beef to me about it. They always said that someday the Jews was gonna make me turn and join the synagogue. So what happens? It ain't me that gets turned, it's the Dutchman. That's some joke."

his recondite duties.* At 10:15 P.M. Bugs Workman and Mendy Weiss strode into the restaurant, empty now of customers except for the men sitting around the large round table in the rear, drew out their weapons—Bugs a .38 revolver, Mendy a sawed-off shotgun—and quietly ordered the help to lie down and say nothing. Then they advanced to the rear table and opened up on everyone there, Abe Landau, Lulu Rosenkrantz, and Abbadabba Berman.

But the main target and justification of the massacre was nowhere in sight. Mendy Weiss, having done what he was assigned to do, no more, no less, fled the premises and leaped into the waiting car and sped away. Bugs Workman, now flourishing a .45, ran to the toilet, kicked open the door and shot the Dutchman who, blithely unaware of the commotion outside, of the angel of death closing in on him, was micturating in one of the urinals. As the Bug retreated toward the door Rosenkrantz and Landau gathered up their remaining strength (Abbadabba's was ebbing away on the floor) and fired the last rounds of their lives at the murderer who disappeared into the night.

On leaving the Palace Chop House Bugs Workman discovered that the car and his partner Mendy were gone. So he kept running through empty lots and swamps, arriving in New York City the next morning in quite a state. He was hopping mad, of course, the more so when he learned through the grapevine that Mendy Weiss was claiming credit for gunning down the Dutchman and his confederates. A serious altercation developed between the two killers, so serious Lepke himself had to settle it. This he did at a "peace conference" which he presided over—not for nothing was he known as "the Judge"—convincing them that for gangdom, for the community of gang/syndicates, the important desideratum was getting the job done, not who did it, that there was gratitude and honor and reward enough for both of them.

Just before dying the Dutchman gave the world a tantalizing in-

---

* According to the policy sheets that were found that evening, Schultz had a total income of $827,253 for the previous seven weeks and payments to winners of $313,712. His own personal share, apart from an enormous expense account, came to $148,369.

sight into his soul. In his semiconsciousness he called up an extraordinary babble of metaphors and figures; a kaleidoscope of images passed in review. A police reporter was present to record it all. Writers on crime have ever since tried in vain to make sense of this rich soliloquy, finding clues in a word, a phrase, a name, anything that might yield a hidden link in the chain of associations.* But the Dutchman's final remarks should be appreciated for what they are: an eloquent juxtaposition of symbols marking his descent into Hades or Nighttown. Here is a sample of it:

"Please Mother! You pick me up now. Please, you know me. Oh, Louie, didn't I give you my doorbell? Everything you get, the whole bill. And did you come for the rest in the doctor's office, sir? Yes, I can see that. Your son-in-law, and he isn't liked is he? Harry, does he behave? No, don't you scare me; my friends think I do a better job. Oh, the police are looking for you all over; please be instrumental in letting us know. That wouldn't be here; they are Englishmen and they are a type I don't know who is best, they or us. Oh, sir, and get the doll a roofing. Please. You can play jacks, and girls do that with a soft ball and do tricks with it. Please; I may take all events into consideration; no, no. And it is no; it is confused and it says no; a boy has never wept ... nor dashed a thousand kim.... Did you hear me? Now leave it or take it. No, I might be in the playing for all I know. Come on over here; come on over. Oh, Duckie, see we skipped again."

And so the labor of decades was undone with a single blow. Dutch Schultz and his lieutenants were dead or scattered to the winds. His vast empire was carved up among the gang/syndicates in accordance with their prior consent, each securing its aliquot portion:

---

* A case in point. Investigative reporter Hank Messick discerns a connection between the Dutchman and the Cleveland gang (the "Silent Syndicate") led by Dalitz, Rothkopf, Tucker, and Kleinman. He singles out one brief sentence from the deathbed statement—"Please crackdown on the Chinamen's friends and Hitler's commander"—to prove circuitously (it would take us too far afield to reconstruct it here) how deeply concerned the Dutchman was about them, how greatly he feared their seizure of his Coney Island race track in Cincinnati, which lay within their demesne. Messick can infer this because the Clevelanders did eventually take possession of the track. But that inference rests on retrospective proof, there being no evidence that the Dutchman in fact feared them. And neither Schultz's biographer Paul Sann nor anyone else draws such an inference.

Lepke the restaurants and cafeterias, Longy Zwillman the northern New Jersey distributorships, Luciano and his associate Michael "Trigger Mike" Coppola the Harlem numbers, the Clevelanders the Coney Island track, and so on. Carthage had to be destroyed.

n̈

▬▬▬▬▬▬ Thomas E. Dewey found himself in an admirable position. The darling of the New York City Republican or legal-corporate establishment was now, in the summer of 1935, Special District Attorney with a sweeping mandate from the governor to pursue racketeers and other kinds of criminals. The meaning of Dewey's appointment could not be mistaken. It was intended to carry forward the assault on corrupt politics that had driven one mayor, Jimmy Walker, into exile and brought about the election of a progressive reformer, Fiorello LaGuardia. But these changes, startling in themselves, only pointed up the deeper truth: that the "invisible government"—the nexus between the Tammany machine and the large-scale practitioners of vice and crime—was still secure, still untouched by the comings and goings of mayors and governors and reformers of every stripe. Tammany Democrats still selected the municipal judges and county district attorneys and police hierarchs (except the commissioner) and the other lesser officials responsible for enforcing the law. And, as we noted, it was the temerity of this invisible government that caused the Manhattan grand jury, a body of middle- and upper-class citizens, to "run away" from the incumbent district attorney who was little more than a front for the bosses, and insist on his replacement. Nor could the governor refuse, whatever his misgivings, for if the public perceived him as Tammany's friend his political career would be over forthwith. And so Dewey was given his singular authority to complete the task of municipal reform.

Dutch Schultz was to be the first of Dewey's targets: Schultz the rich patron and beneficiary of Jimmy Hines and, through Hines, of the clubhouses, judges, and police. Dewey's main and ultimate target, however, was not Schultz, despite his great fame. It was Lepke, the reigning monarch of the industrial rackets and one of the council of princes who presided over the gangster kingdom. Lepke, or the "L and G" team, had become quite notorious by now, even though—or precisely because—they were so clandestine, so elusive. Dewey believed that bringing them to book would expose the whole intricate pattern of criminality, embracing unions and businessmen and politicians and the gang which ran its own paramilitary force of thugs and murderers and possessed an income of incalculable size, the substance of incalculable corruption.

So Dewey set his army of investigators and prosecutors loose on Lepke and Gurrah. He used the same techniques that he had used earlier as federal attorney. He went after hundreds of witnesses; anyone who had anything to do with Lepke was brought in for questioning, threatened with indictments, put under terrific pressure to talk. Phones were tapped extensively and unrestrictedly. Raids were conducted on union and company offices in the middle of the night and their books seized. No lead was neglected or slighted. And, adding yet another arrow to his quiver, Dewey induced the state legislature to pass a special law that enabled a prosecutor to join in a single indictment everyone connected with an alleged crime, however remotely or indirectly or inadvertently, in effect making the crime an all-inclusive conspiracy.*

Just how formidable Dewey could be—therefore how prophetic the Dutchman had been—became ominously clear by the way he disposed of Lucky Luciano who had come into his line of fire quite by accident. During a routine inquiry into New York's enormous prostitution trade Dewey learned that the great Luciano, *primus inter pares* among Italian gang/syndicate bosses, could somehow be implicated in it. The implication was exceedingly tenuous. It seems that several of the petty gangsters in that racket, those who extorted money from or gave protection to the "bookers" (in effect, booking

---

* Dewey argued in behalf of the "joinder" law as follows: "A new type of criminal exists who leaves to his hirelings and frontmen the actual offenses, and rarely commits an overt act himself. The only way in which the major criminal can be punished is by connecting him to these various layers of subordinates and the related but separate crimes in his behalf." True enough. But given Dewey's reasoning, what then becomes of due process? How are prosecutors themselves bound by the law? How is the distinction to be made between the "connecting" and the assumption of a conspiracy?

agents who brought the prostitutes to the madams, each madam having her own set of clients), had dealings with Luciano: they paid him off in turn as protection from other gangsters. Luciano's role was simply to keep the peace and ensure that there were fair shares for all: in reality he had no more to do with prostitution as such than the cop on the beat who was also being paid off.

The point here is that Dewey discovered the fragile link and went after Luciano like a tiger. Operating in strictest secrecy, Dewey's men on the night of January 3, 1936, swooped down on the whole "ring" of prostitutes, madams, pimps, bookers, and gangsters and jailed them all, threatening each with long prison terms if they did not talk and promising complete exoneration and other rewards if they did. And that was how he persuaded such madams as Nigger Ruth, Sadie the Chink, Jenny the Factory, Polack Frances, Silver-Tongued Elsie, Gashouse Lil, Frisco Jean, and Cokey Flo to testify. (One can imagine the press coverage as Dewey called on each of them respectfully, deferentially, a gentleman through and through, to tell her heart-rending story to the grand and petit juries.) Also dutifully "singing" for Dewey were such bookers as Peter Belitzer, Jack Ellenstein, Al Weiss, and David Marcus, all risen from the slums of their youth, earnest seekers of a modest competence in life who had advanced a stage or two beyond the pimp or cadet level. They and many others, sixty-six to be precise, built a strong circumstantial case against Lucky, but it was no more than circumstantial, or rather inferential, since no one proved that Lucky was actually in charge, that indeed he had anything to do with the business.

But Lucky, like Waxey a few years before, played wonderfully into Dewey's outstretched hands. Dewey had argued that beneath the facade—for Lucky was now "Mr. Charles Ross" of the Waldorf-Astoria, with his own elevator, thirty-ninth floor suite, catering service, etc.—lay the murderous street gangster and underworld hierophant, a man therefore capable of any crime, including the most sordid and despicable, namely running New York's prostitution racket. It was to dispel this impression that Lucky took the stand. A battle of wits ensued between Dewey and an upstart, arriviste ethnic gangster, this one born in Sicily. To say Lucky was no match would be an understatement: he helped transmute what might have been a vague presumption of guilt into unquestioned certitude, the irreducible evidence being the character of the man.

The following exchange was typical. Why, Dewey, asked, did he, Lucky Luciano, need so many guns and ammunition for his personal use? Because, Lucky replied, he liked to hunt, "to shoot birds." "What kind of birds?" "Peasants." The jury and the public laughed uproariously, reminding everyone of Waxey Gordon's gaffes two years before.

Dewey's campaign could not have succeeded more splendidly. The mighty Luciano, who had helped transform syndicated crime in America, received thirty years, tantamount to life, an unprecedented term for a gangster of his stature.* And yet he was only an "excursion from Dewey's chief objective" (to quote Dewey's official biographer): Lepke and the industrial rackets. By this time, by the spring of 1936, if not earlier, Lepke and Luciano might have had second thoughts about having turned down the Dutchman's wild proposal of assassination.

To most people's surprise Dewey was just then upstaged, at least momentarily. The federal district attorney, anxious to make *his* mark and demonstrate his concern for the racketeering evil, suddenly put Lepke and Gurrah on trial—for violating the Sherman Anti-Trust Act, of all things—specifically for conspiring to restrain trade in rabbit skins through their control of the Protective Fur Dressers' Corporation, thereby reducing competition and fixing prices. The in-

---

* One would think that Luciano would have stoically accepted his fate, Dewey having vanquished him in the eternal struggle of the strong and the weak, the winners and the losers. Not at all, if we are to believe his *Last Testament*. Luciano complains about the unfairness of his trial and conviction. That would be equivalent to a gambler complaining about the wrong turn of the dice. Luciano comes across as a crybaby when he says: "After sittin' in court and listenin' to myself being plastered to the wall and tarred and feathered by a bunch of whores who sold themselves for a quarter, and hearin' that no good McCook [the judge] hand me what added up to a life term, I still get madder at Dewey's crap than anythin' else. That little shit with the mustache comes right out in the open and admits he got me for everythin' else but what he charged me with. I knew he knew I didn't have a fuckin' thing to do with prostitution, not with none of those broads. But Dewey was such a goddamned racketeer himself, in a legal way, that he crawled up my back with a frame and stabbed me."

teresting question is why the government chose to go after "L and G" for that particular crime. If anything, they should have been congratulated; they accomplished what the government, the New Deal administration, had endeavored to do in every industry. The New Deal's centerpiece, the National Industrial Recovery Act, had sought to bring stability, i.e., reduce competition, and fix prices too, and in much the same fashion that Lepke's protectives had (minus the brutality of course). And what was more, the offenses for which "L and G" were charged bore a maximum sentence of only two years. The federal prosecutor, or the Justice Department, was determined to get them for something, anything, however trivial, or even praiseworthy from a strictly economic point of view. At the very least a march would be stolen on Thomas E. Dewey who had until then monopolized the headlines.

The trial, which took place in late October 1936, was as brief as it was undramatic. Several fur manufacturers bravely testified that gangsters—no one actually saw Lepke and Gurrah—had forced them to join one of the protectives, had so terrorized the industry (some witnesses recounting the beatings, the acid throwings, the dynamiting of property) that the mere utterance of their names had been sufficient to ensure compliance. Others admitted at the same time that the protective, because it did restrain trade, benefited everyone, workers and employers as well as the mob. But none of these witnesses could prove that the defendants had established or ran the protective. That is, not until the union's secretary-treasurer, Jacob Potash, took the stand. Risking his life (how close he came to losing it he never realized), Potash told of meeting Gurrah during negotiations with the head of the protective and being at that time informed by the head that Gurrah, or rather the team of Gurrah and Lepke, was the real boss. Potash's testimony "provided the vital missing link for the prosecution." Both men were found guilty as charged and given the maximum two-year term.

Now as far as Dewey was concerned the affair had not turned out so badly after all. Lepke and Gurrah would be incarcerated while he continued to gather evidence against them; the more time he had to do so the better his case would be. He could even bend the whole affair to his advantage. He happened to be uncomfortable in his present position, kept on the string as he was by the governor, a Democrat, who disliked and distrusted him. Wishing to be his own man, Dewey cast his eye on the Manhattan District Attorney's office, the one held by Tammany's William C. Dodge. If everything went right Dewey might win that office in the November 1937 election. He would run, that is, as the man who was seeking the people's support to finish off the racketeers—chief among them the celebrated Lepke—once and for all, a job that only he, Dewey, was competent and independent enough to undertake.

This explains the great press war that Dewey mounted against Lepke throughout 1936. Hardly a day passed when the Special District Attorney did not fail to reveal the enormity of Lepke's empire and announce his intention of taking it apart industry by industry, from baking to cloaks and suits, and bringing all the culprits to heel. The drumbeat of publicity grew louder and louder, drowning out other local problems, competing even with important national and international issues for attention (1936 being the year when the American people had to pass judgment on President Roosevelt and the New Deal, when Hitler and Mussolini were consolidating their victories in preparation for others to come, when the Spanish Civil War had just gotten under way). So loud was the publicity that Governor Lehman, running for re-election, also "declared war" on the racketeers (i.e., Lepke) and authorized Dewey to empanel a second grand jury and therefore try the criminals in two courts simultaneously. And Mayor LaGuardia, not to be outdone, formed what one reporter called a "civic vigilante committee," a group of distinguished businessmen who were expected to prevail upon their brethren in the garment and baking and building and other racket-infested industries to appear before Dewey's grand juries and talk or confess freely. LaGuardia had already asked important labor leaders in those industries to do the same.

Meanwhile, the public was treated to a discussion of racketeering that it had never heard before, such discussions on the subject—and they were extensive—having been confined until then to occasional books and articles, most of them of an abstract nature. What the public learned now, what the literature had already established, was that racketeering was hardly distinguishable from ostensibly legitimate practices in certain industries; for example, the highly competitive and deliquescent ones,* located in large cities and dominated by Jews and Italians and Irish, the predatory ethic of the marketplace calling forth its appropriate response and character type. Lepke and Gurrah and the lesser gangster-racketeers thus came to seem even more threatening than they were. For they were perceived as operating within the system, surreptitiously giving the orders to no one knew how many unions and companies and politicians. They were perceived as especially satanic, especially dangerous, because so masterfully concealed and disguised.†

But what the public was persuaded to believe bore little relation to the truth. And the truth was that tremendous changes, most of them salutary, had been taking place in the industries susceptible to racketeering, that a new arrangement or equilibrium between the racketeers on the one hand and the companies and unions on the other was coming to pass. We saw how the New Deal, in effect imitating Lepke, had sanctioned the establishment of industry-wide cartels or protective associations; the same National Industrial Recovery Administration also sanctioned, and also for the sake of stability and harmony and efficiency, the establishment of industry-wide unions, the two sides, organized employers and organized workers, to adjudicate such differences as might arise between them through collective bargaining.

Overnight the various garment unions burgeoned to full strength, to upwards of 400,000 members in each of the larger ones, the International Ladies Garment Workers Union and the Amalga-

---

* Mayor LaGuardia's definition of a racket was as good as any: "It is an organization of groups or individuals who through duress, violence or threat of violence exact or extort money from others. As nearly as I can explain it, and without intending to cast any suspicion upon legitimate business, I would say that it bears the same relation to crime as corporations and trusts bear to individual business. When the smaller units of crime are merged in a larger unit we have racketeering."

† Here is how Dewey put it: "Only in the cruder and more primitive rackets are violence and threats still necessary or the shakedown plain and brazen. Legal means are customarily used to achieve illegal objectives. A well-devised cloak of respectability and legitimacy is generally present. The innuendo and the veiled threat are sufficient to exact payment."

mated Clothing Workers. And more than anything else it was the astonishingly augmented power of the unions that brought about the desired stability once and for all in their respective industries. Lepke's men, hundreds of them, had to accommodate themselves to that gigantic fact, to the new order of things, the new equilibrium. They were "in place" as union operatives and as manufacturers and middlemen; they had to assimilate themselves into the industry on that industry's terms or get out altogether, because the services they once provided were no longer needed. Most of them would, in the ordinary course of events, cease to be gangsters, becoming an organic part of the world on which they had once preyed. Time legitimates everything, as the whole history of venture capitalism from its early lawless buccaneer and slaving days attests, and it would have made the gangsters scattered through the garment and bakery and other industries paragons of respectability in the space of a single generation. Would it be too far-fetched to imagine Lepke and Gurrah in old age as prosperous retired clothing manufacturers, noted philanthropists as well, prominently associated with the major fund-raising drives, their salad years of murder and mayhem consigned to long-forgotten newspapers and books?

Dewey's crusade, urged on by the hysteria he helped whip up, threatened to destroy that equilibrium, that uneasy modus vivendi, that assimilative process. He applied excruciating pressure on Lepke's associates, past and present, major and minor, in each of the rackets, promising all of them immunity from prosecution in exchange for information and the willingness to testify for the state when the time came. How successful Dewey was—how many of Lepke's men he persuaded to "sing"—is impossible to know. In a sense it hardly matters. The very act of going after them the way he did: calling them in repeatedly, threatening them with dire punishment, never ceasing to harass them, and when these failed, indicting them en masse—this very act generated powerful currents of fear and suspicion, the object of which was to force Lepke and Gurrah to respond precipitately, to commit a blunder that might break the case (or cases) against them wide open.

But not in his wildest imaginings could Dewey, nor anyone else, have expected Lepke and Gurrah to respond as they did. They came up with a strategy of self-defense, or rather of counterattack, that was as daring and ruthless as only they were capable of devising. If, they decided, the appeals court upheld their convictions, they would break bail and hide. (The court did uphold Gurrah's early in 1937 but ordered Lepke retried; he fled in July, just before the second trial began.) Then came the breathtaking part of the scheme: the systematic purging of the ranks by fire and sword, the execution of each and all of the talebearers, or at least enough of them to terrify the rest into silence, no matter what Dewey might throw at them. Once the carnage was over, once the hysteria had died down and the crusade had run its course—Dewey having presumably moved on by then—the fugitives could safely surrender, serve their brief sentences, and return to the bosom of their empire. Such were the fantastic lengths they were prepared to go to save themselves.

Obviously the success of their scheme depended on the full support of the gang/syndicates; it could not even have been conceived without their aid. They were not going to fail one of their highest-ranking comrades. For if Lepke went, could any of them doubt that Dewey would not rapidly carry his onslaught into their citadels? Sustaining Lepke in his hour of crisis was a matter of collective security. That was why the gang/syndicates saw to it that he and Gurrah were safely harbored (this responsibility being entrusted to Albert Anastasia, the most brutal of enforcers and one of Lepke's admirers and friends), that their territorial integrity remained inviolate while they were on the lam, and, above all, that the ghastly plan, the reign of death, was carried out to the letter.

Murder Incorporated was the title of the band of men assigned to do the deed. Murder Inc. was of course not their official title; it was the title the world would one day confer on them—none was more appropriate—in recognition of their unspeakable labors. No grand guignol theater could have invented anything quite like Murder Inc. Its history beggars description.

$$...$$

m

There is, to begin with, the mise en scène, the neighborhood from which the members of Murder Inc. emerged, the vaulting arch of communities that extended from the East River, more exactly the Williamsburg Bridge, deep into Brooklyn's vast interior plains and that compassed what had once been such quiet, sparsely settled villages as Williamsburg, Brownsville, and East New York. From the turn of the century on, the Lower East Side had been sending more and more of its inhabitants into these outposts, first Williamsburg, then Brownsville, then East New York. Within a generation they had become sprawling replicas of the parent, their combined populations numbering over half a million Jews by 1930. (Italians were streaming in as well, forming companion neighborhoods, replicas of their own parent community.) To be sure these Brooklyn ghettos were not as densely packed and noisome as the Lower East Side had been, but they were oppressive enough and they came to breed a distinctive underworld culture of their own; they were at least as depraved and vice-ridden and violently competitive, and what is more, lacked the institutional constraints—e.g., the trade unions, the Socialist movement, the settlement houses—that were present on the Lower East Side even in its worst days. These Brooklyn enclaves had a frontier quality about them.

Their streets brought forth a uniquely sordid and brutalized set of criminals who survived in the usual way, by extorting, selling alcohol and drugs, serving as schlammers for companies and unions and, as occasion warranted, thieving and murdering. And like street criminals everywhere they coalesced into gangs in order to preserve or expand their territories. Here again the Italian and Jewish gangsters found common ground, cooperating or merging more and more often, subordinating their ethnic differences to larger economic and jurisdictional needs. Yet the Brooklyn gangs, perhaps because they were so diverse, separated by such distances, could never get beyond the rudimentary stage of organization. They could never rival the well-structured gang/syndicates that flourished across the river and elsewhere. (Which was why Brooklyn always suffered a brain drain, its more talented children, the likes of Johnny Torrio, Al Capone, Frankie Yale, Bugsy Siegel, seeking their destiny in the other metropolitan centers of America.) And so the Brooklyn underworld, numerous, savage, inchoate, came inexorably under the control or hegemony of the New York gang/syndicates. The predominantly Italian sections (for they overlapped) acknowledged the redoubtable

Joey Adonis' leadership while the predominantly Jewish sections acknowledged Lepke's.

It took Lepke a few years to achieve his power in Brooklyn. The industrial rackets had given him his foothold there, Jake the Bum Wellner's painters' local being only one of his operations. The hundreds of tiny runaway garment manufacturers that had set up shop in the fastnesses of Williamsburg discovered they could not run away after all, Lepke having found them and made himself their protector. From this secure base he advanced steadily in every direction, muscling in wherever opportunities presented themselves. With imperial finesse he took advantage of Brooklyn's inveterate disorders, the endless conflicts of its street gangs. The Shapiros and the Ambergs, for example, were two such murderous gangs that had fallen out over a division of neighborhood spoils. Lepke threw his enormous weight behind the Ambergs, and in the summer of 1931 Irving and Meyer Shapiro were slain; their brother William fell a year later. The Ambergs' turn was next. By the end of 1935 Lepke and his local allies had eliminated all of them, one by one: Joseph and Louis (nicknamed "Pretty," a ferocious gunman), then Hyman (widely known as "Hymie the Rat"), and finally Oscar, who simply disappeared into the earth. With the Ambergs gone the neighborhood was pacified; at least much of the intramural warfare had ceased. Lepke had established his primacy.

He had done it with the assistance of a remarkable band of killers, an amalgam of young Italians and Jews. As products of the same environment they, Italians and Jews both, were equally barbarous, each representing the lowest level of abomination to which gangsterism in America had sunk. Because several of them later sang freely, omitting scarcely a note, we know something about them, the Jews in particular. They had started out in the 1920s as conventional thugs and strong-armers, pulling down a meager income, hustling for every cent they earned. Then the time of troubles began: the Castellammarese War (Masseria versus Maranzano, Maranzano versus Luciano) and, closer to home, the struggle first between the Shapiros and the Ambergs, then between the Ambergs and the Lepke-Gurrah empire.

A great demand arose for top-grade killers, or "hit men." Also for the accompanying technicians: the "finger men" who studied the habits of the intended victims, plotted their assassination, and pointed them out; the "wheel men" who stole and concealed and drove the cars which bore the hit men to and from their destination; plus such exotic specialists as "evaporators" who were responsible for getting rid of the car and every other trace of incriminating evidence. The killers stood at the top of this gruesome hierarchy. They commanded an enviable salary, paid by Lepke and the gang/syndicate community, from $100 to $250 a week, depending on how reliable and skillful they were, this apart from whatever other "pickings" or sources of income they could lay their hands on.* The highest priced were those with the largest number of murders to their credit.

By 1936 Hershel or Harry "Pittsburgh Phil" Strauss could boast of a score or more; so could Motel or Martin "Bugsy" Goldstein; and Albert "Allie Tick Tock" Tannenbaum (a college boy!), Abraham "Kid Twist" Reles, Abraham "Pretty" Levine, and Irving "Knadles" Nitzberg had almost as many, and so had numerous others. These privileged warriors enjoyed a great prestige in their neighborhood circles. They swaggered through Brownsville and East New York streets with their vassals and hangers-on, wore the best, or loudest, clothes, and had the girls and cars of their dreams. But their very success defined their tawdry limits. When all was said and done they were nothing more than professional assassins. They were too crude to come within miles of the gangland summit occupied by Lepke and the syndicate leaders, by those who presided over vast business concerns. In that sense they were a monstrous throwback to the old Lower East Side gangsters from Monk Eastman to Little Augie. They "never rose from Brownsville flats to penthouses, as have oth-

---

* Meyer Berger wrote: "Murderers' apprentices—'punks' to the trade—go on the payroll at $50 a week. They start with piddling chores—stealing cars to transport corpses after murders, swipe extra license plates.... The curriculum covers techniques in 'schlamming' (severe beating), and 'skulling' (assault just short of murder), and conduct in police lineups in event of arrest. Serious students, if they show an aptitude, are privileged in their senior year to attend undergraduate murder clinics; to watch *cum laude* men ... operate with ice pick, bludgeon and cleaver. Talented young men can advance rapidly. A hard-working, conscientious trooper, first class, subject to call at any hour of day or night for professional duty, gets from $100 to $150 a week. Real artists ... get around $200. Troop bosses ... command $250 and pickings."

er city gangsters," according to the *New York Post*. "They never became angels for Broadway shows; they never opened any big post-Prohibition night clubs; they never acquired large legitimate business interests." They were, in sum, "only big shots in a small and poor territory."

The institution that came to be known as Murder Inc. consisted, then, of just this cadre of prize executioners—Reles, Goldstein, Strauss, Tannenbaum, Levine, Nitzberg, and many others—abetted by various partners and subordinates, Jewish and Italian both, all citizens of the same neighborhoods, all performing their jobs according to an elaborate and arcane division of labor. With their black bags containing the appurtenances of their trade (a rope, an icepick, a knife, a gun), they would travel around the country on special assignment for their employers, the gang/syndicate leaders. Kid Twist Reles and, on the Italian side, one Harry "Happy" Maione served as the intermediaries, passing down the orders or contracts they received from on high and working out the precise details of the execution. The chief authority on the subject attributes a thousand murders to the gang, and while this may be an exaggeration, the number, whatever it was, must have been gigantic by any reckoning, even by the standards of the times. Certainly no one in America was more fiendishly expert in their profession than they.

For almost three years, 1936 to 1939, Murder Inc. cut a broad swath of terror through Lepke's great empire, extinguishing anyone suspected of talking to Dewey, setting examples, proving that he, Lepke, was as omnipresent and cruelly vindictive as ever.

Lepke's first victim, Joseph Rosen, was no gangster at all. It was his misfortune to have once crossed Lepke's path. That was in 1932 when Rosen owned a small trucking company which did business with runaway garment shops in Pennsylvania and New Jersey. Lepke was then attempting to organize those shops; at any rate he organized the truckers who serviced them. Not Rosen: he was forced out, ruined. Lepke did try to help him in various ways, but to no avail. At loose ends, Rosen took to blaming Lepke for his plight, his family's destitution, the hopelessness of his prospects. Even the candy store he bought in Brownsville failed to placate him. All this time Lepke tolerated Rosen, even passing off the remarks openly directed against him as justified; they were only words.

When Dewey's men visited Rosen early in 1936, Lepke grew alarmed. He sent Rosen money and arranged for him to leave town. Soon Rosen was back: he needed more money; his complaints assumed an ominous tone. Lepke could take it no more. "That son of a bitch, that bastard," Lepke was quoted as saying, "is going around Brownsville and shooting off his mouth that he is going to Dewey." And so the death sentence was pronounced. Mendy Weiss, who a year earlier had helped destroy Dutch Schultz's gang in the Palace Chop House, and two other Murder Inc. killers were the hit men; Paul Berger was the finger man; Sholem Bernstein the wheel man; and Louis Capone (no relation to Al) the planner of the escape route. We have dwelled on these sordid trivial details of poor Rosen's murder—which went off flawlessly in his little candy store on the night of September 13, 1936—because his undying spirit would later return to haunt Lepke and the other participants to their very grave sites.

Next, it was George Rudnick's turn. Rudnick, a very low thug in Lepke's garment industry operation, was seeing Dewey, or so it was believed. (He had been spotted talking to a detective.) Not only did he have to die; he had to be an example. So, on May 11, 1937, Reles and Pittsburgh Phil Strauss, Happy Maione, and Frank "the Dasher" Abbendado brought the hapless Rudnick to a favorite neighborhood garage and strangled him.

Problems immediately arose. First there was the problem of how to write the note warning other "stool pigeons" that a similar fate awaited them. "We didn't know how to adjust the typewriter ribbon," Reles later said. "I held it and Strauss typed the note. Then we argued about spelling the word 'friend.' Strauss said it was 'f-r-e-i-n-d.' I said it was ... 'f-r-i-e-n-d.' We tore up two notes and finally we argued so much that I let it go Strauss' way. It was a lousy job." Then there was the problem of Rudnick himself: they heard him moan as they were stuffing his body into the car. "Strauss said, 'De bum ain't dead yet,' and jabbed an icepick in his throat. Maione hit him across the head with the meat chopper, and then Maione said, 'That oughta fix de bum up.'" And so it did.

The abortive assault on Max Rubin several months later deserves particular attention. Rubin had been one of Lepke's most important functionaries. An ex-cutter in men's garments, he had advised Lepke on how to proceed in that industry and several others. Rubin was a master tactician, and for services rendered enjoyed "no show" positions in several union locals. Dewey appreciated Rubin's value too—no one would have been a better catch—and put terrific heat on him. It would be best, Lepke informed Rubin, if he went on an extended vacation, returning only after the heat had dissipated. "That man," Rubin would say years later, "had an obsession that if we went away he'd be safe."

Lepke spared no expense to ensure Max Rubin's happiness wherever he might find it. He sent Rubin to Saratoga, but Rubin could not abide the place. Rubin found Salt Lake City intolerable. Neither could he stand New Orleans, where Frank Costello and Dandy Phil Kastel offered him a job in their slot machine empire. Rubin missed his family too much and returned to New York.

He had disobeyed his boss. One night he was picked up and driven to a secret rendezvous. It was "raining pitchforks," he recalled. Lepke, standing under an awning, asked him why he had not stayed away as instructed. "Lepke," he said, "I want to come home. I'm lonesome. I don't like running around the country. I want to see my family. You can trust me."

"How old are you?" Lepke asked.

"Forty-eight."

"You've reached a ripe old age."

Lepke then turned on his heels and vanished into the darkness.

Rubin of course understood that he was a marked man and he hid from his pursuers. But on October 1, 1937, Reles and others caught up with him and promptly shot him in the head at close range. Miraculously he lived.

For Dewey the shooting of Max Rubin could not have come at a more propitious time. Only a few days before, Max Silverman had been arrested in Los Angeles, rushed to New York, and indicted along with the missing leaders, Lepke and Gurrah, for their part in the bakery racket. (Earlier in the year the other executives of Local 138 and Max's son Harold had been convicted of the same offense.)

And a day before the assassination attempt Dewey announced that Lepke and Gurrah would be charged in absentia for extortion and racketeering in men's clothing. The bullets that struck down Max Rubin therefore gave Dewey the opportunity he sought to dramatize the campaign he was busily waging for Manhattan District Attorney.

His radio speech of October 4, amply headlined and commented on, conveyed the sense of enveloping crisis. The gangsters, Lepke and Gurrah chief among them, were on the run and would scruple at nothing to hold on to what they had. Dewey likened them, Lepke in particular, to Tammany Hall, reinvoking the System in its crudest form. (One could almost hear the ghost of the sainted Reverend Parkhurst saying amen in the background.) Dewey asked the people of Manhattan to give him the mandate to complete the job and so bring his onerous duties to a close, for he wanted nothing more than to retire from public life, go back to his law practice and the warmth of his family whom he had too long neglected. "I intend to see that the grip of the underworld is broken in the next four years." That was the promise on which he concluded his talk.

Manhattan voters were convinced: they elected Republican Dewey by a landslide. Given New York City's politics it amounted to a miracle. The stage was set for the final act of the drama: the young paladin, hardly thirty-five, versus the most fearsome gangster alive.

The pursuit of Lepke and Gurrah began in earnest. New York City offered a $5,000 reward for the capture of each of them; this was matched by the federal government. A tremendous international manhunt got under way. Reports circulated that they were in Warsaw plotting to kidnap Mme. Jeanette Suchestro, Prince Radziwill's fiancée, that they had been sighted in Puerto Rico, Canada, Cuba, Vermont, that they were here, there, everywhere. These reports, growing more and more farfetched and ludicrous, remained a press staple for the duration of their flight. In fact, they had never left New York City, Brooklyn to be exact, where friends and relatives and henchmen took excellent care of them and where, it seems, they could have remained on the lam indefinitely.

But Gurrah, a sick man, could hold out no longer, and on April 14, 1938, he turned himself in unconditionally. "I got a bad reputation from the newspapers," he said as he went off to jail. "They arrest me because they want to be District Attorney, or even Governor. They don't go after the little fellows. They go after big shots like me because the publicity I get is worth maybe $50 million." No one could accuse Gurrah of false modesty. Nor, for that matter, of false prophecy.

The search thus concentrated on Lepke alone, the public's interest in him excited by his apparent ability to be in three or four places at once and by the steady increase in the reward, ultimately $50,000, divided equally between the city and federal governments. His face was seen everywhere—on handbills and movie screens and newspapers across the country. He became the most wanted man in America, in the world, perhaps in history.

And as Lepke's notoriety rose, so did Dewey's status. It was apparent to state and nation that Lepke was escaping from Dewey, and for good reason. Dewey was convicting everyone in sight, including Tammany's own Jimmy Hines, the partner of Dutch Schultz and many another racketeer. But Lepke was Dewey's meal ticket to higher office, perhaps to the highest; Lepke was the best Republican hope to come along in years and Dewey was going to exploit him for all he was worth. And so within a year of making his promise to break the underworld's grip on New York City Dewey became the Republican candidate for governor.

The Democrats knew that only one man could defeat Dewey, namely the popular incumbent Herbert H. Lehman, and Lehman had already announced his intention of retiring after this his third (two-year) term. But the Democrats, from President Roosevelt on down, prevailed on Lehman to run again. So he did, on his record, his irreproachable integrity as man and politician. Dewey campaigned on his by now familiar theme, maintaining that the only way to unseat the invisible government and extirpate the System was through the governor's office, that while Lehman was well-meaning and honest he was, after all, a Democrat, a fatal limitation given the task at hand. And indeed Dewey came within an ace of winning, the margin of difference between him and Lehman being 64,000 votes, a mere 1.5 percent of the total cast. It was an amazing show of strength, so amazing it thrust Dewey forward overnight as a possible presidential candidate of the resurgent Republican Party. He was man of the hour.

The fugitive Lepke was central to these vast designs and calculations. Having invested so much in Lepke's downfall and having drawn so many dividends from it, Dewey was not about to fail now, not at any cost. More and more implacably he closed in on Lepke's men, indicting them wholesale, whether or not he had a case against them, all this in preparation for Lepke's inevitable capture.

And resisting just as implacably, Lepke, with gang/syndicate acquiescence, sent Murder Inc. on a rampage, slaughtering informers, active or potential or suspected, it made no difference, and those among the innocent who happened to be caught in the line of fire. Eleven people that we know of were thus dispatched in a little less than a year: on August 21, 1938, Hyman Yuran, Lepke's partner in a dress concern, his body flung into a lime pit near Loch Sheldrake, New York; on November 10, 1938, Leon Sharff along with his wife, whose misfortune it was to be with the victim when the bullets struck; on January 28, 1939, two old-time comrades going back to the Little Augie era, Isadore Friedman (Danny Field to friend and foe) and Louis Cohen, sometimes Kushner, yes, the very Cohen-Kushner who fifteen years earlier had audaciously killed Kid Dropper and had served such a brief stretch for it; on January 29, 1939, Albert "Plug" Shuman, one of Lepke's ancients, taken for a ride by Murder Inc.'s best hit men, Allie Tick Tock Tannenbaum and Knadles Nitzberg; on March 30, 1939, Joseph Miller, another one of Lepke's business partners; on April 28, 1939, Abraham "Whitey" Friedman, a notorious plug-ugly (once Kid Dropper's companion in arms); on May 25, 1939, Irving Penn, who had nothing to do with Lepke or the rackets—he worked for a music company and was an altogether respectable citizen—but who made the fatal error of looking like and living in the same Bronx apartment house as the intended victim, Philip Orlovsky (the same crook ousted back in 1931 as boss of the cutters' local in men's clothing), the murder taking place on the day Orlovsky was to secretly appear for questioning in Dewey's office; on the same day, May 25, Morris Diamond, office manager of Teamster Local 138; on November 23, 1939, Harry "Big Greenie" Greenberg, a specialist in stink bombs and acid disfigurations, who had tried to blackmail

Lepke and failing this had settled down in Los Angeles where he was slain by Allie Tannenbaum and several local gangsters. Greenberg was the last victim Lepke served up to Moloch in his attempt to save himself from Dewey's outstretched arms.

Let us pause here to consider what took place between Dewey's appointment as special prosecutor in 1935 and Big Greenie Greenberg's death. At least thirteen people were executed in that period.* And while it is true that all but three were deep-dyed gangsters, the price—from a strictly utilitarian point of view, the cost-efficiency factor let us say—was grotesquely high, scandalously high. How much responsibility for this mass murder can be imputed to Dewey's handling of the whole affair? A great deal, we contend. Dewey chose to play Lepke's own game, the game of intimidating witnesses: letting the world know that he was putting pressure on them, indicting them, perhaps targeting them for death. The game, then, was this: Would Dewey be able to force so-and-so to talk and seek his, Dewey's, protection? Or would Lepke be able to demonstrate to so-and-so the folly of yielding to Dewey, whatever the pressure, by silencing the most egregious of the informers, exactly those whose testimony Dewey had openly solicited? The body count tells us the enormity of Dewey's failure, the extent of his inability to play the game on which he had embarked.

This is our retrospective judgment, made forty years after the event, all the protagonists having since died. It certainly was not the public's judgment at the time. If anything, the murders vindicated the great prosecutor, revealing to one and all what he—and society— were up against. Our argument is that Lepke's bestiality could have been contained, that political zeal and opportunism had much to do with unleashing it, that Dewey failed those whose safety he should have guaranteed. The ambit of responsibility for the crimes extends well beyond the murderers, from Lepke on down.

---

* "It is apparent," Dewey informed the public after the ninth victim—the innocent Irving Penn—had been struck down, "that the Lepke mob is waging a war of extermination against its former and some of its present members."

We do not know precisely why Lepke surrendered and why just then—August 24, 1939. This much we do know, that the strains within the gang/syndicate ranks over what should be done with Lepke's empire were growing intolerable. Despite the reign of terror, despite the conscientious efforts of the leaders, the empire was becoming harder to keep intact; it was falling away at the edges, the prey of hungry rivals. Luciano may be telling the truth when he claims that several gang/syndicate leaders met at Thomas "Three-finger Brown" Lucchese's behest (Lucchese, an important Mafioso, had a strong interest in the industrial rackets, especially garments) to discuss the possibility of temporarily dividing the empire, holding it in escrow so to speak, until Lepke beat the rap. Lepke, we are told, would have none of this and after insisting that garments and baking belonged to him and no one else, stormed out of the room. Now one would think that Lepke's enemies at this point would have taken measures to put him out of the way, seizing by force what they could not seize by acquiescence. But he also had his friends, or rather the enemies of his enemies, and chief among these was the fast-rising Albert Anastasia who was charged with Lepke's personal safekeeping and with ensuring that Murder Inc. carried out its orders. Lepke's assassination would have set off a fratricidal conflict in the gang/syndicate community.

Luciano goes on to say that Lucchese, Costello, and others brought the vexing problem directly to him at Dannemora prison. Modest as always, Luciano asserts that he solved it in a trice. The solution, or double cross, went as follows: first, to induce Lepke to give himself up to the federal authorities, specifically J. Edgar Hoover, the FBI's boss, by promising him, Lepke, a deal: Lepke would be told—i.e., led to believe—that if he served his federal sentence Dewey would drop the charges against him; second, to inform Dewey that Lepke would soon be in his clutches, available for full political exploitation, and that it was Lucky Luciano who had masterminded the betrayal (the quid pro quo being obvious); and third, to inform Dewey also that the gang/syndicates in general would handsomely support Dewey for governor—his office for the asking—once he had prosecuted the great Lepke.

"So Frank [Costello] went back to New York," Luciano writes, "with a guarantee from me to Dewey that not only would he get all our backin' to run for governor next time, but also that Lepke was gonna be turned over to him on a silver platter, with my compliments, plus evidence." This explanation, so implausible on its face, so tainted by the character of its author (Luciano conceives everyone else in this world to be a thief and liar, he alone being honest because he alone is willing to admit that he is a thief and liar), is corroborated by Hank Messick, Lansky's biographer. It was Lansky, Messick maintains, who inveigled one of Lepke's close henchmen, Morris "Moey Dimples" Wolensky, to convince Lepke that the deal had been made, that the "feds" would never turn him over to Dewey, that he would go free after serving a brief sentence.

Anastasia, it is said by way of further corroboration, tried vainly to dissuade Lepke from taking up the offer, arguing that it was a trick, perhaps perfidy. Years later, presumably at Lepke's request, Anastasia avenged the wrong by murdering Moey Dimples; gangsterdom recognizes no unwitting acts of treason. Did Lepke and Anastasia ever find out who had put Moey Dimples up to it? Probably not. And if they did find out what could they have done about it? How could they, or Anastasia alone, have gone after Lansky and Luciano—that is, the entire gang/syndicate leadership? Lepke had been sacrificed and that was that.

The most sensational part of the case, the act of surrender itself, is a matter of public record. On August 5, 1939, Walter Winchell, the king of gossip columnists and news broadcasters—no one had a larger national audience at the time than he—received an anonymous call (from Anastasia) to the effect that Lepke "wants to come in" but feared he would be shot "while supposedly escaping." Joyously anticipating the scoop of the year, of a lifetime, the thrill of being himself a maker of events, Winchell, on one of his broadcasts, promised to relay back to Lepke J. Edgar Hoover's assurance of safe conduct to a federal jail. It was universally known that Winchell and Hoover were the best of friends, that they often shared the same high table at New York's Stork Club. Each helped the other in important ways: Hoover gave Winchell delicious tidbits on the private lives of famous people; Winchell adulated Hoover repeatedly, serving as coryphaeus and press agent in the national celebration of "America's top cop."

That assurance Winchell conveyed in his next broadcast. The elaborate and slightly ludicrous arrangement, a study in diplomatic protocol, took several weeks to complete.

Early in the evening of August 24, Winchell received the telephone call he was waiting for. He was told to drive at once to Proctor's Theater in Yonkers, New York. Just as his car approached the theater another car full of men drew up alongside; one of them, his face covered by a bandana, instructed Winchell to turn back to New York and stop at a drugstore on Eighth Avenue and Nineteenth Street; there he was to wait in one of the phone booths. At 9:00 P.M. a customer in the drugstore nonchalantly walked over to Winchell and whispered a message into his anxious ear: he must tell Hoover by phone to be at Fifth Avenue and Twenty-ninth Street between ten and ten-twenty; Winchell himself must go immediately to Madison Avenue and Twenty-third Street. There, at 10:15 P.M., Louis Lepke Buchalter, heavier now and graced by a mustache, introduced himself and entered Winchell's car. Two minutes later they met Hoover who was sitting alone in the rear of his limousine.

"Mr. Hoover," said Winchell, "this is Lepke."

"How do you do," said Hoover.

"Glad to meet you," said Lepke. "Let's go."

The rest is pure melodrama, the resolution of an interminably complicated plot. Soon after turning himself in Lepke realized that he was caught in a labyrinth of deceptions (Anastasia having been proved correct) and that he was finished, condemned to spend his life in jails; that at the very least.

The federal government, it transpired, wanted first of all to arraign him for his part in a large drug operation, the largest since Arnold Rothstein had tried his hand at it. After Rothstein's assassination in 1928 a new ring had been established by the infamous Jacob "Yashe" Katzenberg, Rothstein's helpmate, who undoubtedly knew more about procuring heroin in Asia and smuggling it into the United States than anyone else in the world. Not for nothing did the League of Nations call Katzenberg an "international menace." It was a strange and buffoonish sort of ring consisting of small-time Lower East Side crooks—Nathan Gross, David Dishback, Jacob Livorsky, Louis Kravitz, Benjamin Shisoff, and others (one of whom, Shisoff, also owned a Coney Island frozen custard stand)—who were sent on buying trips to various exotic countries. By 1935 Lepke had muscled his way into the ring and quickly enlarged its scope. In return he kept better than a third of the profits. The trick of course was to bribe the customs officials, a complicated scheme in itself. Between December 1935 and February 1937, so federal narcotics agents estimated, the outfit smuggled 665 kilograms (1,465 pounds) of heroin into New York City from Tientsin, China, via Marseilles. The amount was worth millions by the time it was cut in the ring's own Bronx processing factory and sold to distributors and street gangs.

What Lepke also learned was that as soon as the federal government was done with him it would give him over to Thomas E. Dewey who, flattered by fresh court victories, was now openly seeking the Republican presidential nomination. If, that is, he could get the public's complete attention. Lepke was making splendid copy, appearing daily on the front pages of the newspapers. But other events were reducing the great gangster to size. Lepke had surrendered a few days after the Hitler-Stalin pact had been signed, therefore a few days before the German army invaded Poland and thus ushered in World War II. Domestic affairs suddenly seemed trivial, though criminals like Lepke continued to fascinate the public and continued to win their share of space on the front page. Stories about them, however, were growing less significant in the nature of things, and Dewey could no longer hope to capitalize on them quite so advantageously as before. Still, Lepke was invaluable to him.

The federal narcotics trial of Lepke and accomplices (Max Schmuckler, Morris Sweden, David Kardonick) took place in December 1939. It was open and shut, Yashe Katzenberg—who was behind bars on another rap—and lesser culprits admitting everything. The jury easily convicted the defendants and Lepke received fourteen years, these in addition to the several he owed the federal government for breaking bail.

The moment Lepke was sentenced Dewey took possession of him and hustled him over to the state court a block away to be tried, along with his satrap Max Silverman, president of the Flour Truck-men's Association, for racketeering in the baking industry. (He was not charged with ordering the local's ex-president William Snyder murdered back in 1934 because that was too difficult to prove.) Dew-ey had little trouble establishing Lepke's guilt, especially since the union officials were willing to testify in exchange for immunity, lay-ing the full obloquy on the two defendants. Wolfie Goldis, the boss who had replaced Snyder, was a star witness. ("You're a dirty rat," Lepke stood up and shouted—an uncharacteristic loss of cool for him—when Dewey triumphantly brought Wolfie into court.) So was Samuel Schorr, the business agent. Testifying too was Max Rubin, who among other things told of how Lepke had befriended leading Tammany politicians, how he had then negotiated in his behalf with recalcitrant employers. Especially interesting were the confessions wrung from the owners of the region's largest bakeries: Gottfried's, Levy's, Fink's, California Pies, Rockwell's, Dugan's. And while they all blamed Lepke for beating and blasting them into submission they omitted to say how much they may have gained from the protectives he maintained and from the sweetheart contracts Teamster Local 138 signed with them. At any rate, Lepke was found guilty in due course and received yet another thirty years (Silverman received twenty to thirty), these to begin after he had served his federal terms.

But Providence was not through with him; the worst blows, all unanticipated, were yet to fall.

While Lepke was being tried by Dewey a scarcely noticed item ap-peared in New York newspapers. On February 2, 1940, Brooklyn po-lice arrested three gangsters, Kid Twist Reles, Bugsy Goldstein, and Anthony "the Duke" Maffetore, for allegedly murdering a petty hoodlum named Alexander "Red" Alpert more than six years before. This arrest, which was to ramify so widely, was itself the culmina-tion of a whole history.

The Brooklyn district attorney who ordered their arrest, William D. O'Dwyer, represented Tammany's best hope of a smashing come-back after its long years of exile and disgrace. He justified that hope. O'Dwyer had emigrated from Ireland as a lad and had been a policeman, a lawyer, and a judge before being elected Brooklyn district attorney. He was a man of infinite charm and a demonstrated vote-getter in the most populous of the city's boroughs. Who better than he to challenge the invincible Mayor Fiorello LaGuardia in the next election? And so in the early months of 1940, immediately after taking over the scandal-filled office of Brooklyn district attorney—probably no office in the land was more corrupt—O'Dwyer announced that he would crack down on the criminals of Williamsburg, Ocean-hill-Brownsville, and East New York. This he did in the most loudly publicized way possible. Acting under the extremely broad provisions of a temporary vagrancy law, police descended on the neighborhoods, picking up hundreds of suspected "hoods" (the official term used) who "hung out" in candy stores, poolrooms, bars, and street corners and threw them in jail for up to three months. O'Dwyer came across as a fierce law-and-order man who, regardless of cost and constitutional niceties, would wrest Brooklyn from the gangsters much as Dewey wrested Manhattan from them.

One day while this well-advertised campaign was going ahead full force, O'Dwyer's office received a letter from a Riker's Island prisoner, Harry Rudolph by name. "I am doing a bit here," he wrote. "I would like to talk to the District Attorney. I know something about a murder in East New York." Rudolph was referring to the murder of his friend Red Alpert. And even though Rudolph was a notoriously unreliable fellow whose testimony would never stand up in court his lone accusation enabled O'Dwyer to put the three gangsters whom Rudolph named, Reles, Goldstein, and Maffetore, behind bars for a while.

How surprised and delighted O'Dwyer was therefore when Duke Maffetore began to sing. Obviously Maffetore had no idea how flimsy the evidence against him and the others was. Hoping to save his skin he implicated all of his Murder Inc. associates. One of them, Pretty Levine, an awesome killer, promptly confessed as well. Soon Happy Maione, Pittsburgh Phil Strauss, and Frank the Dasher Abbendado were arrested. Finally, with the heavens collapsing all around him, Abe Kid Twist Reles succumbed.

Reles was an especially valuable catch because he ranked highest in Murder Inc.'s chain of command: he (and Maione) had been in constant touch with the gang/syndicates above them. Reles knew more than anyone else. And what was more, he possessed a superhuman memory, photographic in its precision, and an equally remarkable facility with words. He was the perfect "stool pigeon" or "canary." His pregnant wife, we are told, extracted a promise from O'Dwyer to treat Reles leniently—indeed to exonerate him altogether—if he spoke the whole truth and agreed to testify in all subsequent trials. Reles' confession filled thousands of pages, solved or cleared up or explained countless murders—the Shapiro brothers', the Amberg brothers', Lepke's confederates', and many, many others—and sent the police scurrying in every direction to dig up bodies and arrest still more members of Murder Inc. With the result that one more "stoolie" came forward, the dread assassin Allie Tick Tock Tannenbaum, who also had quite a story to tell and who also received immunity.

Everything Reles, Levine, Tannenbaum, and the others said immediately became public knowledge, and District Attorney O'Dwyer became the hero of the moment, eclipsing even Dewey for the time being, making him a potent threat indeed in the mayoral election to come. The more so after he began sending the killers to the chair, a host of them, in one show trial after another: Strauss, Goldstein, Maione, Levine, Maffetore (hard as they tried these last two could not save themselves), Nitzberg, and Abbendado. O'Dwyer was making good his promise; he was wiping out Murder Inc., the immensity and brutality of whose crimes strained the nation's credulity. What prosecutor anywhere could boast of such a record? What more convincing proof could one find that he represented a new breed of Democratic politician, as clean and straight and trustworthy as his Republican opponent across the river?

We have, by the way, Reles and Tannenbaum to thank for clearing up the Dutch Schultz matter. On the strength of the evidence or leads they furnished, a New Jersey court tried Bugs Workman in June 1941. (Mendy Weiss was then on the lam, hiding out in Kansas City where he posed as an executive of a mining company.) When his alibi failed Workman threw himself on the mercy of the court and was given a life sentence.

The truly sensational news O'Dwyer kept for last, for the coping stone of his achievement. In early April 1941 he announced that he was indicting Lepke, Mendy Weiss (who had just been apprehended),

Louis Capone, and Philip "Little Farfel" Cohen for the murder of Joseph Rosen in his Brownsville candy store on the night of September 13, 1936—Lepke for having ordered it, Weiss and two other hit men (Pittsburgh Phil Strauss and one James Ferraco), both deceased, for having carried it out, Capone and Cohen for having assisted in their separate and subordinate capacities. With great fanfare O'Dwyer personally traveled to Washington to arrange Lepke's transfer to Brooklyn, the completion of which was itself a public event. Lepke's appearance in court produced bedlam; the room was jammed with reporters, officials, and policemen, scores of them lining the walls and occupying the front seats and forming an impenetrable cordon around the villain, the putative mastermind of Murder Inc., his lawyers, his wife and brother. ("This is ridiculous," the judge shouted to O'Dwyer. "Why don't you send for a company of Marines?") But not until the summer did the trial get under way. By then O'Dwyer had removed himself from the case because, as expected, he was running for mayor.

Meanwhile, dominating the headlines, was the approaching apocalypse. Hitler's Wehrmacht was smashing deep into the Soviet Union and from all signs would soon win its greatest victory; his empire, unprecedented in history, would extend from the English Channel to the Siberian steppes, from the Baltic to the Black seas. And on the other side of the world Japan was advancing across Southeast Asia; it was only a question of time before the United States would be at war. Yet Lepke's trial captured its fair share of public attention. The recitation of his escapades seemed to bring Americans— certainly New Yorkers—back to the scenes of a less troubled era, to a time when the public had actually been concerned about racketeering and gang warfare and political corruption. The three-month trial—which ended on the eve of Pearl Harbor—can be said to have provided a respite, a piece of nostalgia. In that sense the outcome scarcely mattered to Lepke and his loved ones. He was hors de combat whatever the verdict, condemned either to remain in jail for the rest of his life or die at the hands of the state executioner. His trial provided an occasion for reviewing the blithely innocent past.

The prosecution's case was very fragile. Since there were no witnesses to the murder (Weiss would not confess and the other gunmen had gone to their reward), the evidence necessarily had to rest either on inference or on the testimony of highly tainted participants in the act, chief among them Sholem Bernstein, the wheel man, who, like Reles and Tannenbaum, had been singing steadily in one trial after another, but unlike them was an inveterate liar. Reles and Tannenbaum also testified that Lepke had ordered Rosen's death and that Weiss had pulled the trigger, but they had neither taken part in the crime nor witnessed it; their corroboration therefore meant little. More damaging evidence came from Paul Berger, a member of the "L and G" organization, who claimed that Lepke got him to point out Rosen to Weiss two days before the shooting. Yet one could not exactly regard Berger as a reliable witness either: he had turned state's evidence only after he himself was indicted for the murder. Louis Capone's offense was to lay out the escape route for Sholem Bernstein. Little Farfel Cohen was separated from the case for technical reasons.

Everything, then, turned on motive—on why anyone would want Joseph Rosen, candy-store proprietor, slain. The absence of an intelligible motive was Lepke's primary defense, his lawyers arguing (he did not testify) that the lowly penurious Rosen meant nothing to a man like Lepke and could not conceivably have been a threat to Lepke's well-being. The prosecution on the contrary sought to establish the connection between the two men: between the onetime owner of a delivery truck that served runaway clothing manufacturers and the gang boss who was attempting to force those runaways into line, for the benefit both of the union and the manufacturers. Rosen was a casualty of Lepke's expanding operation. This uncovering of motive led to a fascinating inquiry into racketeering in general, into Lepke's relation to the men's clothing industry in particular. Here Max Rubin, who had been shot in the head in 1937, and the renegade Paul Berger were indispensable sources of knowledge, each having been an insider, Rubin as business agent of the Clothing Drivers and Helpers Union (one of his many hats), Berger as Lepke's trusted intermediary between the employer protectives and the Amalgamated Clothing Workers. Their testimony revealed how vulnerable Lepke was even to a minor and transient figure like Rosen. For Rosen had the power to name others, ultimately to unravel the whole skein. Why else did the big man go to such lengths to mollify Rosen, offering this "nobody" jobs, handouts, trips abroad, anything to keep him quiet? By thus placing the murder in its larger criminal context their testimony clinched the case for the state. With the motive established beyond doubt, the burden fell inexorably on Lepke and the defendants to prove their innocence, an impossible task no matter how many contradictions and ambiguities and mendacities their lawyers brought out. A reader of the trial is bound to conclude that Lepke went to the chair because he was Lepke. And because his fellow defendants were associated with him, or associated with his associates, they had to go too.

Not that he and they had any kicks coming. By their code of ethics society would have been justified to stand them against a wall and shoot them. To them due process was nothing more than an aspect of the tooth-and-claw game of life itself, another piece of hypocrisy. They recognized no exceptions to the law of the jungle, in court and out. Their enemies had beaten them and that was that.

The trial was interrupted by an astonishing occurrence, the strange death of Abe Kid Twist Reles. That event has been mired in controversy to this day. Most writers on organized crime assume that he was the victim of a conspiracy. The profusion of coincidences easily lend themselves to such an assumption. Reles was staying in a suite on the ninth floor of the Half-Moon Hotel in Coney Island. He was guarded twenty-four hours a day by a contingent of detectives specially assigned to District Attorney O'Dwyer under the supervision of Captain Frank Bals. Their charge of course was never to let Reles out of their sight, not even for an instant. According to the official account, the six detectives on duty in the early morning of November 12, 1941, happened to be asleep, all of them. They therefore could not have known that Reles, seeing his opportunity for escape, had tied several bedsheets together and climbed out of his bedroom window. While he was lowering himself to the windows below the sheets separated and he fell to the parapet six stories below. That was the official version. (For their dereliction the six officers were demoted, hardly the worst of punishments.)

There was naturally a tremendous outcry, the official story being taken as an insult to the public's intelligence. The obvious questions were raised. If all the detectives were asleep—itself an incredible coincidence—why was at least one of them not in Reles' bedroom? After all, Tannenbaum and Bernstein, the other kept witnesses, attested to the fact that the police guarding them were never absent from their bedrooms. If Reles wished to escape in this way why was he found so far from the wall—a full eight to sixteen feet away? This suggests that he either jumped or was thrown out of the window. But if he jumped—if he wanted to commit suicide—why would he have bothered with the sheets? If it was murder, who did it? Was it the detectives? Indeed, why not the detectives since they perhaps feared that Reles would eventually go after them? He seemed to know of every payoff, every collusive act in his neighborhood between the gangsters and the police. (Hence the saying that made the rounds even before he died: "This bird can sing but he can't fly."*) Lucky Luciano, at least, has no doubt that the detectives did it, Captain Bals, he claims, having received $50,000 for the defenestration. "The way I heard it was that Bals stood there in the room and supervised the whole thing. Reles was sleepin' and one of the cops gave a tap with the billy and knocked him out. Then they picked him up and heaved him out the window."

Bals had his own theory. Reles, he maintained, wanted to trick his guardians by lowering himself to the next apartment down, coming back up the stairs and appearing at the front door. It was all for laughs. Bals advanced this astonishing explanation in 1951 before a Senate committee investigating organized crime. The senators dismissed it with the contempt it deserved, and they even came to regard Bals as a hostile witness. One of the senators, Charles Tobey of New Hampshire, could take it no longer and, speaking for the rest of the committee, told Bals: "The whole thing, from the standpoint of the citizen and the country, as well as New York, is a tawdry mess, smells under heaven; and I don't believe that honest truth has ever been told about it; probably won't be until the day of judgment. Why, it's ridiculous. Six policemen going to sleep at the same time and you in charge of them. Why, it's ridiculous. O. Henry in all his wonderful moments never conceived of such a wonderful silly story as this."

---

* After the event another saying took its place: "The only law that got him was Newton's law of gravity."

w

With Lepke's conviction and Reles' death the epoch that began with Dewey's investigation of the industrial rackets came to a close. The district attorneys carried everything before them. O'Dwyer could claim that he destroyed Murder Inc. and brought the most infamous gangster of the age to heel. For his labors a grateful city would present him with the cynosure of his ambitions, the mayor's office (though not until 1945). And Dewey, the darling of the Republican Party, became governor of New York by a landslide in 1942. The boy prosecutor from Owosso, who owed so much to the big city's pullulating ethnic underworld, the very Babylon of his youth, now commanded the future if anyone in America did. From Waxey Gordon to the White House was a stupendous leap, but he was on the verge of accomplishing it.

Lepke himself refused, or was not permitted, to withdraw into obscurity and there await his extinction. His life dragged on and on like an interminable epilogue which keeps reminding the audience of the play they have just seen.

It was not until October 30, 1942, that the seven-member State Court of Appeals handed down its decision. And an extraordinary one it was. Three of the judges concluded that while the state's evidence and the behavior of the prosecutor and presiding judge left a good deal to be desired, the trial had been fair and the conviction should stand. Two other judges found the conduct of the trial outrageous and favored giving the defendants "a fair chance to defend their lives before another jury." A sixth judge wanted to go further. He thought the trial "so grossly unfair as to leave the defendants without even a remote outside chance of any free consideration by the jury of their defenses, so unfair in fact as utterly to render without force the presumption of innocence to which every person charged with a criminal offense is entitled until his guilt is established beyond reasonable doubt," and he favored throwing out the case altogether. The swing vote was cast by Chief Judge Lehman (the governor's brother).

Lehman's views were odd, to say the least. They amounted to this: yes, the trial was poorly conducted; all the damaging testimony had come from "degraded criminals whose credibility [was] impeached, if not completely destroyed, by the cross-examination, in which they admitted a callous disregard of every law, human and divine," and, like the defendants, they too belonged to a "gang engaged in criminal practices nefarious even beyond the imagination of any fiction writer unless he had the genius of a Balzac"; and the jury's verdict was wrong, too, so wrong "I might have been unwilling, if I had been a member . . . to concur in it." These errors notwithstanding, Lehman concluded, "the conviction should stand, the sentences be carried out." One senses from Judge Lehman's muddled and vacillating opinion that the prospect of giving Lepke and the others a second chance, or, worse, exonerating them outright, was simply unthinkable, that procedural standards had to yield to larger considerations of the public good. Practical reality then, not scrupulous adherence to law, sealed Lepke's fate.

But the epilogue, instead of ending then and there, went on to assume a drama of its own. Political exigencies explain why. When Dewey was elected governor (in the same week that the Court of Appeals reached its decision) he instantly became an adversary of the Roosevelt administration which, quite obviously, he wished to replace with his own two years later. Lepke was a pawn in that emergent struggle for power.

As soon as all appeals had been exhausted Dewey publicly demanded that President Roosevelt turn Lepke over to the State of New York, Lepke being still under federal jurisdiction with many years left on his narcotics rap. The governor even accused the President of wanting the gangster to remain under federal lock and key and thus out of further harm's way. Why was Roosevelt reluctant to give up Lepke? Did he and the Democrats have something to fear? These and other such questions were implied in Dewey's demand.

"It is surprising to me that you should choose to communicate with the President or with me on this important matter through the medium of the press," responded the U.S. Attorney General, Francis K. Biddle, in an open letter to Dewey (thereby also communicating through the medium of the press). Biddle promised that Lepke would be transferred at once if Dewey could assure the President that he, Dewey, was "ready to carry out the death sentence." It was a subtle riposte. Suppose, Biddle was saying in effect, Lepke somehow escaped the sentence: how, then, would the federal government get him back? Dewey's reply was just as shrewd. He would give no assurances. His demand for the killer was unconditional. "The Governor may not bind his conscience or limit the exercise of his duty." If the President chose to keep—that is, to protect—Lepke he alone must bear the responsibility for it.

It was apparent that Dewey was winning this conflict of the missives, this skirmish for public opinion, and that the longer it continued the more suspicions it would arouse, all of them redounding to Dewey's advantage. By now Roosevelt had cause to fear Dewey, so refreshingly young (barely forty) and clean, such a prodigious vote-getter. It was generally assumed that he would be Roosevelt's opponent in the coming election, the toughest one yet for the old campaigner by all accounts. So, unwilling to let the sordid and embarrassing affair drag on any longer, Roosevelt ordered Lepke sent to New York state without conditions, to be disposed of as Dewey saw fit.

Dewey's strategy was precisely to let it drag on and on. He granted Lepke, and his partners Weiss and Capone, one reprieve from execution after another. Dewey's hope was that Lepke would sing in return for a commutation of his sentence, or something even better. And what a song Lepke could have sung! He would have been the greatest apostate in the history of American crime. Who among his compatriots at the summit of gangsterdom would have been safe? Few indeed. But Dewey was not primarily interested in this sort of confession. Dewey was after much larger game. Now that he was governor, not prosecutor, what he sought from Lepke was an exposé of the Amalgamated Clothing Workers of America, specifically of its president, Sidney Hillman. In the first place, Hillman was a powerful member of Roosevelt's wartime administration and inner political circle. And secondly, Hillman symbolized the role that unions in general had come to play in the government—and in the Democratic Party, a role, according to Dewey, that was far too influential for the nation's good. This was standard Republican rhetoric. But if, in addition, Dewey could establish a link between Hillman, and perhaps other union leaders as well, and Lepke the industrial racketeer and murderer, than he would have his issue, at the very least *an* issue, in the 1944 election. That issue, the linkage of crime with Democratic politics, he had brilliantly parlayed so far. Why not parlay it once more, now that all the chips were on the table, with Lepke again as his winning suit?

Whether in fact Lepke could have brought down Hillman and hurt Roosevelt badly, even enabling Dewey to win, the world will never know because Lepke refused to say a single word about anyone. Why he refused is conjectural too. At bottom, he might have refused for no other reason than pride and character—his commitment to the one moral truth of his life, the one that distinguished him from the canaille of his profession, the likes of Reles and Tannenbaum, namely his solidarity with his comrades of the gang/syndicates, the very solidarity they had shown him in his hour of need.

Lepke's last days on earth were a well-publicized charade. Rumors kept cropping up that he was softening, that he was asking to see important people, that a sensational break was about to occur. And indeed he did see important people, among them New York District Attorney Hogan (who had replaced Dewey in that office) and his staff. They spent several hours together, Lepke talking freely about numerous things, appearing to be cooperative. He said nothing of value. "Lepke," said Hogan, "knew what he was doing every minute, even though he was two days away from the electric chair.... He knew just how far to go—and we knew pretty fast that we weren't going to get anywhere with him." Hillman's—and David Dubinsky's—name did come up in the conversation, but Lepke claimed that he hardly knew them or anything about them. In the words of Hogan's assistant: "I got the impression that we were talking to a man who was utterly desperate and frantically trying to save himself but at the same time would only tell us things we already knew."

Always the statesman or "judge," Lepke demanded that the execution be postponed while a special commission investigated the whole case. This was the burden of his final message to the world, issued by his wife the day before his execution. Not the world at large so much as *his* world, the gang/syndicate underworld, his comrades and friends in particular. It was to them that he addressed his comforting statement, his assurance that they had nothing to fear on his account, that he was still the same old Lepke, that so far as they were concerned he was already a corpse. "I am anxious to have it clearly understood that I did not offer to talk and give information in exchange for any promise of a commutation of my death sentence." *Perinde ac cadaver.*

There was nothing for the authorities to do then but carry out the dread consummatory act. On the night of March 4, 1944, before a blue-ribbon audience gathered in Sing Sing's famous death chamber, the three men, Capone, Weiss, and Lepke, were in that order successively ushered in, strapped to the surreal chair standing in the middle of the room, and electrocuted, the entire ritual lasting no longer than three or four minutes for each of them. Only Weiss interrupted it to say his piece: "I am here on a framed-up case and Governor Dewey knows it. I want to thank Judge Lehman. [Obviously an ironic thrust.] He knows me because I am a Jew. Give my love to my family and everything." Lepke as ever showed not a trace of emotion or humility, though according to one reporter he lacked the "calm disdain" of old, the "cocksureness that amounted to impudence" as he went to his doom, the rabbi's prayers ringing in his ears. The detailed account of the executions that filled the newspapers gave the public a last glimpse into the uncomplicated past, an age that had long since expired.

Lepke lived long enough to witness the collapse of his empire. Many of his associates, those who persisted in their gangsterism, gravitated toward other regions of power, serving other criminal masters such as Thomas Lucchese and Johnny Dio and Jimmy Hoffa and his underworld friends in and out of the Teamsters Union. The rest held on to their positions in painting, baking, trucking and garments, and simply grew old in them. If they went straight it was because they were left alone; salutary neglect had saved them. Gurrah was again tried, in the summer of 1943, and convicted of racketeering and extortion in men's clothing, the testimony laying bare once again, though reported now in the back pages of newspapers, the whole mammoth system of protectives, gangster-run locals, and sweetheart agreements that the two men had wrought so carefully over the years; this time he was given another long stretch—in effect a death sentence. Gone by then was the last vestige of a legacy. Even that had been taken from them.*

As expected, Dewey easily won the 1944 Republican nomination. And while he lost the election—Americans were not about to "change horses in midstream" and throw off their great leader—Dewey put up a better fight against Roosevelt than any previous Republican had. Nothing therefore prevented him from running again four years later, Roosevelt having died only months after his fourth inauguration. The Democratic Party in general appeared more vulnerable now than at any time since the start of the Great Depression.

President Harry S. Truman was deeply unpopular, so unpopular that it seemed for a while his fellow Democrats might even refuse to nominate him. If anything was certain in American politics, as the 1948 campaign got under way, it was Thomas E. Dewey's prospective triumph. But Providence turned a wrathful face toward the young governor (though all of forty-five he looked no different than when he had prosecuted Waxey Gordon a millennium before), and delivered the most astonishing upset in American history. The voters palpably disliked what they saw of candidate Dewey, preferring the combative little man from Missouri, with all his faults, or precisely because of them. Lepke's shade, wherever it was, in whatever circle of damnation it resided, must have smiled sardonically.

---

* While Lepke languished in jail the motion-picture racket, which he was so instrumental in creating, fell apart also. Its downfall began modestly when the Screen Actors' Guild exposed the International Alliance of Theater and Stage Employees for what it was; it exposed, that is, the illicit affair between IATSE's boss, Willie Bioff, and the movie moguls, notably Joseph Schenck. Treasury agents picked up the lead and got Schenck (by prosecuting him for tax fraud) into admitting everything. Bioff and Browne, nominal president of IATSE, went to jail following a celebrated trial in New York City. Unwilling in the end to take the rap, Browne and Bioff later admitted everything too, revealing in finely spun detail how they became the mere creatures of the Capone mob, how the money they extorted from the studios was passed on to their superiors. Capone's heirs, to make a long story short, found themselves behind bars soon after; and one of them, Frank the Enforcer Nitti, committed suicide rather than serve more time. But thanks to a scandalously indulgent federal judge they served only a few years of their ten-year sentences. Nor was this the end of it. Many years later Bioff's enemies discovered his whereabouts—he had made a new life for himself in Arizona as a businessman (he was an acquaintance of Barry Goldwater, among others)—and blew him to smithereens. Browne lived out the rest of his days in peace.

SIX

THE WORLDS OF
MEYER LANSKY

i

October 24, 1918, had been a typical day in the life of young Meyer Lansky. He had spent most of it working in the tool-and-die shop near his Lower East Side home and now toward evening was walking home through familiar streets. He heard screams coming from an abandoned tenement house. The good Samaritan, crowbar in hand, found his way to the apartment where the cries had come from. He flung open the door and beheld a violent little drama in progress: a woman was lying on the floor, her face bloodied, while a young man chased a boy around the room. Without a second's hesitation Lansky leaped into the fray and brought the crowbar down on the young man's head. As he did so, the police arrived and arrested everyone.

At the Fifth Street station house the police pieced together the following story. The young man, Salvatore Lucania, resident of Little Italy (and notorious years later as Lucky Luciano), had caught his girl making love in the empty apartment with the lad, Benjamin Siegel, resident of Williamsburg, Brooklyn, and was taking revenge on both when Lansky burst in on them. The police pressed charges against Lansky: his was the only crime they had witnessed. But thanks to Siegel's testimony Lansky was let off by the kindly judge with a two-dollar fine and an admonition to behave himself.

That event, trivial in itself, assumes importance in retrospect because it brought Meyer Lansky and Benjamin Siegel (and also Lucky

Luciano) together for the first time. It marked the beginning of one of the exceptional friendships in American crime, the only one comparable to it in the chronicles of the Jewish underworld being Lepke and Gurrah's. But unlike Lepke and Gurrah, Lansky and Siegel—aged sixteen and twelve respectively—were not yet criminals.

Lansky had not yet made up his mind what to be; the struggle for his soul was still going on. So far as his parents, the Luchowljanskys, were concerned, he was still Maier, the boy they had brought to America from Grodno, Poland, in 1911 with their two younger children, the boy who had done well in public school and was now taking up a trade, preparing for an honorable and secure future. If there was a darker side to this Lower East Side youth, if, despite his size (never more than five feet four and one-half inches), he was as tough as any kid in the vicinity or in any of the street gangs to which he belonged, if he was attracted to the underworld culture that flourished everywhere and even to the high-stepping vice lords and gangsters who shamelessly flaunted their success, if their Maier had such inclinations—and how many boys his age did not also have them?—he would surely overcome them, and indeed was overcoming them, as witness his commitment to tool-and-die making. His parents obviously could not have realized how easily he would yield to those darker inclinations. They could not have known that in Benjamin Siegel he had found the stimulus he needed to set him on the course of criminality.

Siegel seems to have needed less stimulus, to have already—by twelve!—traveled far on the path of delinquency, to have had a fairly good idea of what to do with his life. His neighborhood, situated on the Brooklyn side of the East River and not without its own savageries, was too limited to contain his vast ambitions. And Siegel by then may already have acquired the nickname that galled him to the end of his days, Bugsy, which he despised and which one called him to his face at one's peril, meaning "bold" and "intrepid" and "wildly unpredictable." And so, from this adventitious discovery of each other, emerged the team of Bugs and Meyer. Something immense was born in the realm of gangsterdom.

They became professional in the time-honored way, engaging in such illicit neighborhood practices as gambling, purveying contraband goods, stealing, renting out and chauffeuring getaway cars, schlamming. Yet as far as we know they never joined the gangs that presided over the Lower East Side streets, neither Kid Dropper's nor Little Augie's nor any of the lesser ones, though they may have worked for them at some time or other. Even as youths Lansky and Siegel were exhibiting, for anyone who cared to notice, the independence that would distinguish them in the years ahead.

Even so they would probably have gone straight sooner or later (and posterity would have heard no more of them) as had multitudes of young Lower East Side criminals before them, but for the maleficent *deus ex machina* which entered their lives at that critical instant, just as they were passing from adolescence to manhood. It was Prohibition that brought out their criminal talents so egregiously, that justified and rewarded them so fulsomely.

We will recall how those talents flowered during the 1920s—how both young men started out as shotgun riders, specialists in the dangerous occupation of transporting booze; how, prospering steadily, they created a formidable little gang of their own; how they allied with young Italian gangsters, Frank Costello and Joe Adonis but chiefly Lucky Luciano (who held no grudges and admired these brave, resourceful Jews), all eager like themselves to break down the ethnic and religious constraints imposed by the old-world ghetto mentality of their forebears and by many of their contemporaries as well, specifically the Mustache Petes; how, ascending to wholesale bootleg status, Bugs and Meyer were admitted into the newly formed community of gang/syndicates that was attempting to regulate alcohol traffic in the regional arc embracing the Great Lakes and Atlantic Coast states and, more generally, to nurture the delicate art of cooperation and mutual assistance; how they helped Luciano and the other young Mafia Turks wipe out the leading Mustache Petes, in particular Masseria and Maranzano and their henchmen, thus hastening the triumph of the gang/syndicate community and everything it represented. Prohibition had been kind to Lansky and Siegel. It made them rich and respected; it gave them a place of honor among the hierophants of gangsterdom. And they were still very, very young.

The commonly held view is that Lansky was the brains, therefore the senior partner. It is an impression deduced mostly from the contrast in their personalities. Lansky was (and is) the very model of conventional virtue. Nightclubs and women and fancy clothes, the signs and baubles of success in the profession, attracted him hardly at all. He felt no need to compensate by swagger and ostentation and a brave display of power for his modest size and undistinguished looks. When not working he usually stayed at home with his wife and children. He kept his own counsel and spoke softly and to the point. He was the quintessential gangster-bourgeois.

Siegel was truer to type. Nicely built, ruggedly good-looking, by the cinematic standards of the day, and always nattily dressed, he unfailingly drew attention to himself wherever he went, whatever he did. He gambled heavily and was an insatiable womanizer despite his wife and children. He was impetuous and quick to take offense, passing easily from rage to violence. Now these personality differences, interesting in themselves and the source of much copy, should not deceive us. Both men were exceedingly smart and exceedingly ruthless, and their friends and co-workers knew better than to draw invidious distinctions between them. Their qualities of mind and character, not the superficialities of style and manner, accounted for the astonishing success of their joint enterprise.

The repeal of Prohibition in December 1933 (with the ratification of the Twenty-first Amendment) could not have come as a surprise to Lansky and Siegel and the rest of the bootlegging fraternity. The Democrats had made Repeal a cardinal issue of the 1932 presidential campaign, and Roosevelt's smashing victory had been the confirmation of its triumph. Bootleggers, then, had ample time to make the transition. Or so one would think. But then again how do people, practically speaking, prepare for such a disaster? For the loss of a livelihood, a trade, a universe of associations and hopes? What are they to do? Some bootleggers returned to the life of the streets, wearily trying to resume where they had left off thirteen years before. Others tried to go straight, no easy task for men in their thirties and forties seeking to breach the tightest job market in America's history and with no end of the malaise in sight.

Compared to them, Lansky and Siegel and the other gang/syndicate leaders and their lieutenants enjoyed certain competitive advantages. Their accumulated wealth, their connections, their muscle, enabled them to seize and enlarge on whatever opportunities were available. The richest of the gangsters, Zwillman, Nig Rosen, Dutch Schultz, the Purples of Detroit, the Four from Cleveland, King Solomon's men in Boston (though Solomon himself was rubbed out in 1934), Kid Cann's in Minneapolis, they and their Italian friends and allies moved with *force majeure* into a host of operations whose yield depended on the amount of capital they invested in them: slot machines, numbers (Dutch Schultz's success being paradigmatic), race tracks, gambling joints, the sale and/or manufacture of alcoholic beverages, and other perfectly legitimate businesses, these along with such familiar standbys as loan-sharking, racketeering, drug-selling, and strong-arming. The gang/syndicates demonstrated again, this time in the lean and cruel years of the 1930s, that the laws of capitalism applied as much to them as to the rest of America.

What interests the historian is the *difference* between Lansky and Siegel and their compatriots in high crime. Lansky and Siegel, it should be emphasized, had never been proprietors of a territory, a landed estate. The splendid shotgun-riding gang they had mustered in the 1920s had served other gangs and wholesalers of booze and had dissolved when it was no longer needed. So that from one point of view Repeal left them particularly vulnerable to the hurly-burly of chance: unlike the other bosses they could exploit no given area over which they were suzerains—as the Dutchman, say, could (until his demise) exploit the Bronx and Harlem, Kid Cann greater Minneapolis, Longy Zwillman all of northern New Jersey, the Cleveland Four Ohio and parts of Kentucky, King Solomon's epigone rural Massachusetts, and so forth. Yet from another point of view Lansky and Siegel could count themselves fortunate in having neither gang nor territory of their own, in being confined by no topographical and financial obligations. They were thus free to go wherever their destiny or fancy bore them, wherever the spirit of enterprise summoned them. This freedom explains why they came to play the role they did in the decades ahead, as the advance guard of the gang/syndicate community.

n

No one in America, it seems, was busier in the 1930s than Meyer Lansky, ambassador extraordinaire of organized crime. Here is a checklist of some of his endeavors at that time.

With a number of his colleagues, among them Bugsy Siegel, Frank Costello, and Joey Adonis, he owned shares in Capitol Wines and Spirits, a giant New York distributor. Everything was legal except the concealment of the investors' names. When their identities were finally revealed (in 1945) they sold out at a huge profit.

Lansky joined the Cleveland outfit—Dalitz, Tucker, Kleinman (who happened then to be in jail), Rothkopf, and the Polizzis—in building a series of distilleries strung across the northern tier of the country from Ohio to New Jersey, the largest illicit operation of its kind uncovered by revenue agents. It was titled the Moloska Corporation (for molasses, the substance it distilled), and among its front men was Lansky's father-in-law, Moses Citron, a wholesale produce dealer. The government eventually confiscated its assets, but not before it had sold millions upon millions of gallons of alcohol to American liquor manufacturers.

Lansky was instrumental in converting Hot Springs, Arkansas, from a venerable watering hole into an up-to-date casino gambling town—though it never lost its quaintness—and an ideal refuge for syndicate gangsters on the lam. Lansky's influence was less overt, less conspicuous than elsewhere, but it was no less important. The man who ran the Hot Springs affairs was Owney "the Killer" Madden, one of the few WASP syndicate chieftains, who for years, indeed ever since his murderously delinquent youth (when he was not in jail), had captained a powerful West Side Manhattan gang. What Lansky did was help finance the creation of an extravagantly appointed casino, the Southern Club, and further help to plan its amazingly successful career. Like Costello, Madden remained to his last breath (he died peacefully in old age) a loyal subaltern of the gang/syndicates.

Lansky was a partner in the enormously lucrative slot machine business that Frank Costello opened in New Orleans. How this came about is a complex and controversial matter. It deserves retelling.

Early in 1934, shortly after he took office, New York's Mayor Fiorello LaGuardia declared war to the knife against the gangsters, Luciano and Costello in particular. He conducted a magnificently publicized campaign against slot machines, many of them Costello's, destroying a goodly number of them in the process. (The papers were full of pictures of the mayor, sledgehammer in hand, standing over the fallen machines.) Within a year, though, Costello had managed to transfer a thousand of them—this for starters—to New Orleans, where they quickly became the rage, and had placed his sidekick, Philip "Dandy Phil" Kastel, a Lower East Side crook of ancient lineage, in charge of the operation.

In dispute are the circumstances under which the penetration of New Orleans was effected. In dispute, to be more precise, is the role that the great Huey P. Long played in the whole affair. Long, the "Kingfish," wielded such power over Louisiana—he had been governor and now was senator—as Tammany in its palmiest days would have envied. His ambitions were illimitable. That he would try to wrest the presidency from Franklin D. Roosevelt was a foregone conclusion; that he might succeed could not be dismissed—certainly Roosevelt did not—for he had a national following. Long, of course, needed money, lots of it, and he hardly scrupled over how or from whom he got it. So it was that he and Costello, united by common interests, struck up their extraordinary bargain: for granting permission to install the slots Long, as a first step, was to be paid an annual fee of thirty dollars for each machine.

Accounts differ mainly on how they met. According to one version Long, while visiting New York, "went into the powder room of one of them clubs . . . and somebody punched him in the mouth and Costello, that is one of Costello's friends, saved him from getting a beating, and he became very, very friendly with Costello." Messick informs us that the altercation took place in a toilet of the New Yorker Hotel, that Long, drunk as usual, had urinated on a gentleman who was in his way, that the gentleman happened to be Trigger Mike Coppola the infamous gangster, that Coppola promptly knocked the Kingfish to the floor and took his gun out for the coup de grâce (Long's bodyguards, who accompanied him everywhere, having scattered like chaff), but that Costello intervened just then to save his life. Another version claims that Long was caught in a New York hotel room in flagrante delicto and that Costello burned the prints in exchange for the slot machine rights. And yet another version—Costello's—has it that Long simply came to him, the biggest man in the business, with a straightforward offer he could not refuse.

All of these accounts Long's best biographer, T. Harry Williams, calls into question by pointing out that the Kingfish lacked the power even to make the deal, New Orleans being run at the time by his blood enemy, one Semnes Walmsley, that therefore there probably never had been anything between Long and Costello. But the question, persuasive on its face, does not hold up under examination. Williams neglects to say that the operation, under the name of the Pelican Novelty Company, was incorporated by the state legislature, which Long owned completely, as a legitimate or licensed form of gambling: some of its profits were earmarked for charity, the relief of widows and orphans and paupers. Obviously, there was nothing Semnes Walmsley could do about it; challenging a state law would have been an imprudent act, to say the least. Our own assumption is that the deal was consummated between the two men, though exactly by what means and under what terms remains in dispute.

How much did the Pelican Novelty Company contribute to the needy and destitute folk of Louisiana? By Costello's own admission a grand total in eleven years of $600. How much the gang/syndicates and the Long organization (the Kingfish was assassinated in September 1935) together took in is incalculable. What is clear is that Lansky, as the gang/syndicates' representative, kept a close watch on everything and saw to the proper distribution of the profits.

But above all there was Lansky's pioneering effort at the edge of the Southern rim. His bootlegging ventures as a shotgun rider and wholesale importer of booze had taken him to many places. One can assume that wherever he went he unobtrusively made friends and kept his eyes open, especially after it had become apparent that Prohibition was doomed. Lansky was always thinking ahead.

Florida was one such place. Despite the Depression sizable numbers of tourists continued to spend their money down there, in and around Miami in particular. Only one mobster of any standing laid claim to the territory, a New Yorker named Anthony "Little Augie

Pisano" Carfano. After several reconnoitering expeditions Lansky set up shop in Broward County, directly above Miami (which is in Dade County). If Little Augie objected to this intrusion—we are told he did—the gang/syndicates of course overruled him and at Lansky's request proclaimed all of Florida, including Carfano's very bailiwick, to be wide open. Lansky established, and had his brother Jake operate, "The Farm," a nightclub and casino prominently located on Hollandale Boulevard, Broward County's main thoroughfare; besides gaming tables, The Farm provided the sole source of racing data for local bookies, Carfano among them, this thanks to the peculiar relationship, already touched upon, between the gang/syndicates and Moses Annenberg, America's sole retailer of that data. Lansky also poured money into Florida's two race tracks, Tropical Park and Gulfstream, and into a dog track as well, the Hollywood Kennel Club. Before long, suffice it to say, a bevy of gangsters from New York, Cleveland, Chicago, Detroit, Philadelphia, and elsewhere (their names are entirely familiar to us) who held shares in these properties were visiting Florida regularly to see for themselves what Lansky had wrought in their behalf. It was the merest beginning of a great hegira.

Lansky's vision was large enough to also compass the best of America's good neighbors, the republic of Cuba. He had long been struck by Havana's beauty, its magnificent beaches and climate, its young prostitutes, its well-heeled American *colons*, its easy-going Latin ambience, and he had decided that here too was a vast potential, a fecund source of wealth. So, while buying molasses for his distillery plants, he took over the Hotel Nacional's plush gambling casino (too expensive for any but the richest Cubans) and acquired the lease to operate the Oriental race track. These Cuban endeavors were yielding no enormous returns. Not yet anyway. They were liens on the future, down payments on what he regarded as the solidest of investments.

At the very least Lansky demonstrated that these rural and foreign extremities, so far from the beaten path, offered ideal environments in which to conduct business. They offered long-term political stability, that elusive sine qua non of everything else. He effortlessly bought out Broward County's police chief, Sheriff Walter Clark, an amiable man who had quit being a butcher for politics, winning re-election every time he ran. The people obviously approved of an arrangement, however debauched, that brought in money and created jobs and lent excitement to their otherwise dull and humdrum lives. (Years later a Senate committee investigating organized crime asked Clark why he gave Lansky and the other gangsters completely free rein. Clark guessed it was because he was a "liberal," not an uptight Puritan, in his attitude toward innocent pleasures, and he went on to say that his liberality obviously reflected the will of his constituents. The committee also wanted to know how someone who never earned more than $3,500 a year, and with a family to support, could have become such a wealthy man. Sheriff Clark was less glib in answering that one.)

In Cuba, Lansky dealt with another kind of boss, ex-army sergeant Fulgencio Batista, who late in 1933, and with the help of the United States, made the law himself, giving the stamp of legitimacy to whatever he authorized. He and Lansky were the closest of friends. Catching the vision Lansky outlined, Batista would rent Havana to the American underworld, not at once but bit by bit and for as long as he could. In return Lansky and his associates would build up the tourist industry as only they knew how, and the whole island, from Batista to the humblest *campesino* (though in unequal measure), would enjoy the blessings of their largesse.

Such, then, was the range and diversity of Lansky's business activities of the 1930s. He more than anyone else grasped the emergent possibilities of gangster-capitalism. He advanced the ethic of rational self-interest, the ethic of community, beyond the stage it had reached in late Prohibition, when the gang/syndicates drew together and attempted to form cartels. That attempt arose as a self-protective device, as a means of guaranteeing to each gang/syndicate its share of the alcohol market; none was given what it already did not have, or had not won by main force. It was an attempt, in sum, to preserve the status quo. Now, in the 1930s, their task was to *acquire* markets for their surplus capital, to supply other illicit services to masses of people, and chief among these was gambling, gambling of all sorts, slot machines and numbers and bookmaking and race-track betting and casinos.

This new or second stage in the evolution of gangster-capitalism required a high degree of planning and self-regulation. The gang/syndicates had to police themselves, bringing into play all the arts of statesmanship they had learned. They had to decide, for example, how many points or percentages, say, in a given casino or track, each gangster or group of gangsters was entitled to have in a freshly opened territory. Such decisions required a good deal of tact, intelligence, command of the economics involved and, most important, a close kinship with the gang/syndicate leaders, the "old boy" network. Many gangster-statesmen possessed these virtues—Moe Dalitz, Frank Costello, Joey Adonis, Longy Zwillman come to mind—but none possessed them to quite the extent that Lansky did. None was as ubiquitous as he, his ubiquity being itself the measure of his status among his peers, the confidence and trust he inspired. He was everywhere at once, acting simultaneously in his interest and in the gang/syndicates', always seeking to maintain the balance between competition and cooperation, between individual greed and the well-being of the community.

There is no need to exaggerate Lansky's power in order to appreciate his importance. Some writers, none more blatantly than his biographer Hank Messick, would like us to believe that Lansky in the 1930s became the boss of bosses, or better yet—a more suitable image—chairman of the board of the "NCS" (National Crime Syndicate), that in his quiet relentless way he manipulated everyone. It would be closer to the truth to say, as mobster Vincent Teresa does in his recent confession, that Lansky performed his statesmanly function on sufferance, because his comrades allowed him to, because he brought them gifts from afar. Had he betrayed their trust, overstepped his limits, they would have removed him in a trice and replaced him with another statesman. Whether this other person would have been his equal is a subject on which we are unable to speculate, Lansky providing the only standard of excellence we have. What can be stated with reasonable certainty is this: with his brilliant understanding of gangster-capitalism and his preternatural shrewdness Lansky made himself increasingly useful to the gang/

syndicate community—indispensable would be a mite too strong—
and so came to hold a unique position of authority within it, one he
has held ever since.

Lansky unquestionably owed much of his success to his special
friendship with Lucky Luciano. It has been observed here how that
friendship ripened over the years, how each assisted the other at
critical intervals, none being more critical than the Castellammarese
War. That bloody conflict eventuated in Luciano's spectacular rise to
preeminence in the Italian-American underworld, at least in greater
New York. To be more exact, Luciano became first among equals in
the collegial system of governance that replaced the authoritarian
system which the Mustache Petes, embodying outmoded Sicilian values, had tried to retain. Closer ties to Jewish gangsters were among
the changes institutionalized by the new order, and no two men were
closer than Luciano and Lansky. Despite his far-flung interests, his
continental responsibilities, Lansky spent most of his time in New
York, within earshot of his Italian compatriots, Luciano above all,
without whose support he could have achieved nothing. And even
after he went to jail in 1936, Luciano remained first among equals.
An endless procession of colleagues, including of course Lansky,
made regular pilgrimages to Dannemora, the North Country's
walled fortress, keeping him abreast of events and receiving his
opinions or decisions—as though he were still holding forth at the
Waldorf-Astoria as Mr. Charles Ross.

How close they were may be judged from Lansky's role in
springing Luciano, a controversial issue to this day. Lansky's biographer contends that he was the prime mover because as always he
foresaw events. "Dewey put him in," Lansky is quoted as assuring
the gang/syndicates, "Dewey can get him out." Luciano contends
that *he* was the prime mover, the seer, the omnicompetent force who
directed everything. If the exaggerations and posturing are pared
away we are still left with the fact that Lansky did have a considerable part in the affair, as arranger or intermediary. Its broad outline,
if not its details, are well known.

The Second World War was the providential act which set everything in motion. New York was the single busiest port in America,
the one from which most merchant vessels and troopships departed
for Great Britain and elsewhere beyond the Atlantic. Security of

course greatly concerned the federal government, hundreds of men and millions of tons of material having been sunk just off the East Coast by Nazi U-boats, some of the loss being attributable to spies who had learned the sailing schedules along with other vital data. Now it was universally assumed that the Mafia controlled the International Longshoreman's Association of the Port of New York, and so the commanding officer of the Third Naval District concluded that the best way to improve security was to win the cooperation of the ILA. (It never occurred to the Navy to appeal directly to the patriotism of the longshoremen. There is an implied racism here: Italians equal Mafia.)

In the spring of 1942, the head of Naval intelligence operations for the Third District called on the New York District Attorney for help. The D.A. got in touch with Joseph "Socks" Lanza, boss of the Fulton Fish Market on the East River. Lanza, a tertiary figure in the gang/syndicate order, could not do very much and referred the government officials to Luciano. This they did through one of Luciano's lawyers in the 1936 trial, Moses Polakoff, who happened also to be Meyer Lansky's lawyer. It was Lansky who conveyed the government's message to Luciano, secured Luciano's agreement to do whatever he could in behalf of the war effort, and as Luciano's emissary worked closely with the ILA leaders. Luciano granted the government one more favor: he saw to it—again through Lansky—that his Sicilian Mafia *paisanos* lent the American and Allied expeditionary forces every assistance (quite valuable as it turned out) when they landed there in September 1943.

What Luciano demanded in return, or what promises were made to him, is unclear, at least from the written record. All the officials concerned—the district attorney, Governor Dewey, the Navy—later denied making any promises, consenting to any arrangement, though they naturally told Luciano that his contributions to the war effort would be taken into account when he appealed for clemency or parole. And despite Hank Messick's claim that the fix had been on all along, that Luciano's work was no more than a "gimmick" whereby "Dewey would be justified in freeing him"—despite this claim the evidence bears out Dewey's account in full. In 1945 Dewey handed Luciano's petition for release to the State Parole Board. The Board recommended that he be rewarded for his tremendous help in defeating the Axis powers and for his exemplary behavior in prison. Americans were euphoric in these last days of the war, full of gratitude to those who helped win it, and it was understandable that Dewey would accept the Board's recommendation and pardon even the most notorious of the men he himself had prosecuted. Certainly no one in authority disagreed with Dewey at the time.

The pardon was conditional. Luciano had to return to Italy and remain there for the rest of his life. And so when he left jail in January 1946 he was taken to a Brooklyn pier where a ship was waiting to whisk him away. But not before a splendid party was held at dockside, with only the most intimate of Luciano's comrades present, Lansky among them. He and the other gang/syndicate leaders assumed as a matter of course that the chief would soon be back, if not in the United States then at the very least in Cuba. For it was plain that his exile to Italy would stretch the leading string too thin, that so far as the exercise of his power was concerned he would have been better off in Dannemora, only a few hours from New York City. And sure enough—to conclude the Luciano saga—he did enter Cuba a year later, in February 1947, and with Lansky at his side set about gathering up the threads of his power.

Suddenly topflight criminals from all over the United States were arriving in Havana. The reason, according to the head of the Federal Narcotics Bureau, was that Luciano "had developed a full-fledged plan. . . . The Isle of Pines, south of Cuba, was to become the Monte Carlo of the Western hemisphere. Cuba was to be made the center of all international narcotics operations." This claim, even though it comes from such a high and worthy source, is vastly overblown, based as it is on conspiratorial inferences, nothing more. The grain of truth is that Havana was to be Luciano's headquarters for as long as necessary; his ultimate objective was to return to New York. At any rate, his presence in Havana was played up extensively in the American press and assumed scandalous dimensions, causing the State Department to inform the Cuban president that Luciano had to go at once. Reluctantly, the president complied and Luciano was deported again. He would never leave Italy after this and gradually his authority as *primus inter pares* in the Italian-American underworld withered away.

Messick quotes from a secret Narcotics Bureau memo sent by

one of its agents in Italy on December 4, 1951. "Lucky Luciano," the memo goes, "came to an understanding with Mafia elements in the U.S.A.," the burden of which was this: "If anyone in the U.S.A. interfered or muscled in on Lansky's activities Lucky Luciano would take appropriate strong actions from Italy." How Luciano would take such "appropriate strong actions from Italy" is unexplained. The memo accepts Luciano at his own valuation, a serious error. This does not mean that it lacks significance. Luciano, as we interpret the statement attributed to him, was entreating or advising his American comrades to leave Lansky alone so that he might go on serving as their statesman, bringing his well-tempered wisdom to their councils. Luciano was thinking not so much of Lansky's welfare as that of the community of gang/syndicates.*

World War II was Lansky's vindication. The economy was booming for the first time since the 1920s. People were earning more money than ever before, with little to spend it on apart from necessities (which were cheap, thanks to price controls). It was a situation made to order for the gambling impresarios, that is, for the gang/syndicates across the country but nowhere more so than on Florida's "Gold Coast," Lansky's satrapy embracing Dade and Broward counties. (Cuba was moribund in those years; only Americans on government business were permitted to go there.) The profits Lansky made during the war convinced him that something enormous was gestating in the American womb, a new America was in the offing, an America seeking hedonic release of every kind, hungering to spend and be entertained, an America which would insist on gambling in style, in the largest, most exquisite surroundings, in rococo palaces of consumption. This was the America he envisioned.

---

* Yet Messick tells us that Lansky did not hesitate to betray Luciano in Cuba—one more betrayal that Messick ascribes to the hero of his book. After "Lucky had received the pledges of allegiance from all ranking members of the Honored Society," Lansky "sent an informer to have a talk with a Federal Narcotics agent in Havana." Messick offers no corroboratory evidence for this extraordinary piece of treachery except to cite the statement by the Commissioner of Narcotics: "I had received a preliminary report through a Spanish-speaking agent I had sent to Havana." But nowhere in the commissioner's statement is there the intimation that this Spanish-speaking agent had spoken to one of Lansky's informers.

Its realization had to wait until the war ended. With labor and materials in short supply he could not enlarge his operations anywhere near the bounds of their possibilities. The expansion thus got under way in 1946. Within a year Lansky had under his thumb such lucrative "rug joints" as the Colonial Inn, the Green Acres, and the Club LaBoheme, along with interests in tracks and book-making parlors and real estate, huge amounts of the latter on the Gold Coast, soon to be the most desirable part of Florida. Not only were tourists now coming down by the millions every winter, spending money with profligate abandon—for the postwar boom continued unabated—but the gang/syndicate leaders, more and more of them, were buying homes and real estate of their own, settling as near as they could to the site of their investments. Kid Cann, his brothers and in-laws, Joey Adonis, Trigger Mike Coppola, Louis Rothkopf and Sam Tucker of the Cleveland gang, Nig Rosen and his Philadelphia allies, Joe Linsey and Hyman Abrams from Boston, representatives in fact from "practically all the large towns located east of the Mississippi River"—they, like Lansky, all became Floridians for at least part of the year. Under Lansky's tutelage the Gold Coast, with Greater Miami at its epicenter, was emerging as the provincial gangster capital of the United States.

The Gold Coast was wide open to insiders—members of the gang/syndicate community in good standing—but closed to outsiders. If an outsider dared poach on the sacred turf he was dealt with summarily. The Club LaBoheme affair is a savage illustration. In 1946 John "Big Jack" Letendre with a partner launched the Club, a plush casino in the heart of "Lanskyland." Letendre had money and connections: he was a prominent Rhode Island Republican who read the future as clearly as Lansky did and who wanted to exploit it too. He was offered a quarter of a million dollars in cash to sell his casino and leave at once. He refused. Weeks later Big Jack was gunned down near his Woonsocket, Rhode Island, home. The upshot: "when Club LaBoheme opened for the winter [1947] season Jake Lansky was running it . . . " After that no one else made Letendre's error.

There were lesser provincial capitals as well, all of them located in America's southern tier: Havana (about which more shortly); Hot Springs, managed by Owney Madden; New Orleans, or rather nearby Jefferson Parish where Costello and Kastel—and Lansky—now owned the Beverly Club, a very fancy casino; and Los Angeles and tiny Las Vegas, both handled by Bugsy Siegel. All were in the position to seize hold of the coming revolution, the pent-up desire of Americans to gamble. And all had one thing in common: Lansky's presence. He ensured that the revolution would benefit the community he represented, however remote he was from the fields of action.

One problem troubled Lansky above every other in this new world of crime over whose emergence he presided. It was especially vexing because it involved his oldest and best friend, his comrade-in-arms since youth—none other than Bugsy Siegel. And it was a problem that required immediate attention. Its genesis lay in the remarkable personality of Bugsy Siegel himself and in the turn his career had taken.

Siegel had always wanted to go to Hollywood, confection of his dreams or fantasies, perhaps to try his hand at acting, a wish we are told he never ceased to entertain. By 1933 he was there often, surveying the terrain, learning about the illicit opportunities that might be available to him. His guide and helper on these visits was George Raft, a rising star in the Hollywood firmament. Raft, who had once been something of a petty gangster, scarcely more than a hanger-on in Owney Madden's outfit, found himself at the beck and call of junketeering big-timers like Siegel. Though he had scant choice in the matter Raft used his role to good account. Being seen in their company was worth a ton of press releases: it enhanced his image as the actor who played himself—gangster parts being his genre—the man who was at least as tough off the screen as he was on it. (Could Jimmy Cagney or Paul Muni or Edward G. Robinson or Humphrey Bogart claim as much?) By 1936 Siegel had shaken New York's dust from his feet and had settled with his family in Hollywood, apparently for good.

Of course, while he was taking this step in his own behalf (the decision to go West being his alone*), he was also taking it on behalf

---

* The point deserves emphasis because some writers would have us believe that Siegel was dispatched to California on assignment as it were, every deed being explained by the omnipotence of the "National Gang Syndicate."

of the gang/syndicate community to which he belonged and on whose support he relied. Which meant that Southern California's gangsters, gamblers, underworld figures in general, chief among them Jack Dragna, would have to acknowledge Siegel's primacy, at the very least accommodate themselves to his presence, much as Little Augie Carfano had had to accommodate himself to Lansky's presence in Florida. There was little else they could do about it.

Siegel made his presence felt with a vengeance. He had a mansion built according to his specifications on one of Hollywood's fanciest streets. He joined the Hillcrest Country Club. He contributed bountifully to both local political parties. His two daughters went to the best private schools. He got Raft to introduce him to the Hollywood illuminati, from the moguls Jack Warner and Harry Cohn to such screen idols as Clark Gable, Jean Harlow, Cary Grant, Marlene Dietrich, Charles Boyer, and Fred Astaire, among others. Those who did not know him by reputation found this "sportsman" who had arrived from nowhere rather intriguing. Soon he was seeing them more and more intimately. That was because his mistress was one of Hollywood's most extravagant party-givers, the Countess Dorothy DiFrasso, wife of a penurious Italian aristocrat and daughter of Bertrand Taylor, whose huge fortune she had inherited.* She took Siegel under her care and made a minor celebrity of him. Her solicitude, we might add, hardly prevented him from having affairs with numerous other women, mainly aspiring young actresses. But concealed from the Hollywood tinsel world was Siegel's circle of business associates.

---

* Siegel's biographer Dean Jennings recounts an incident involving the Countess DiFrasso that might have earned Siegel a place, or at least a footnote, in world history. In the spring of 1938 the two lovers traveled abroad—he posing as a baronet—and ended up in her husband's family villa outside Rome. It happened that two of Hitler's closest henchmen, Joseph Goebbels and Hermann Goering, gangsters of an infinitely deadlier sort than Bugsy, were staying at the villa, part of which the Italian dictator Mussolini had requisitioned for their convenience. When Siegel learned who the other guests were he went into a paroxysm of rage and announced to Countess DiFrasso that he would kill the Nazi anti-Semites then and there. She, of course, dissuaded him from what would have been an act of suicide. Even if he had gone through with it nothing much would have changed; Goebbels and Goering would have been replaced by Nazi hierarchs equally murderous. But the thought of Siegel rubbing them out remains a delightfully tantalizing one.

They included several of the most vicious gangsters to be found anywhere—Mickey Cohen, a bandit of unusual depravity and cunning, and Frankie Carbo, who had not yet taken possession of the prizefight racket, to name only two. With their help and with the cooperation of Jack Dragna, Siegel cast his net wide, drawing in every mode of gambling from dog tracks to offshore yachting casinos, from numbers and bookie establishments to slot machines. How much Countess DiFrasso and the Hollywood crowd knew about the real Siegel, Bugsy, not Benjamin, is problematic. So long as he kept out of trouble he was safe. If anything, the sinister intimations and rumors that circulated behind his back whetted the prevailing interest in him, making his company more desirable.

One day in October 1939 Siegel learned through the underworld grapevine that Harry "Big Greenie" Greenberg, an old Lower East Side chum and one of Lepke's prize schlammers, was actually living in the neighborhood, or rather hiding out there. For, as Siegel knew, Big Greenie had crossed Lepke, that is, had threatened to see District Attorney Thomas E. Dewey about a few matters of racketeering, and ever since had been fleeing his Murder Inc. executioners. Siegel immediately informed his gang/syndicate comrades (Lansky, Zwillman, Anastasia, Adonis et al.) of the apostate's whereabouts. They decided that the death warrant still held. Siegel, who loved the *Sturm und Drang* of violence, the ineffaceable thrill of the hit—this despite his high gangland station—swung into action and on the night of November 22, 1939, with his associates slew Big Greenie Greenberg in traditional style.

That murder would have gone unsolved but for the dissolution of Murder Inc., more precisely the confessions of Kid Twist Reles and Tick Tock Tannenbaum, Reles in this instance having received and conveyed Lepke's original order, Tannenbaum having stalked his quarry from city to city and having accompanied Siegel and the others on the final mission. Their confessions enabled the Los Angeles grand jury to charge Siegel and several others with the murder.

Here then was sensational news indeed, the local press sparing none of the lurid details. Here was a prominent sportsman, a happy addition to Hollywood society, who turned out to have been a part of the conspiracy, coast to coast it now transpired, that included Lepke

Buchalter, until recently public enemy number one, and his team of Murder Inc. assassins—and who knew what other dreadful criminals? The real Siegel, Bugsy Siegel, was thus unmasked and paraded before the people of Southern California. Who among the Hollywood elect he had charmed at parties and race tracks and clubs had realized that this man was one of America's foremost gangsters?

But the affair in the end worked to Siegel's advantage because it demonstrated how much power and influence he commanded.* The original indictment in what seemed an open-and-shut case was thrown out because Brooklyn District Attorney O'Dwyer would not allow Reles and Tannenbaum to testify against Siegel in the upcoming trials; the songbirds, he claimed, were too precious to be let out of his sight even for a moment (though he had previously allowed them to appear before the Los Angeles grand jury). And a year later, after O'Dwyer did suddenly announce during his mayoral campaign that he would let them testify, and after the Los Angeles prosecutor did accordingly reindict Siegel (and Frankie Carbo) for the crime, Abe Reles was silenced by defenestration—while in O'Dwyer's custody, as we have already mentioned—a deed that finished the case for good, two witnesses being required under California law to substantiate a murder charge. On the face of it Siegel was simply the beneficiary of an astounding run of good luck. Insiders knew or assumed better: such a farrago of coincidences scarcely occurs in the lives of ordinary crooks but occurs all too often in the lives of gang/syndicate leaders.

By the time Siegel beat the rap the public had lost much of its interest in his putative misdeeds. For by then, February 1942, the war had broken out and the local folk had more important things to worry about: the possibility, for example, that Japan would attack them just as she had attacked Pearl Harbor a few months before (a worry which assumed psychotic dimensions and led to the removal and internment of California's entire Japanese-American population). Fa-

---

* "The searing publicity," Siegel's biographer observes, "inflicted no permanent damage and, as one could expect, it gave him an even more glamorous cloak in the movie colony." But the colony also learned to keep a healthy distance from him.

mous gangsters, whatever else might be said of them, were at least homegrown patriots, a comforting presence in the face of the threat from abroad, actual or fancied. So the heat was off Bugsy Siegel for the duration.

It is safe to assume that he was doing at least as well as any of his gang/syndicate associates, including his chum Lansky on the other side of the continent. No area of America burgeoned so spectacularly as Los Angeles and environs, Los Angeles itself being a clutch of suburbs, its population doubling and redoubling thanks to the military facilities and munitions and aircraft factories that mushroomed overnight. It was an environment in which Siegel and his mob thrived. His prosperity arose in the first place from the sheer scale of his operation, the number of tracks and casinos in which he held an interest and the myriad bookmaking joints whose lay-off bets he handled; and in the second place from the new venture on which he embarked, one that requires a bit of telling.

In 1939 Moses Annenberg, now an old man facing jail for tax fraud, had "walked away" from his racing news monopoly, the Trans-National, in effect leaving it in the hands of his assistant James Ragen, who renamed it the Continental Press. But the Capone gang had contested this arrangement and had set up its own rival organization, the Trans-American. A violent struggle for control of the wires ensued, in the course of which Ragen was assassinated. Siegel, who threw in his lot with the Capone mob, was Trans-American's west coast boss. Through his strong-armers, Mickey Cohen prominent among them, he saw to it that the bookies fell in line. So many of them did by 1945, the year the war ended, that Siegel was pulling in above $25,000 a month, so it has been generally estimated, from selling the wire news alone. It was only one component of his expanding fortunes.

Siegel's wartime success forms the backdrop for his greatest accomplishment, the one that earns him his place of honor in the literature of organized crime, indeed in the history of American culture. We refer to his seminal role in the creation of Las Vegas.

The facts are clear enough. Gangsters had had their eyes on Nevada since 1931 when the state legislature, desperate for taxable revenues, legalized gambling. The drawback was that Nevada was a huge desert wilderness whose whole population, under a hundred thousand then, could fit into a big city neighborhood. The only part of the state that did well was way up north in and around Reno, and that largely because of Reno's easy divorce procedure, and the only casinos there were, like the patrons themselves, rather straight and conservative. Las Vegas, which lay in the heart of the south Nevada desert, was at that time just a "cowpoke town," in Dean Jennings' words, "where gambling was just another Saturday night diversion for ranchers, toothless bearded prospectors, workers from nearby Boulder Dam," where "Paiute Indians occasionally wandered through the dusty downtown streets, and it was not uncommon to see a wrinkled squaw with a baby in a basket on her back." But by 1945 changes could already be seen in this "cowpoke town." Las Vegas was, after all, a railroad and interstate highway junction, and it had a modest airport. It was potentially within striking distance of the Los Angeles megalopolis three hundred and fifty miles due west. In fact, more and more Los Angelenos were making their way to Las Vegas and were gambling in one or another of its little clubs, such as the El Dorado, the Golden Nugget, the Frontier Turf, the Las Vegas, in several of which, it so happened, Bugsy Siegel owned shares. No one therefore was better able than he to recognize and measure the significance of the change, the increase in the number of patrons visiting the "cowpoke town."

Like Lansky and others Siegel felt in his bones that America at large—not merely his fellow Los Angelenos—was ready for the grand epoch of debauchery to come. But none of them, not even Lansky, had his audacity, his sense of the grandiose, his courage (or foolhardiness) to attempt the really big move. None had his genius.

In the summer of 1945, the war having drawn to its apocalyptic end in the skies above Hiroshima and Nagasaki, Siegel's gang/syndicate comrades gave him the go-ahead, promising him the financial support he needed to build a casino in the desert. Now nothing could stop him; he was a fury. He formed the Nevada Projects Corporation, its shares nominally divided among assorted criminals, notably himself and Lansky, and the usual front men, and from a widow bought thirty acres of wasteland outside Las Vegas. Every detail of the construction from the foundation to the last touch he personally oversaw, making certain throughout that there would be no delays, no shortages of material and skilled labor, both of which were still very hard to come by, so that the casino-hotel would open on schedule in the Christmas week of 1946. And throughout he refused to compromise with the standards he had set: he was going to have a fountain and a reflecting pool at any cost—the image of an oasis could not be tampered with—a garbage disposal unit in each of the ninety-two suites, the best plumbing money could buy and other such accouterments.

His Flamingo, for that is what he chose to call it, was going to be an extension of its planner and builder, Benjamin Siegel, was going to tower over the barren land like a palace, eclipsing the dusty run-of-the-mill joints nearby, the Frontier Turf, the Golden Nugget, the El Dorado and the rest, the very mention of whose names conveyed to the world all that one needed to know about them. No wonder the Flamingo ran up a bill of four million dollars by the time it was completed, an astronomical amount compared to the original estimates. Financially, his great dream was also a great nightmare.

But after a false start in which everything went wrong—the fountain failed to work, the weather was poor, the crowds were thin, the hotel portion remained closed for repairs—and which forced a two-month postponement, the Flamingo managed to catch on, attracting a steady and growing clientele to its one-armed bandits and gaming tables, its nicely appointed rooms, its star-besotted nightclub, its general ambience of extravagant fun. By June 1947 it was clearing $300,000 a month. Bugsy Siegel's brightest anticipations had already come to pass and it was, manifestly, only the beginning. He was triumphant.

Yet this very triumph proved his unseating because it brought to a head the conflict that had been germinating for some time between him and his gang/syndicate compatriots, led by Meyer Lansky. To them he seemed less and less the Bugsy Siegel of old. The Flamingo was eliciting features of his character—his single-mindedness, his obstreperousness, his megalomania—which they no longer found so endearing when directed against them. The conflict itself turned on fundamental issues of right and prerogative, territory in a word. The gang/syndicate leaders felt that Las Vegas, now that its future was settled, should be as wide open as the Gold Coast, available, that is, to members of the community, certainly to those who had backed the Flamingo and seen it through every vicissitude. Now obviously Siegel could not object to reasonable claims. What he did object to was the gang/syndicates' attempt to vest decision-making in themselves, in the collectivity, thereby reducing him in status from lord of the Western marches to one among many. Such in his view was the depth of their ingratitude. Who discovered Las Vegas? Who else but he was entitled to guide its future, and, yes, for the common good as well as his own? They regarded *him* as the ingrate, for without them his dream of a desert paradise would have been nothing more than a mirage.

Their distrust inevitably gave rise to a more serious grievance. They were coming to believe that he might be cheating them. So they carefully watched his every move, relying on information supplied by his own circle of friends and assistants. They also kept a weather eye on Siegel's latest love, Virginia Hill, who seemed to have a magical hold over him, who at any rate meant more to him than any other woman ever had (causing his wife at last to bid him adieu). This fact might not have surprised the gang/syndicate leaders, for Virginia Hill was hardly a stranger to them; some knew her charms firsthand. Since arriving in Chicago in the early 1930s, a teen-age beauty fresh from rural Alabama, Ony Virginia Hill (she soon dropped the Ony) had consorted with an army of gamblers, crooks, politicians, actors, entertainers, and businessmen, marrying and divorcing a few of them along the way, enabling her to indulge always in her incredibly outsized wants—her Cadillacs and jewelry and homes and wardrobe. She could claim, rightly to judge from her conquests, that she was worth every penny of the expense she incurred, that the man was lucky indeed who received her favors. It is generally believed that she met Siegel in New York City during the war, while she was keeping company with Joey Adonis. Whether theirs was love at first sight is not known, but love it was from the moment their affair began. Fierce and unruly and punctuated by breakdowns, it managed to endure and led even to marriage. The Flamingo, with its specially built penthouse, was Siegel's monument to their love, his own Taj Mahal.

Siegel's comrades may have disliked Virginia Hill, or blamed her for the changes that had come over him, but she was after all his woman, his cross to bear. Until, that is, she was sucked directly into their quarrel with him. Why, they wondered, was she going abroad so often? Was she carrying money—*their* money—to Swiss or other European banks? Was Siegel therefore preparing to pull out unannounced or sell his shares in the Flamingo—after robbing them, his partners—on the pretext of starting a new life, even of going straight? Such questions his comrades were asking more and more insistently.

The crisis, according to the omniscient Hank Messick, broke on June 16, 1947, the day Virginia Hill suddenly flew to Paris. That was the signal for Meyer Lansky to visit Las Vegas to have it out once and for all with his ancient pal. A few days later Lansky reported his findings to the other hierarchs in council assembled. Their decision followed as a matter of necessity. Their justice was swift.

It was Siegel's custom when staying in Los Angeles to spend his nights at Virginia Hill's Hollywood home (a bitter paradox for Siegel to swallow: she hated the Flamingo and avoided it as much as possible). There, on the night of June 20, shrouded in darkness outside the living-room window, his murderers lay in wait. Well-informed about his habits, they must have expected him to do exactly what he did: sit on the sofa with his back to them, furnishing a perfect target for the .30 caliber rifle they had brought. Many shots were fired but the bullet that struck him in the head, coming out through an eye, killed him instantly. The gruesome spectacle of Bugsy Siegel lying dead, covered with blood, was flashed to newspapers across the country.

That same night, about the time the police arrived on the scene and before anyone else had officially been notified of the assassination, three of Siegel's former henchmen, Morris Sidwirtz (known to the profession since his Lower East Side days as Moe Sedway), Morris Rosen, and Augustus "Gus" Greenbaum, a gangster chieftain of some renown in Phoenix—he had emigrated there from Chicago in the 1920s—announced to the Flamingo employees that henceforward *they* would be in charge. The announcement went uncontested be-

cause the employees understood at once that Siegel's invisible partners back East had ousted him for reasons known only to
themselves. Another Siegel underling, John "Fat Irish" Greenberg,
demonstrated his fealty to the new regime—and his instinct for self-
preservation—by turning over to it the $600,000 Siegel had entrusted
in his care. What Siegel had intended to do with this huge sum, keep
it for himself, as his comrades suspected, or enter it in the books, will
never be discovered. The employees must also have realized—they
were not in that line of work for nothing—that their self-styled
bosses, Sedway, Rosen, and Greenbaum, were themselves hired
hands and that the real boss, whose spirit everyone felt no matter
how far away he happened to be or how infrequently he showed up,
was of course Meyer Lansky.*

. . .

m

In their most grandly optimistic moments Lansky and
Siegel, gangster-capitalists par excellence, had actually underesti-
mated the passion of Americans to gamble casino-style. Not only did
more Americans have more money than ever before, they were willing more than ever to consume rather than save, and what is more to
consume without guilt or apologies or remorse. And in pursuit of
their pleasures, especially the legally forbidden ones, they were willing also to go further and further away from home. Long-distance
travel had ceased to be an impediment to masses of Americans; during the war, roads and planes and airports had been vastly improved,

---

* As for Virginia Hill, the rest of her sad life can be encapsulated in a footnote, Siegel's departure from history being hers as well. She had sound reason at first to believe that his killers would go after her next. But the gang/syndicate chiefs left her
alone: eliminating her would not restore to them a farthing of the money that may
have been stolen, assuming she had it or knew where it was. She may, it is also possible, have made a deal with them, but of this we know nothing. In any case, she was or
soon became a very sick woman; her cycles of manic-depression drove her to the edge
of suicide several times. Heroically she tried to make a new life for herself. She married an Austrian ski instructor, settled down after a fashion, and even had a child. But
the Furies never ceased to pursue her. In 1966, at the age of fifty, she succumbed to
them at last, dying of an overdose of sleeping pills in the woods outside Salzburg, Austria.

setting the stage for the great transportation revolution that followed. By the late 1940s one could spend one's brief vacation anywhere one wished in the forty-eight states, and "rug joints" like the Green Acres and LaBoheme and the Beverly Club and the Flamingo and others along the fast-rising southern tier could hardly keep up with the business that engulfed them. The conundrum facing Lansky and the syndicates in fact was what to do about this extraordinary phenomenon, this passion to gamble. It was, as we shall see, a conundrum that taxed his ingenuity to the utmost.

Many Americans, though, were unhappy with what they were witnessing. The success of gambling, the expansion of the gang/syndicate empires deep into the hinterlands, far beyond familiar urban precincts, called forth a hostile counterresponse, though compared to the early 1920s, when nativism swept everything before it, the movement that now arose was mild and temperate. Mainly it was led by big-city crime commissions (made up primarily of Mugwump types, mostly WASP and Republican and upper middle class) and the American Municipal Association. From their frequent deliberations came startling news on the dangers of organized crime, particularly in the field of gambling. Papers, magazines, radio, bestselling books (television had not yet arrived) picked up the stories, shaping them to their requirements, that is, to the dictates of an inflamed public. So that by 1950 a sharply honed image had come into national focus: a monstrous conspiracy of evil, composed exclusively of Italians, variously titled the Mafia, the Unione Siciliana (or Honored Society), the Black Hand, the Comorra, directed in any case by a tiny cabal whose power and influence reached into every community in the land, whose aim was nothing less than the subversion and conquest of the American people, and whose prime minister was none other than New York's Frank Costello. An immensely successful book published in 1950, *Chicago Confidential!*—its authors Jack Lait and Lee Mortimer were gossip columnists for the Hearst chain—even claimed that the Mafia's "tentacles" held in thrall "the Cabinet and the White House itself, almost every state capitol, huge Wall Street interests" and had important connections in "Canada, Latin America, England, France, Italy, Turkey, Greece, China and Outer Mongolia, even through the Iron Curtain into the Soviet Union."

These fantastic charges transport us directly into the kingdom of paranoia: a response that was out of all proportion to the actual threat posed by organized crime. One reason such a distorted response emerged at this time was undoubtedly the fact that some Americans, a large number of them at any rate, felt uneasy about Italian-Americans. For Italian-Americans, the nation's second largest ethnic group, were at last coming into their own, acquiring economic security, even affluence, and moving into better neighborhoods or out of the cities altogether. And they were becoming a political force to reckon with; more and more of them were holding office. So, by the usual logic of bigotry, the rise of the Mafia was attributed to the rise of the Italian-American community.

This was exactly how Lait and Mortimer saw it. "The Italian voting bloc now controls some of the largest cities in the country," they wrote in *Washington Confidential!*, a rehash of their Chicago book. "Too many of their men in office have ties to the Mafia. They can count on the votes of their countrymen in nominations and elections. The mass of Italians are bartered back and forth and usually can be delivered by Black Hand threats in Italian neighborhoods, by appeal to blood relationships and national pride, or through the pages of Italian-language newspapers."

The conspiratorial way of thinking reflected in this passage had by now grown congenial to Americans. Before the specter of organized crime engaged their passions, they had become convinced that home-grown Communists and their sympathizers were taking over the country by stealth, or selling it down the river to Russia, much as their comrades presumably had done in so many other countries, China most recently. Senator Joseph McCarthy of Wisconsin did not usher in the psychosis that gripped the nation (1950 being the year he announced himself to the world): he was only more outlandish and adept—for a while—in exploiting it; with the result that history, which is rarely just, has made him the scapegoat and symbol of that whole era, that whole matrix of crimes against civil liberties and due process of law.

Under the circumstances, it was for the anxiety-ridden a short leap from the Communist threat to the Mafia threat. And if the occasion required it, the two could be united in one grand diapason of evil. Here, for example, was how the chairman of New York's Anti-Crime Committee put it in March 1951 before an audience of millions: "Joe Stalin, if he had planned it that way, could not find a speedier and surer way to defeat the democracies than by subsidizing these gangsters and foul politicians. Actually, as I have seen in other countries how closely the gangsters and Communists work together, I wonder if the Soviet is not, at least in some measure, inciting these vermin [the Mafia] to defile our system of law and order."

One of the perplexing questions of the period is why the FBI saw no pressing danger in organized crime, nothing to compare to the danger it saw in Communism and indeed in anything left of center on the political map. No one preached the gospel of conspiracy more vehemently than its chief J. Edgar Hoover. What makes the question especially intriguing is that Hoover paid so little attention to organized crime, indeed so little that one could accuse him of dereliction of duty. The answer obviously is that he thought it constituted no immediate danger to established order. Or, as some have argued, he assumed that gang/syndicate members (as distinguished from lone desperadoes of the Dillinger stripe) were in fact pillars of the status quo. They at least had a vested interest in the health of the free enterprise system, in America's triumph over Communism and for that matter over Socialism and liberalism too—over anything that might remotely threaten their specific opportunities. Intelligent gangsters from Al Capone to Moe Dalitz and Meyer Lansky have always been fierce, voluble defenders of the capitalist faith, and to that extent they were and are J. Edgar Hoover's ideological kinsmen.*

Congress was of course not slow to reflect the national mood, and a host of senators and representatives sought to look into and expose—that at a minimum—the dark regions of organized crime in America. This clearly was what the public wanted and it was what the politicians gave them. One of the first to offer a resolution, on

---

* Some would go further in explaining the "pattern" of indifference, the FBI's unwillingness for decades to take on the gang/syndicates. Messick writes, "John Edgar Hoover has received support, as well as more tangible rewards, from right-wing businessmen who, in turn, have dealt directly and indirectly with organized crime figures who have not been disturbed by John Edgar Hoover."

January 5, 1950, to be exact, was a freshman senator from Tennessee, Estes Kefauver. An unabashed progressive, Kefauver had pulled off something of a miracle a little more than a year earlier when he singlehandedly defeated Boss Crump's candidate. (That candidate committed the fatal error of describing Kefauver as a coon that was about to be skinned. For the rest of the campaign Kefauver wore a coonskin cap wherever he went as his crown of distinction: if it was good enough for Davy Crockett it was good enough for him and the people of Tennessee.)

Kefauver demonstrated that he was an astute and persevering man by getting the Senate gerontocracy, after much pulling and hauling, to act on his resolution to set up a "Special Committee to Investigate Organized Crime in Interstate Commerce" and to appoint him its chairman. Now the Senate's Democratic leaders hardly wanted such a committee established—it could bring no conceivable benefit to the party—and even less one chaired by a newcomer whose reliability had yet to be tested, who indeed already gave cause for apprehension. They were forced to do something because Kefauver had masterfully bent the public's fear of crime to his advantage. The Senate leaders hoped that he and his four committee colleagues, all as obscure as himself, would soon bore the public and that the proceedings would die of inanition, hardly lasting out the year.

Like the country at large, the Kefauver Committee assumed that organized crime meant Mafia and Mafia meant Frank Costello. The assumption, though, was vague and abstract. How precisely did the Mafia operate? How did it threaten to undermine the lives of Americans? The Committee easily located the answer to these questions: it lay in the Mafia's putative control of the racing wire service. The Committee labored endlessly to build up its theory—and a frightening theory it was, as frightening as anything Lait and Mortimer had dredged up. It went as follows.

When Moses Annenberg gave up his racing wire company in 1939, a struggle ensued over proprietorship. The gang/syndicates, represented by the Capone outfit—with whom Annenberg had had an amicable arrangement for decades—staked their claim through their own company, Trans-America. Annenberg's deputy, James Ragen, staked his claim through his company, Continental Press. Before Ragen himself was murdered in August 1946 he had dictated a very long disordered account, widely publicized, of how his Capone gang enemies, led by Jake "Greasy Thumb" Guzik, Anthony Accardo, and Murray "the Camel" Humphries (a Jew, an Italian, and a WASP, incidentally), were conspiring to destroy him. The wire service war explained to the Kefauver Committee's satisfaction the motive behind several of the other sensational murders that had taken place since 1946, above all Bugsy Siegel's. Was it a coincidence that Siegel was Trans-America's West Coast agent? Everything fit beautifully. By monopolizing the racing wires the Mafia would be in the position to insinuate itself in every neighborhood, town, and village across the country. It was exquisitely diabolical.

Between May 1950 and September 1951 the Committee visited scores of cities from coast to coast and heard six hundred witnesses, including most of the powerful gangsters of the day. It was an astonishing spectacle. Never before did so many criminals pass in review before the general public; never before were so many put on display singly or in tandem as members of a single community of outlaws. Though with few exceptions they were still in their forties—they all belonged to that extraordinary generation which had been born around the turn of the century and had made its mark in bootlegging—some were already legends, even to the untutored masses: e.g., from Chicago, Tony Accardo, Paul the Waiter Ricca, Louis New York Campagna, Cherry Nose Gioe, the Fischetti brothers, Guzik, and Humphries; from Los Angeles, Jack Dragna and Mickey Cohen; from New Jersey, Joey Adonis and Longy Zwillman and the Moretti brothers; from Philadelphia, Nig Rosen; from Cleveland, Al and Chuck Polizzi, the Andreola brothers, and the Big Four (Dalitz, Rothkopf, Kleinman, and Tucker); from New York, Frank Erickson, Meyer Lansky, and of course Frank Costello, whose testimony brought the proceedings to a climax (whose supreme moment—the climax within the climax as it were—came when, claiming to be unwell, he simply rose and left the hearing room, an unprecedented act of defiance that was to call forth a contempt citation and eventually an eighteen-month prison sentence). And the public, far from being bored with the hearings, as the wise old Senate leaders had hoped, found them more and more fascinating. Wherever it went the Kefauver Committee was a sensation, especially after its hearings began to be televised in February 1951. They drew an incredible audience, the largest ever to witness such an event, turning the participants into national celebrities overnight.

The success of the hearings could also be ascribed to the marvelous contrasts they evoked. There was the contrast between the senators themselves. Standing out like a beacon of fairness and intelligence was Estes Kefauver. (In this respect how different he was from Senator McCarthy and the other congressmen of both houses who were busy investigating "subversives.") He was usually well-prepared; his questions were probing and directed to some discernible purpose. His colleagues—Senators Charles W. Tobey of New Hampshire, Herbert O'Conor of Maryland, Alexander Wiley of Wisconsin, and Lester Hunt of Wyoming—contributed little, their remarks being more often than not inane and pointless. Wiley and Hunt, both sonorous and distinguished-looking, as senators should be, were out of it altogether; O'Conor took scant interest when he did show up (until, that is, he became chairman toward the end); and Tobey, who did take a keen interest (as he proved by removing his jacket and donning a green eye shade) fell back on jeremiads, empty moral pronouncements, thereby assuming the role of the "conscience" of the Committee. There was the contrast—it could not have been more artfully designed—between Kefauver, tall, Lincolnesque, benign, and chief counsel Rudolph Halley, short, combative, sharp-tongued, a street-wise New Yorker who gave the witnesses no respite, no quarter, forcing them to seek comfort in Kefauver's gentle embrace. And then there was the contrast between the senators in general, all, except O'Conor, exemplifying the virtues of rural and small-town and WASP America, and the gangsters, almost all of them immigrants and the children of immigrants, none having had more than the rudiments of a formal education. To be watched and judged by the world in this setting was for most of them a humiliating experience. Their carriage, demeanor, speech—some spoke in guttural foreign accents—pointed up the poverty of their lives, a poverty which no amount of acquired wealth or hired legal talent could conceal. They were stripped naked.

Within weeks after the hearings opened it became plain that there was precious little to the wire service affair. The war, it transpired, had hardly been a war at all; it had ended amicably, Trans-

America and Continental having quietly merged years before. Also, the wire services proved to be no sinister operation (though the people running it were sinister enough), only a service sold to customers, the bookmakers of America. Almost despite itself the Committee stumbled on the fact that casino gambling was organized crime's main source of revenue, that in such wide-open territories as Florida's Gold Coast, the parishes surrounding New Orleans, the Ohio River and Great Lakes regions, and above all Las Vegas, the gang/syndicate leaders took scrupulous care to cooperate with each other, determining who invested what amount of capital and received what share of the profits, and that as in the olden days of bootlegging so now large-scale entrepreneurs had worked out a rational arrangement for allocating capital and controlling the market. Such was the nature of the "conspiracy"—a far cry from the theory that had prompted the investigation. Foiled in its quest, the Committee was reduced to asking Italian mobsters, whose police records filled pages, if they belonged to or knew anything about the Mafia, Black Hand, and so on.

That the Mafia was hardly the point at issue—in the form the Committee imagined at any rate—was blatantly obvious from the number of Jewish gangsters who appeared before it, gangsters as rich and powerful as the most notorious of the Italian witnesses. With the exception of King Solomon's men—Joe Linsey, Hyman Abrams, and Louis Fox (Kefauver having inexplicably omitted Boston from his itinerary)—and Kid Cann, just about every important Jewish gangster testified. And on the whole they comported themselves very well. They pictured themselves as men who after a few youthful peccadilloes and false starts were trying earnestly to make a go of it in business. There was of course some truth in this misrepresentation. Detroit's Bernstein Brothers, retired Purples, were raising horses and selling real estate in California; Moe Dalitz, besides running a huge Las Vegas hotel with his partners, had many legitimate concerns in Cleveland and Detroit, from scrap iron and laundries to steel mills; Nig Rosen had dress factories in the Bronx and Pennsylvania; Longy Zwillman rented cigarette vending and washing machines and sold cars, among other things; Lansky lamented his failure in selling jukebox television to bars and restaurants ("We should have gone into the home set end, and maybe I would have been a rich man today"); and so on and on went the parade of gangster-entrepreneurs.

When pressed hard and forced to admit that they were still friendly with "known underworld figures," were indeed still engaged in illegal activities, they shifted ground, pleading for sympathy, claiming they were trapped, overwhelmed by circumstances. Addressing Moe Sedway, Bugsy Siegel's ex-sidekick and now one of the Flamingo's bosses (he also had risen to considerable respectability: he was in 1950 the chief fund-raiser for the Nevada United Jewish Appeal), Senator Tobey said with unflagging righteousness: "You are in cahoots with a lot of people like Bugsy Siegel, and you wonder whether it all pays or not or what it amounts to, and why men do these things. I look upon these people in my state of New Hampshire that till the soil and make $2,000 a year as a lot richer than these people down here. They have peace of mind and can look everybody in the eye."

"Senator," Sedway replied, "you can see what it got for me, three coronaries and ulcers."

Tobey asked: "What does it all amount to? Why do men play the game this way? What makes it attractive to them? What is the matter with men?"

Sedway: "Just go into that type of business and you get into it and stay in it."

Tobey: ". . . when decent men want to make a living, these men peel it off. They are rich. . . . They may have money but that is all they have got."

Sedway: "We don't get as rich as you think we do. This is hard work. I work pretty hard in this business."

Tobey: "If you put the talent you have got toward constructive things in life, producing something that makes real wealth and human happiness, men would arise and call you blessed. We find these men all over the country. What has come over the world? What are the dangers: Love of money and power. There are some finer things in the world."

Sedway: "You asked me if I would want to do it all over again. I would not do it again. I would not want my children to do it again."

The Committee more than met its match in the likes of Dalitz, Lansky, and Zwillman. Their intelligence and wit and self-possession were always in evidence; they said only what they wanted to though they were never at a loss for words; they confronted their interlocutors as equals.

In one exchange Tobey asked Zwillman, the most polished of gangsters, "Is it true that you have been known in New Jersey for a long time as the Al Capone of New Jersey?"

Zwillman laughed. "That is a myth that has been developing, Mr. Senator, for a good many years, and during the time when I should have had sense to stop it, or get up and get out of the state, I did not have the sense enough, until the point where it blossomed and bloomed. . . . I am not that, I don't intend to be, I never strived to be, and I am trying to make a living for my family and myself. But these rumors go around. They accuse me of owning places. I walk into a restaurant and I own the restaurant. I walk into a hotel and I own the hotel. I take a shine twice, and I own the bootblack too."

"Well," said Tobey, "those are the penalties of greatness."

Tobey, incidentally, was roundly put in his place (and so by implication was the Committee) during Lansky's interrogation. His lawyer, Moses Polakoff, had also once been Lucky Luciano's lawyer. When he learned this Tobey lost his patience. "How did you become counsel for such a dirty rat as that [Luciano]? Aren't there some ethics in the legal profession?"

Polakoff then read the senator an elementary lesson in the Bill of Rights. "I don't want to get into a controversy with you about that subject at the present time, but under our Constitution every person is entitled to his day in court. . . . When the day comes that a person becomes beyond the pale of justice, that means our liberty is gone. Minorities and undesirables and persons with bad reputations are more entitled to the protection of the law than so-called honorable people. I don't have to apologize to you . . . or anyone else for whom I represent."

"I look upon you in amazement," said Tobey.

Polakoff had the last and best word: "I look upon you in amazement, a senator of the United States, for making such a statement."

The only prominent Jewish gangsters who defied the Committee *tout court* were Kleinman and Rothkopf of Cleveland, both of whom read identical statements protesting that they could not receive a fair hearing, the publicity being what it was, and would be maligned and ridiculed whatever they said, thereby articulating what every other recalcitrant and humiliated gangster must have felt. "I am not an actor, and have no experience as a public speaker. . . . My manner of sitting, of talking, using my hands, the clothes I wear, may all be the subject of movies and unfavorable comment, and may be used against me. My voice, which is not trained, may make an unfavorable impression, and my entire appearance, as given or compared to others, may be distorted." And further: "The television hearings in New York City were referred to as being bigger than the World Series. The *New York Times*, the *World-Telegram*, the *Journal-American*, and even Washington papers reported that in theaters, stores and other places business declined because of the television show. Saloons and restaurants were jammed. . . . In the Cleveland press Saturday evening, along with a story about me, by cartoon it was suggested that my TV debut might even replace Kukla, Fran and Ollie. [Laughter.]"

Kleinman and Rothkopf preferred jail on a contempt of Congress citation, if it should come to that, to testifying before the Committee. The Committee did of course cite them and so did the Senate. But they never served their sentences because the courts in 1952 declared that they were right, that the hearings were conducted in such a way as to violate their constitutional rights. (The courts for that matter threw out most of the Committee's contempt citations, Costello's being the notable exception.)

Now there was some value to holding America's top gangsters up for display and ridicule, inquiring into their life histories, giving the public an idea (not enough) of who they really were beneath the personas they adopted. And it was useful to see how insufferably corrupt small-town police and politicians could be, how poorly "grass roots" democracy resisted the blandishments of the urban and ethnic underworld. But those accomplishments were trivial when measured against the ambitious goal the Committee had originally set for itself—the unraveling of the Mafia plot to bring down America. Its failure was inevitable given that goal and given therefore its approach to the problem of organized crime, its assumption, namely, that America consisted of two nations, the gangsters and their allies on the one hand and the decent plain folk on the other. Senator Tobey, always the Committee's Polonius, is worth quoting here: "Benedict Arnold rides again in this country. When men are guilty of some of the things brought to light here today they come pretty near being treason in my judgment, beyond peradventure. The time will come—and I pray to God it has—when the American people will rise up and sound a warning note to this type all over the world and say, 'Hold! Enough!' Russia may flay us in the papers tomorrow and tear America and crucify her by words and editorials. But what we have heard here today is not America. If you want to know what America is, go out in the hinterlands of this country, to the farm homes and the village homes, to the men who come home at night to greet their wives and little children, who pay their taxes and worship God according to the dictates of their own consciences, and love America—and there are 10,000 times as many of them as there are crooks who came before us."

The Committee, then, never heard a point of view or approach other than its own. It never entertained the possibility that gangsters were at bottom middlemen who took the risks, and won the rewards, of satisfying the needs of upper-world citizens, often enough the very men "who come home at night to greet their wives and little children," that organized crime was in fact an expression of, not a departure from, conventional American morality, that there might be reasonable alternatives to yet more punitive legislation, the vain hope that all would be redeemed by a yet stricter enforcement of the law.

By the time the Committee expired on September 1, 1951, the public seemed no longer to regard organized crime as an immediate threat, or even to care about it. To the very end, though, the Committee stuck to its original position or dogma. In its third and last interim report it still insisted, in the teeth of its own experience, despite all the hearings it held, that "there is a sinister criminal organization known as the Mafia, operating throughout the country with ties to other nations. . . ." But these phrases were stale and flat and without conviction, and by then few were listening anyway.

ẇ

━━━━━━━━ The Committee's antics might have amused Meyer Lansky and several of his gang/syndicate colleagues—those not humiliated or held in contempt of Congress. Less amusing to them were the economic consequences of the hearings. Wherever Kefauver went (and with him the television cameras and the press) the illicit operations had to close down, at least until the heat wave was over. In some instances the adverse effects were permanent, with reform administrations and new laws and zealous investigative reporters making it intolerable for the gamblers to resume their operations. The Cleveland syndicate, whose casinos extended down Ohio and into Kentucky, some of them as opulent as any in the country, was hurt badly, losing millions in revenue and capital. For all its ineptitude and wrongheadedness the Kefauver Committee taught Lansky and the Clevelanders and the gang/syndicates in general a truth they would never forget: that their investments were unsafe wherever gambling was illegal, no matter how thoroughly they had corrupted the politicians and law-enforcement and judicial agencies. In fact, the *illusion* of security embodied in, say, Sheriff Walter Clark of Broward County, was especially dangerous since it led to massive expenditures of fixed capital—buildings, equipment, and so forth— which became worthless the moment something went wrong. This was an old story to experienced criminals. Only now the stakes were inordinately high, and the gang/syndicates, like their big-business counterparts, could not afford to take chances.

Yet they still had a distance to go before the full force of that illusion could be brought home to them. Lansky and his partners still had to learn that even where casino gambling was legal and conditions otherwise optimum—a friendly government, a happy population—well-laid and lavishly financed plans might go awry, catastrophically so. The Cuban debacle afforded a notorious case in point.

One can understand why Lansky turned his attention to Cuba. Since the 1930s he had neglected that island paradise, maintaining only a modest operation there. For one thing, the war had devastated the tourist trade. For another, Lansky's old friend Fulgencio Batista was no longer dictator; far from it. Having given up the presidency during the war (under U.S. pressure), Batista left Cuba altogether and settled in Florida, though at a discreet distance from Broward County. He never ceased plotting his return home however. His opportunity came in 1952 while he was running as one of Cuba's presidential candidates. On March 11, three months before the election, with the polls showing Batista hopelessly trailing the others, the army overthrew the regime and made him Cuba's boss once again, this time without even the pretense of democracy. What he could not get legitimately he would get illegitimately. Tyrants are no different than gangsters.

And so it was that the Florida Gold Coast moved to Havana, Batista granting Lansky and the gang/syndicates carte-blanche rights to the city. The promise of decades ago, when Lansky had planted his first seeds there, now yielded a rich harvest. Under Batista's ukase only clubs worth more than a million dollars could install casinos, effectively giving Lansky and his friends monopoly status—this in addition to the tax write-offs, the investment of Cuban government funds in the building of gangster-controlled hotels and casinos (as much as one half the cost), and other subsidies and incentives as well. In return, the illusion of security being complete, the gang/syndicates poured vast amounts of money into Havana, one edifice after another rising up to accommodate the burgeoning crowds of Americans for whom Florida had become too staid: the monumental Riviera (Lansky officially serving as master of the kitchen), which in the first three months of its existence grossed over two million dollars, the Capri (featuring George Raft as greeter and host), the Sevilla Biltmore, the Havana Hilton, the Montmartre, and, not to be outdone, the Nacional, Lansky's initial conquest way back when he was buying molasses. These properties were divided up in the customary fashion, Lansky recommending who came in on what terms, the community of gang/syndicate leaders giving their approval. Particularly heavy investors were the Clevelanders—Sam Tucker, the eldest, was their man in Havana—whose store of venture capital seemed inexhaustible. But so rapid was the expansion, so eager were Americans to visit Havana and enjoy its amenities, that few mobsters were denied, though naturally the chieftains, Lansky's comrades of olden days, received the largest share.

And of course Batista and his family and courtiers were extravagantly rewarded too, he with a percentage of the take, not off the top but sufficiently close to make him very rich, or much richer than he already was, his brother-in-law with one half of the slot machine earnings, and so on. The mounting profits sustained all the quid pro quos.

A plausible case could be made—certainly the Batista regime and its apologists made it—to justify the presence of American gangsters and, yes, even the system of pay-offs: it was the price that had to be paid for the accompanying benefits to the Cuban masses. But the swelling band of Batista's critics argued that the costs to Cuba far outweighed the benefits. How much of the profits remained in the country? How useful to a poor people was that section of the economy which drew its income from gambling? How healthy was it to have so many women, often girls who had scarcely reached puberty, emigrate from the countryside to become whores in the big city? And what was a Cuban to think of a government leagued with America's worst elements, the very ones who had been paraded before the Kefauver Committee only a few years before? These were questions asked by all Cubans who opposed Batista, more and more of whom were joining or supporting the movement to oust him that Fidel Castro led. Ever since he and his handful of followers launched their guerilla assault in 1956, Castro had exploited the gangster issue for what it was worth. And as that handful grew into an army, Lansky and his co-proprietors witnessed a startling re-creation of something they had witnessed many times before in their careers: an upsurge of reform, perhaps even something worse (for beyond the loss of property there was one's life and liberty to worry about), was threatening their interests, revealing anew how vulnerable they were and how easily they could still be taken in by appearances.

The denouement is well known. Castro seized power in January 1959, the Batista government disintegrating, unable to muster a defense. Nor was it long before Castro demonstrated how serious he was about reform, or rather revolution. He mercilessly drove out the gangsters, forcing them to run for their lives, literally that; those who dawdled were rounded up as enemies (Jake Lansky, for one, spent a month in a Havana jail). Everything the gang/syndicates had invested, yes, everything, was confiscated and nationalized. (As for Batista, he retired to a villa in Franco's Spain; his wealth was beyond the reach of the revolution.) Lansky and his friends offered a prize— some claim as much as a million dollars—to anyone who would assassinate Fidel Castro. Small wonder that some prominent gangsters (not Lansky though) cooperated with the CIA in its extraordinary attempts over the years to kill him, all other attempts to bring him down having failed, most notably the Bay of Pigs invasion of April 1961. As we have seen, it was not the first time the United States government had called upon the underworld for help in a crisis.*

Reliance on the friendship and power of a foreign tyrant was an error that Lansky and his cohorts would try to avoid henceforth, especially now that opportunities for the worldwide expansion of casino gambling were opening up as never before. The 1960s were an era of uninterrupted prosperity in the United States and throughout the West, prompting Lansky to go further and further afield, creating what became in effect his own multinational operation. He might very well, as some contend, have established beachheads in England, Beirut, Hong Kong, and the Bahamas, for he was relentless and never let any possibility escape him. But he had also become warier and more cautious. He made certain that the risks were minimal. Rather than move in wholesale, as he and his compatriots had done in Ha-

---

* A Senate Foreign Relations subcommittee headed by Idaho Senator Frank Church in 1975 identified two hierarchs in the Chicago gang/syndicate who worked with the CIA on this project, John Roselli and Sam Giancana, both of whom were later executed gangland style. One can only infer that their comrades punished them for having done what they did without the Mafia's authorization or for having gotten caught and so becoming targets for further investigation. A word finally on the ludicrous methods the CIA used, through its underworld associates, in its efforts to kill Castro: special foot powder, exploding cigars, poisoned food, and other such sophisticated devices. Perhaps Roselli and Giancana were slain because they were such a bumbling disgrace to the good name of the Mafia.

vana, the Florida Gold Coast, Ohio and Kentucky, and elsewhere, Lansky tended increasingly to rent his services, employing his magnificent skills to set up and manage the casinos, nothing more. This represented on the multinational level a further rationalizing of the gambling business. Even so the hazards were considerable. Under the best of circumstances there could be no guarantee against war and revolution and a hundred other disasters to which foreign operations were heir. Ultimately no foreign government could be trusted. The celebrated Bahamian incident provided an object lesson.

For years the Bahamas had whetted Lansky's appetite. Their pleasant weather and relaxed tempo, their British upper-class civility, complete with agreeable black natives, would have made them a good place for tourists to visit and enjoy had they been properly developed, had the torpid colonial authorities ever sought to change things. In the last few years, though, a transformation had been taking place, and Lansky was as aware of it as anyone whose livelihood it was to follow such matters. A spanking new community had just been built on Grand Bahama Island called Freeport, literally that, because companies from all over the world were invited to do business there without fear of taxes or regulations. For whatever reason, the recession that struck in 1958 perhaps, few companies took the bait. Bank notes were falling due; the venture was threatening to be a monumental white elephant.

Lansky showed up at precisely the right instant—the summer of 1961—with a tried and true plan of his own. He proposed this: instead of concentrating on industry Grand Bahama's Freeport should encourage the ingathering of the tourists (Cuba now being off-limits to them) and to that end put up a lavish hotel according to his specifications. The political boss of the Islands, a huge, corrupt hulk of a man named Sir Stafford Sands (Justice Department lawyers would refer to him one day as "King George's revenge," an allusion to the fact that Sir Stafford traced his ancestors back to American Tories who had fled the Revolution), consulted with his fellow oligarchs, the Bay Street Boys, leaders of the ruling United Bahamian Party, and found the scheme to his liking. Because conditions were so favorable, because the Bahamian government seemed impregnable, Lansky was willing to pay the price: $1.8 million to Sands alone.

If Lansky had known how desperate Sands was he might have bought the big man more cheaply. The fact was that Sands could not allow Freeport to go under, for then everything would become known: how it had started as a dream by one Wallace Groves, an American expatriate who had once served three years in a Federal penitentiary for mail fraud, how Sands and the Bay Street Boys had then enacted a law virtually giving away an immense tract of Grand Bahama—eventually 150,000 acres—to Groves, and how Groves, thus granted extraterritorial rights and assuming the role of absolute despot, had engineered the whole project. Sands had good reason to panic should Freeport come a cropper; the ensuing scandal would be his disgrace and undoing. He needed Lansky much more than Lansky needed him.

At any rate, by the time the Lucayan Beach Hotel opened in January 1964 its success was foregone because by then Grand Bahama Island was experiencing a boom. It had been discovered. Not only were more and more American tourists arriving there; more and more people were seeking land to buy on or near the beachfront (the value rising to thousands of dollars a foot). It was the Gold Coast and Havana redivivus, and Lansky and his men enjoyed a double triumph: earning a fortune in real estate and at the same time fleecing the players at the hotel.

But just when everything was going so well—Sands had seen to it that yet another fabulous hotel-casino would be built in the future, this one on Paradise Island smack in the heart of gorgeous Nassau Bay—just then an ominous and all too familiar cloud appeared in the distance. Native Bahamians, led by the Progressive Liberal Party, rose in protest against the despoliation of their country. That Sands and his Boys were less than impregnable was soon obvious. Good investigative reporting, especially by the *Wall Street Journal*, brought out the magnitude of the chicanery, the whole sordid relationship between Sands and Groves and Meyer Lansky.

Shocked colonial authorities ordered a special election held on January 10, 1967. To everyone's surprise the Progressive Liberals won and their leader, Lynden O. Pindling, became prime minister. A month later a royal commission inquired into the affair and the authorities were shocked anew. For Groves and Sands, needless to say, it was the end of the line. (A not altogether unhappy ending for them, each getting out with his untold millions.) It might also have been the end of the line for Lansky—if Pindling had been Castro and the Progressive Liberals revolutionaries. But what they wanted was merely a share of the gambling profits as tax revenue for sorely needed social projects. Driving out such a valuable goose, along with the tourists who nourished it, was the least of their intentions. So the casinos throve as always at Lucayan Beach and Paradise Island, now under the protection of a government untainted by colonialism or racism. It had worked out tolerably well for Lansky.

The last chapter was still to come however. It might be titled "Rendering the Lansky Connection Invisible," or "The Ascendancy of the Corporate Image," or "The Emergence of Resorts International."

In the early 1960s the Mary Carter Paint Company—an improbable name for a company that sold many things besides high quality paint, a conglomerate in short, albeit a small one by the standards of the day—bought land in the Bahamas and built the Paradise Island hotel and casino. (Among the distinguished guests who attended the January 1968 gala opening was Richard M. Nixon who was about to launch his campaign for President.) In 1970 Mary Carter Paints metamorphosed into Resorts International, and to burnish its image hired ex-Justice Department crime fighters and formed its own international detective agency—all impressive on the face of it. But the fact was that between Mary Carter (or Resorts International) and Meyer Lansky there existed a linkage, a bond. The manager of the Paradise Island casino, to take a flagrant example, was one of Lansky's trusted functionaries, Edward Cellini. Only after Cellini's credentials were publicized—and this only under duress—did Resorts International remove him from the premises, shifting him at that simply to a less conspicuous position. Now the relations between Lansky and the company may have amounted to nothing more than a reasonable quid pro quo, Lansky lending his expert knowledge in exchange for a fee; a straight business deal, in other words. To whom, after all, should Resorts International have turned? And there is certainly no proof that the master criminal was behind the corporation, or even that he owned shares in it, or if he did how many. Supposing he did own shares, indeed did secretly run the company—what then? Would Resorts International be any different than it is? Would it be any less accountable to its stockholders, the Securities and Exchange Commission, the American Stock Exchange, and numerous other public and private agencies? In any event, Lansky retained a very lucrative interest in the Bahamas both for himself and for the gang/syndicates.

Still, it had been a close call. And there was no guarantee that the natives would remain acquiescent, that the Progressive Liberal government might not be replaced by a radical one. When all was said and done the fact that forced itself on Lansky and the gang/syndicates, the profound and irreducible truth, was this: the only secure place on earth was right here in the United States—in Las Vegas, where gambling was legal. Compared to that fact, that truth, everything else was incidental.

No one, not even Bugsy Siegel at his most euphoric, could have imagined what would become of his dream. Even before his murder (as noted) his Flamingo was thriving; and by the end of that year, 1947, control having passed to Lansky and the gang/syndicates, it was clearing upwards of four million dollars, paying off manyfold the original expenditures that he, Siegel, had once squandered so freely. And the Flamingo gave only a hint of what lay ahead. In its vicinity, on either side of the main highway out of town, hotels sprang up with frantic speed and urgency, as though animated by the spirit of Bugsy Siegel, each surpassing its predecessors in size and extravagance, the cost of its entertainment, the glittering magic it offered to the swelling crowds who came from every corner of America. And so the world beheld the Las Vegas Strip, an endless succession of bright-lit castles of joy—the Thunderbird, the Desert Inn, the Sands, the Sahara, the Riviera, the Dunes, the Royal Nevada, the Tropicana, later the Stardust and Caesar's Palace and still others to come. It was a miracle of American civilization.

Las Vegas demonstrated that legality could work entirely to the advantage of the underworld, the local, state, and federal taxes, whatever they were and even if paid, being an expense worth suffering in payment for the benefactions legitimacy conferred: immunity from citizen reformers and eager prosecutors, freedom from corrupt officials and tinhorn dictators and natural catastrophes. Furthermore, many Las Vegas gangsters, transmogrified into respectable businessmen (e.g., Moe Sedway), were sought after, feted, embraced. Nevada politicians outdid themselves in soliciting their support, privately if not publicly, and therefore in securing favors for them. By the early 1950s what had once been a desert outpost now had a major airport, an extensive highway network, limitless access to scarce water reserves, civic and convention centers—all of these government-subsidized.* Legalized gambling was the greatest boon that the gang/syndicates ever experienced, eclipsing the alcohol trade at its apogee.

And while no change of appearance and venue could erase their past nor completely hide their network of associations they did learn from Lansky to move circumspectly in this new Arcadia, to avoid suspicion, Bugsy Siegel being an unforgettable lesson in how not to behave. The gang chieftains who invested their fortunes in Las Vegas casinos used every legal subterfuge, manufacturing in the process an ingenious labyrinth of corporate dummies and fronts. One of the nominal owners of the Thunderbird, which opened with trumpets and fanfare in 1948, was Nevada's ex-lieutenant-governor Clifford A. Jones; the real boss of course was Meyer Lansky. Two years later Wilbur Clark's Desert Inn opened to still louder acclaim, for it was then without question the world's premier "rug joint."

---

*   The prime mover in bringing about these internal improvements—without which there would have been no Las Vegas—was, let it be noted for the record, one of America's redoubtable politicians of the 1940s and 1950s, Nevada's Senator Patrick McCarran, senior Democrat and ofttimes chairman of the Judiciary Committee. A ferocious anti-Communist during the height of the Cold War, McCarran was only slightly less demagogic than Joseph McCarthy, his Wisconsin colleague. (McCarran sponsored the infamous Internal Security Act of 1950 which ordered "subversive" organizations to register with a government review board and authorized the building of concentration camps in the event of a "national emergency"—this along with other similar pieces of repressive legislation that bore his name.) He regarded Nevada's leading gamblers as his friends and honored constituents. And why not? By his lights they were the solidest of Americans, invincible anti-Communists, assets to community and nation. They presided over his state's one growth industry; they put Nevada on the map of the world.

Clark had been a knockabout gambler and hustler of large ambitions who, like Bugsy Siegel, had dreamed of building such a place of his own and indeed had raised enough money to start it on its way but no more than that; only the foundation was laid. The rest of the capital came from the Cleveland gang—Dalitz, Rothkopf, Kleinman, and Tucker and their Mayfield Road Italian comrades led by Big Al Polizzi. They generously cut Clark in for a quarter of the shares and made him the Desert Inn's front man.

And so it was in every instance, for every Las Vegas hotel built during those formative years. If from time to time the truth did leak out, scandalizing the public, arousing the usual indignation, and even if as a consequence the regulations handed down by the Nevada Gaming Commission grew steadily tougher, enabling officials to summarily dispossess, i.e., deny a license to, anyone with a criminal record, or anyone who consorted with known criminals*—so did the gang/syndicate capitalists rely more and more on artful stratagems of concealment, always managing to stay ahead of the law which otherwise protected their interests so well.

They—more accurately Lansky—developed a whole range of stratagems. Skimming, for example, evolved into an exact science. This was inevitable: the less money a casino registered as income the less taxes it paid; the avoidance of taxes gave a considerable advantage, the minimal rate being over fifty percent of gross profits. To get an idea of the amounts involved, assume that the Flamingo in 1965 actually took in $10,000,000; with total taxes of fifty-two percent the Flamingo would have been left with $4,800,000. But suppose that $3,000,000 was skimmed; the Flamingo would then have $6,360,000 after taxes, a difference—in that one hotel—of $1,560,000. That this is a modest example of what actually happened may be gathered from the federal government's 1970 indictment of Lansky and several associates for skimming $36,000,000 over the previous ten years *from the Flamingo alone*. Beleaguered by illness, Lansky never

---

* Not until 1959 was the Nevada Gaming Commission formed and granted the plenary authority to license or not to license. The day-to-day investigative function of the Commission is vested in the Gaming Control Board. It must be emphasized that the more stringent the controls over gambling the more advantageous it can be to the underworld, the better the cover.

stood trial. Others took the rap: one of them, Samuel Cohen, served a year; another, Morris Lansburgh, served five months.*

The skimming devices were ingenious, trying to keep or hide the cash received being too crude, tax officials and other government authorities always being present for the counting. To mention a few: the "kickback skim," whereby the gaming table operatives received large bonuses and remunerations and kicked them back; the "junk skim," whereby a group of high-rollers were brought to Las Vegas (or the Bahamas or anywhere else in the world for that matter) by a "travel agent" or "sporting club," all expenses, including the sum to be bet, prepaid to them, the agent or club; and the "credit skim," whereby losers were allowed, or encouraged, to sign IOU's, the checks for which, made out much later, rarely appeared on the books.

(Skimming is a universal practice. As people from doctors to waiters can testify, any cash transaction lends itself to skimming, and except in outlandish instances—a Park Avenue specialist reporting only $50,000 for a given year, say, or a waiter at the Four Seasons only $10,000—there is little the Internal Revenue Service can do about it. What distinguishes casino skimming from other forms is scale and magnitude and therefore the need to develop elaborate techniques such as the ones cited above.)

The next stratagem followed logically. With vast sums of hot money at his disposal Lansky willy-nilly became an international banker; or, rather, he shaped to his purposes the system of international banking that emerged in the age of multinational corporations. His men refined the techniques for conveying the hot money from the United States to foreign, primarily Swiss, banks. These specially trained couriers had to be men of exemplary character and intelligence; it was absolutely essential that they arouse no suspicions, that they have the ability to handle any emergency, that they could be completely trusted. The model of them all was the legendary John

---

* The case was finally thrown out in 1974. The judge took pity on Lansky. "The court finds it is almost a certainty that this elderly and seriously ill defendant will never be well enough to undergo the rigors of the trial in this complex case."

Pullman, a Rumanian-Jewish immigrant who had been nurtured in Kid Cann's Minneapolis gang and worked out of Montreal. When the Canadian Mounties caught up with him in 1967 he fled to Lausanne, settling there comfortably as Lansky's Swiss ambassador. Pullman and his fellow couriers would deposit upwards of $250,000 at a time in numbered accounts, and to ensure that the owner could never be traced and that his money was available to him at a moment's notice, they would deposit it in the name of a dummy corporation registered in Liechtenstein, which dummy corporation would in turn belong to another dummy corporation registered in, say, Panama or the Bahamas. The cover was thus foolproof, as the authorities were the first to admit.*

Circumstances might also require Lansky's men to move quickly—couriers taking at least a day to reach their destinations—and so they had their own international banks, among them the Bank of World Commerce, headquartered in Nassau, and the Exchange and Investment Bank of Geneva, or they entered into close working relations with reliable (i.e., crooked) houses, notably the International Credit Bank of Switzerland and Overseas Investors Corporation, also of Switzerland, both of which finally collapsed under the weight of scandal, but not before their assets were pillaged and ransacked, the latter's by Robert S. Vesco.

Lansky's devices might seem mysterious, even magical, to rank-and-file gangsters, but his object was luminously clear, so clear his underworld friends, or friends of his friends, near and far, sent him their hot money to dispose of as only he knew how, depending on him to do for them what they could not do for themselves. That object was to convert the money into capital, thereby making it available to them for reinvestment, as the seed of new personal wealth. "Stash-

---

* So that, according to two experts on the recondite subject of "dirty money," even if American investigators "are able to penetrate Swiss banking secrecy and, with the cooperation of the Swiss authorities, obtain bank records they believe to be crucial to the dirty money scheme, these Swiss records are rendered worthless. All they will indicate is that the suspicious account is owned by the Liechtenstein company named, for example, Highlo. But who was Highlo? The answer to that question is in the file cabinet of the Liechtenstein lawyer who represents Highlo."

ing" (hiding the hot money in drawers and mattresses and back-yards) was as obsolete as the Mustache Petes who had practiced it. Even the possibility of personally consuming it, or a fraction of it, was out of the question, an invitation to every prosecutor in the neighborhood to snoop about and establish a case for tax evasion if nothing else. In plain language, unless the money was "laundered" it was lost, denuded of its value. Meyer Lansky showed his underworld comrades how the laundering should be done. In this too he was a pioneer.

A pioneer in the broadest sense. By the 1960s very respectable people and institutions were laundering their money "in the snows of the Alps" as a matter of course and for a variety of reasons. Thousands of individuals, many of them pillars of respectability, avoided taxes by keeping their money in Swiss banks or in Swiss branches of American banks.* Also, the CIA, and perhaps other government agencies as well, pays for clandestine operations with laundered money. So have many of America's largest corporations. Watergate revealed the extent to which these corporations financed President Nixon's 1972 re-election campaign through Swiss, Panamanian, Bahamian, and other accounts, all dummies of course. The extent to which they bribed leading politicians in other countries, for example, the prime ministers of Italy and Japan, Prince Bernhard of the Netherlands among others, with laundered funds was brought out later; but by then the astonishment had worn off. How amusingly naïve therefore Nixon himself was (or appeared to be, for he knew he was being taped) in his famous discussion with John Dean on March 21, 1973, on how best to continue buying off the Watergate defendants. Dean: "It will cost money. It is dangerous. People around here are not pros at this sort of thing. This is the sort of thing Mafia people can do: washing money, getting clean money and things like that. We

---

* United States Attorney Robert Morgenthau said in December 1969: "I find it shocking that an American bank, by opening a branch abroad, can lend its facilities to citizens who are defrauding the revenue and violating our laws and then successfully deny its obligations to make account records available to the Department of Justice by claiming that the laws of a foreign country would be violated."

just don't know about those things because we are not criminals and not used to dealing in that business."

To which Nixon replied, "Maybe it takes a gang to do that."

Lansky's universe, then, to bring it down to the present, can be reduced to a single word: convergence—the coming together of the upper and underworlds. How much the underworld depends on legitimate institutions such as the international banking system to advance its illegitimate ends is fairly obvious. What is more, those ends have been growing less and less illegitimate. After all, the aim of converting ill-begotten wealth into fresh capital is to be able to invest it in legally sanctioned business enterprises. Not that gangsters, having done so, cease to be gangsters; often, as in the case of pizza dough and mozzarella cheese and wholesale meats, to cite a few that have come to light in recent years, they muscle in and establish rackets in the customary way. Nor do we doubt Charles Grutzner's claim, drawn from the best law enforcement and regulatory agencies in the land, that "organized crime today owns or has decision-making influence in *50,000 commercial and industrial companies.*" Investigative reporters, especially for the *Wall Street Journal*, have been exposing the business side of organized crime with unflagging assiduity for years. But taking them all in all, what do such revelations and exposés tell us? They tell us that nothing can stop the historic process now under way to bring gangster-businessmen into the mainstream of American capitalism. It is a process that may take time to complete, the space of another generation perhaps, but completed it will be. And when it is, organized crime will have joined the Mustache Petes among the reliquaries of the past.*

The convergence is coming from the direction of the upper world

---

* The Mafia, according to Thomas P. Puccio, head of the Justice Department's organized crime strike force for New York, is "more sophisticated than it has ever been, involving itself more and more and more in legitimate business. . . . They have learned over the years how to clean up their money" and they now own a variety of enterprises: hotels, bars, construction and trucking and private carting companies and the like. Legitimacy, Mr. Puccio complains, has made the Mafia "almost impregnable."

as well. Lansky's—organized crime's—ancient hope of getting casino gambling legalized may have arrived. For good or ill Americans no longer regard gambling as a cardinal vice or as a vice at all. Is it too far-fetched to predict that more and more communities, each desperate for new tax revenues, will follow the example of Atlantic City, New Jersey, where a single casino run by Resorts International took in more money in its first year (1978–79) than the four largest Las Vegas casinos took in during that same year—a total of $222 million? Is the country becoming Las Vegasized? Defining the convergence of upper and nether worlds in these terms we can understand why casino gambling is now big business indeed. "Entertainment" conglomerates like MGM today own the largest establishments in Las Vegas. Bugsy Siegel's Flamingo is now the Las Vegas Hilton. And as the newspapers tell us daily, the rush is on in Atlantic City, one "entertainment" conglomerate after another—Bally, Playboy, Hilton, Caesar's Palace, Holiday Inn—having already staked its claim to this reborn Eldorado on the sea. Will New York City be far behind? Will other tourist and entertainment centers across the land? The point need not be labored. America is embracing Bugsy Siegel's vision; his martyrdom was not in vain.*

The question universally asked is how much influence or power Meyer Lansky and his minions exercise over these conglomerates, at least over their casino operations, how much of the usual skimming, laundering, and other stratagems of predation take place. To us this is a fruitless question because it fails to account for the dynamics of convergence, the tendency of the American economic and political system to (a) force the criminals to play by the rules and in so doing (b) make them ex-criminals sooner or later. Even if the worst is imagined—if Lansky and his associates own considerable shares in, say, Resorts International, and he and his apparatchiks work with,

---

* The president of Caesar's World, William H. McElnea, was only speaking the truth when he recently pointed out to a distinguished Wall Street audience: "Various levels of government have recognized the public benefits to be derived from legalized gaming, and there is rapidly growing public acceptance of gaming as a legitimate business operation as well as a legal enterprise. The combination is creating a vast new market for our industry."

are consulted by, and, yes, have power and influence over, its executives—if all this is granted *ex hypothesi*, the fact remains that the
company must still be run as a business, profits must still be earned,
stockholders satisfied, and the regulations laid down by a plethora of
government agencies observed. In the end the system swallows up
the gangsters in its gigantic maw, leaving behind only the traces of
their errant careers.

$\mathcal{V}$

Jewish gang/syndicate chieftains are no more.
Lansky is the exception, and properly speaking he has only a team of
experts in the arcana of crime; he depends on the gang/syndicates he
serves for such coercive power as he may occasionally require. The
gang/syndicates are now Italian from top to bottom; nary a Jew is to
be found in their ranks. The Teamsters Union, though, still has several Jewish middle-range bosses who are closely connected with the
Mafia in their communities: above all, Paul and Allen Dorfman and
Alvin Baron of Chicago; William and Jackie Presser of Cleveland;
Harry Davidoff and Abraham Gordon of New York. Back in the
1950s, we should add, a goodly number of Lepke's New York operatives, those involved in his several trucking rackets, such as Davidoff and Gordon among many others, played a decisive role in
handing the Teamsters International over to James S. Hoffa and the
gang/syndicates with which he was allied, which he faithfully served
until his imprisonment, and which eventually executed him for reasons that have not yet become wholly clear. This takeover of the
largest and most important union in the land was one of the Mafia's
supreme accomplishments.

And even if Lansky is as awesome as he is reputed to be he is by
now scarcely more than a lonely isolated old man on the criminal
landscape of America. He bears the mark of Cain and knows no
peace. Government investigators (and sometimes reporters too)
watch and trail him without letup. Nor is he welcome anywhere else
on earth. In 1970 he sought asylum in Israel under the Law of Return, which gives every Jew a right to settle in the Promised Land (a
right that his old friend Joseph "Doc" Stracher, once a prominent

Newark hood, had exercised years before). Did Lansky intend to retire in Israel in good faith? Or was he planning to use Israel as a cover for his worldwide operations? Obviously the Israeli government, urged on by the United States, assumed the latter. Since no other country would have him he went back home to Miami Beach to face—and ultimately survive—a sea of troubles. Along with the $36 million skimming indictment were two other charges: that on fleeing to Israel he refused to honor a grand jury subpoena and should therefore be held in contempt of court; and that he had evaded paying taxes on about $100,000 he had earned in 1967 and 1968. On the contempt charge he was tried, convicted, and sentenced to a year and a day in jail. The appeals court, however, threw out the conviction, ruling that the government had not established its case, that he had not "willfully and contemptuously" refused to comply with the subpoena. The tax evasion charge he easily beat in a short trial which the government prosecutors obviously botched, relying as they did on a discredited, or highly questionable, Mafia informant. Meanwhile, Lansky was undergoing open-heart surgery, and was still recuperating when he attended court for his second trial. The removal of the skimming indictment wiped the slate clean.

Absolved, vindicated, Meyer Lansky lives out his remaining days in modest, amply guarded surroundings; he is to all appearances just another retired senior citizen from the fleshpots of New York. To the cognoscenti, those who know something of his career, his wealth, reputed to be around $300 million (making him one of the wealthiest men in the world), is not the most impressive measure of his achievement. It is the fact that in his more than sixty years as a criminal—since that fateful day he met Bugsy Siegel—he has spent a total of three months and sixteen days in jail.

But he has his epigones. Among these pride of place by every account reputedly belongs to Alvin I. Malnik, graduate of Miami Law School and at forty-eight an attorney-businessman of far-ranging interests. When asked if he is Lansky's "heir apparent" Málnik replies, "What's been reported about me is almost total fiction. I'm neither a crook nor a part of the Mafia. People have heard so many bad things about me that when they see me for the first time they're surprised I don't wear a mohair suit and I'm not smoking a big cigar." This is certainly true. Miami Beach's Club 41 and its companion restaurant,

The Forge, both of which he owns, testify to Malnik's exquisite taste. Not only does he select and arrange their "colorful murals, tapestries and wood carvings," he is himself something of an artist who takes very seriously his sculpting and interior decorating. The old-fashioned gangster stereotype he conjures up scarcely applies to anyone involved in corporate and multinational crime.

That Malnik has been closely associated with Lansky's organization or apparatus for the last twenty years is a matter of public record, and it would be tedious to recite it. (The government once tried him for tax evasion but lost the case because its illegally procured wiretaps could not be used as evidence—wiretaps that trace in rich detail the character of Malnik's associations.) Law enforcement officials seem to agree with the Italian underworld—to quote one of its members who turned informer—"that dealing with Al Malnik was the same as dealing with Meyer Lansky."*

To judge from Malnik's more recent ventures one must conclude that he is a chip off the old block; Lansky himself could not have carried them off more dexterously. Consider the "Cove Associates" affair. Cove Associates is the name of a company chartered in Florida whose owners are Malnik and—talking of epigones—Alan and Joel Cohen, sons of Samuel Cohen, the very person sent to jail for his part in the $36-million skim. In 1975 Cove bought two "honeymoon" hotels in the Pocono Mountains, a lovely resort area northwest of Philadelphia. The seller happened to be Caesar's World, parent company of the fabled Caesar's Palace of Las Vegas (and soon to be of another palace in Atlantic City). The terms were generous indeed: Cove paid $15 million for the hotels, only to lease them back to Caesar's World for twenty years at the generous rate of $177,500 a month ($2,130,000 a year); of this amount $121,000 a month ($1,452,000 a year) went to the lender of the $15 million, leaving Malnik and the Cohen brothers $56,500 a month ($678,000 a year) to do with as they saw fit. That very question brought the Securities and Exchange Commission into play, Caesar's World being a public corporation. The government's

---

* To be more precise: "Al Malnik was an employee of Meyer Lansky and the purpose of his association with Meyer Lansky was that Al Malnik would convert illegal cash by laundering it in various real estate ventures."

suspicions deepened when it learned the source of the $15 million, namely the Teamsters Union's Central States, Southeast and Southwest Areas Pension Fund. Now it is a notorious and universally acknowledged fact that the immense pool of wealth—a minimum of $1 billion—fell into the hands of the gang/syndicates (through their control of its trustees) and that they drew on it heavily for many of their investments, resulting in a substantial drain on its resources. The Teamster Pension Fund, in other words, has given the underworld access to a vast quantity of clean money, or rather capital, that finds its way to the likes of Alvin Malnik.*

Nor was this the first time Malnik, the Cohens, and the Teamsters collaborated. Years earlier Malnik and the Cohens, through a company named COMAL, bought the posh Sky Lake Country Club in North Miami along with considerable land adjacent to it thanks to loans from the Teamster Pension Fund. In 1971 Caesar's World leased the Club and 320 acres from COMAL for a tidy sum; three years later it bought the land outright for $20 million and assumed the entire Pension Fund debt. Tne extent of the collaboration might be gauged by yet another fact that has come to light. Malnik and the Cohens own two thirds of a famous North Miami condominium-hotel complex, the Cricket Club. The other third, it transpires, belongs to the chairman of the board of Caesar's World, Clifford Perlman. Now it must be emphasized that these transactions are legal (unless proved otherwise), that the underworld aspect is far removed indeed, the gang/syndicate leaders in Chicago, Detroit, Cleveland, and elsewhere who dominate the Teamsters International being separated from them many times, that, in fine, they exemplify nothing so much as the effects of convergence, the fusion of modern capitalism and modern criminality. In this sense can Alvin I. Malnik be regarded as Lansky's "heir apparent."

Apart from Malnik (and the Cohen brothers) one is hard put to find many more epigones. Perhaps Allen R. Glick qualifies. This thirty-eight-year-old lawyer from Pittsburgh has certainly had a meteor-

---

* One fact will show how susceptible to loss or destruction this vast pension fund is. As of 1974, 58.3 percent of its assets were tied up in mortgages, some of them poor risks and at best low yielding. Compare this to the 1.8 percent of all pension funds tied up in mortgages.

ic rise. He had been working for a San Diego real estate firm in the early 1970s when, inexplicably, he was able to buy almost half of its stock for a mere $2,500, becoming by that single stroke a millionaire. In Las Vegas shortly afterward he set up his own company, Argent (Allen R. Glick Enterprises), and promptly became principal shareholder of the Stardust and Fremont hotels at a cost of $62 million. This the Teamster Pension Fund covered with a loan to Argent of $62.7 million—on top of the $15 million it had already lent him. By 1976 Argent owed the Fund $146 million all told. One has the impression that it is all a game of musical chairs, the same property being sold back and forth to different companies, maintaining appearances and justifying the use of further Pension Fund moneys. (Consider this sequence of events: Argent bought the Stardust and Fremont hotels from a company called Recrion which had bought them from Parvin-Dohrmann which originally had bought them from Moe Dalitz* and the legatees of the Cleveland syndicate. Parvin-Dohrmann had once also owned the Flamingo before selling it to one of Lansky's friends, Lansky receiving $200,000 as a finder.)

Allen R. Glick, then, was obviously being groomed for higher responsibilities by Lansky and the underworld powers that be. But his promising career may have run aground. For one thing, the Justice Department believes that a Chicago gangster, Anthony "Tony the Ant" Spilotro, enjoys an "intimate relationship" with Glick; if so, the Nevada Gaming Commission will have to remove Glick's license, thus finishing him in Las Vegas for good. For another thing, there is the murder—still being investigated in 1979—of his former business partner, one Tamara Rand, in November 1975, as she was about to be questioned by Justice Department lawyers. Allen R. Glick's fate hangs in the balance.

We can, if we wish, call up other young Jews in organized crime and put them on display. But to what purpose? They are obscure and they are few in number and they are very uninteresting.†

---

* Eased out of Las Vegas in 1966, Dalitz lives in graceful old age as the manager of the huge and opulent Teamster-owned LaCosta Hotel and Country Club, just north of San Diego.

† Here is the place to mention a well-known figure who falls somewhere between being a contemporary and an epigone of Meyer Lansky. We refer to Sidney Korshak,

It is a fading memory enveloped in twilight now: the Lower East Side of Maier Luchowljansky's childhood, where Big Jack Zelig and his men (Lefty Louie, Whitey Lewis, and Gyp the Blood) still commanded the streets, taking up where Monk Eastman and Kid Twist had left off, where the whores and gun-mols and cadets and gamblers and guerillas and life-takers met at Segal's Cafe and in scores of hangouts like it, where youth gangs abounded on every block, where aspiring criminals learned the techniques of survival and with luck and audacity and brains achieved success as well. But the Lower East Side and every other urban ghetto—Chicago's and Philadelphia's and Cleveland's and Boston's and Detroit's and Newark's—once tenanted by Eastern European Jews are gone, and so are all the children of the underworld, those who fell in battle and those who died peacefully in the bosom of respectability, the anonymous mass and the privileged few. That past is vanquished. Meyer Lansky is the last of its heroes.

---

now seventy-three, a paradigm if anyone is of how convergence works its destiny in America. According to correspondent Seymour Hersh of *The New York Times*, Korshak made his way up from the Chicago ghetto with the help of the Capone mob. Back in the early 1930s as a lawyer fresh out of the University of Wisconsin and DePaul he represented local gangster-controlled unions in fixing public officials and setting up sweetheart arrangements with employers. Decades later Korshak settled in Los Angeles and there again served as intermediary between gangster-led unions and business. He was instrumental, for example, in channeling Teamster Pension Funds to the right places, especially the burgeoning Las Vegas casinos. Meanwhile he prospered. Always he paid his taxes—a total of $2.9 million out of a reported $4.5 million earned between 1963 and 1969. Much of that stupendous income came from perfectly legitimate sources, Korshak's stock in trade being his contacts, his exceptional ability to bring the affluent segments of the upper and underworlds together. So it is that his company, Associated Booking Corporation, is now the country's third largest booking agency, that he represents over one hundred corporation clients, among them Gulf and Western, Schenley Industries, the Los Angeles Dodgers, and the Madison Square Garden Corporation. And though modesty is hardly one of Korshak's virtues—his mansion is worth more than a million dollars, and he flaunts his Rolls-Royce, Mercedes, Jaguar, and Cadillac—like Alvin Malnik he cannot be called vulgar: his wine cellar has few equals, and Chagalls and Renoirs grace his walls. But when all is said and done, and with due respect for Hersh's admirable effort, Sidney Korshak must be seen for what he is, no more no less: as a servitor of the gang/syndicates, not one of its members and certainly not one of its leaders.

AFTERWORD
TO THE
MORNINGSIDE
EDITION

i

In *The Rise and Fall of the Jewish Gangster in America,* I tried to show that an underworld subculture took root in the Eastern European ghettoes of America around the turn of the century. It was a subculture that produced a farrago of young criminals who went on to prosper in the roaring twenties due mainly to Prohibition. The capital that they amassed enabled them, organized by now into a loose arrangement of gang/syndicates, to prosper still further by entering other flourishing rackets, especially gambling, after Prohibition ended in 1933. This subculture for all intents and purposes died out when that extraordinary generation did. The "fall" of the Jewish gangster is a metaphor. Mostly, he just faded away.

What was true when this book appeared in 1980 is truer even today. The two surviving argonauts have since gone to their reward—in 1990, Moe Dalitz who cut his teeth with Detroit's Purple Gang and came into his own with the Cleveland Four prior to moving on to Caesar's Palace and La Costa Country and in 1983, Meyer Lansky, a towering figure in the history of the American demi-monde, who was condemned, following his expulsion from Israel, to live out the rest of his life in quiet, modest retirement. And, the young men such as Alvin I. Malnik and Allen R. Glick who, as I mentioned in the book, were being groomed for a place in the gang/syndicate hierarchy have disappeared entirely from view. Hardly anything remains today of the fantastic world I described. This also applies to Italian-American gangsters. The historic tendency of illicitly-begotten wealth to find legitimate outlets ("primitive accumulation") has accelerated since 1980. New punitive legislation and a growing number of important defectors willing to testify against their former associates have helped federal prosecutors send more and more Mafia bosses to jail for interminable stretches. Above all, the absence of an Italian-American underworld subculture is drying up the pool of new recruits. The inevitable consequence is that other ethnic and racial minorities (African Americans, Hispanics, and Asians) have been emerging from their ghetto enclaves to make their mark on the criminal landscape. They are keeping faith with a grand American tradition.

Also worth noting in this backward glance is an event I could not imagine happening; I still rub my eyes in disbelief. I am referring to the transformation of the Teamsters Union. Readers will remember that the gang/syndicates effectively controlled the Teamsters, the largest union in America, and freely drew on its gigantic pension fund to help finance their ventures such as Las Vegas. The union, moreover, was never so corrupt as in the 1980s when its Mafia directors brazenly made Jackie Presser its president. Quite an honor for a Jew. But, they would not have honored him had he not been a member in good standing with the Cleveland mob. Meanwhile, his friend Allen Dorfman, a long-time intermediary between the union and the Chicago mob, was gunned down because he presumably was talking to the authorities. Presser, an acknowledged FBI informer, might have suffered the same fate had this 300 pound leviathan not died a natural death. Outraged public opinion compelled the federal government to intervene by first securing the union's pension fund against further peculation and, then, by supervising a union election (the rank and file had never voted before) that resulted in the ouster of the old guard and the triumph of an intrepid band of reformers. Although these actions were a significant step in cleaning up the Teamsters, much work remains to be done. Gangsters or their collaborators are still in charge of many Teamster locals and eliminating them poses a daunting challenge to union reformers and federal officials alike.

ü

▬▬▬▬▬▬▬ Several books including two on Meyer Lansky have been published since mine. Actually *Meyer Lansky, Mogul of the Mob* was published in 1979. However, I could not make any use of it because my book had already gone to the printer.

Meyer Lansky, Mogul of the Mob by Israeli journalists Dennis Eisenberg, Uri Dan, and Eli Landau claims to at last give us a truthful account of what this master criminal did and what he knew about the mob. Their lengthy interviews with him during his stay in Israel is something of a coup; we meet a human being for the first time. He is full of new information about his grandparents and parents; his childhood in Grondo, Poland; his emigration to America; his Lower East Side youth; his introduction to gambling and other vices; his lifelong friendship with Bugsy Siegel and Lucky Luciano; and the like. However, this canny old gangster tells us precious little about what we really want to know. The specificities are lacking. He artfully serves up one vague generality and self-exalting platitude after another, each duly recorded by his interlocutors. For example: "The advice I always give my friends and family and anyone who wants to listen is: Never play the dice and cards and the roulette wheel or anything else if you dislike losing. Games of chance are for those who are greedy." And again "if you think ahead and carefully plan whatever you are going to do, whatever activity it is, you can win. It's the fools who rush in unprepared . . . they are life's suckers." One thing I did learn from the book is that Lansky and his street comrades used to call the great Arnold Rothstein "the PhD," short for "papa hat gelt," papa has money.

More formidable by far is Robert Lacey's *Little Man: Meyer Lansky and the Gangster Life.* Lacey has certainly done his homework. No source or document escaped his eagle eye; he even managed to interview Lansky's widow and children. His biography puts the others in the shade. And yet, for all its virtues, it too disappoints. It rehashes the oft-told story of organized crime in the Lansky epoch, from the 1920s through the 1960s, authoritatively to be sure, but it is short on new revelations or fresh insights. However, Lacey does pique our curiosity. He challenges the universally held assumption that Lansky left behind a fortune, hundreds of millions of dollars perhaps. It is more likely, Lacey contends or rather speculates, that Lansky left behind nothing. What is the evidence? The straitened, even pathetic condition of his widow and children, one of whom, disabled from birth, died in a miserable welfare institution. Is it conceivable that the venerable gangster exhausted his genius on behalf of his colleagues while neglecting his own interests? More believable is the possibility that the millions he did stash away were either looted or are in the possession of family members who, for obvious reasons, can not easily spend it. One can speculate endlessly.

Two books of a different sort that appeared in the 1980s, both models of scholarship and published by university presses, also deserve mention.

Alan Block's *East Side—West Side* (University of Wales Press) deals with Jewish gangsters as part of the general organized crime scene in New York City between 1930 and 1950. His focus is sociological. Thus, the incidents and personalities he takes up (many of the same ones I do) merely illustrate broader and more significant themes: how a complex system inextricably unites organized crime to politicians and respectable clientele behind a cover of law and morality and how a hideous "social world" that is deliquescent, treacherous, and murderously violent feeds that system. The paradox is that Block's study comes most alive when it details the machinations of its protagonists during those turbulent years, the Jewish and Italian gangsters and their Irish and WASP coadjutors. The material is too rich to be reduced to a general schema.

"Jewish crime" between 1900 and 1940 is the subject of Jena Weissman Joselit's *Our Gang* (University of Indiana Press), the dates being inseparable from her schema. She relates the Jewish community's response to Jewish crime; that is the two changing together, pari passu, during the years in question. She demonstrates that as Jewish gangsters become more professional and brutal—Lepke's associates and Murder Inc. carried out the worse deeds in the 1930s—the community at large was less concerned than in earlier years about what the outside world thought because, by then, Jews were better adjusted to American life, more self-confident, and more at ease with themselves. The interplay between criminals and community also requires Joselit to get into the always fascinating details of how the gangsters conducted their sordid business. This she does deftly, never straying from her solidly documented sources.

Both authors, Block and Joselit, make us aware of how much more work should be done on the history and sociology of the Jewish underworld, especially beyond the precincts of New York City. Some of America's most prominent Jewish gangsters, as readers of my book will recall, came out of the fleshpots of Newark, Philadelphia, Detroit, Cleveland, Chicago, and Minneapolis. How useful it would be to have academically authorized studies of these individuals, their gangs, and the remarkable subcultures from which they sprang.

In 1989, E. L. Doctorow brought out a gangster novel, *Billy Bathgate*, about a latter-day Huck Finn from the Bathgate district of the Bronx, where Dutch Schultz and his gang hold sway. The Dutchmn takes a shine to Billy, a fetching lad, whose keen recollections many years later give us an all too vivid picture of the gangster's vaunted sadism and cunning. Billy, ingratiating as he is audacious (he makes love to the boss's mistress) witnesses these deeds first hand and emerges from the relationship with the Dutchman well prepared for the life that lies ahead of him. I know of no other gangster novel written by a major writer that is built on real life gangsters and their deeds. But, the Dutch Schultz portrayed here is simply too loathsome to be credible. As a result, we loose interest in young Billy as well.

In his powerful short stories, Issac Bael shows us what a great writer can do with real-life gangsters. However, at his worse, Benja Krik of Odessa could not hold a candle to such

New York counterparts as Big Jack Zelig, Kid Dropper, Gyp the Blood, Bugsy Siegel, Lepke Buchalter, and Abe Kid Twist Reles. Will any of them find their Babel?

• • •

m

It never occurred to me when I wrote my book that the movies would discover Jewish gangsters to the extent that they did in the last decade. Paving the way for them was Francis Ford Coppola's enormously popular *Godfather* films in the 1970s, based on Mario Puzo's enormously popular and quite conventional novel of the same name. By emphasizing the ethnic background of the gangster-heroes and the deprivations they undergo as a reviled minority and how organized crime became the lever which lifts the Corleones out of poverty and anonymity, the movie raised the genre to a level it had never attained. Whereas the famous old gangster movies, notably *Little Caesar* and *Scarface*, at once romanticized and vilified their lead characters by proving that crime did not pay (a favorite film maxim of the 1930s), *Godfather I* and *II* delivered an ambiguous message. The Corleones were gangsters but they were also decent businessmen engaged in outlawed commodities, except drugs—far more decent than the politicians, clients, and assorted hangers-on who surreptitiously consort with them. For the Corleones crime does pay, as it does for most real life gangsters.

Incidentally, Samuel Roth, the Jewish gangster in *Godfather II*, who was brilliantly played by Lee Strasberg is an obvious stand-in for Meyer Lansky. In his perfidy, his fiendish manipulation of the trusting Corleones and other paisans, he is the most execrable character of all. So taken by the performance was Lansky, this according to Robert Lacey, that he called Strasberg to both compliment him on his performance and complain about how unfairly it depicted him. What Lansky probably did not realize was that Strasberg brought it off so well because he was so free to "invent" a universal Jewish gangster type; he was not doing Lansky. To this point I will return in a moment.

The best of the Jewish gangster movies without a doubt is

Once Upon a Time in America (the three hour uncut version) made by the great Italian director Sergio Leone. It traces the underworld careers of a gang that grew up on the Lower East Side before World War I by concentrating on two members, the fastest of friends, who were played by Robert DeNiro and John Woods. The contrast between the idyll of struggling ghetto youth and the corruption and betrayals of success can not be more starkly conveyed. The movie is so convincing and hangs together so well because, like the *Godfather* cycle, its characters are archetypes or composites; they are not taken from real-life figures. We watch a believable story unfold; we are not asked to measure the screen characters against actual gangsters of lengendary reputation.

The failure of the movie *Bugsy* reinforces this point. We are given to believe that only an actor like Warren Beatty, who is himself somewhat of a legend as far as women are concerned, can do justice to the redoubtable Bugsy Siegel. It fails because we, the audience, are already supposed to now about: (1) Siegel's monstrous temper, love of violence, and appetite for women; (2) his stormy affair with the only woman, Virginia Hill, who was his match; (3) his genius in building the Flamingo Hotel and, thus, creating what we now know as Las Vegas; and (4) his suicidal defiance of the gangster/syndicates, his old pal Lansky included. The problem is that we may not know these things and wonder why this man behaves in such contradictory and implausible ways. The contradictions and implausibilities that defined the real-life Siegel do not work cinematically, where characters must be sharply delineated on their own terms. Sharp delineation of character, the presentation of a readily understood *type* is just what Coppola and Leone achieve along with the best of the classic gangster films. It is better artistically to have single dimensional portraits a la Edward G. Robinson, Paul Muni, Jimmy Cagney, George Raft, and Humphrey Bogart than labored efforts at verisimilitude. The movie is the thing, not the legend.

A still more egregious failure along these lines is the film version of *Billy Bathgate*. Dustin Hoffman's portrayal of Dutch Schultz borders on psychopathy. This dominates the proceedings and overwhelms poor Billy and everyone else. The film might have approached its target had it not departed as far from the book as it did and not reduced the Dutchman to a stock character in the tradition of *Little Caesar, Scarface,* and *Angels With Dirty Faces.*

Yet another failure is Coppola's ambitious and expensive try at historical representation, *The Cotton Club.* Once again the reigning gangsters are legends to those in the know, from Bob Haskin's Owney Madden, the well-liked partner in the Harlem club, to the ineffable Dutchman (Allen Garfield) portrayed as a bloodthirsty maniac. And once again, the attempt at verisimilitude makes the movie implausible, often incomprehensible. The best part of *The Cotton Club* is the dancing of the Hines brothers and the music, especially by Duke Ellington.

My book figures in a strange film of the late 1980s, Jean-Luc Godard's *Lear,* as a prop. Don Learo (Burgess Meredith) is an Italian gangster who, we gather from the vaguest of allusions, is King Lear and a Mafia godfather and maybe Meredith himself of *Winterset* fame more than half a century ago, all rolled into one—a typical Godardian exercise, in short. In several scenes, Don Learo conspicuously carries a copy of my *The Rise and Fall of the Jewish Gangster in America.* With the book under his arm, he is shot and killed. Godard saw that the copy I lent him got back to me, its cover streaked with an ineradicable red substance. No matter. I cherish this souvenir of my name in film.

w

The republication of *The Rise and Fall of the Jewish Gangster in America* is, if I may say so, long overdue. And, I would like to thank Columbia University Press for doing it. Too few libraries still possess copies as many were evidently expropriated for personal use. I suppose I should be flattered by this display of cupidity. Clearly, the subject has not ceased to provoke interest. And, to John Michel I owe a special thanks. He is an ideal editor, savvy, wise, and patient. I count myself lucky that our paths crossed.

NOTES

Full publication information on sources cited in these notes can be found in the Bibliography.

page no. **Introduction.   Some Questions of Motive and Method**

xiv   A year after the Jewish Museum exhibit was held, Allon Schoener compiled a book, *Portal to America: The Lower East Side, 1870–1925*, which includes much of its material.

xvi   "Jewish criminals": Moses Rischin, *The Promised City*, p. 90.

xvii   "But in the life of the immigrant community": Irving Howe, *World of Our Fathers*, p. 101.

xvii   On crime and ethnic upward mobility in America, see, for example: Daniel Bell, "Crime as an American Way of Life," *Antioch Review*, June 1953; Joseph L. Albini, *The American Mafia: Genesis of a Legend*; Francis A. J. Ianni, *Black Mafia: Ethnic Succession in Organized Crime*; and Humbert S. Nelli, *The Business of Crime*.

One.   The Old Neighborhood

1   On Abe Shoenfeld's undercover work in general, see Chapter Two, pp. 79–80, and Arthur A. Goren, *New York Jews and the Quest for Community*, pp. 169–72. Goren also briefly describes Shoenfeld's life and career, pp. 162–63.

2–4   Segal's Cafe and its "habitues" are taken whole from Magnes Papers, Story #6, SP 126 (listed in Bibliography under Judah P. Magnes).

4–5   The Solomon, or Boston, brothers and their spouses are the subject of Magnes Papers, Story #83, SP 127.

5–6   Portraits of Lower East Side "hangouts" and brothels and gambling joints and their numerous habitués lie scattered in the "stories" Shoenfeld drew up and comprise SP 125 through SP 139 and F 46–L 16, pp. 1–11 of the Magnes Papers.

6   Vigilante group can "be formed in 4 hours": Magnes Papers, Story #6, p. 2, SP 125.

7–8   On New York prostitution at this time: Robert Ernst, *Immigrant Life in New York City 1823–1863*, pp. 58–59; William W. Sanger, *History of Prostitution*, pp. 459–60, 559–61; and John H. Warren Jr., *Thirty Years Battle with Crime*, pp. iv, v.

8   On Jewish prostitution: Maude E. Miner, *The Slavery of Prostitution*, p. 35; Frank Moss, *The American Metropolis*, vol. 3, pp. 221–23; and *Report of the Special Committee of the Assembly Appointed to Investigate the Public Officers and Departments of the City of New York and of the Counties Therein Included*, vol. 2, pp. 2002–4, 2033–34 (hereafter referred to as Mazet Committee Report).

8   Survey (1909) of prostitutes: *Importation and Harboring of Women for Immoral Purposes*, Reports of the U.S. Immigration Commission, pp. 62, 64–65.

8–9   On Bedford Hills survey: George T. Kneeland, *Commercialized Prostitution in New York City*, pp. 164, 180, 200–202.

8n   "The greatest evil": University Settlement Society of New York, *Year Book (1899)*, p. 37 (hereafter referred to as *USSNY Year Books* or *Reports* with year of publication specified).

9   Charity work by Jewish organizations: National Council of Jewish Women, *Yearbook, New York Section, 1904–5*, p. 11; and Hawthorne School, *Third Annual Report (1910)*, p. 12.

9–10   "The horrors of the sweatshop": William McAdoo, *Guarding a Great City*, p. 145.

10n   Miner, p. 35.

10n   "The 'new Jewish woman' ": Charlotte Baum, Paula Hyman, and Sonya Michel, *The Jewish Woman in America*, p. 89.

11   On Rosie Solomon and Jennie Silver: Magnes Papers, F 46–L 16, pp. 17–20.

11n   Maimie Pinzer, *The Maimie Papers*, introduction.

12   On prostitution in "the back rooms of stores": *USSNY Year Book (1897)*, p. 37; Magnes Papers, F 46–L 16, pp. 15–16.

12   "The other member of the household": Committee of Fourteen, *The Social Evil in New York City*, p. 12.

12   The "hideous women swarming": Moss, vol. 3, pp. 221–22.

12	"Almost any child": Committee of Fifteen, *The Social Evil*, 1912 edition, p. 158.
12n	"A hundred women": Benjamin Antin, *Gentleman from the 22nd*, p. 30.
13	" 'Oh, Meester Report!' ": Lincoln Steffens, *Autobiography*, p. 245.
13	"The worst sin": *USSNY Report for 1900*, pp. 11–12.
13	On Raines Law hotels: Willoughby Waterman, *Prostitution and Its Repression in New York City 1900–1931*, pp. 31–32; and Committee of Fourteen, p. 38.
13–14	"The average citizen goes there": Committee of Fifteen, *The Social Evil*, 1902 edition, p. 62.
14	Cadet "is a young man": Committee of Fifteen, 1912 edition, p. 156.
14	Encountering "a young gentleman": Marcus E. Ravage, *An American in the Making*, p. 115.
14–15	"Beware of those who": *Statement and Recommendations Submitted by Societies and Organizations Interested in the Subject of Immigration*, Reports of the U.S. Immigration Commission, p. 47.
15	"He took the girl": *Importation and Harboring of Women for Immoral Purposes*, pp. 119–20.
15n–16n	Rosie who "worked for years": Michael Gold, *Jews Without Money*, p. 21.
16	The "young people in Jewtown": Jacob Riis, *How the Other Half Lives*, p. 82. On Lower East Side dance halls in general: Verne M. Bovie, "The Public Dance Halls of the Lower East Side," *USSNY Year Book (1900)*, p. 31.
16–17	"If you walk along": Belle Lindner Israels, "The Way of the Girl," *Survey*, p. 494.
16n	"By occasional visits": Committee of Fifteen, 1912 edition, p. 157.
17	"You cannot dance": Israels, p. 495.
17	Dance halls as "gathering places": Bovie, pp. 32–33. On reforming dance halls: Kneeland, pp. 67–73; and Committee of Fourteen, p. 51.
17	"In one you see": Bovie, p. 34. On procurers in general: Committee of Fourteen, pp. 60–61.
18	On Motche Goldberg: Howard B. Woolston, *Prostitution in the United States*, pp. 91–92.
18–19	"There are large numbers": *Importation and Harboring of Women for Immoral Purposes*, p. 77.
18n	The "rage for redheaded": Nell Kimball, *Nell Kimball, Her Life as an American Madam*, p. 229.

19   On cadets hiring enforcers: Committee of Fourteen, p. 65.

19n   Legalizing prostitution: Committee of Fifteen, 1902 edition, pp. 177–78.

20   On Lower East Side gambling: Andy Logan, *Against the Evidence*, p. 60.

20–21   For a description of stuss: Diagram Group, *The Way to Play*, p. 207; and Herbert Asbury, *Sucker's Progress*, p. 18.

21   Poolrooms on the Lower East Side and elsewhere: Logan, p. 60; Josiah Flynt, "The Pool-Room Vampire," *Cosmopolitan Magazine*, February 1907, pp. 336–37, 514–15; Flynt, "Allies of the Criminal Pool-Room," *Cosmopolitan Magazine*, September 1907, p. 57; Mark Sullivan, "The Pool-Room Evil," *Outlook*, p. 212; and McAdoo, pp. 206–7; Magnes Papers (in which 180 neighborhood poolrooms are listed), F 46–L 16, p. 22.

21n   "To justify the expenditure": R. F. Foster, *Foster's Complete Hoyle*, p. 534.

21n   "Harry Green is an ex-pickpocket": Magnes Papers, F 46–L 16, pp. 22–23.

22   "The man who goes to a race-track": Sullivan, p. 215.

22   "Gambling Commission": *The New York Times*, March 9, 1900.

22–23   Big Tim Sullivan and the "smart young Jewboys": Logan, pp. 53, 60.

22n   Jobs for the faithful: McAdoo, p. 193; and Logan, p. 56.

23   On neighborhood casinos: Logan, p. 69.

23   On Rothstein's launching: Leo Katcher, *The Big Bankroll*, pp. 17–18, 24–29.

23   "Sometimes he even took": Carolyn Rothstein, *Now I'll Tell*, pp. 19–20.

23   "I always gambled": Katcher, *The Big Bankroll*, p. 20.

23–24   On Rothstein's rise in the Tenderloin: Logan, p. 152; and Katcher, *The Big Bankroll*, pp. 63, 65–70.

24   On the tradition of Canfield and Churchill: Asbury, *Sucker's Progress*, pp. 419–69; and on Jews making their mark uptown: Logan, pp. 65, 152. The relation between Lower East Side gamblers and enforcers was brought out in the *New York World*, July 24 and 27, 1912.

24n   Pocket billiards game: Katcher, *The Big Bankroll*, pp. 53–56.

25   On Harry Joblinsky and Abe Greenthal and other fagins: Frank Moss, vol. 3, p. 168; and Ande Manners, *Poor Cousins*, p. 235.

26   On Mother Mandelbaum: Moss, vol. 3, pp. 209–10; Nell Kimball, p. 175; and Prison Committee of the Association of Grand Jurors of New York County, *Criminal Receivers of the United States*, p. 11.

26   On notorious arsonists of the Lower East Side: *The New York Times*, January 20, April 23, 1894, and July 18, 1895, and January 30, 1896. On Isaac Zucker: *The New York Times*: December 18, 22, 23, 24, 29, 30, 31, 1896.

26n   "The energy of her character": Lewis E. Lawes, *Cell 202, Sing Sing*, pp. 485–86.

26n   "Many of the 400": *The New York Times*, April 20, 1911.

27   Eastman "began life with": Herbert Asbury, *The Gangs of New York*, p. 278. For some newspaper accounts of Eastman's gang: *The New York Times*, September 17, 18, October 3, 1903.

27n   On Eastman's feud with Paul Kelly: Asbury, *The Gangs of New York*, p. 280.

28   On Eastman as a bouncer: Alvin Harlow, *Old Bowery Days*, pp. 440–41.

28   On Silver Dollar Smith: Abraham Cahan, *The Education of Abraham Cahan*, p. 290; and M. R. Werner, *Tammany Hall*, p. 382.

28   "Once I saw him": Cahan, p. 290.

28–29 On Eastman gang and Rothstein: Katcher, *The Big Bankroll*, p. 23. On Eastman's downfall: *The New York Times*, February 3, 5, March 5, April 13, 14, 15, 20, 1904; and Asbury, *The Gangs of New York*, pp. 286–87.

29–30 On Kid Twist: Asbury, *The Gangs of New York*, pp. 287–92; and George Kibbe Turner, "Tammany's Control of New York by Professional Criminals," *McClure's*, June 1909, p. 123.

29n   Eastman's last years and death: Asbury, *The Gangs of New York*, pp. 295–98; and *The New York Times*, December 27, 1920.

30   "No 'wop' and no 'mick' ": Joel Slonim, "The Jewish Gangster," *Reflex*, p. 38.

30   Kid Twist's comeuppance: Asbury, *The Gangs of New York*, pp. 292–95; and *The New York Times*, May 15, 1908.

30–31 On Big Jack Zelig and his gang: Asbury, *The Gangs of New York*, pp. 328–35; Logan, pp. 24–25, 72–73; Harlow, p. 519; and *The New York Times*, October 6, 1912.

32   Zelig's troubles: Werner, *Tammany Hall*, p. 506; Logan, p. 131; and the *New York World*, October 6, 1912.

32–33 On Dopey Benny's early years: *The New York Times*, August 10, 14, 1913, and January 14, 1914.

32n   "I want you to stop": *The New York Times*, October 6, 1912.

33   On trade unions and conflicts with manufacturers: Rischin, pp. 243–57; Melech Epstein, *Jewish Labor in USA*, pp. 388–89; Hyman Berman, "Era of the Protocol," pp. 75–76; and Cornelius Willemse, *Behind the Green Lights*, pp. 283–84.

34–36 On Dopey Benny's operation, and Yoski Nigger's and Joe the

Greaser's as well: Harold Seidman, *Labor Czars*, pp. 46–50; and Asbury, *The Gangs of New York*, pp. 283, 358–59, 361–64. Also, *The New York Times*, March 6, 25, 1913, and December 20, 1914, and May 12, 13, 14, 15, 1915.

36   "The age of maximum criminality": E. H. Sutherland, *Principles of Criminology*, pp. 87–88.

36*n*   Statistical analysis of Jewish criminals by Francis J. Oppenheimer, "Jewish Criminality," *The Independent*, p. 642.

37   On the prevalence of street gangs: Harry Roskolenko, *The Time That Was Then*, p. 18; and the College Settlement Association, *Eighth Annual Report*.

37   Conflict "so fraught with heart-rending consequences": Morris Raphael Cohen, *A Dreamer's Journey*, pp. 98–99.

37*n*   "We saw it everywhere": Steffens, pp. 244–45.

37*n*   "Often some of the more": Committee of Fourteen, pp. 61–62.

38   "The boy's mother": Frederick A. King, "Influences in Street Life," *USSNY Year Book (1900)*, p. 32.

38   "If Division Street": Eddie Cantor, *Take My Life*, p. 16.

39   "The distracted storekeeper": Eddie Cantor, *My Life Is in Your Hands*, pp. 40–41.

39*n*   "Thousands of children": Frank Simonds, "The Relation of Children to Immoral Conditions," *USSNY Year Book (1900)*, pp. 34–35.

39*n*   "Jewish boys of this class": Frederick A. King, p. 32.

40*n*   "A group of women": McAdoo, p. 157.

41   On the Hawthorne School: Hawthorne School, *First Annual Report (1908)*, p. 9; and *Third Annual Report (1910)*, p. 12.

41   On the work of Lower East Side settlement houses: Rischin, pp. 206–9.

41*n*   Juvenile Court figures appear in *American Hebrew*, December 19, 1909, p. 1.

42   "True, these institutions": A. H. Fromenson, "East Side Preventive Work," *National Conference of Jewish Charities, Proceedings*, pp. 116–24.

42*n*   "This was the greatest": Harry Golden's preface to Hutchins Hapgood's *Spirit of the Ghetto*, p. xiii.

43*n*   "Why should it not be the purpose": *USSNY Report for 1910*, p. 23.

page no.   **Two.   The Mugwumps and the Jews**

44   On the beginning of Parkhurst's crusade: Charles H. Parkhurst, *Our Fight with Tammany*, pp. 4–5.

44   The police "existed for the purpose": Parkhurst, p. 5.

45	On the Mugwump as a type: Richard Hofstadter, *The Age of Reform*, pp. 139, 141–43.
45–46	"There is no such organization": London *Review of Reviews*, October, 1897, quoted in Werner, *Tammany Hall*, pp. 449–50.
46	The "lying, perjured, rum-soaked": Parkhurst, pp. 14, 18; and *The New York Times*, February 15, 1892; *New York World*, February 15, 1892; *New York Tribune*, February 15, 1892.
47	"The best employment": Parkhurst, pp. 41, 44.
47–48	Parkhurst's travels through the underworld: Charles W. Gardner, *The Doctor and the Devil*, pp. 52–54, 57.
48	On Parkhurst's March 13 sermon: Parkhurst, p. 78; and *The New York Times*, March 14, 1892. The ditty is found in M. R. Werner, *It Happened in New York*, p. 50.
48n	A young man "whose face was painted": Gardner, p. 57.
49	On Parkhurst's effect and the emergence of the Lexow Committee: *The New York Times*, January 26, 1894; and Werner, *It Happened in New York*, p. 59. The committee hearings are published as *Report and Proceedings of the Senate Committee Appointed to Investigate the Police Department of the City of New York* (hereafter referred to as Lexow Committee Report).
49	For insights into the city's night life, see, for example, the testimony of Captain Schmittberger, Lexow Committee Report, vol. 1, pp. 25–26; and vol. 5, pp. 71–79.
50–51	Mrs. Urchittel's testimony: Lexow Committee Report, vol. 3, pp. 2733–38, 2961–64.
51–52	Return of Urchittel children: Lexow Committee Report, vol. 4, pp. 3639–40; and *New York World*, October 20, 1894.
53	Lower East Side overcrowding: Robert W. DeForest and Lawrence Veiller, *The Tenement House Problem*, vol. 1, frontispiece: "The Most Densely Populated Spot in the World—the Lower East Side of New York."
53–54	On Big Tim Sullivan: Logan, pp. 55–57; and Harlow, pp. 487–92.
53n	"Whenever they vote": Harlow, p. 505.
54	"I was born in poverty": Werner, *Tammany Hall*, p. 503.
54–55	"The habits and modes of": *USSNY Report for 1897*, p. 27.
55	"It is not possible": *USSNY Report for 1897*, p. 47.
55–56	"Ignorance, prejudice, stubborn": Moss, vol. 3, pp. 159–61, 235.
56–57	On Murphy's reign: Allan Nevins and John A. Kraut, eds., *The Greater City: New York 1898–1948*, pp. 61–78.
57–58	"Wherefore it is not": Theodore A. Bingham, "Foreign Criminals in New York," *North American Review*, pp. 383–84.
58	On the rise of American nativism at this time: John Higham, *Strangers in the Land*, pp. 158–61.

59	On protests by Jewish newspapers and organizations: Goren, pp. 26–27; and *The New York Times*, September 2, 7, 11, 16, 1908.
59	Bingham's apology: *The New York Times*, September 17, 1908.
59n–60n	On the crude use of statistics: Goren, pp. 146–47. The Immigration Commission survey: *Immigration and Crime*, Reports of the U.S. Immigration Commission, pp. 90, 94, 101.
60	On the organization of the Kehillah: Goren, pp. 30–56; and the *Jewish Communal Register of New York City 1917–18*, pp. 49–51.
61–64	Turner's article on Tammany control is in *McClure's*, June 1909, pp. 117–34.
64–67	Turner's second article is in *McClure's*, November 1909, pp. 45–61.
67–68	S. S. McClure's response is in *McClure's*, November 1909, pp. 117–28.
68–69	On reaction to Turner's piece: Goren, pp. 236–39.
69–70	The pro-Tammany view: *Warheit*, October 20, 1909; the Socialist view: *Forward*, October 26, 31, 1909.
69n	Prostitutes in night court: *Warheit*, October 28, 29, 30, 1909.
70	On Jewish prostitution in Chicago: *Chicago Daily News*, September 25, 1909; Herbert Asbury, *The Gem of the Prairie*; and John Landesco, *Organized Crime in Chicago*, pp. 30–31.
70	"The facts that were uncovered": *Forward*, September 7, 1909.
70	On London meeting of Jewish representatives: *Official Report (Private and Confidential) of the Jewish International Conference on the Suppression of the Traffic in Girls and Women* (hereafter referred to as Jewish International Conference).
70–71	"I wish I had time": Jewish International Conference, pp. 34–36.
71–72	On the absence of a Jewish prostitution trust, ring, or cabal: Kneeland, pp. 171–72; and *Importation and Harboring of Women for Immoral Purposes*, pp. 76, 77–78.
73	On Rosenthal's murder: *The New York Times*, July 17, 1912.
73	"And the time and place selected": *New York World*, July 17, 1912.
73	"I knew him as a boy": *New York World*, July 17, 1912.
74	Sullivan's insanity: Werner, *Tammany Hall*, p. 509.
74	Breaking the case open and indictments: *New York World*, July 30, 31, 1912; and Logan, p. 139.
75	"One thing is clear": *The Outlook*, August 3, 1912, p. 739; also, *Literary Digest*, July 29, 1912, p. 136, and August 10, 1912, pp. 205–7.
75	"Zelig will never see": *The New York Times*, October 6, 1912. On Zelig: Logan, pp. 137, 172.

76   On "the New York gunman": Richard Harding Davis, "The Defeat of the Underworld," *Collier's*, November 9, 1912, p. 11.

76   Rosenthal-Becker affair and the Jewish community: Goren, pp. 154–58.

76   "The divine word": quoted in Goren, p. 155.

77   For the religious argument: *Tageblatt*, July 26, 30, 1912; and *Morgen Journal*, August 1, 2, 1912; for Socialist argument: *Forward*, July 20, 23, 27, 31, 1912.

77–78   For uptowners' argument: Goren, pp. 157–58.

77n   Rabbis closing their "eyes to the departure": quoted in Goren, p. 272.

78   On the difficulty of establishing a Kehillah: Goren, pp. 247–48.

78–79   On Judah P. Magnes's life in general see Norman Bentwich, *For Zion's Sake: A Biography of Judah P. Magnes*.

79   To "stir the conscience": *The New York Times*, July 29, 1912.

79   On the exact nature of Shoenfeld's assignment: Goren, pp. 163–64, 169–72.

79–80   On differences between Magnes and mayor: Goren, pp. 176–81.

79n   "All these young men": *The New York Times*, July 29, 1912.

79n   "With the civilian branch": Bingham, p. 394.

80–81   On the conduct of the trials: Logan, pp. 172–209.

81   On final disposition of the case: Logan, pp. 234–327.

81   On the triumph of the Mugwumps: Nevins and Kraut, *The Greater City*, pp. 84–86; Henry H. Curran, *Pillar to Post*, pp. 150–62; and *Special Committee of the Board of Alderman Appointed to Investigate the City's Police Department Pursuant to the Resolution of August 4, 1912*. 6 vols.

82   Yoski Nigger's arrest and confession: *The New York Times*, March 6, 25, August 24, 1913.

82   "I said, 'I always' ": *The New York Times*, December 20, 1914. On the arrest of Joe the Greaser and his sidekicks: *The New York Times*, December 20, 22, 1914, and May 29, 1915.

82–83   On shootouts and the murder of Straus: Willemse, pp. 290–91; and *The New York Times*, January 11, 14, 16, 1914.

83   "Last July it was": *The New York Times*, January 24, 1914.

83   On Appellate Court's decision: *The New York Times*, May 30, 1914.

84   On arrests of Benny's cohorts: Willemse, pp. 297–98; and *The New York Times*, May 28, 1915.

84   On trial and acquittal of Jew Murphy and Waxey Gordon: Willemse, pp. 298–302.

84   On Benny's confession: *The New York Times*, May 12, 1915.

84   "They knew I knew": *The New York Times*, May 20, 1915.

84–85   On arrest of union leaders and response by left and by Perkins: *The New York Times*, May 12, 13, 14, 16, 1915.

85   On prosecutor's case: *New York World*, September 24, 1915; and *The New York Times*, September 24, 25, 28, 1915.

85–86   "I was not interrupted": Morris Hillquit, *Loose Leaves from a Busy Life*, pp. 138–40.

86   On dropping the case: Harold Seidman, pp. 286–87; and Asbury, *The Gangs of New York*, p. 368.

86   On Benny's going straight: Willemse, p. 302.

87   On population change: New York Bureau of Jewish Social Research, *Jewish Communal Survey of Greater New York*, pp. 3–7.

page no.   **Three.   Breaking Out**

90   On Chicago's Jewish quarter: Ira Berkow, *Maxwell Street*; Philip Bregstone, *Chicago and Its Jews*, p. 6; Irv Kupcinet, *Kup's Chicago*, pp. 19–21; Edith Abbott, *The Tenements of Chicago 1908–1935*, pp. 85–86; Clifford Shaw, *Delinquency Areas*, p. 49; and Jane Addams, *Twenty Years at Hull House*, pp. 99–100.

90   "Murderers, robbers and thieves": *Chicago Tribune*, quoted in Stephen Longstreet, *Chicago 1860–1919*, p. 423; see also Asbury, *The Gem of the Prairie*, pp. 211–12.

91   On Philadelphia Jews: Charles S. Bernheimer, *The Russian Jew in the United States*, pp. 51–52; Edwin Wolf, *Philadelphia, Portrait of an American City*, p. 39; Sam Bass Warner, Jr., *The Private City*, p. 183; and American Guide Series, *Philadelphia*, pp. 441–43.

91   On Cleveland Jews: Wellington G. Furdyce, "Immigrant Colonies in Cleveland," *Ohio State Archeological and Historical Society*, pp. 333–35.

91   On Boston Jews: Albert Ehrenfried, *A Chronicle of Boston Jewry*; Arnold A. Weiden, *The Early Jewish Community of Boston's North End*; and Isaac Goldberg, "A Boston Boyhood," *The American Mercury*, pp. 354–61.

91   Dorchester "with its dreary massed": Francis Russell, *The Great Interlude*, p. 93.

91   On Detroit Jews: David M. Katzman, *Before the Ghetto*, pp. 58–59; Henry J. Meyer, "A Study of Detroit Jewry, 1935," *Jewish Population Studies*, p. 115; and Robert A. Rockaway, "The Detroit Jewish Ghetto Before World War I," *Michigan History*, Spring 1968, pp. 28–36.

91   On Minneapolis Jews: Albert A. Gordon, *Jews in Transition*, pp. 19–20.

94   On Waxey Gordon's Lower East Side career: Craig Thompson and Allen Raymond, *Gang Rule in New York*, p. 27; and Magnes Papers, Story #871, SP 136.

95   On "Big Maxey" Greenberg in St. Louis: *The New York Times*, December 2, 1933.

95   On the reason for Greenberg's visit to New York: Hank Messick, *Secret File*, pp. 58–59; and Katcher, *The Big Bankroll*, pp. 232–33.

95–96   On Black Sox scandal: Katcher, *The Big Bankroll*, pp. 138–48. On Rothstein's reputation as a sportsman: *The New York Times*, September 7, 1921; and *New York Tribune*, September 7, 1921.

96   On Rothstein's relations with gangsters: Katcher, *The Big Bankroll*, pp. 23, 279–80.

96n   Rothstein's wife "might have as dinner guests": Rothstein, p. x.

97–98   The operation is explained by Katcher, *The Big Bankroll*, pp. 233–36.

98   On Waxey's bootlegging business: *The New York Times*, September 25, 27, 1925.

98   Waxey's transformation: Thompson and Raymond, pp. 29–30.

99   Capture of Waxey: *The New York Times*, September 25, 27, October 9, 21, 31, November 1, 1925, and December 2, 1933; and Elmer L. Irey, *The Tax Dodgers*, p. 139.

99   Waxey's luck, the fate of Fuhrman: *The New York Times*, January 7, February 9, 1926.

100   Waxey's re-emergence in Hudson County: *The New York Times*, May 2, November 21, 1933; John Starr, *The Purveyor*, pp. 12–18, 28–30; Joseph Driscoll, "Men of Action," *New Outlook*, p. 27; and Irey, pp. 138–53.

100n   "To accommodate the hoodlums": Irey, p. 140.

101n   "They tell me": Herbert Asbury, *The Great Illusion*, p. 228.

102   "The stills and the raw materials": Asbury, *The Great Illusion*, p. 229.

103   On Dutch Schultz's early years: Paul Sann, *Kill the Dutchman!*, pp. 105–8, 112–14; and J. Richard "Dixie" Davis, "Things I Couldn't Tell till Now," *Collier's*, July 29, 1939, p. 38.

103–4   On the Purples: Driscoll, p. 28; Hank Messick, *Silent Syndicate*, pp. 47–49; Nelli, p. 170; and Albini, pp. 202–4.

104   On the Cleveland Four: Messick, *Silent Syndicate*, pp. 4–52; *Hearings Before the Special Committee to Investigate Organized Crime in Interstate Commerce* (hereafter referred to as Kefauver Committee), Part 7, pp. 32–33; and "Murder in Cleveland," *Cleveland Plain Dealer*, December 26, 27, 28, 29, 1933, January 2, 3, 4, 1934.

104 On Kid Cann's outfit: Nicholas Gage, *The Mafia Is Not an Equal Opportunity Employer*, pp. 44–45.

104 On Leon Gleckman: Messick, *Secret File*, pp. 55–56.

104 On King Solomon's men: Nelli, p. 169. On Reinfeld-Zwillman: Messick, *Secret File*, pp. 277–78.

104–5 On Boo Boo Hoff and Nig Rosen: Driscoll, pp. 27–28; and Kefauver Committee, Part 1, pp. 744–45.

105–6 The Jewish Twentieth Ward Group: *Official Records, National Commission on Law Observance and Enforcement* (hereafter referred to as Wickersham Commission), vol. 4, p. 304. On Samuel "Nails" Morton in particular: Asbury, *The Gem of the Prairie*, p. 343.

106–8 On the success of the Cleveland Four: Messick, *Silent Syndicate*, pp. 52–72, 81–85; his account is based largely on "Murder in Cleveland," the *Plain Dealer* series already referred to.

108 On the rise of the criminal syndicate: Albini, pp. 205–6.

108*n* "A multiplication of units": Frederick M. Thrasher, *The Gang*, p. 439.

109*n* Rothstein "taught me how": Martin A. Gosch and Richard Hammer, *The Last Testament of Lucky Luciano*, p. 41 (hereafter referred to as Luciano's *Testament*).

110 On Broadway nightclubs in the 1920s: Stanley Walker, *The Night Club Era*, pp. 77–102, 243; and Asbury, *The Great Illusion*, pp. 201–8.

111 "A Jewish crime wave": *The New York Times*, January 5, 1930.

111*n* The Cleveland policy "black-list": Wickersham Commission, vol. 10, p. 193.

112–13 Excerpt from *The Saturday Press*: Near v. Minnesota, *U.S. Reports*, pp. 724–27.

113–14 Minnesota statute and Supreme Court decision: Near v. Minnesota, *U.S. Reports*, pp. 701–23. On Near v. Minnesota see: *New York University Law Quarterly*, 9, September 1931, pp. 64–81; *Yale Law Journal*, 40, December 1931, pp. 262–71; and *Columbia Law Review*, 31, November 1931, pp. 1148–55.

114–15 On the tendency toward cartelization: Andrew Sinclair, *Era of Excess*, p. 222. On Johnny Torrio: Kenneth Allsop, *The Bootleggers*, pp. 41–90; and Wickersham Commission, IV, pp. 375–76.

114*n* "Minneapolis is the capital": Carey McWilliams, "Minneapolis: The Curious Twin," *Common Ground*, p. 61.

114*n* Torrio, "The father of": Irey, p. 151.

115 On Big Seven: Irey, p. 160; Luciano's *Testament*, p. 94; Sid Feder and Joachim Joesten, *The Luciano Story*, pp. 63–64; and James M. Wanless, "Order in the Underworld," p. 36.

115 Consortium control was "so complete": Messick, *Secret File*, p. 96.

115–16 On Atlantic City conference: Nelli, pp. 214–15; *The New York Times*, May 16, 18, 1929; and Virgil W. Peterson, *Barbarians in Our Midst*, p. 213. On Nucky Johnson: Irey, pp. 245–70.

116 It "was time to stop": John Kobler, *Capone*, p. 258.

117–18 On Moses Annenberg and his empire: Irey, pp. 215–224; Luciano's *Testament*, pp. 123–24; and John T. Flynn, "Smart Money," *Collier's*, January 13, 1940, pp. 9–10, 51–53; January 20, 1940, pp. 20, 54–57; January 27, 1940, pp. 16, 34–40; and February 3, 1940, pp. 18, 48–51.

117 On Chicago newspaper wars: Ferdinand Lundberg, *Imperial Hearst: A Social Biography*, p. 149.

117n "Reporters might compete": Messick, *Secret File*, p. 155.

118–19 On the Sam Bloom affair: Hank Messick, *Lansky*, pp. 31–33; and Luciano's *Testament*, pp. 96–97.

119n On Zwillman's career as shotgun rider: Messick, *Secret File*, pp. 277–78.

120 On collaboration between second generation Italian and Jewish gangsters: Francis A. J. Ianni, *A Family Business*, p. 56.

120–21 On Luciano's relations with Jews: Luciano's *Testament*, pp. 13, 41.

120n "Manpower for the syndicates": Nelli, p. 101.

121 On Costello's relations with Jews: Leonard Katz, *Uncle Frank*, p. 46; and Luciano's *Testament*, pp. 39–40, 47.

121 On Dutch Schultz's Bronx legion: Sann, pp. 109–13.

122 On the transethnic solidarity of the Purples: Messick, *Silent Syndicate*, pp. 53–54.

122 On the transatlantic solidarity of the Philadelphia gang: Kefauver Committee, Part 1, pp. 774–75.

122 On Waxey Gordon's gang: *The New York Times*, November 29, 1933; and Starr, pp. 28–30.

122 "To me, the whole": Luciano's *Testament*, pp. 88–89.

123 On the myth and fancy of the Castellammarese War: Dwight C. Smith, Jr., *The Mafia Mystique*, pp. 233–34.

124 On the "Twenties Group": Nelli, p. 200; and David Ben Chandler, *Brothers in Blood*, p. 135.

124 On Salvatore Maranzano: Nick Gentile, *Vita di capomafia*, p. 203.

125 On the murder of Masseria: *The New York Times*, April 16, 1931; and Luciano's *Testament*, pp. 131–32.

125 On planning Maranzano's assassination: Luciano's *Testament*, p. 139.

125n Imperative "to rid the Italian": Wanless, p. 152.

125–26   The attack on Maranzano: Gentile, p. 205; *The New York Times*, September 11, 1931; and *Hearings Before the Permanent Subcommittee on Investigations of the Committee on Government Operations*, p. 162 (hereafter referred to as McClellan Committee II).

126   On the so-called purge of Maranzano's men: Burton B. Turkus and Sid Feder, *Murder Inc.*, p. 87; Donald R. Cressey, *Theft of the Nation*, pp. 44–45; and Nelli, pp. 182–83.

126*n*   The Cressey thesis: "Methodological Problems for the Study of Organized Crime as a Social Problem," *Annals of the American Academy*, p. 111; also Annelise Graebner Anderson, *The Business of Organized Crime*, pp. 9–33; and Mark H. Furstenberg, "Violence and Organized Crime," *Crimes of Violence*, pp. 911–13.

127   On the gathering at the Congress Hotel: Gentile, p. 207; Luciano's *Testament*, p. 145; and Messick, *Lansky*, pp. 57–58.

127   On the imminence of Capone's trial: Irey, p. 25ff.

127*n*   On the view that the Mafia is a myth: Smith, *The Mafia Mystique*. There is a middle-of-the-road position defended by: Ralph Salerno and John S. Tompkins, *The Crime Confederation*, pp. 85–89; and Albini, p. 47.

page no.   **Four.   Lepke's Rise: The Chronicles of Labor**

129–32   On Lepke's parents, youth, and early life in crime: "Probation Report," *People of New York Against Louis Buchalter et al.*, and *The New York Times*, October 16, 1935, and July 8, 1936, and August 13, 25, 1939, and March 5, 1944.

133   On Gurrah's early years: Federal Bureau of Investigation, *The Fur Dress Case*, p. 26 (hereafter referred to as F.B.I. Report #60–1501).

133   The "bloodiest New York has known": Willemse, p. 317.

133   On Kid Dropper: *The New York Times*, August 29, 1923.

133–34   He "appeared along Broadway": Asbury, *The Gangs of New York*, p. 369.

134   On Little Augie: *The New York Times*, January 11, 1914, and October 17, 1927; and Willemse, p. 339.

134   Attack on Dropper: *The New York Times*, August 31, 1923; and Thompson and Raymond, p. 231.

135   The death of Kid Dropper: *The New York Times*, August 29, 30, 1923; and Willemse, pp. 332–35.

135   "Well you ——": Willemse, p. 335.

135–36   On Kushner-Cohen: *The New York Times*, August 30, 1923; Thompson and Raymond, p. 232; Willemse, p. 336; and Morris Markey, "Gangs," *Atlantic Monthly*, March 1928, p. 299.

136 On postwar recession: Joel Seidman, *The Needle Trades*, pp. 142–43.

137 Representing the Socialist point of view: Benjamin Stolberg, *Tailors' Progress*, p. 138; and David Dubinsky and A. H. Raskin, *A Life with Labor*, p. 68. Representing the Communist: Philip S. Foner, *The Fur and Leather Workers' Union*, pp. 83–84, 396–97.

138–39 On 1926 ILGWU strike and the role of Little Augie on the one side and Legs Diamond on the other: Joel Seidman, pp. 157–67; Stolberg, pp. 123–39, 141–44; and Dubinsky and Raskin, pp. 62–70.

139 Communists decide to sue for peace: Dubinsky and Raskin, pp. 68–69.

140 "Rothstein's first assignment": Dubinsky and Raskin, p. 69.

140 "More probably this astute": Dubinsky and Raskin, p. 69.

140–41 On *quid pro quo*: Harold Seidman, p. 118.

142–43 On Brooklyn painters' war: *The New York Times*, June 18, August 17, 27, October 27, 1927, and May 1, October 3, 1937; Thompson and Raymond, pp. 234–35; and Harold Seidman, pp. 165–71.

143–44 Little Augie's execution and funeral: *The New York Times*, October 16, 18, 1927; Thompson and Raymond, p. 235; and Fred P. Pasley, *Muscling In*, pp. 127–28.

144 Disposition of Lepke, Gurrah, Little Hymie: *The New York Times*, October 26, November 5, December 11, 1927.

157 On Communists vs. anti-Communists in furs: Foner, pp. 110–13; and Benjamin Gitlow, *I Confess*, p. 344.

157–58 On situation in fur industry: Joel Seidman, pp. 169–73.

158 The formation of protectives and accompanying violence: F.B.I. Report #60–1501, pp. 9–11; and *The New York Times*, October 28, 29, 1936.

158 Foner's estimate: Foner, p. 398.

158*n* On Longy Zwillman's cooperation: F.B.I. Report #60–1501, pp. 13–14.

159 On the unemployment fund: *The New York Times*, October 27, 1936.

159–60 The bloodiest encounter: *The New York Times*, April 25, 1933, and April 23, May 7, 1942; and Foner, p. 401.

159*n* "Well, we'll be together": Foner, pp. 400–401.

160 On Lepke's penetration of men's clothing: F.B.I. Report #60–1501, pp. 9–10; *The New York Times*, July 8, 1936, and August 13, November 2, 1939, and June 26, 29, 1943; and Turkus and Feder, p. 332.

161–63 On Hillman's response to Local 4: Matthew Josephson, *Sidney Hillman, Statesman of American Labor*, pp. 329–38; and John Hutchinson, *The Imperfect Union*, pp. 76–78.

163 On Lepke and Luciano; Turkus and Feder, p. 86; *The New York Times*, August 15, 1939; and *Hearings Before Select Committee on Improper Activities in the Labor and Management Field* (hereafter referred to as McClellan Committee I), p. 6691.

163–64 Lepke's tactful handling of situation: Turkus and Feder, pp. 86–87.

164 "You think this is a clothing": Feder and Joesten, p. 83.

164–65 Lepke's arrangement with the Amalgamated: Court of Appeals, Brooklyn, New York, *People of the State of New York Against Louis Buchalter et al.*, May–June 1942, pp. 1323–77; Turkus and Feder, pp. 340–43; and *The New York Times*, June 17, 1938.

165 On Lepke's power in women's clothing: *The New York Times*, February 11, 1938, and December 2, 4, 1942, and July 2, 1943.

165 On Five Borough Association: *The New York Times*, May 11, 1933, and June 3, 5, 1937; Thomas E. Dewey, *Twenty Against the Underworld*, pp. 304–9. On Dio and Lepke: McClellan Committee I, pp. 3690, 3697.

166 "What did I do": Dewey, p. 309.

166 On Lepke and the hat, cap, and millinery industry: Harold Seidman, p. 195; and Donald B. Robinson, *Spotlight on a Union*, pp. 161–64, 168–73.

166n On $25,000 offer to Lepke: Robinson, pp. 173–74.

167–68 Lepke's takeover of the bakery and flour industry: "Probation Report," pp. 9–15; Harold Seidman, pp. 121–24; and *The New York Times*, September 26, 28, 1937, and February 3, 7, 8, 9, 10, 11, 15, 16, 1940.

167n "You're marked lousy": *The New York Times*, February 7, 1940.

168–69 On the shooting of Snyder: *The New York Times*, September 14, 1934; Thompson and Raymond, pp. 247–48; Rupert Hughes, *Attorney for the People*, pp. 119–20; and Dewey, pp. 299–300.

169–71 On Lepke's relations to movie industry and the takeover in general by the Capone mob: Irey, pp. 271–88; Hutchinson, pp. 130–33; Carey McWilliams, *The Education of Carey McWilliams*, pp. 86–91; Turkus and Feder, p. 346; and *The New York Times*, October 7, 8, 9, 27, 28, 30, November 4, December 22, 1943.

172n On Lepke and pocketbooks: *The New York Times*, January 23, 1942.

172n–173n "For them unrestricted": Harold Seidman, pp. 264–65.

page no. **Five.   Lepke's Fall: The Chronicles of Thomas E. Dewey**

175–76 On Dewey's Owosso childhood and background: Stanley Walker, *Thomas Dewey, An American of This Century*, p. 33.

176 On Medalie and his appointment: Dewey, p. 76.

176n   "I did bring with me": Dewey, p. 20.

177   On the Seabury investigation and its effect: Charles Garrett, *The LaGuardia Years: Machine and Reform Politics in New York City*, pp. 76–79.

177   On Medalie and Dewey: Walker, *Thomas Dewey*, p. 35.

177–78   The conviction of Capone: Irey, pp. 25–65.

178   On Dewey's thoroughness and executive abilities: Dewey, p. 120; Hughes, pp. 48–49; and Irey, pp. 135–36.

178n   "Dewey was the perfectionist": Irey, p. 135.

178–79   On war between Waxey and the Dutchman: Messick, *Secret File*, pp. 66–67; Starr, pp. 45–55; and Irey, pp. 144–45.

179   "It is extremely difficult": Irey, p. 145.

179–80   Waxey's capture: Messick, *Secret File*, pp. 68–69; and *The New York Times*, May 22, 1933.

180–81   Waxey's trial and conviction and Dewey's triumph: Walker, *Thomas Dewey*, p. 41; Dewey, p. 118; Irey, pp. 147–53; Thompson and Raymond, pp. 29–30; and *The New York Times*, November 21, 25, 28, 30, December 1, 2, 1933.

180n   Luciano's claim: Luciano's *Testament*, p. 140.

182   On Dutch Schultz's inner circle: Sann, pp. 40, 197.

182   "His murderous reputation": J. Richard "Dixie" Davis, *Collier's*, July 29, 1939, p. 38.

182n   "Mr. Mayor, I think you and I have got a common interest": quoted in Sann, pp. 221, 225–26.

183–84   On the numbers racket: Sann, pp. 159–60.

184   On Dutch Schultz's moving in on Harlem rackets: Sann, pp. 161–64.

184   On Schultz and Jimmy Hines: Sann, pp. 186–87.

184–85   "I soon learned": J. Richard "Dixie" Davis, *Collier's*, July 22, 1939, p. 40.

185   At least "it ensures the players": Sann, p. 176.

185–86   Rigging the game: Sann, pp. 213–15.

186   On Schultz and the restaurant racket: Sann, pp. 18, 234; and Dewey, pp. 282–91.

186   On Schultz hiding out: Sann, pp. 199–206; and Polly Adler, *A House Is Not a Home*, pp. 233–34.

187   "It was as simple and undramatic": J. Richard "Dixie" Davis, *Collier's*, July 22, 1939, pp. 10, 38. Moving the trial upstate: Davis, *Collier's*, August 12, 1939, p. 16.

187   On the rebellious grand jury: *The New York Times*, May 14, 15, 16, 23, 1935.

188   On Lehman's appointment of Dewey: *The New York Times*, June 25, 26, 28, 29, 30, 1935; Dewey, pp. 155–73; and Allan Nevins, *Herbert H. Lehman and His Era*, pp. 179–82.

188–89   On the plan to assassinate Dewey: Turkus and Feder, pp. 134–39; and Sann, pp. 278–79.

189   "I suppose they": quoted in Sann, p. 279.

189–90   The murder of Weinberg: J. Richard "Dixie" Davis, *Collier's*, August 12, 1939, p. 29; Luciano's *Testament*, pp. 182–84; Feder and Joesten, p. 97.

190   On the need to kill Schultz: Dewey, pp. 274–75.

190n   "And then I'll be damned": Luciano's *Testament*, p. 41.

190–91   On Workman and the death of Schultz and his cohorts: Sann, pp. 270–75.

191   The altercation and Lepke's settlement: *The New York Times*, June 7, 8, 1941.

191n   On the policy sheets: J. Richard "Dixie" Davis, *Collier's*, August 19, 1939, p. 13.

192   Schultz's dying soliloquy is presented whole in Sann, pp. 60–68.

192n   Messick's far-fetched interpretation: Messick, *Silent Syndicate*, p. 150.

194n   "A new type of criminal": Hughes, p. 87.

194–96   On the arrest, trial, and conviction of Lucky Luciano: Philip James McCook, *The Days of My Age*, p. 223ff.; Hughes, pp. 79–111; Dewey, pp. 184–269; and *The New York Times*, April 2, May 12, 14, 15, 17, 19, 21, 22, 26, June 4, 8, 19, 1936.

196   Only an "excursion from": Hughes, p. 114.

196n   "After sittin' in court": Luciano's *Testament*, p. 224.

197   Effect of NIRA on garment unions: Stolberg, p. 255.

197   Trial and conviction of Lepke: *The New York Times*, October 27, 28, 29, 30, 31, 1936; and Foner, p. 413.

198   On the beginning of Dewey's campaign: e.g., *The New York Times*, December 5, 16, 1935, and April 30, 1936.

198–99   Lehman's and LaGuardia's war on racketeering: *The New York Times*, August 11, 16, 1936; and Nevins, *Herbert H. Lehman*, pp. 182, 186. On the general preoccupation with the subject: Murray I. Gurfein, "Racketeering," *Encyclopaedia of the Social Sciences*, 13, pp. 45–49; G. L. Hostetter and T. Q. Beesley, "Twentieth Century Crime," *The Political Quarterly*, pp. 403–22; "Implications of Labor Racketeering," *Columbia Law Review*, June 1937, pp. 993–1004; and Louis Adamic, "Racketeers and Organized Crime," *Harper's Magazine*, September 1930, pp. 404, 411–16.

199n   "It is an organization": *The New York Times*, December 6, 1936.

199n   "Only in the cruder": Hughes, pp. 45–46.

200   Dewey's excruciating pressure: Dewey, pp. 309–13.

201   Anastasia's responsibility for protecting Lepke: *The New York Times*, April 18, 1941.

202   On the street life of Williamsburg, Brownsville, East New York: John Harlan Amen, *Report of the Kings County Investigator 1938–1942*, pp. 124, 138–39; see also: Alter F. Landesman, *Brownsville*, pp. 329–35.

203   On Lepke's supremacy over the Jewish sections: Court of Appeals, Brooklyn, New York, *People of the State of New York Against Irving Nitzberg*, September–October 1941, pp. 158–61.

203–5   On Murder Inc.—how it emerged, its character and organization and ruthlessness: *The New York Times*, February 3, April 7, May 16, 1940, and November 14, 1941; Leo Katcher and Malcolm Logan, "Murder Inc.," *New York Post*, April 8–13, 1940; Turkus and Feder, pp. 7, 9–12, 104, 179; and Joseph Freeman, "How Murder Inc. Trains Its Killers," *American Mercury*, October 1940, pp. 155–62.

204n   "Murderers' apprentices": Meyer Berger, "Murder Inc.," *Life*, September 30, 1940, p. 90.

204–5   They "never rose from": Katcher and Logan, *New York Post*, April 13, 1940.

205–6   On the whole Rosen affair: Court of Appeals, Brooklyn, New York, *The People of the State of New York Against Louis Buchalter et al.*, May–June 1942, pp. 1323–77 and *The New York Times*, October 2, 1941.

206   Rudnick's murder: *The New York Times*, May 16, 1940.

207   "That man had an obsession": *The New York Times*, February 13, 1940.

207   "Lepke, I want to come home": *The New York Times*, November 4, 1941.

207–8   The attack on Rubin: *The New York Times*, October 2, 1937. The arrest and return of Silverman: *Times*, September 26, 28, 1937. Dewey's radio speech: *Times*, October 4, 1937.

208   On reports of Lepke's whereabouts: *The New York Times*, April 15, 16, 1938.

208–9   Gurrah's arrest: *The New York Times*, April 16, 1938. "They arrest me because": *Times*, June 18, 1938.

209   On Lehman and Dewey in 1938: Nevins, pp. 194, 196; Dewey, p. 437; and *The New York Times*, November 10, 1938.

210–11   Hyman Yuran: *The New York Times*, April 16, 1940; Leon Sharff and wife and Danny Field and Louis Cohen: *Times*, June 14, 1939; Plug Shuman: *Times*, September 27, 1941; Joseph Miller and Whitey Friedman: *Times*, June 14, 1939; Irving Penn: *Times*, July 28, 1939; Morris Diamond: *Times*, June 14, 1939; Big Greenie Greenberg: *Times*, November 25, 1939; and Dean Jennings, *We Only Kill Each Other*, pp. 82–85.

211–12   On the problem of keeping Lepke and the double cross: Luciano's *Testament*, pp. 241–43; Messick, *Lansky*, p. 100; Turkus and Feder, pp. 351, 359–61; and Starr, p. 138.

211*n*   "It is apparent": *The New York Times*, July 29, 1939.

212–13   "So Frank went back to New York": Luciano's *Testament*, p. 243.

213–14   On Lepke's surrender: *The New York Times*, August 25, 1939; *New York Daily Mirror*, August 26, 1939; and F.B.I. Report #60–1501, pp. 44–45.

214–15   On Lepke and drugs: Andrew Tully, *Treasury Agent*, pp. 50–58; Kefauver Committee, Part 7, pp. 1079–81; and *The New York Times*, December 1, 2, 7, 8, 13, 19, 20, 24, 1939, and January 3, 1940.

216   On Lepke and baking: Court of Appeals, New York, New York, *People of the State of New York Against Louis Buchalter*, January 16, 1940; and *The New York Times*, January 25, February 3, 7, 8, 9, 10, 11, 13, 16, April 6, 1940.

216–17   Arrest of Brooklyn gangsters: *The New York Times*, February 3, 1940.

217   On O'Dwyer's political appeal: *The New York Times*, June 5, August 26, November 9, 1939.

217   On O'Dwyer's crackdown: Turkus and Feder, pp. 27–29; and *The New York Times*, January 4, February 3, 4, 1940.

217   "I am doing a bit here": Turkus and Feder, pp. 30–31.

217–18   On Reles and the other informers: Turkus and Feder, pp. 63–64, 67–70; and *The New York Times*, March 18, 24, 1940.

218–19   Indictment of Lepke: *The New York Times*, April 16, 1941.

219   "This is ridiculous": *The New York Times*, May 10, 1941.

219–21   The trial: *The New York Times*, October 25, 28, November 8, 11, 1941.

221   On death of Reles: *The New York Times*, November 14, 15, December 6, 1941; and Turkus and Feder, pp. 438, 443–58.

222   "This bird can sing": *The New York Times*, November 14, 1941. "The way I heard it": Luciano's *Testament*, p. 253.

222   On Bals's testimony: Kefauver Committee, Part 7, pp. 592–93, 1123. "The whole thing": Kefauver Committee, Part 7, p. 1119.

222*n*   "The only law": *The New York Times*, November 14, 1941.

223–24   On Court of Appeals decision: Buchalter *v.* New York, *New York Supplement, 2nd Series*, pp. 181–245.

224   Dewey's demand: *The New York Times*, November 23, 1943.

224–25   "It is surprising to me": *The New York Times*, November 30, 1943; "The Governor may not": *Times*, December 1, 1943.

225   Lepke's return to New York State: *The New York Times*, January 18, 1943.

225   Dewey's strategy: *The New York Times*, March 4, 1944.

226   "Lepke knew what"; "I got the impression": Sann, pp. 285–86.

227   "I am anxious"; "I am here": *The New York Times*, March 5, 1944.

227   Gurrah's 1943 trial: *The New York Times*, July 2, 10, 16, December 21, 1943.

228n   Demise of the motion-picture racket: McWilliams, *The Education of Carey McWilliams*, pp. 90–91; Hutchinson, pp. 133–38; Irey, pp. 282–88; and *The New York Times*, October 7, 8, 9, 27, 28, 30, December 15, 22, 1943.

page no.   **Six.   The Worlds of Meyer Lansky**

229   On October 24, 1918, incident: Messick, *Lansky*, pp. 19–20.

230–31 On Lansky's and Siegel's youth: Messick, *Lansky*, pp. 17–25; and Jennings, pp. 32–33.

231–32 On contrast between Lansky and Siegel: Katz, p. 144; and Ed Reid and Ovid Demaris, *The Green Felt Jungle*, p. 19.

232   On the return of bootleggers to streets: William F. Whyte, *Street Corner Society*, p. 112.

233   On Zwillman, Rosen, Schultz, Solomon's men, Purples, Cleveland Four, Kid Cann: Hank Messick, *The Private Lives of Public Enemies*, pp. 245–46; Messick, *Silent Syndicate*, pp. 89–92; Messick, *Secret File*, pp. 115–18; Gage, pp. 44–45; and Kefauver Committee, Part 1, pp. 744–45, Part 7, pp. 33–34, 138–45.

234   On Capitol Wines and Moloska: Messick, *Lansky*, pp. 67–70.

234   On Owney Madden and Hot Springs: Driscoll, "Men of Action," *New Outlook*, p. 30; Messick, *The Private Lives of Public Enemies*, pp. 86–87; and Messick, *Lansky*, p. 85.

234–35 On Costello and Huey Long and the slot machines of New Orleans: *The New York Times*, January 2, February 17, 18, October 14, 1934 (on LaGuardia's war on slots).

235–36 Long "went into the powder room": Katz, pp. 98–99; Messick, *Lansky*, pp. 81–82 (on toilet encounter); Kefauver Committee, Part 7, pp. 918–19, Part 2, p. 187; T. Harry Williams, *Huey Long*, pp. 824–25; and Hamilton Basso, "The Death Agony of Huey Long," *New Republic*, January 1, 1936, pp. 215–18.

236–37 On Lansky in Florida: Messick, *Lansky*, pp. 87–89. On Anthony Carfano: Driscoll, p. 30.

237–38 On Sheriff Walter Clark: Kefauver Committee, Part 1, pp. 126–34, pp. 452–75.

238   On Batista–Lansky friendship: Mario Llerena, *The Unsuspected Revolution*, p. 17; and Messick, *Lansky*, p. 89.

240   On closeness of Lansky and Luciano: Rodney Campbell, *The Luciano Project*, pp. 76, 85.

240   "Dewey can get him out": Messick, *Lansky*, p. 121. On Luciano's claim to omnicompetence: Luciano's *Testament*, pp. 265–72, 276–77.

240–42 On the circumstances of Luciano's release: Kefauver Committee, Part 7, pp. 1188–95; Norman Lewis, *The Honored Society*, p. 17; and Dewey, pp. 269–70.

241   On Lansky's extraordinary role in the affair: Campbell, pp. 85–88, 96–110.

242   On Luciano in Cuba: Feder and Joesten, pp. 230–35, 242–47; Kefauver Committee, Part 7, p. 1183. He "had developed a full-fledged": Messick, *Lansky*, p. 136. On notoriety of his presence in Havana: *The New York Times*, February 22, 23, 24, 25, 1947.

243   "Lucky Luciano came to an understanding": Messick, *Lansky*, pp. 137–38.

243–44 On Lansky's Florida operation: Herbert Asbury, "America's Number One Mystery Man," *Collier's*, April 12, 1947, pp. 16–17, 26.

243*n* "Lucky had received the pledges": Messick, *Lansky*, p. 136.

244   On the gangster emigration to the Gold Coast: Kefauver Committee, Part 1, pp. 161–63. On Big Jack Letendre: Messick, *Lansky*, pp. 140–43.

245   On Raft and Siegel: Reid and Demaris, p. 20; and Gage, p. 67.

246   On Siegel's primacy over Dragna: Reid and Demaris, p. 217. Siegel's effect on Hollywood: Jennings, pp. 38–39, 46–47. On Dorothy DiFrasso: Jennings, pp. 39–40.

246*n* On Siegel, Goebbels, and Goering: Jennings, pp. 76–77.

247   The assassination of Greenberg: Jennings, pp. 82–85; and *The New York Times*, November 25, 1939, and August 29, 31, 1940.

247–48 Siegel's indictment for murder and his victory: Turkus and Feder, pp. 277–278, 280–83; and Jennings, pp. 120–21, 128.

248*n* "The searing publicity": Jennings, p. 123.

249   Siegel's empire: Jennings, p. 139.

250   Siegel's earnings: Jennings, p. 141; and Reid and Demaris, p. 17.

250   A "cowpoke town where gambling": Jennings, p. 149; on early Las Vegas, see also: Rufus G. King, *Gambling and Organized Crime*, p. 120; and Russell Elliott, *History of Nevada*, pp. 277–85.

250–51 Siegel and the rise of the Flamingo: Jennings, pp. 150–51; David W. Toll, *The Compleat Nevada Traveler*, pp. 226–29; and Reid and Demaris, pp. 26–27.

251–52 Siegel vs. the gang/syndicates: Reid and Demaris, p. 19; and Messick, *Lansky*, pp. 147, 150–51.

252   On Virginia Hill: Jennings, pp. 86–94, 108–114; and Kefauver Committee, Part 7, p. 1163.

253   On the crisis coming to a head: Messick, *Lansky,* pp. 150–51; and Kefauver Committee, Part 7, p. 1155.

253   On Siegel's murder: Kefauver Committee, Part 10, pp. 714–16, 898; Jennings, pp. 202–3; and *The New York Times,* June 22, 1947.

253   On new management at Flamingo: Reid and Demaris, pp. 34, 40–41.

254   On Fat Irish Greenberg: Jennings, pp. 194–95.

254n   On the rest of Hill's life: Messick, *Secret File,* pp. 202–20; Jennings, pp. 215–20, 232–52; and *The New York Times,* March 23, 1966.

255   On America's preoccupation with crime: William Howard Moore, *The Kefauver Committee and the Politics of Crime,* pp. 29–41; and *Newsweek,* January 13, 1947, pp. 24–25.

255   "The Cabinet and the White House": Jack Lait and Lee Mortimer, *Chicago Confidential!,* p. 176.

256   "The Italian voting bloc": Jack Lait and Lee Mortimer, *Washington Confidential!,* pp. 185–86.

257   "Joe Stalin, if he had": Spruille Braden quoted, Kefauver Committee, Part 7, p. 1604.

257   On Lansky's patriotism and the right-wing character of gangsters in general: Gage, pp. 52, 54.

257n   "John Edgar Hoover has received": Hank Messick, *John Edgar Hoover,* p. 94.

258   On Kefauver and the emergence of his committee: Moore, pp. 42–73; and Joseph Bruce Gorman, *Kefauver: A Political Biography,* pp. 35–63, 74–78.

258–59   The Committee and the racing wire conspiracy: Moore, pp. 74–113.

259–60   The Committee's work: Gorman, pp. 79–102.

259   Costello's defiance: Kefauver Committee, Part 7, p. 1177.

260   These observations are drawn from my own experience as an indefatigable watcher of the Kefauver Committee's hearings on television. I was then twenty years old and remember them as vividly as yesterday—testimony to the power of their effect.

261–62   On the Bernsteins: Kefauver Committee, Part 2, pp. 171, 182, 188–92; on Dalitz: Part 10, pp. 910–18, 925; on Rosen: Part 11, pp. 72–75; on Zwillman: Part 12, pp. 623–24; and on Lansky: Part 7, pp. 602–3.

262   "You are in cahoots": Kefauver Committee, Part 10, p. 90.

263   "Is it true": Kefauver Committee, Part 12, p. 617.

263   "How did you become counsel": Kefauver Committee, Part 7, pp. 151–52.

264   "I am not an actor": Kefauver Committee, Part 12, pp. 630–31, 637–39.

265   "Benedict Arnold rides again": Kefauver Committee, Part 7, p. 1719.

265   "There is a sinister": Kefauver Committee, Third Interim Report, p. 2.

265   Several excellent critiques of the Committee's work and its reports came out in the early 1950s: Daniel Bell, "Crime as an American Way of Life," *Antioch Review*, June 1953, pp. 131–54; Rufus G. King, "The Control of Organized Crime in America," *Stanford Law Review*, December 1951, pp. 52–67; and H. H. Wilson, "The Pressure to Buy and Corrupt," *The Nation*, July 2, 1951, pp. 45–48.

266–69   On Lansky, the syndicates, and Cuba: Messick, *Lansky*, pp. 193–98, 221–22; Messick, *Silent Syndicate*, pp. 271–80; Hugh Thomas, *Cuba*, pp. 972, 1027; Llerena, pp. 17–18; Gage, p. 65; and Vincent Teresa, *My Life in the Mafia*, p. 220.

269–70   On Lansky's expansion abroad: Gage, pp. 66–67, 154–56; Messick, *Lansky*, pp. 237–38, 241; and Teresa, pp. 216–17.

269*n*   On fate of Roselli and Giancana: *The New York Times*, February 25, 1977.

270–72   On Bahamian affair: Gage, pp. 65–67; Messick, *John Edgar Hoover*, pp. 229–33; Bill Davidson, "The Mafia: Shadow of Evil on an Island in the Sun," *Saturday Evening Post*, February 25, 1967, pp. 27–33; Peter J. H. Barratt, *Grand Bahama*, pp. 93–100; Michael Craton, *A History of the Bahamas*, pp. 289–91; and *Wall Street Journal*, October 5, 1966.

272–73   On Resorts International and its putative linkage to Lansky: Messick, *John Edgar Hoover*, pp. 233–36; and *Wall Street Journal*, January 5, 1979. On Cellini as Lansky's cohort: Teresa, p. 217.

273–74   Rise of Las Vegas: Rufus G. King, *Gambling and Organized Crime*, pp. 121–22; Gilman M. Ostrander, *Nevada, The Great Rotten Borough, 1859–1964*, p. 212; Reid and Demaris, pp. 152–53; and Wallace Turner, *Gambler's Money*, pp. 94–129.

274–75   On the Desert Inn and the Cleveland Four: Kefauver Committee, Part 10, pp. 52–53; Messick, *Silent Syndicate*, pp. 251–52; and Reid and Demaris, p. 63.

274*n*   On McCarran: Wallace Turner, pp. 9–10; and Reid and Demaris, p. 152.

275   On skimming in general: *The New York Times*, August 6, 1966; Wallace Turner, p. 4, 26–27; *Life*, September 1, 1967, p. 51, and September 8, 1967, pp. 91–102; *Time*, August 22, 1969, pp. 18–27; and Teresa, p. 212.

275–76   On Lansky's indictment: Clark Mollenhoff, *Strike Force*, pp. 188–89; *Wall Street Journal*, December 15, 1976; *The New York*

Times, April 15, 1976; and Jerome H. Skolnick, *House of Cards*, p. 130.

276   On the various kinds of skimming: Davidson, pp. 33–34; on the junket skim in particular: Teresa, pp. 209–21.

276–77   On couriers and their work: Thurston Clarke and John J. Tighe, Jr., *Dirty Money*, pp. 91–94, 118; on Pullman in particular: Gage, p. 57; Messick, *Secret File*, pp. 201–9; and *The New York Times*, March 2 and December 1, 1969.

276n   "The court finds it": *The New York Times*, August 23, 1974.

277   On crooked Swiss banks tied to Lansky: Robert A. Hutchison, *Vesco*, p. 50; Jim Hougan, *Spooks*, p. 212; and Gage, pp. 56–57.

277n   Even if they "are able to penetrate": Clarke and Tighe, p. 118.

277–78   On laundering: Gage, pp. 56–57; Clarke and Tighe, pp. 16–17; and T. R. Fehrenbach, *The Swiss Banks*, p. 141. On corporate laundering and bribing see a fine recent book: David Boulton, *The Grease Machine*.

278n   "I find it shocking": *The New York Times*, December 5, 1969.

279   On Mafia investments in legitimate business: Chandler, pp. 201–3; Clark and Tighe, pp. 130–34; *The New York Times*, June 12, 1978, and June 14, 1979; Francis A. J. Ianni, "Authority, Power and Respect," ed. Simon Wittenberg, *The Economics of Crime and Punishment*, p. 139; Anderson, pp. 74–135; and Peter D. Andreoli, "Organized Crime Enterprises—Legal," ed. S. A. Yefsky, *Law Enforcement Science and Technology*, pp. 22–27.

279   On the view that the Mafia takes over business rather than other way around: Jonathan Kwitny, *Vicious Circles*.

279   Claim that "organized crime today owns": Charles Grutzner, "What Is Organized Crime?," *Harvard Business Review*, March–April 1970, p. 49.

279n   The Mafia is "more sophisticated": *The New York Times*, August 6, 1978.

280   On the phenomenal success of Atlantic City: *The New York Times*, July 12, 1979.

280   On New York's increasing interest in gambling: *The New York Times*, July 10, 1979.

280   On gambling as big business: Paul W. Sturm, "Casinos—Corporate Style," *Forbes*, June 12, 1978, pp. 29–31; *U.S. News and World Report*, May 29, 1978, pp. 35–36.

280   On organized crime and Atlantic City: Howard Blum and Jeff Gerth, "The Mob Gambles on Atlantic City," *The New York Times Magazine*, pp. 10–15, 20, 26–51; and Michael Dorman, "The Mob Wades Ashore in Atlantic City," *New York*, January 30, 1978, pp. 40–44.

280*n*   "Various levels of government": quoted by Heywood Hale Broun, "Gambling as a Virtue: Rendering Unto Caesar's World," *The Nation*, June 16, 1979, p. 721.

281   On ex-Lepke operatives in Teamsters: McClellan Committee I, pp. 4097–99, 13224, 13229–31, 13535, 13971–74; Walter Sheridan, *The Fall and Rise of Jimmy Hoffa*, pp. 27–28. On the Dorfmans and Baron and the Pressers: Steven Brill, *The Teamsters*, pp. 36, 200–61, 321–52.

281–82   On Lansky's troubles with Israel: *The New York Times*, November 12, 1970, and June 10, 17, July 3, August 23, September 25, 1971, and January 13, June 9, September 12, 14, 1972.

282   On the contempt charge: *Miami Herald*, February 29, June 15, 1973; and *The New York Times*, December 7, 1974. On the tax evasion trial: *Miami Herald*, July 18, 19, 20, 21, 24, 26, 1973; and Thomas Plate, *Crime Pays*, pp. 161–62.

282   Profile of Lansky (marking his seventy-fifth birthday): *Miami Herald*, March 27, 1977.

282–83   "What's been reported about me": *Wall Street Journal*, December 15, 1976. Also on Malnik: Messick, *John Edgar Hoover*, pp. 210–19; *The New York Times*, April 17, May 31, 1979; and *Wall Street Journal*, January 5, 1979; Blum and Gerth, p. 38.

283*n*   "Al Malnik was an employee": *The New York Times*, April 17, 1979.

284   On the gang/syndicates' possession of the Teamster Pension Fund: Brill, pp. 206–14; *Wall Street Journal*, May 13, 1978; and *Newsweek*, November 24, 1975, pp. 89–91.

284–85   On Allen R. Glick's career and spectacular rise: Skolnick, pp. 205–11; *Time*, March 14, 1977, p. 21; *Wall Street Journal*, December 27, 1976; *Washington Post*, August 24, 1978; and *The New York Times*, July 24, 1978.

284*n*   Statistic is presented in *U.S. News and World Report*, July 12, 1976, p. 74.

285   On Lansky and Parvin-Dohrmann: Gage, p. 63; Messick, *Lansky*, p. 152.

285*n*   On Dalitz today: Brill, pp. 11, 250.

285*n*   On Korshak: Seymour Hersh's eye-opening series in *The New York Times*, June 27, 28, 29, 30, 1976.

BIBLIOGRAPHY

This bibliography lists only those works already cited in the Notes. Except for *The New York Times* and specific references to the *New York Post* and *Cleveland Plain Dealer*, no newspaper articles have been included in the bibliography, nor have all of the magazine articles. Newspaper and magazine articles not included here can be found, with appropriate dates, in the Notes themselves.

Abbott, Edith. *The Tenements of Chicago 1908–1935*. Chicago, 1936.

Adamic, Louis. "Racketeers and Organized Labor." *Harper's Magazine*, 161. September 1930.

Addams, Jane. *Twenty Years at Hull House*. New York, 1916.

Adler, Polly. *A House Is Not a Home*. New York, 1953.

Albini, Joseph L. *The American Mafia: Genesis of a Legend*. New York, 1971.

Allsop, Kenneth. *The Bootleggers*. New York, 1969.

Amen, John Harlan. *Report of the Kings County Investigator 1938–1942*. New York, 1942.

American Guide Series. *Philadelphia*. Philadelphia, 1937.

Anderson, Annelise Graebner. *The Business of Organized Crime*. Palo Alto, California, 1979.

Andreoli, Peter D. "Organized Crime Enterprises—Legal." In *Law Enforcement Science and Technology*, edited by S. A. Yefsky. London, 1967.

Antin, Benjamin. *Gentleman from the 22nd*. New York, 1927.

Asbury, Herbert. "America's Number One Mystery Man." *Collier's*, 119. April 12, 1947.

———. *The Gangs of New York*. New York, 1928.

———. *The Gem of the Prairie*. New York, 1940.

———. *The Great Illusion.* New York, 1950.
———. *Sucker's Progress.* New York, 1938.

Barratt, Peter J. H. *Grand Bahama.* London, 1972.
Basso, Hamilton. "The Death Agony of Huey Long." *New Republic,* 85. January 1, 1936.
Baum, Charlotte; Hyman, Paula; and Michel, Sonya. *The Jewish Woman in America.* New York, 1976.
Bell, Daniel. "Crime as an American Way of Life." *Antioch Review,* 13. June 1953.
Bentwich, Norman. *For Zion's Sake: A Biography of Judah P. Magnes.* New York, 1954.
Berger, Meyer. "Murder Inc." *Life,* 9. September 30, 1940.
Berkow, Ira. *Maxwell Street.* New York, 1977.
Berman, Hyman. "Era of the Protocol." Ph.D. dissertation, Columbia University, 1956.
Bernheimer, Charles S. *The Russian Jews in the United States.* Philadelphia, 1905.
Bingham, Theodore A. "Foreign Criminals in New York." *North American Review,* 88. September 1908.
Blum, Howard, and Gerth, Jeff. "The Mob Gambles on Atlantic City." *The New York Times Magazine.* February 15, 1978.
Boulton, David. *The Grease Machine.* New York, 1979.
Bovie, Verne M. "The Public Dance Halls of the Lower East Side." *Year Book, University Settlement Society of New York (USSNY).* New York, 1900.
Bregstone, Philip. *Chicago and Its Jews.* Chicago, 1933.
Brill, Steven. *The Teamsters.* New York, 1978.
Broun, Heywood Hale. "Gambling as Civic Virtue: Rendering unto Caesar's World." *The Nation,* 228. June 16, 1979.
Buchalter *v.* New York. *New York Supplement, 2nd series,* 39 (289).

Cahan, Abraham. *The Education of Abraham Cahan.* Philadelphia, 1969.
Campbell, Rodney. *The Luciano Project.* New York, 1977.
Cantor, Eddie. *My Life Is in Your Hands.* New York, 1928.
———. *Take My Life.* New York, 1957.
Chandler, David Ben. *Brothers in Blood.* New York, 1975.
Clarke, Thurston, and Tighe, John J., Jr. *Dirty Money.* New York, 1975.
Cohen, Morris Raphael. *A Dreamer's Journey.* Boston, 1949.
College Settlement Association. *Annual Reports.* Cambridge, Massachusetts, 1897–1910.
Committee of Fourteen. *The Social Evil in New York City.* New York, 1910.
Committee of Fifteen. *The Social Evil.* New York, 1902.

_____. *The Social Evil*. Edited by E. R. A. Seligman. New York, 1912.

Court of Appeals, Brooklyn, New York. *People of the State of New York Against Irving Nitzberg*. September–October 1941.

Court of Appeals, Brooklyn, New York. *People of the State of New York Against Louis Buchalter et al*. May–June 1942.

Court of Appeals, New York, New York. *People of the State of New York Against Louis Buchalter*. January 16, 1940.

Craton, Michael. *A History of the Bahamas*. London, 1968.

Cressey, Donald R. "Methodological Problems for the Study of Organized Crime as a Social Problem." *Annals of the American Academy*, 374. November 1967.

_____. *Theft of the Nation*. New York, 1969.

Curran, Henry H. *Pillar to Post*. New York, 1941.

Davidson, Bill. "The Mafia: Shadow of Evil on an Island in the Sun." *Saturday Evening Post*, 240. February 25, 1967.

Davis, J. Richard "Dixie." "Things I Couldn't Tell till Now." *Collier's*, 103–4. July 22, 29, August 5, 12, 19, 26, 1939.

Davis, Richard Harding. "The Defeat of the Underworld." *Collier's*, 50. November 9, 1912.

DeForest, Robert W., and Veiller, Lawrence. *The Tenement House Problem*. 2 vols. New York, 1903.

Dewey, Thomas E. *Twenty Against the Underworld*. New York, 1974.

Diagram Group. *The Way to Play*. New York, 1977.

Dorman, Michael. "The Mob Wades Ashore in Atlantic City." *New York*. January 30, 1978.

Driscoll, Joseph. "Men of Action." *New Outlook*, 102. November 1933.

Dubinsky, David, and Raskin, A. H. *A Life with Labor*. New York, 1977

Ehrenfried, Albert. *A Chronicle of Boston Jewry*. Boston, 1963.

Elliott, Russell. *History of Nevada*. Lincoln, Nebraska, 1973.

Epstein, Melech. *Jewish Labor in USA*. New York, 1950.

Ernst, Robert. *Immigrant Life in New York City 1825–1863*. New York, 1949.

Feder, Sid, and Joesten, Joachim. *The Luciano Story*. New York, 1954.

Federal Bureau of Investigation. *The Fur Dress Case*. Report #60-1501. United States Department of Justice. Washington, 1939.

Fehrenbach, T. R. *The Swiss Banks*. New York, 1966.

Flynn, John T. "Smart Money." *Collier's*, 105. January 13, 20, 27, February 3, 1940.

Flynt, Josiah. "The Pool-Room Vampire." *Cosmopolitan Magazine*, 42. February 1907.

————. "Allies of the Criminal Pool-Room." *Cosmopolitan Magazine*, 43. September 1907.

Foner, Philip S. *The Fur and Leather Workers' Union*. Newark, 1950.

Foster, R. F. *Foster's Complete Hoyle*. New York, 1914.

Freeman, Joseph. "How Murder Inc. Trains Its Killers." *American Mercury*, 51. October 1940.

Fromenson, A. H. "East Side Preventive Work." *National Conference of Jewish Charities, Proceedings*. New York, 1904.

Furdyce, Wellington G. "Immigrant Colonies in Cleveland." *Ohio State Archeological and Historical Society*, 45. October 1936.

Furstenberg, Mark H. "Violence and Organized Crime." *Crimes of Violence*, vol. 13. National Commission on Causes and Prevention of Violence. Washington, 1967.

Gage, Nicholas. *The Mafia Is Not an Equal Opportunity Employer*. New York, 1971.

Gardner, Charles W. *The Doctor and the Devil*. New York, 1894.

Garrett, Charles. *The LaGuardia Years: Machine and Reform Politics in New York City*. New Brunswick, New Jersey, 1961.

Gentile, Nick. *Vita di capomafia*. Rome, 1963.

Gitlow, Benjamin. *I Confess*. New York, 1940.

Gold, Michael. *Jews Without Money*. New York, 1965.

Goldberg, Isaac. "A Boston Boyhood." *The American Mercury*, 17. July 1929.

Gordon, Albert A. *Jews in Transition*. Minneapolis, 1949.

Goren, Arthur A. *New York Jews and the Quest for Community*. New York, 1970.

Gorman, Joseph Bruce. *Kefauver: A Political Biography*. New York, 1971.

Gosch, Martin A., and Hammer, Richard. *The Last Testament of Lucky Luciano*. Boston, 1975.

Grutzner, Charles. "What Is Organized Crime?" *Harvard Business Review*, 48. March–April 1970.

Gurfein, Murray I. "Racketeering." *Encyclopedia of the Social Sciences*, 13. New York, 1934.

Hapgood, Hutchins. *Spirit of the Ghetto*. New York, 1966.

Harlow, Alvin. *Old Bowery Days*. New York, 1931.

Hawthorne School. *Annual Reports*. New York, 1906–14.

Hearings Before Select Committee on Improper Activities in the Labor and Management Field. U.S. Senate, 85th Congress, 2d Session. (McClellan Committee I.) Washington, 1958–59.

Hearings Before the Permanent Subcommittee on Investigations of the Committee on Government Operations. U.S. Senate, 88th Congress, 1st Session. (McClellan Committee II.) Washington, 1963.

Hearings Before the Special Committee to Investigate Organized Crime in Interstate Commerce. U.S. Senate, 81st Congress, 2d Session. (Kefauver Committee.) Washington, 1951.
_____. *Third Interim Report.* Washington, 1951.
Higham, John. *Strangers in the Land.* New Brunswick, New Jersey, 1955.
Hillquit, Morris. *Loose Leaves from a Busy Life.* New York, 1934.
Hofstadter, Richard. *The Age of Reform.* New York, 1956.
Hostetter, G. L., and Beesley, T. Q. "Twentieth Century Crime." *The Political Quarterly,* 4. July–September 1933.
Hougan, Jim. *Spooks.* New York, 1978.
Howe, Irving. *World of Our Fathers.* New York, 1976.
Hughes, Rupert. *Attorney for the People.* Boston, 1940.
Hutchinson, John. *The Imperfect Union.* New York, 1970.
Hutchison, Robert A. *Vesco.* New York, 1974.

Ianni, Francis A. J. "Authority, Power and Respect." In *The Economics of Crime and Punishment,* edited by Simon Rottenberg. Washington, 1974.
_____. *Black Mafia: Ethnic Succession in Organized Crime.* New York, 1974.
_____. *A Family Business.* New York, 1972.
Immigration and Crime. Reports of the U.S. Immigration Commission. Senate Document 750, 61st Congress, 3d Session. Washington, 1911.
"Implications of Labor Racketeering." *Columbia Law Review,* 37. June 1937.
Importation and Harboring of Women for Immoral Purposes. Reports of the U.S. Immigration Commission. Senate Document 753, 61st Congress, 3d Session. Washington, 1911.
Irey, Elmer L. *The Tax Dodgers.* New York, 1948.
Israels, Belle Lindner. "The Way of the Girl." *Survey,* 22. July 3, 1909.

Jennings, Dean. *We Only Kill Each Other.* Englewood Cliffs, New Jersey, 1967.
Jewish Communal Register of New York City 1917–18. New York, 1918.
Josephson, Matthew. *Sidney Hillman, Statesman of American Labor.* New York, 1952.

Katcher, Leo. *The Big Bankroll.* New York, 1958.
Katcher, Leo, and Logan, Malcolm. "Murder Inc." *New York Post.* April 8, 9, 10, 11, 12, 13, 1940.
Katz, Leonard. *Uncle Frank.* New York, 1973.
Katzman, David M. *Before the Ghetto.* Urbana, Illinois, 1973.
Kimball, Nell. *Nell Kimball, Her Life as an American Madam.* New York, 1970.

King, Frederick A. "Influences in Street Life." *Year Book, University Settlement Society of New York (USSNY)*. New York, 1900.

King, Rufus G. "The Control of Organized Crime in America." *Stanford Law Review*, 4. December 1951.

———. *Gambling and Organized Crime*. Washington, 1969.

Kneeland, George T. *Commercialized Prostitution in New York City*. New York, 1913.

Kobler, John. *Capone*. New York, 1971.

Kupcinet, Irv. *Kup's Chicago*. Cleveland, 1962.

Kwitny, Jonathan. *Vicious Circles*. New York, 1979.

Lait, Jack, and Mortimer, Lee. *Chicago Confidential!* New York, 1950.

———. *Washington Confidential!* New York, 1952.

Landesco, John. *Organized Crime in Chicago*. Chicago, 1968.

Landesman, Alter F. *Brownsville*. New York, 1968.

Lawes, Lewis E. *Cell 202, Sing Sing*. New York, 1935.

Lewis, Norman. *The Honored Society*. London, 1964.

Llerena, Mario. *The Unsuspected Revolution*. Ithaca, New York, 1978.

Logan, Andy. *Against the Evidence*. New York, 1970.

Longstreet, Stephen. *Chicago 1860–1919*. New York, 1970.

Lundberg, Ferdinand. *Imperial Hearst: A Social Biography*. New York, 1936.

McAdoo, William. *Guarding a Great City*. New York, 1906.

McClure, S. S. "The Tammanyizing of Civilization." *McClure's*, 34. November 1909.

McCook, Philip James. *The Days of My Age*. New York, 1965.

McWilliams, Carey. *The Education of Carey McWilliams*. New York, 1979.

———. "Minneapolis: The Curious Twin." *Common Ground*, 7. Autumn 1946.

Magnes, Judah P. *The Magnes Papers*. The Central Archives for the History of the Jewish People, Jerusalem, Israel.

Manners, Ande. *Poor Cousins*. New York, 1972.

Markey, Morris, "Gangs." *Atlantic Monthly*, 141. March 1928.

Messick, Hank. *John Edgar Hoover*. New York, 1972.

———. *Lansky*. New York, 1971.

———. *The Private Lives of Public Enemies*. New York, 1973.

———. *Secret File*. New York, 1969.

———. *Silent Syndicate*. New York, 1967.

Meyer, Henry J. "A Study of Detroit Jewry, 1935." In *Jewish Population Studies*, edited by Sophia M. Robison. New York, 1943.

Miner, Maude E. *The Slavery of Prostitution*. New York, 1916.

Mollenhoff, Clark. *Strike Force*. Englewood Cliffs, New Jersey, 1973.

Moore, William Howard. *The Kefauver Committee and the Politics of Crime.* Columbia, Missouri, 1974.

Moss, Frank. *The American Metropolis.* 3 vols. New York, 1897.

"Murder in Cleveland." *Cleveland Plain Dealer.* December 26, 27, 28, 29, 1933; January 1, 2, 3, 4, 1934.

National Council of Jewish Women. *Yearbook, New York Section, 1904–5.* New York, 1905.

Near *v.* Minnesota. *U.S. Reports,* 283, Washington, 1931.

Nelli, Humbert S. *The Business of Crime.* New York, 1976.

Nevins, Allan. *Herbert H. Lehman and His Era.* New York, 1963.

Nevins, Allan, and Kraut, John A., eds. *The Greater City: New York 1898–1948.* New York, 1948.

New York Bureau of Jewish Social Research. *Jewish Communal Survey of Greater New York.* New York, 1928.

The New York Times. (Dates specified in notes or in the text itself.)

Official Records, National Commission on Law Observance and Enforcement. 4 vols. Senate Document 307. (Wickersham Commission.) Washington, 1931.

Official Report (Private and Confidential) of the Jewish International Conference on the Suppression of the Traffic in Girls and Women. (Jewish International Conference.) London, 1910.

Oppenheimer, Francis J. "Jewish Criminality." *The Independent,* 65. September 17, 1908.

Ostrander, Gilman M. *Nevada, The Great Rotten Borough, 1859–1964.* New York, 1966.

Parkhurst, Charles H. *Our Fight with Tammany.* New York, 1895.

Pasley, Fred P. *Muscling In.* New York, 1931.

Peterson, Virgil W. *Barbarians in Our Midst.* Boston, 1952.

Pinzer, Maimie. *The Maimie Papers.* Edited by Ruth Rosen and Sue Davidson. Old Westbury, New York, 1977.

Plate, Thomas. *Crime Pays.* New York, 1975.

Prison Committee of the Association of Grand Jurors of New York County. *Criminal Receivers of the United States.* New York, 1928.

"Probation Report." *People of New York Against Louis Buchalter et al.* Court of General Sessions. January 26, 1940.

Ravage, Marcus E. *An American in the Making.* New York, 1936.

Reid, Ed, and Demaris, Ovid. *The Green Felt Jungle.* New York, 1963.

Report and Proceedings of the Senate Committee Appointed to Investigate the Police Department of New York. 5 vols. (Lexow Committee.) Albany, 1895.

Report of the Special Committee of the Assembly Appointed to Investigate the Public Officers and Departments of the City of New York and of the Counties Therein Included. 5 vols. (Mazet Committee.) Albany, 1900.

Riis, Jacob. *How the Other Half Lives.* New York, 1890.

Rischin, Moses. *The Promised City.* Cambridge, Massachusetts, 1962.

Robinson, Donald B. *Spotlight on a Union.* New York, 1948.

Rockaway, Robert A. "The Detroit Jewish Ghetto Before World War I." *Michigan History,* 52. Spring 1968.

Roskolenko, Harry. *The Time That Was Then.* New York, 1971.

Rothstein, Carolyn. *Now I'll Tell.* New York, 1934.

Russell, Francis. *The Great Interlude.* New York, 1964.

Salerno, Ralph, and Tompkins, John S. *The Crime Confederation.* New York, 1969.

Sanger, William W. *History of Prostitution.* New York, 1858.

Sann, Paul. *Kill the Dutchman!* New Rochelle, New York, 1970.

Schoener, Allon. *Portal to America: The Lower East Side, 1870–1925.* New York, 1967.

Seidman, Harold. *Labor Czars.* New York, 1938.

Seidman, Joel. *The Needle Trades.* New York, 1942.

Shaw, Clifford. *Delinquency Areas.* Chicago, 1929.

Sheridan, Walter. *The Fall and Rise of Jimmy Hoffa.* New York, 1972.

Simonds, Frank. "The Relation of Children to Immoral Conditions." *Year Book, University Settlement Society of New York (USSNY).* New York, 1900.

Sinclair, Andrew. *Era of Excess.* New York, 1964.

Skolnick, Jerome H. *House of Cards.* Boston, 1978.

Slonim, Joel. "The Jewish Gangster." *Reflex,* 3. July 1928.

Smith, Dwight C., Jr. *The Mafia Mystique.* New York, 1975.

Special Committee of the Board of Aldermen Appointed to Investigate the City's Police Department Pursuant to the Resolution of August 4, 1912. 6 vols. New York, 1913.

Starr, John. *The Purveyor.* New York, 1961.

Statement and Recommendations Submitted by Societies and Organizations Interested in the Subject of Immigration, Reports of the U.S. Immigration Commission. Senate Document 764, 61st Congress, 3d Session. Washington, 1911.

Steffens, Lincoln. *Autobiography.* New York, 1931.

Stolberg, Benjamin. *Tailors' Progress.* New York, 1944.

Sturm, Paul W. "Casinos—Corporate Style." *Forbes,* 121. June 12, 1978.

Sullivan, Mark. "The Pool-Room Evil." *Outlook,* 77. May 28, 1909.

Sutherland, E. H. *Principles of Criminology.* Chicago, 1934.

Teresa, Vincent. *My Life in the Mafia*. New York, 1973.

Thomas, Hugh. *Cuba*. New York, 1971.

Thompson, Craig, and Raymond, Allen. *Gang Rule in New York*. New York, 1940.

Thrasher, Frederick M. *The Gang*. Chicago, 1927.

Toll, David W. *The Compleat Nevada Traveler*. Reno, 1976.

Tully, Andrew. *Treasury Agent*. New York, 1958.

Turkus, Burton B., and Feder, Sid. *Murder Inc*. New York, 1951.

Turner, George Kibbe. "The Daughters of the Poor." *McClure's*, 34. November 1909.

_____. "Tammany's Control of New York by Professional Criminals." *McClure's*, 33. June 1909.

Turner, Wallace. *Gambler's Money*. New York, 1965.

University Settlement Society of New York (USSNY). *Year Books* and *Reports*. New York, 1897–1911.

Walker, Stanley. *The Night Club Era*. New York, 1933.

_____. *Thomas Dewey, An American of This Century*. New York, 1944.

Wanless, James M. "Order in the Underworld." Ph.D. dissertation, Columbia University, 1974.

Warner, Sam Bass, Jr. *The Private City*. Philadelphia, 1968.

Warren, John H., Jr. *Thirty Years Battle with Crime*. Poughkeepsie, New York, 1874.

Waterman, Willoughby. *Prostitution and Its Repression in New York City 1900–1931*. New York, 1932.

Weiden, Arnold A. *The Early Jewish Community of Boston's North End*. Waltham, Massachusetts, 1962.

Werner, M. R. *It Happened in New York*. New York, 1957.

_____. *Tammany Hall*. New York, 1928.

Whyte, William F. *Street Corner Society*. Chicago, 1943.

Willemse, Cornelius. *Behind the Green Lights*. New York, 1931.

Williams, T. Harry. *Huey Long*. New York, 1969.

Wilson, H. H. "The Pressure to Buy and Corrupt." *The Nation*, 173. July 2, 1951.

Wolf, Edwin. *Philadelphia, Portrait of an American City*. Harrisburg, Pennsylvania, 1975.

Woolston, Howard B. *Prostitution in the United States*. New York, 1921.

ACKNOWLEDGMENTS

It is a pleasure to thank first of all the great institutions whose debts I have incurred so lavishly: the New York Public Library, particularly its Jewish Division; the Columbia University Library, mainly its Special Collections and Rare Books Division; the Central Archives for the History of the Jewish People in Jerusalem, in particular Hadassah Assouline, for generously allowing me to see and use part of its Judah P. Magnes Papers; and *The New York Times,* the absolutely indispensable newspaper of record for the period and subject covered in this book.

I am grateful to Herbert Asbury's *Gangs of New York* for enabling me to draw on its collection of mug shots—Monk Eastman's, Jack Zelig's, Lefty Louie's and Gyp the Blood's, Dopey Benny's, Kid Dropper's, and Little Augie's—all of which had been supplied by the New York City Police Department and are now unavailable.

It is a pleasure also to thank my friends, those who read portions of the manuscript with an acute eye, those who asked questions and offered advice, or those who patiently heard me out, encouraging me at the very least to struggle on to the end: I mean Ralph DellaCava, Jay Dreyer, Richard Elman, Ray Franklin, Herb Hill, Walter Kendall, Al Nash, Nancy Partner, George Rawick, Sol Resnik, Peter Schwab, Dan Seidman, B. J. Widick, and Mike Wreszin.

I profited from the expert knowledge and detailed criticisms offered by Jenna Weissman Joselit, who is completing her own study of crime in the Jewish community.

My editor, Tom Wallace, deserves special thanks: he was a model of patience, understanding, intelligence, good temper, and, when the occasion required, firmness.

Acknowledgments

My largest debt, one I cannot ever repay, I owe to my wife, Edith Firoozi Fried. She has shared the burdens of this book every step of the long, arduous course despite the demands of her own work, and I hardly exaggerate (though she may think so) in saying that it could not have been done without her.

INDEX

Workman, Charles ("the Bug"),
190–91, 218
World of Our Fathers (Howe),
xvi–xvii
World Series of 1919, fixing of, 95–96
World War I, 87

Yale, Frankie, 202
Yanish (thief), 4
Year Book of University Settlement
Society of New York:
1899, 8n
1900, 39n
Yiddish press, 69, 76, 78
"Yoski Nigger," *see* Toblinsky, Joseph

"Young Turks," 123–28, 231
Yuran, Hyman, 210

Zelig, Big Jack, 2, 3–4, 30–32, 34, 40,
74, 75, 76, 80, 82
gang of, xvii, 31–32, 33, 102, 130
Zerilli, Joseph, 122
Zionism, 58, 87
Zucker, Isaac, 26
Zweibach, Max ("Kid Twist"), 29–30,
34, 82
gang of, xvii, 29–30, 63, 102
Zwillman, Abner ("Longy"), 104,
115, 116, 119n, 121, 158n, 193,
233, 239, 249
Kefauver Committee and, 261, 263